Shooting Blanks at the Anzac Legend

Australian Women's War Fictions

SYDNEY STUDIES IN AUSTRALIAN LITERATURE

Dr Meg Brayshaw, Series Editor

The Sydney Studies in Australian Literature series publishes original, peer-reviewed research in the field of Australian literary studies. It offers engagingly written evaluations of the nature and importance of Australian literature, and aims to reinvigorate its study both locally and internationally.
SUP thanks Professor Robert Dixon, Founding Editor.

Dedicated to Elizabeth Webby

Shooting Blanks at the Anzac Legend

Australian Women's War Fictions

Donna Coates

SYDNEY UNIVERSITY PRESS

First published by Sydney University Press

Sydney University Press
Gadigal Country
Fisher Library F03
University of Sydney NSW 2006
Australia
sup.info@sydney.edu.au
sydneyuniversitypress.com.au

 A catalogue record for this book is available from the National Library of Australia.

NATIONAL
LIBRARY
OF AUSTRALIA

ISBN 9781743329245 paperback
ISBN 9781743329252 epub
ISBN 9781743329030 pdf

Cover image: Barbara Hanrahan, *Poppy day* (1982). Screenprint on paper, 75.9 x 57.2 cm. Collection of the Australian War Memorial ART29757
Cover design by Miguel Yamin

We acknowledge the traditional owners of the lands on which Sydney University Press is located, the Gadigal people of the Eora Nation, and we pay our respects to the knowledge embedded forever within the Aboriginal Custodianship of Country.

Some quotations from scholarly sources may contain terms or views that were considered acceptable within mainstream Australian society when they were written, but may no longer be considered appropriate. The wording in these quotes does not reflect the views of Sydney University Press or the author.

Acknowledgements

I would like to pay tribute to some of my Australian home-front allies. Most important would be the well-known Elizabeth Webby, whom I had the good fortune to meet within months of completing my dissertation. We connected for the first time in 1992 at a war memorial conference in Canberra, and then a few weeks later, when we were both back in Sydney, she invited me to a lovely lunch on the campus, during which time I discovered that as the Chair of Australian Literature, there was very little, if anything, that Elizabeth was not fully aware of. More than once, if I could not locate the information I needed back in Canada, I would email Elizabeth and voila! within a matter of hours, she would have sent a response that fulfilled my request. Over the years – virtually every year from 2000 onward – she helped arrange office space for me (as did both Robert Dixon and Brigid Rooney during their terms of office), and before long we became good friends. Elizabeth often took me to literary events that I would never have known about, let alone been invited to. We also spent many hours together in darkened theatres, most often the Belvoir.

While there are a lot of "Australian allies" who made my yearly visits to the lucky country pleasurable by providing me with a place to live, often for several weeks (Mike and Vicki Woolley from Canberra, and Ruth Law and Gary Steed from Sydney), one of the greatest pleasures is also meeting "overseas/out of country allies" – that is, people from around the world who have consistently supported my work over the years. My list includes Nic Birns (New York), with whom I have been attending conferences for decades, as well as Jatinder Mann (England), Daniel McKay (New Mexico), Janet Wilson (England and Auckland), and Anna Branach-Kallas and Marzena Sokolowska-Paryz (Poland). "Home-front allies" at the University of Calgary, such as Judy Zhao, who without complaint always promptly found the research materials I needed, and Karen Preddy, who then cheerfully helped me (repeatedly) figure out how to incorporate them into my work, have been equally co-operative. So, too, has Sydney University's Press Naomi van Groll: she deserves a medal for her consistently helpful editing and being such a great pleasure to work with from such a distance. I salute my son Jeremy and his partner Andrea, who have remained optimistic that I would eventually make "the big push" and finally finish the "war with words," a long overdue project that I have no regrets about having embarked upon. It has taught me (and I hope many others) a lot about the need for women to speak their peace.

Donna Coates, August 2023

Many of the chapters contained within were originally published as journal articles or conference papers. I thank the journals for permission to reproduce and rework them for this book.

Table of Contents

Introduction

Over the years of my academic career, which I came to late in life, I have been frequently asked why I have chosen to teach and write about women's responses to twentieth-century wars in both Canada, the United States and Australia (and occasionally New Zealand). It's a story I have told several times (parts of which have already been published), so please accept my apologies for any repetition.[1]

My round-about tale begins when I persuaded my (ex)husband, who did not like to travel, that we should take advantage of a teacher-exchange program to Australia, which would offer us and our sons (aged ten and sixteen) the opportunity to experience life in another country for a year. Surprisingly, he accepted, but only, I suspect, because we had recently attended a gathering of teachers where a good-looking blond, tanned young man had just recently returned from a one-year teaching stint in Queensland. Over the course of the evening, he repeatedly informed the crowd that his duties as an educator were far from arduous: at one point he claimed that he just "sent the kids to the beach" every morning and then delighted in basking in the sun and sand himself!

On the strength of that "evidence," my husband agreed to go to Australia, but a few months before we were scheduled to leave, one of his relatives encouraged us to come to Ottawa for a few days because he had just landed a job which gave him entry to most of the city's museums and he was keen to show us around. We duly travelled to Ottawa and went to quite a few of the museums, but the only one I remember vividly was the Canadian War Museum, and then only because the few staff members on the site kept apologising for the scarcity of expositions, the overall shabbiness of the place and consequently the dearth of visitors. Historian Tim Cook refers to the war museum, created in 1942, as a "nondescript and inefficient building"[2] and adds that in 1998, the newly appointed director-general and CEO of the forthcoming new museum, J.L. Granatstein, also had little good to say about

---

1   Cited in "All You Have to Do Is Look," Nicolas Birns Interviews Donna Coates, *Antipodes* 43.2 (December 2020), 222–32.

the original, which he claimed was "stodgy, boring and dull. Its exhibits are tacky. As a museum, it's just appalling".[3] (A much larger and more comprehensive new museum opened in Ottawa in 2005.)

We duly began the first leg of our adventure at the end of December, which was fortuitous because we were obliged to follow the Australian school year that would not officially begin until late February, thereby leaving us nearly two months to acclimatise and to travel around the country before tackling serious work. At the time, I lamented that the system was grossly unfair, given that our exchanges were compelled to arrive in Canada in early January and be prepared to teach within days, when the weather that month was frequently the worst of the year. Temperatures often dipped below minus twenty or worse, and the newcomers had virtually no time to adapt to the harshness of the cold. Accordingly, those of us heading Down Under were asked to leave our refrigerators full of food so that the new arrivals would not have to venture out immediately unless absolutely necessary. But unlike our counterparts, we were able to get off to a fine start by spending a few relaxing days in the colourful and exotic (to us) Fiji ahead of making our way to Sydney, where we planned to sightsee for a few days before touring Canberra and Melbourne on the way to Adelaide, where my husband would be teaching. (Not, notably, carefree, laidback Queensland.) After only a few days in Sydney I had fallen in love with everything in the city and the country: I revelled in its doggedly persistent hot weather; its sandy, readily accessible beaches; its friendly people; its dangerously delicious wine; its numerous good-looking men; and its dazzling architecture like the famous Opera House and the Harbour Bridge (best known as the Coat Hanger).

Strangely, however, almost everyone we spoke to in Sydney urged us to make the Australian War Memorial our first stop in Canberra, and because of their insistence, we obeyed. We learned it had opened in 1941, but unlike its dismal Ottawa counterpart of similar vintage which the historian Cook has already claimed resembled a dingy 1940s bungalow, the daunting Australian museum was a glorious art deco structure with spectacular spaces that others have described as part shrine, part world-class museum, but with plenty of additional features such as an outdoor sculpture garden. Clearly, funding had not been a problem. Accordingly, we watched as hundreds of people, including a surfeit of children, busily explored dozens of engaging exhibitions or quietly read through extensive archives. Because there was so much to see, both indoors and out – and even though no one in either of our families had ever expressed any interest in war or the military – we were so impressed that we spent part of the next day strolling along the lengthy Anzac Parade (with the Australian parliament buildings clearly visible

2   Tim Cook, *The Fight For History: 75 Years of Forgetting, Remembering and Remaking Canada's Second World War* (Toronto, Canada: Penguin, 2020), 177.
3   Cook, *The Fight For History*, 396.

in the distance), where dozens of displays continued to pay tribute to the sacrifices Australians had made at the numerous battles they have fought (and died) in.

After our two visits to the museum, I began to ponder why Australians should pay so much attention to honouring their men (and occasionally women) who sailed away to war when Canadians, for the most part, did not. When Anzac Day (25 April), which commemorates the landing at Gallipoli (despite its having been declared a military disaster), rolled around, I was astonished because the event was so entirely unlike its Canadian equivalent, which reveres their veterans chiefly on Remembrance Day. On 11 November (a holiday in only a few provinces), Canadians gather typically in small groups (they are getting larger, however), listen to a few brief speeches, adhere to the required two minutes of silence, and then either witness or participate in the laying on of wreaths at memorials.[4]

But on Anzac Day in Adelaide, I watched as thousands of Australians attended the lengthy morning parade and then went on to celebrate further when the pubs opened and the solemnity of the morning gave way to boozy celebrations on the streets. I was unaware at the time that many of those thousands might also have attended the early morning dawn ceremony to commemorate the time of the landing in Gallipoli. I admit that I thought people were exaggerating when they tried to convince me of those facts, which I found inconceivable. It was not until some years later, on another visit to Australia, that I attempted to get to the dawn ceremony in Sydney, but I could not get near the site because crowds had assembled much earlier. And in case you labour under the impression that this custom must surely have waned by now, you would be very wrong indeed, as historian Anna Clark records that "the numbers of those who attended the Dawn Ceremonies are steadily increasing: an estimated 50,000 attended the ceremony at Melbourne's Shrine of Remembrance in 2014".[5] But having come from a country where many continue to perceive of themselves as inhabitants of a "peaceable kingdom," I thought it was time to begin seriously investigating why, given so many obvious similarities between the two countries, there should be such disparities in their treatments of war.

Little did I know that my having signed up for a full-year course on Australian literature at the University of Adelaide would prove to be so momentous to my future career on the subject of war. The course, taught mainly by writers (poets taught poetry, playwrights taught drama, for example), was ideal. At the end of the second semester, I produced an essay on the Australian writer Shirley Hazzard's *The Transit of Venus*, which my professor thought was first-rate. In his written comments, he claimed that I "wrote like an angel" (the kind of praise no one in Canada had ever given me), awarded the paper a very good grade, and suggested I submit it for publication at a small university press (which unfortunately had just

---

4   Australian Remembrance Day observances are like those in Canada.
5   Anna Clark, "The Place of Anzac in Australian Historical Consciousness", *Australian Historical Studies* 48, no.1 (2017): 137.

closed). I was thrilled with the professor's comments, but troubled when I stumbled upon a brief interview with Hazzard in the *Bulletin*, where she declared that her novel was all about war, but because few people envisage that women writers ever tackle war as their subject, they tend to ignore that topic altogether.[6] My quick re-reading of the novel demonstrated conclusively that there were references to war on virtually every page, but I, too, had barely noticed them (and obviously neither had my professor). Up until that point, I had been teaching as a poorly paid sessional instructor at several post-secondary institutions in Calgary; much as I enjoyed the teaching, I knew if I wanted to keep working as an academic (and now admittedly spurred on by a subject I wanted to pursue), I would have to get a PhD.

Before we left Australia, I asked the aforementioned professor to list a few war novels by Australian women worthy of study, but after a long pause, he mentioned only Dymphna Cusack and Florence James' World War II novel titled *Come in Spinner* (1951), and then likely only because the unabridged edition had been recently re-issued and subsequently adapted into a popular television series. After returning from Australia, I was accepted into the PhD program at the University of Calgary, but my search for sources continued to be as challenging as they had been in Australia. When I asked a well-read Canadian professor to suggest a few titles on women's wartime fictions, after giving it virtually no thought, he advised me to drop the topic because he could not identify any! On my third try, this time prepared to insist that it was unfathomable that women would have let three world wars – I intended to focus on the First and Second World Wars and the Vietnam War – go by (Korea remains the forgotten war) without writing a word, I had no need to worry when a much younger professor found my proposal intriguing. When I informed him that I had been told that I might not find any books, he replied that "They are there, and you will find them. You just have to look," and of course, how right he was! But regrettably, he died not long after he had agreed to be my supervisor, and not surprisingly, I was assigned to someone who had no interest in or knowledge of the topic. It was again fortunate that the Head of the English Department insisted that because no one in the faculty was familiar with Australian writing, mine would have to be a comparative study and include Canadian women writers. I was not troubled by the additional work because I assumed that since both these countries were settler societies whose inhabitants spoke (mostly) the same language, paid tribute to the same monarch, and were equally comprised of small populations eager to rush to the defence of Mother England during her time of need in spite of being vast distances from the fields of battle, I would just be writing

---

6   For a much lengthier analysis on why women's voices have been suppressed on the topic of war, see my general introduction to a seven-volume series titled "Catch 22", which I wrote for the first volume of Routledge Press' *Women and War: History of Feminism* (xi–xxvii). My introduction, which appears in "Women and War from the Middle Ages," is edited by Jaclyn Carter and Timothy Duffy (2020).

"ditto" much of the time. But comparative studies are useful for what they reveal: rather than similarities, I found, almost exclusively, differences.

Near the beginning of my studies at the university I was again fortunate to receive a small scholarship that enabled me to conduct research for a few months at the magnificent National Library of Australia in Canberra. Several of the librarians took an interest in my topic and cheerfully helped me find many of my resources, but before too long, I began to feel a bit at sea, largely disappointed by the several-dozen World War I books I had been reading, and then uncertain how to respond to them. My discomfort did not last long, however, because another stroke of luck occurred when an Australian academic at the Defence Force Academy recommended that I should read the work of the much-admired historian and war correspondent C.E.W. Bean (whom I had never heard of), and he was right. I learned then that Australian women writers did not write their own novels but had them written for them by the dominant ideology (that would primarily be Bean), which permitted only one voice, a single interpretation of the war which essentially glorified the Anzacs' (which stands for the Australian and New Zealand Army Corps) participation in the hostilities. Bean worshipped "the noble bushman" (even though most came from cities), his physical appearance, temperament, democratic values, as well as his love of, and success on, the battlefield. Following Bean's lead, more than a dozen women writers set much of the "action" of their fictions at Gallipoli, and because they were merely reflecting Bean's vision of the men who fought in the war, included no strong women in their fiction. Regardless of Australian women's prodigious output – they produced several-dozen novels – much of the majority reflected a unique form of powerlessness.

As I have written elsewhere, unlike their female counterparts in Canada or Great Britain whose novels reflected women's desires to loosen the patriarchal grip on their lives, Australian women's Great War fictions were, like Bean, gripped by the performance of the Anzac, not with the emancipation of women or collective social reform. Rather than chronicling typical concerns over pacifism, prohibition or conscription (words not uttered even once in their fictions), women writers muted their own voices, took their orders from Bean, and marched away to war with their soldiers. Accordingly, their writing (if read at all), was risible; female characters sent letters and presents to their husbands and uttered ridiculous comments such as hoping that their husbands liked their smoking jackets or that they were not too close to danger on the front lines. It is important to stress that these absurd responses were not their fault: from a distance of approximately 12,000 miles, they could only mimic what Bean had informed them of.[7] His popular Christmas book, titled *The Anzac Book: Written and Illustrated in Gallipoli by the Men of Anzac* (1916), depicted soldiers complaining about the weather, or "attacks" from flies or

---

7   Note that Bean was not alone in his worshipping of the "noble bushman"; several British writers such as John Masefield, Compton Mackenzie and Ellis Ashmead-Bartlett also wholeheartedly praised the Anzacs.

fleas, or feeling the pain of "glancing blows to their wrists." Some labelled bomb attacks "inconvenient." Once I became aware of Bean's influence on women writers, I also began to re-read the many-fewer Canadian novels I had finally found, which promoted an entirely different perspective, and the comparative study began to take shape.[8]

My continuing search for women's war fictions eventually led me to a few absorbing novels by Australian women writers who did not follow (or perhaps had never heard of) Bean's work and hence produced unique anti-war books. One was M.L. (Mollie) Skinner, whose *Letters of a V.A.D.* (1918) features a nurse who privileges her career over marriage, and her second novel, the hilarious *Tucker Sees India* (1937), depicts a man who does not want to fight, but both novels have been unjustly neglected. I have argued elsewhere that both such atypical works deserve a prominent place in Australian war writing, as does Lesbia Harford's *The Invaluable Mystery*, whose novel, written in the 1920s but not published until 1987, previous editors had rejected, at least in part, because there were no Anzacs in the book. Furthermore, Harford had the courage to suggest that in the absence of men, the home front could become a radical site for women.

But perhaps the best ways to elucidate how valiant these rebels were is to survey the works by Canadian women writers. Even though they produced a much smaller opus, none of their books privilege the life of soldiers; rather, these writers insisted that attention must be paid to women, whose female characters look to the future and visualise a better world where women are fully participating members of Canadian society. The best known of the Canadian writers at the time was L.M. Montgomery, whose *Rilla of Ingleside* (1920) incorporates the responses of those usually ignored in wartime such as children, animals, and even enemy Germans, and which I regard as the best Canadian wartime novel ever written. I also discovered another powerful novel by Nellie McClung, titled *The Next of Kin: Those Who Wait and Wonder* (1917), which insisted that women writers' work shared a common purpose, which was to recognise the marginalisation of women's voices in wartime, to show women how to write themselves into an intensely male-dominated discourse, and at the same time to teach women how to secure powerful positions in their society.[9]

Around the time that I was nearing completion of my dissertation, the head of the department who had insisted upon the comparative study came across an organisation titled the American Association of Australian Literary Studies (AAALS), which was holding a conference on Australian writing in Bloomington,

---

8 Once I was back in Canada, the head of the graduate department advised me to concentrate solely on the World War I fictions because there were so many emanating primarily from Australia.

9 For a thorough examination of the progressive ideas presented in Canadian women's war writing, see my "The Best Soldiers of All: Unsung Heroines in Canadian Women's Great War Fictions", *Canadian Literature* 151, Winter (1996): 66–99. I have utilised material from this essay in my Conclusion, here titled "Boomerangs do come back."

Indiana, and suggested I might be interested in attending. Indeed I was. It proved to be a terrific experience, especially since after the delivery of my first-ever conference paper, the Canadian scholar Tom Tausky immediately asked to publish it in a new journal he had started called *Australian and New Zealand Studies in Canada*, and he did. Sadly, Tom died not long after. But I was fortunate to have had the opportunity to participate at the gathering because I learned soon after that the conference experience is not always so collegial. I have been occasionally asked if I have encountered negative reactions from Australians who resent a Canadian telling them what they should think about their literature or who question my feminist approach; I am pleased to say, "only rarely." I did, however, face a strong reaction the day I delivered a talk based on a paper recently accepted for publication at a conference being held at the war museum in Canberra. I had only begun to read it when a large man seated in the back row of the room leapt to his feet, shouted "Rubbish," and then rushed to the door and slammed it. Perhaps in bad form, I shouted after him, "Have you read the books yet?" That got a good laugh and we proceeded without him. Surprisingly, the only other criticism I am aware of occurred in Canada at a conference in Kingston, Ontario. During the question period, a Canadian scholar who had done some good work on Australian literature suggested I was being unkind or perhaps even unfair to women writers, but as I pointed out again, since she had not read the books I was referring to, she had only my position – which I explained was reporting their dilemmas and not making fun of them – to rely upon. Otherwise, the scholars I have met Down Under are welcoming, friendly and generally pleased that I have continued to promote their literature.

But what does rankle with me are the numerous historians who persist in writing lengthy essays about how similar the two nations' perspectives are on war. I tire of the academics who try to force the comparisons between Canada and Australia so that responses to World War I are almost identical, when they are emphatically not. Primarily, the Australians wanted to prove to the British that they benefited from having been sent to live in a beautiful sunny country which offered many opportunities for "the good life," whereas Canadians had no need to feel beholden to supreme powers. Moreover, much as Australians continue to idolise the men who fought at Gallipoli (even though it was a catastrophe), Canadians celebrate only their participation at Vimy Ridge, an important battle they won after four days of fighting in 1917. But the continuing reverence for the Anzac is fuelled by the education system in Australia, which ensures that from an early age, virtually every child can offer a history lesson on what happened, what day, the importance of the day, and so on, at Gallipoli. By contrast, I have been teaching adult students for several decades and have only recently encountered a few students who know the basics about Vimy Ridge – where it was fought, what the issues were, and even which war it occurred in! But as of today, most students' knowledge – if they have any at all – ends there. (To be fair, students are not the only ones who remain ignorant about what happened at Vimy: a recent survey revealed that numerous

Canadians thought Vimy was either a mountain range or a famous racehorse!) Significantly, unlike young people in Australia who make their rites of passage through pilgrimages to Gallipoli, which some critics have suggested are now just drunken revelries and not tributes to the sacrifices Australian soldiers made, very few, if any, of my students have been to Vimy and rarely express any desire to go there in the future.

It's also important to stress that while Australians have participated in every major twentieth-century war, Canadians did not sent troops to either Vietnam or Iraq. Although our reputation as "peace-mongers" has slipped, a substantial portion of Canadians continue to believe they live in a "peaceful kingdom" and want to keep it that way. This topic obviously requires much further investigation, but for now, I am repeating two anecdotes I wish to share because they are too good to resist. The first instance, which illustrates that even those Canadians who ought to know their war history do not, applies to then Defence Minister John McCallum, who attempted to atone for his lack of knowledge about the Dieppe raid, which took place on 19 August 1942 (another battle my students know nothing about) by writing a letter to one of the national newspapers, where he succeeded only in making matters worse when he confused Vichy, the seat of the French government that collaborated with the Nazis during World War II, with Vimy, the World War I battle fought at Vimy Ridge![10] The second example illustrates that while the Australian adoration of the Anzac continues, in Canada, newspaper writer Peter C. Newman reminds us that, "This is the only country on earth whose citizens dream of being Clark Kent instead of Superman." And that, I will end by saying, suits me just fine.[11]

---

10   John McCallum, letter to the editor, *National Post*, 1 September 2002.
11   For a lengthy examination of these issues, see my "Happy Is the Land That Needs No Heroes," in *ANGLICA: An International Journal of English Studies, Special Issue: The Great War*, 27, no. 3, (2018):111–42.

Part 1
World War I Fictions

1

The Digger on the Lofty Pedestal

Australian Women's Fictions of the Great War

In his full-length study on Australian war writing, Robin Gerster states: "Australian prose of the Great War was based on one fundamental premise: that Australians excel, even revel, in battle".[1] From this proposition, Gerster advances two related arguments: that Australian war writing is propagandist in its promotion of national sentiment and ideals; and that in its continuing glorification of war, it is anachronistic and out of step with European and American war writing. While I agree with Gerster's theories, I take issue with his almost exclusive use of male war writers to support his thesis. In his examination of World War I prose, he mentions only four women writers – Mary Grant Bruce, Ethel Turner, Gladys Hain, and Angela Thirkell – and omits entirely from his discussion Mabel Brookes, Linda Webb Burge, Ray Phillips, Annie Rixon and Chrystal Stirling, several of whom wrote more than one novel, and whose fiction would have added ammunition to his argument. In overlooking women's valuable contribution to Australian war writing, Gerster succumbs to traditional patriarchal criticism, which assumes that the weaponless are wordless.

Paradoxically, after omitting these important writers from his study, Gerster then gives women (along with a few expatriates and contemporary writers) credit for calling into question national sentiments, stating, "the debunking, anti-heroic, or demythologising literary territory has been with few exceptions occupied ... by women ... unimpressed by male histrionics" (20). But in offering only one novel by English war bride Angela Thirkell as evidence, he undermines his own argument. While he might have added to his discussion Mollie Skinner's *Tucker Sees India*, which atypically features an Anzac who does not want to fight, Gerster is otherwise completely erroneous in his assumptions that women writers deflate national myths or deride heroic posturing; for in their texts, they not only stand by their men, but

---

1   Robin Gerster, *Big-Noting: The Heroic Theme in Australian War Writing* (Melbourne: Melbourne University Press, 1987), 2. All subsequent references are to this edition and appear in parentheses in the text.

fashion them into superhuman legendary figures who excel at combat. In *Broken Idols*, for example, Mabel Brookes elevates her Diggers to "lofty pedestals".[2]

While Gerster notes that the·tendency to "big-note," which he defines as "the giving of extravagant praise to oneself or the exaggeration of one's own importance" is "everywhere evident in First AIF literature" (3), he refers almost exclusively to those writers who either participated directly in combat, gave orders from behind the lines, or were male civilians who jumped on the Anzac adulation bandwagon. Women writers could not swap bayonets for pens, but they could sing the praises of the soldier. In their texts, the figure of the Anzac looms large, his dominating presence firmly establishing that women writers are equally propagandist in promoting cultural stereotypes. Furthermore, because women writers continuously laud the Anzacs' participation in war, their fiction is also anachronistic and out of step with other literary traditions. That several of the most male-dominated texts appeared as late as the 1940s indicates women writers' prolonged enthusiasm for the event, and their slavish devotion to hegemonic tradition.

Whereas Gerster identifies these characteristics in Australian male writing as nonconformist, I suggest that when they appear in women's writing they reflect a unique form of female powerlessness. In shoring up, not shattering, reigning ideologies, their texts differ significantly from those by British, American, or Canadian women writers, which foreground strong women determined to make their part in war matter. In her study of American and British women's war writing, Sandra Gilbert argues that the Great War served to empower women psychologically, economically, and sexually; throughout her essay, Gilbert employs words such as "glee," "exuberance," and "triumph" to describe writers' enthusiastic response to war, which (alas only temporarily) liberated women from cloistered environments, confining clothing, and tedious domestic chores.[3] Canadian writers demonstrate in their texts a less jubilant, more subdued response, but they do reveal women seizing war as an opportunity to loosen the patriarchal grip on their lives. In their women-centred texts, heroines move out of the home and hearth and take up meaningful occupations which give them strength and confidence in their abilities. And amidst the chaos occasioned by war, they insist that the time is ripe to restructure society, to create a "new world order" which incorporates women's voices and values into the design.

---

2   Mabel Brookes, *Broken Idols* (Melbourne: Melville and Mullen, 1917), 35, 49.
3   Sandra M. Gilbert, "Soldier's Heart: Literary Men, Literary Women and the Great War," in *Behind the Lines: Gender and the Two World Wars*, eds. Margaret Higonnet, Jane Jenson, Sonya Michel, and Margaret Collins Weitz (New Haven, CT: Yale University Press, 1987): 197–226. Gilbert's essay should be read in light of the critics who argue that her thesis is biased and her use of examples cavalier. See Jane Marcus (1989): 49–83; Claire M. Tylee (1988): 199–210. My own research reveals that Gilbert disregards Mary Marlowe's *The Women Who Wait* (London: Simpkin, 1918), and Helen Zenna Smith's *Not So Quiet ... Stepdaughters of War* (London: Marriot, 1930; rpt. London: Virago, 1987), presumably because they do not fit her thesis.

But in Australia, women writers are obsessed with hero worship of the Anzac, not with societal reform or the liberation of women. Several women writers – Hain, Burge, Rixon – undergo paper sex changes and send a man off to war, thereby replicating the master narrative of the soldier in the trenches and nullifying their own voices as women, to whom they hand barely speaking parts and walk-on roles in their texts. Other writers – Stirling, Grant Bruce, Turner, Phillips, Brookes – play out a tug of war, a "star wars" battle for centre stage between heroine and hero, from which the Digger inevitably emerges victorious; writers deem his story more worthy of the telling. Annie Rixon for example, begins *The Scarlet Cape* with the story of a resilient young woman who survives deprivation in the bush before courageously making her way to Sydney, where she becomes a nurse. In the first third of the book, the nurse offers a rigorous critique of her profession. But once war breaks out, without any advance warning to her readers, Rixon drops the nurse's story and takes up the Anzac's, to that point a minor character. The switch in point of view is frustrating, since Rixon also sends her nurse overseas, but tells us nothing about her journey, the kinds of duties she performs, or most significantly, how she responds to the death and destruction of the battlefield. In allowing her nurse's voice to evaporate, Rixon denies the legitimacy of a woman's story in war and reaffirms the central importance of the soldier's story in Australian fiction.

Before passing judgement on women writers for acting as publicity agents for the Anzac campaign, it is important to recognise that at the outbreak of World War I, Australian women were particularly defenceless on the home front. A number of forces operated to prevent them from achieving even limited emancipation, in spite of the fact that, as Carmel Shute observes, they were eager to fight for their country in any way they could. Like men, who hastened to enlist in "active" service, women, too, charged authorities' offices and pleaded to be given "active" roles of any dimension, either on the home front or the battlefront. They were consistently counselled, however, to devote their energies to more "appropriate" causes such as knitting, making small domestic sacrifices, nursing the sick and wounded, or acting as society's moral guardians, and to let men get on with the business of war.[4] War offices also issued similar instructions to British, American and Canadian women, but were obliged to rescind the orders when it became apparent that women were needed either to take up jobs in industries created by the war, or those left vacant when men marched away. But in Australia women were compelled to obey male dictates, for, as Michael McKernan comments, there was no large-scale munitions industry in Australia to give Australian women the experience of factory work and no wholesale shortage of labour to force them to men's jobs".[5] Further, because Australian women had achieved suffrage at Federation, there were few vocal women's groups at the

---

4   Carmel Shute, "Heroines and Heroes: Sexual Mythologies in Australia 1914–1918." *Hecate* 1, no. 1 (1975): 14–18.

5   Michael McKernan, *The Australian People and the Great War* (Melbourne: Nelson, 1980), 65–6.

outbreak of war to advance the feminist cause. It was not all quiet on the Australian home front, for although women were denied access to paid employment, Patsy Adam-Smith records that they threw their energies into providing comforts for Australian soldiers. Indeed, women undertook their volunteer tasks with such vigour and enthusiasm that, "as a result of their efforts, Australian soldiers became the best-cared-for body of troops in the Great War".[6] Anzacs truly sprang from "the lucky country," for in real life, they were the best provided-for troops among the Allied Forces, and among literary representations, most revered.

In committing themselves to Anzac aggrandisement, women writers did not go on the warpath to overcome women's oppression, did not deploy their words as artillery to help overcome their marginalisation. Instead, they uphold conventional pursuits for women: rarely do they argue that women's emancipation from marriage and motherhood is possible, or even desirable.[7] Missing from the texts by Hain, Grant Bruce, Turner, Brookes, Burge, Phillips, Rixon and Stirling is a candid confession of women's desire for power and control over their lives; consistently, female characters remain male-identified as wives, sweethearts, or sisters. Moreover, these texts consistently portray women suspended in holding patterns, waiting, in static and silent submission for their loved ones to return. While anticipating war's end (and hence a return to prewar existence), women cling to traditional pastimes: they knit, nurture, weep, and wait. Some female characters engage in occasional volunteer wartime work, but half-heartedly; they view their tasks as diversionary, something to fill in the time or to relieve anxiety, but not as significant donations to the war effort. Moreover, women's volunteer tasks serve as opportunities for writers to give voice to the wounded, but never downhearted, Anzac. Other fictional characters concentrate on recruitment, on getting a man to the front, but their "white-feather" activities are devoid of intellectual underpinnings. No women in these texts emerge from the private sphere to wear the pants, to step into men's shoes for paid employment, or to take up "brilliant careers." Since marriage is the only profession open to women, it matters not if the soldier returns maimed, blinded, armless or legless, for in this society even a husband who cannot wear the pants is better than no husband at all. And because competition for a lifetime partner is stiff, women level much hostility at war brides; they regard one another as enemies, not allies, and routinely choose men as their confidantes. None works collectively to overcome subordination, and any woman who show signs of transgressing social codes is quickly punished and restored to

---

6   McKernan, *The Australian People and the Great War*, 66.
7   Only two novels assert women's right to autonomy and independence. Skinner's *Letters of a V.A.D.* was published initially in England. In her autobiography *The Fifth Sparrow*, she writes that, because she was nursing in India, she did not realise until the spring of 1915 that war was being waged, or that Australians were part of the war effort (95); thus she would have missed much "big-noting." Lesbia Harford's *The Invaluable Mystery*, an unusual woman-centered urban text written during the 1920s, failed to locate a publisher until 1987, when it was accidentally discovered by researchers in the Australian Archives in Canberra.

her proper place as wife and homemaker. As well, women writers create negative views of their sex, illustrating that they have internalised one of patriarchy's basic tenets, misogyny: several characters refer to their sex as useless, and declare women too emotional and irrational to hold public office.

Throughout their brief history, Australian women had been conditioned to think of themselves as the second sex, for they inhabited a patriarchal society which had, since its inception as a penal colony, either ignored them or treated them with indifference and even enmity. A surfeit of critics – Beryl Donaldson Langer, Anne Summers, Miriam Dixson, Dorothy Jones, Susan Sheridan, and Kay Schaffer – have documented Australian women's historically marginal status in their society. Beryl Donaldson Langer contends that women's exclusion from Australian culture and identity became evident in the colonial period, but during the nationalist, myth-making 1890s their absence was explicitly confirmed. Prominent writers like Henry Lawson, Joseph Furphy, Banjo Paterson and Steele Rudd privileged the noble bushman's values of rugged manliness, anti-authoritarianism, ready initiative in a hostile environment and irreverence; at the same time, these writers viewed women as agents of restriction and restraint, as inhibitors of male pleasure, and dismissed them as overly concerned with manners and fashion.[8] Anne Summers writes that male writers of the period were anxious to transpose what they deemed positive male characteristics into a living legend, and they succeeded.[9] And in this society, charges Dorothy Jones, where men mythologise themselves and exclude women, the latter's only defence against isolation is to try to fit themselves into the myth, to be "myth-fits".[10] Some writers, like Barbara Baynton and Miles Franklin, became adept at camouflage; they chose the bush as their setting and depicted, in bush vernacular, typical egalitarian values. In accommodating their writing to the bush, writes Susan Sheridan, they earned approbation from such patriarchal figures as Henry Lawson and A. G. Stephens, editor of the influential and "offensively masculine" *Bulletin* magazine, who praised them for "transcending their female qualities and preoccupations" and contributing to "this masculine construction of 'the Bush'".[11] But Summers argues that, in writing within male tradition, "myth-fits" inevitably suffer: their situation becomes "precarious and almost inevitably dishonest, for by conforming to men's ideals, they are denying something in themselves".[12] They cannot write about the bush as if they are men: rather, they

---

8   Beryl Donaldson Langer, "Women and Literary Production: Canada and Australia", *Australian-Canadian Studies: An Interdisciplinary Social Science Review* 2 (1984), 78.

9   Anne Summers, *Damned Whores and God's Police: The Colonization of Women in Australia* (Ringwood: Penguin, 1975), 36–7.

10   Dorothy Jones, "Mapping and Mythmaking: Women Writers and the Australian Legend", *Ariel* 17, no. 4 (1986), 74. Jones derives this clever term from Thea Astley, who coined it in *A Boat Load of Home Folk* (1968).

11   Susan Sheridan, "'Temper Romantic: Bias Offensively Feminist': Australian Women Writers and Literary Nationalism," in *A Double Colonization: Colonial and Post-Colonial Women's Writing*, eds. Kirsten Holst Petersen and Anna Rutherford (Aarhus: Dangaroo Press, 1986): 54.

12   Summers, *Damned Whores and God's Police*, 40.

are forced to "draw a wider canvas and to write about whole settlements or communities," or to write about individual women as if they are somehow "separated from the norm". Women writers dared not create strong females who might rival the bushman, nor dared they hazard writing honestly about what life in the bush looked like from their more familiar vantage point of the kitchen or child's bedroom.[13] Women were trapped in a Catch-22: if they failed to write about the bush and male experience, they found their work dismissed for being outside the range of serious subjects; if they examined subjects like marriage, pregnancy, sexual hypocrisy, their fictions were deemed not relevant to national literature.[14] Sheridan argues that novels by the 1890s writers Cambridge, Praed and "Tasma" were published in accessible forms, widely circulated, and garnered a large readership,[15] but because women wrote about social life in the cities and the relations between the sexes, they were discredited for writing inferior novels.[16] Jones concurs, finding that women authors who did not extol the virtues of mateship and the bush but chose instead to draw their matter from urban and domestic life found their work "criticized as lightweight, and even un-Australian".[17] Even though these "women's books" were acclaimed on publication,[18] they nonetheless fell rapidly out of sight, whereas those that upheld nationalist masculine values formed the traditional canon.[19]

The advent of World War I compounded this already problematic situation for women writers, because the myth of the noble bushman, on the wane by the beginning of the twentieth century, did not die out as Australian society became increasingly urban, but like a boomerang, zoomed from bush to battlefield, and became entrenched as the myth of the Anzac soldier, or the Anzac legend. Writing against the bush myth had always been difficult for Australian women writers, but writing against this revised, more potent myth was even more intimidating. In the brave new Digger figure's reincarnation, he picked up some stellar new characteristics, while retaining the old. He was newly handsome, cosmopolitan, well-read, suave, charming to women, as well as a ferocious foe. Several critics – Marilyn Lake, Summers, Schaffer – have observed the progression from noble bushman into Anzac, but none has considered the negative impact this mythical figure had on women's wartime literature. This larger-than-life warrior demanded attention, and got it; for in spite of the many obstacles in their path, many female "recruits" attempted the pen. Women writers sublimated their own needs and desires, absented themselves from the war narrative, took the battlefront as their

---

13   Summers, *Damned Whores and God's Police*, 37–8.
14   Langer, "Women and Literary Production: Canada and Australia", 78.
15   Sheridan, "Temper Romantic: Bias Offensively Feminist", 51.
16   Sheridan, "Temper Romantic: Bias Offensively Feminist", 53.
17   Dorothy Jones, "Canon to the Right of Us, Canon to the Left of Us", *New Literature Review* 17 (1989), 72.
18   Sheridan, "Temper Romantic: Bias Offensively Feminist", 51.
19   Jones, "Canon to the Right of Us, Canon to the Left of Us", 73.

focus, and backed the Diggers' attack. In writing about men at war, they would have felt they were tackling serious subject material. But they lost the literary war, for their writing, which meticulously followed the dictates of the dominant ideology, was overlooked. Unlike women writers of the bush, who received praise for adopting the standards and preoccupations that patriarchal society defined for them, women wartime writers were completely ignored. Gerster's omission is proof of that neglect.

Women suffered more than indifference, however, for in "big-noting" the Anzac, they did not write their own texts, but had them written for them by the dominant ideology. Dutiful myrmidons, women writers took their orders from war correspondents C.E.W. Bean and Banjo Paterson and poet C.J. Dennis, and were their mouthpieces, or interlocuters, but not tellers of their own stories. Foregrounding the Anzac, they failed to take up issues considered of special interest to women, such as pacifism or temperance. No female characters discuss conscription, a curious omission since women were intensely involved in the heated debates that proved so divisive on the home front.[20] None challenges the makers of war; none questions how war affects women's lives; none interrogates why men go to war. Ideological discussions on war are brief and sketchy and take place primarily between soldiers. In spite of the fact that women could not have provided soldiers' comforts without superior fundraising, managerial and organisational skills, writers adhered to the patriarchal decree that women must be silent martyrs. Women were never to flaunt their activities, but to dress themselves in the "invisible crown of sacrifice".[21] They were to be "missing" from the accounts of war. Women writers contributed to their own powerlessness by remaining silent in their literature about wartime subsidies and charitable contributions. Whatever male writers said about Australian men at war, women writers mimicked; they did not determine their own views of war, or try to come to terms with what it meant to them as women. Thus their novels are, for the most part, a working out in fiction of a male assessment of Australian soldiers – these men who displayed extreme valour and courage against overwhelming odds, and achieved "nationhood" for Australia.

While it could be argued (and often is) that the significant unifying event in Australian (war) history was the landing at Gallipoli, there is also evidence to suggest that Australian writers like bush poet-cum-war correspondent Banjo Paterson had begun glorifying Australian soldiers' participation in war before the turn of the century. Shirley Walker writes that Paterson's widely circulated dispatches from the Boer War "fostered a mythic view of Australian prowess in

---

20 See Pat Gowland, "The Women's Peace Army," in *Women, Class and History: Feminist Perspectives on Australia 1788–1978*, ed. Elizabeth Windschuttle (Melbourne: Fontana, 1980): 216–33; Darryn Kruse and Charles Sowerwine, "Feminism and Pacifism: 'Women's Sphere' in Peace and War", in *Australian Women: New Feminist Perspectives*, eds. Norma Grieve and Alisa Burns (Melbourne: Oxford University Press, 1986): 42–58; Carmel Shute, "'Blood Votes' and the 'Bestial Boche': A Case Study in Propaganda", *Hecate* 1, no. 2 (1975): 7–23.

21 Shute, "Heroines and Heroes: Sexual Mythologies in Australia 1914–1918", 13.

war based, as was the myth of the 1890s, on courage, equestrian skill, the ability to survive in rugged country, and an aggressive independence".[22] Walker further observes that Paterson's reports reinforced pro-war sentiments at home, and persistently emphasised the value of Australian troops: Anzacs were usually placed in the foremost lines, displayed individual acts of courage, and demonstrated their strengths as bushmen. Paterson also stressed the skill and dedication of stretcher-bearers and doctors. What the correspondent omitted was equally important, however; he suppressed larrikin behaviour and downplayed violence, in particular muting mention of death and stressing grit and heroism instead.[23] Walker concludes that Paterson's writing "fostered the establishment myth – of war as a gallant and necessary enterprise in aid of the Empire, of Australia as a nation moving towards maturity and demonstrating this by the courage of its superior (if somewhat rakish) young men".[24] Bush legend, then, had begun to blur into warrior myth well in advance of World War I.

At the outbreak of war, other prominent myth-shapers like Paterson began to set down equally laudatory descriptions of the Australian male's character and his superb performance in war. Not the least of these men was historian and war correspondent C.E.W. Bean, who was ultimately a journalistic reincarnation of the bush writers. Prior to the war, he had been sent by the *Sydney Morning Herald* to report on bush life, and he liked what he saw; though city-born, like the literary writers of the 1890s, he came to worship the noble bushman, his character and values. When he turned to writing his war dispatches (published at various periods and eventually collected into a twelve-volume set titled *The Official History of Australia in the War of 1914–1918*), Bean transferred what he had observed (or thought he had observed) about the temperament and physical appearance of the Australian bushmen and re-created them as Anzacs. That many of the Anzacs were either British-born or hailed from cities, Bean conveniently overlooked.

One of the aspects of the bush Bean most revered was the healthy environment. Because of the open air, sunshine, and abundant supplies of good food, men from Down Under, Bean pronounced, were physically stronger, taller, better developed and more adventurous than Englishmen, who were cramped in stature as a result of their existence in overcrowded polluted centres. Bean further decreed that besides possessing large frames, all Australian men looked alike: "An active life, as well as the climate, rendered the body wiry and the face lean, easily lined, and thin-lipped".[25] This active life led Australian men to exhibit an independence of

---

22   Shirley Walker, "The Boer War: Paterson, Abbott, Brennan, Miles Franklin and Morant",
      Australian Literary Studies 12 (1985), 209.
23   Walker, "The Boer War", 209.
24   Walker, "The Boer War", 209.
25   Bean, C.E.W., *The Official History of Australia in the War of 1914–1918. The Story of Anzac From
      the Outbreak of War to the End of the First Phase of the Gallipoli Campaign, May 4, 1915*
      (Sydney: Angus & Robertson, 1934), vol. 1: 5. All subsequent references are to this edition and
      appear in parentheses in the text.

character which manifested itself in their aggressiveness, resourcefulness, and vigorous initiative (5), all valuable qualities in time of war. Many of the skills required in combat, Bean further argued, were those that Australian men practiced in civilian (but always bush) life. Bushmen were often called upon to snuff out bushfires, and, more than any other experience, that activity resembled the "fighting of a pitched battle" (47). Bean concluded that "the Australian was half a soldier before the war" (47).

Further, Bean believed that the character of the Australian men that he so admired could be explained in terms of social experience. While bush life was crucial to the formation of character, so too was instruction in a state school system which abolished feudal class distinctions. As a result, socially, "the Australian people came nearer than perhaps any other to forming one class without distinction of birth or wealth" (5). This egalitarian principle found its way into the AIF, where men were promoted from within the ranks (54), and correspondingly took a great dislike to the traditional models of authority followed by the British army (48). The other "law" of behaviour which grew out of egalitarianism was mateship. Bean decreed that a man should at all times and at any cost stand by his mate (6). His central thesis was, then, that the Great War served as a testing ground through which the character of Australian men could be determined, and, according to Bean, they came through with flying colours. Their most significant contribution to the war effort was not destroying the Hun or the Turk, however; it was the "getting of nationhood." Concluding his Introduction to *The Official History*, Bean states, in what is perhaps his most famous proclamation, that "in those days [World War I] Australia became fully conscious of itself as a nation" (xlviii).

When he put down his eyewitness accounts of Australian men at war, Bean had his audience of general readers on the home front firmly in mind; vivid and highly readable prose comes across more like a thrilling novel than a documentary account of military manoeuvres. That women writers read and absorbed his war messages is obvious, for in their texts, they replicate depictions of the Anzacs' physical appearance, their temperament and philosophy, and their love of combat. Bean did not single-handedly turn Anzacs into heroes, however; there was a plethora of myth-shapers willing to "big-note" Australians at war. Other correspondents were equally lavish, arguably more so, in their praise of the Digger, both of his sabre-wielding skills and physical appearance. It is possible to speculate that Bean's accounts of war might have held little sway with the folks at home had they not been supported by foreign journalists, whose reports were available as early as 8 May 1915. Gerster suggests that it was the English correspondent Ellis Ashmead-Bartlett who established the "fanatical tone" of Australian war writing with his "famous Anzac despatch describing a rampaging 'race of athletes' storming the Turkish cliffs and bayoneting everything in its path".[26] Geoffrey Searle notes that both John Masefield

---

26   Gerster, *Big-Noting*, 13.

and Compton Mackenzie added to the deification process by paying cloying tribute to the Anzac physique.[27] In the eyes and ears of the world, the Anzac soldier was a hero, a Greek God, a man more than worthy of the lofty pedestal. This excessive adulation, emanating from overseas correspondents, would have influenced gullible women writers who, situated 12,000 miles from the field of combat, were obliged to rely on second-hand accounts of war.

Their braggadocio about these astral Anzacs takes a variety of forms, but most prominent is his fighting prowess, his capacity for combat, said often to achieve both history for a new nation and international acclaim. In *Broken Idols*, Mabel Brookes, one of the troops' most enthusiastic fans, creates a Digger who boasts to a "mate" that the "glorious" struggle at Gallipoli brought the nation "our first bit of history",[28] and her narrator contends that, even though many are dead and can never comprehend how their country appreciated them, those who return home will do so as the "idols of their land":

> Those men had gone to uphold Australia's flag in the forefront of this world war, and were eminently fitted to symbolize their country in the great meeting of Empire on foreign battlegrounds. Alas! Some were dead, most of them were maimed, broken and war-wearied, but many would return, the idols of Australia, wounded and scarred though they might be through their service with the War God, as Egypt's idols today bear the disfigurements of time. But also like Egypt's idols, they would remain a symbol – erect – immovable – braving the elements – commanding the wonder and admiration of the world.[29]

Brookes is only one voice in a chorus of approval, for in *The Scarlet Cape*, Rixon's narrator also declares that "the name and fame of the Anzac had been flashed from one side of the world to the other",[30] and one of Burge's Anzacs in *Wings Above the Storm* echoes Brookes, remarking to a war correspondent that, "we have no history up to now, and we begin with this war".[31] A common pattern in these texts is for a foreign journalist, whose voice adds weight and authority to the Diggers' reputation, to report on the Anzac's invincibility in combat. In *The Scarlet Cape*, a newsman applauds an Aussie's evil spirit and tenacity in war, for in spite of incurring several wounds, he nonetheless fights at every important battle – from Lone Pine to Pozieres – in which Anzacs take part. Whether bayoneting an enemy in the trenches or shooting down a German from his flying machine, Rixon's Aussie distinguishes himself as a supreme (and flexible) marksman. The reporter deems the Anzac's military might as "superhuman".[32] Burge utilises a similar technique,

---

27 Geoffrey Searle, "The Digger Tradition and Australian Nationalism", *Meanjin Quarterly* 24, no. 2 (1965), 151–2.
28 Brookes, "Broken Idols", 49.
29 Brookes, "Broken Idols", 281–2.
30 Annie Rixon, *The Scarlet Cape* (Sydney: Criterion, 1939), 129.
31 Linda Webb Burge, *Wings Above the Storm* (Melbourne: The National Press, 1944), 195.

except that her Parisian war correspondent praises not only a single champion, but the collective action of Australians. The journalist extolls the Anzacs' courage and dogged determination and testifies that they "profoundly affected the course of the war".[33] Generously, he allows that although the Anzacs clearly won the battles, took the prisoners, and captured the guns, they were at times "aided" by Canadians and Americans![34] (Not, readers will note, Brits.) In other texts, soldiers themselves do the big-noting. Rixon's Aussie observes, without a trace of humility, that the Germans feared the Diggers from Down Under more than troops from any other country.[35] The soldier also acknowledges that the Aussies amassed a considerable death toll, but undercuts the notion of loss by suggesting they incurred few in comparison to the number of casualties they inflicted upon the enemy, often as high as 20–1.[36] Nowhere in his account of the fighting does the Digger lament the loss of life, or concede that victory was achieved at a terrible price. Neither Brookes, Burge nor Rixon address suffering and death as by-products of war. In their texts, characters are more moved by Anzacs' physical accomplishments and the getting of nationhood than they are by any destruction of human life.

In Chrystal Stirling's *Soldiers Two*, victory and achievement take precedence over human loss in war. Her central character, Emily, knows that Australian men have sacrificed life and limb, but she believes that, having been tested and not found wanting, Australians have come to recognise unique strengths and abilities. Without the advent of war, Australians might not have discovered that they are a superior race. To her soldier-husband, Emily writes:

> But, despite the sorrow, who shall say we have not come into our own. Always within us as we fought against fire and flood, against drought and thirst, as we dared a horse to do its worst with us, was the subsconscious [sic] knowledge that we were made for greater deeds ...
>
> And now has come Gallipoli ... Pozieres, which you call "peculiarly ours," and other places which we had scarce been conscious existed, and in some strange way we have emerged into the sunlight ... Our hearts are broken, and yet there is a strange new cheerfulness about us; there is, if I may dare to say it, almost an optimism ...We have lost our own, but we put that aside.[37]

Stirling is responsible for the curious ellipses which permeate her text, but they are not necessarily the mark of a sloppy writer. Rather, the omissions mirror Stirling's elliptical reportage of war. The absence of women is everywhere in these texts,

32   Rixon, *The Scarlet Cape*, 197.
33   Burge, *Wings Above the Storm*, 190.
34   Burge, *Wings Above the Storm*, 193.
35   Annie Rixon, *Yesterday and Today* (Sydney: Criterion, 1940), 109–11.
36   Rixon, *Yesterday and Today*, 112–13.
37   Chrystal Stirling, *Soldiers Two* (Sydney: Bookstall, 1918), 187–8. All subsequent references are to this edition and appear in parentheses in the text.

especially in the telling of the story. When Emily fashions Australians into a "superior race" because they combat fire, flood, drought, thirst, and "dared a horse to do its worst," aside from being poetic, she leaves out women, who were not likely to have fought the elements, or have been part of the "action" on the home front. (Undoubtedly they did fend off fire and flood, but would not have been perceived as equal participants.) On the battlefront, women are definitely "missing," hence Emily's discomfort ("if I may dare to say it") in labelling Gallipoli as "ours," or using "we" in the context of war. Women, absent from Gallipoli and Pozieres, could not share in the claim for nationhood. Only Arthur ("you") can call the battles "ours." There is no "we" possible in a country which insists that in war, and war discourse, women must be missing, absent, never participants. In Australia, only men constitute "the superior race."

Other women writers echo Bean's proclamation that the harsh Australian landscape produces exceptional human beings, but they are all men. The taxing bush environment produces soldiers who look so identical that they appear to have been fashioned on an assembly line or spewed out of a photocopying machine with perfect "Anzactitude."[38] No matter which text they appear in, all Anzacs are hatchet-faced, square-jawed, clear-eyed, and bronzed. One of Burge's Diggers refers to an English soldier as "weedy" and "sick looking," and "about three feet higher than a duck".[39] The healthy Australian climate, replete with abundant sunshine and plentiful food, renders men physically huge, prepares them to withstand hardship and, by extension, the rigours of war. They can fend off bushfires on the home front or deflect bullets on the battlefront with equanimity. According to Stirling's Anzac, their hulking physique makes them able to tolerate the cold in France better than the diminutive English Tommy (155). Women writers go one step farther than Bean in their big-noting, though. Life in the rigorous Australian bush has endowed the Anzac with extraordinary sensory perceptions. One of Brookes' Anzacs has such superior hearing that he can detect impending air raids almost before they happen,[40] and Grant Bruce's soldier possesses such keen eyesight that he can see in the dark, a trait Grant Bruce would have us believe invaluable in war, for his unauthorised night raids are said to strike fear in the hearts of the Huns.[41] That her fighting man marauds unsanctioned is evidence of the dash and initiative men develop surviving in the bush, the way of life so admired by Bean, for Australians who fend off floods and fires and resist droughts become hardy, resilient, and

---

38　This word originated in a 1918 issue of *Aussie* magazine, illustrated and printed in France by members of the AIF. It was used to denote that under fire, soldiers forgot their reputed coolness, and "streaked to the nearest dug-out" (Gerster, *Big-Noting*, 26). Elsewhere in *Aussie*, however, "Anzactitude" was a praiseworthy term, as in "He faced the situation with superb Anzactitude" (27). I am using the term to describe "exactitude," or similarity in appearance and personality.

39　Burge, *Wings Above the Storm*, 82.

40　Mabel Brookes, *On the Knees of the Gods* (Melbourne: Melville and Mullen, 1918), 108. All subsequent references are to this edition and appear in parentheses in the text.

41　Mary Grant Bruce, *Captain Jim* (Melbourne: Ward, 1919), 182.

resourceful. Any other experience, even war, pales in comparison, and accordingly, the Anzac frequently refers to trench life as a "picnic." In Brookes' novels, nothing about war is too disheartening for a Digger, who routinely maintains "high spirits" (99), a "light-hearted manner," and "the ability to enjoy the immediate present," no matter where he might find himself (173). He is often heard cheerfully singing "Australia Will Be There" (171, 183). This refrain, which reverberates throughout the novels, is another notice that women are "missing." Only half of Australia (and in women's minds, the better half) can be "there." Stirling's Anzac, too, emphasises the jaunty approach Australians take to war. In the following passage, her Anzac writes his wife about how cheerfully Aussies respond to combat: "They are in great glee, going into the fray as light-heartedly as to a cricket match" (118). Australian women writers appear to have been seduced by these demi-gods in khaki, for their depiction of them is so commendable and formulaic that their texts take on the flavour of Harlequin romances.

The pronounced tendency to big-note soldiers' physical and temperamental suitability for war is a result of women writers' craving to overcome the perception that Australians spring from lowly convict stock. Several of these novels, particularly those by Brookes and Grant Bruce, are in fact arguably less about war than they are about "writing back" to the Empire;[42] their texts insist that Australians have achieved a cultural and physical superiority despite their inauspicious beginnings. In Brookes' *On the Knees of the Gods*, set in England, it is never clear whether the Anzac's enemy is the Turkish Johnny, the German Hun, or the English Tommy. The major task she gives her central female character, Ernestine Lawry, is to speak in defence of Australians when they are attacked by members of the British upper class. When an aristocrat insinuates that Diggers prematurely evacuated Gallipoli because they lacked stamina, Brookes brooks no slurs on her countrymen. Her central character exonerates them assiduously: "I doubt if any of them are of convict blood. That page of Australia's history has long been turned over and is hidden beneath many others that are inscribed with records of golden deeds".[43] Ernestine then gets her own back, insisting that "Education and environment will produce a far finer *man* than can the average noble family of today. Take our Australians – very few have ancestral homes, or ancient names to burden them, yet you'll find the finest *men* that God ever made among their ranks".[44] In turn, she insists that the English aristocracy has little to be proud of, for it does not produce men who are "good" at war, the criterion for success in Australia. (It will not be lost on the reader that she makes no mention of "fine women.") Rather, Ernestine implies, a form of "tommy rot" has set in. The English woman's son has returned (prematurely, of course) from active service limping and suffering from

---

42   Ashcroft, Bill, Gareth Griffiths, and Helen Tiffin. *The Empire Writes Back: Theory and Practice in Post-Colonial Literatures.* 2nd edition. London: Routledge, 2002.
43   Brookes, *On the Knees of the Gods*, 71.
44   Brookes, *On the Knees of the Gods*, 71; emphasis added.

shell shock. Brookes thus assures her readers that no English Tommy who is, after all, a product of a dismal English climate and social class which tolerates indolence and dissipation, can be a war hero.

In making her Diggers superior to Tommies, Brookes also strives to eradicate the "bad strain," or larrikin reputation which dogged the Australian abroad. Hain joins Brookes in fending off undeserved attacks on soldiers' morality by creating few who fall off the lofty pedestal or heroes who turn hooligan. Yet both writers had their work cut out for them for, as Alistair Thompson points out, in real life, Anzacs deserved their ruffian reputation.[45] Many of the soldiers sent home from Gallipoli had procured VDs, not VCs. Women writers stringently protect their heroes from the charge of moral degeneracy, and either downplay the licentiousness of the troops, or struggle to explain it away. In *Broken Idols*, a woman excuses Aussies for having climbed a harem wall or two or become inebriated because they might be dead the next day.[46] Hain's male narrator suggests that womanisers are only performing favours for lonely, loveless women,[47] thereby bringing a unique interpretation to the refrain, "Australia Will Be There". He further argues that British women are predators, rushing defenceless Anzacs in uniform, whom they apparently find irresistible.[48] In other texts, the rowdy man may simply not have associated with the right people. *On the Knees of the Gods* recounts an instance where an accused murderer (insufficient evidence sets him free) meets a sensitive poet in the trenches; the Anzac laureate teaches the criminal socially valued skills, such as how to fight. Once under a proper influence, the desperado learns patriotic commitment and is cured of his antisocial behaviour.[49] Fearful that their Diggers will be accused of debasement, women writers will not permit them to be less-than-perfect for long; larrikins are either falsely charged or blameless victims of circumstance, which the war helps overcome.

By placing a poet in the trenches with a social outcast, Brookes points to another positive characteristic of Australian men – their espousal of an egalitarian philosophy. According to Bean, whether men were wealthy and educated or rough and poor, they went into the ranks together, unconscious of any class distinction.[50] Hain, Stirling, Phillips, Grant Bruce, Rixon and Brookes follow Bean's lead; in their literary contingents, men enlist without concern for class or rank. One of Brookes' Anzacs, a professional man, earns a substantial income, yet as a private in the army, he peels potatoes in a rough camp.[51] He does not mind taking his

---

45 Alistair Thompson, "Passing Shots at the Anzac Legend", in *A Most Valuable Acquisition: A People's History of Australia Since 1788*, eds. Verity Burgmann and Jenny Lee (Ringwood, Vic: Penguin, 1988), 196.

46 Brookes, *Broken Idols*, 189.

47 Gladys Hain, *The Coo-ee Contingent* (Melbourne: Cassell, 1917), 10.

48 Hain, *The Coo-ee Contingent*, 97.

49 Brookes, *On the Knees of the Gods*, 179–80.

50 Bean, *Official*, 45.

51 Brookes, *On the Knees of the Gods*, 57.

orders from a civilian who blacked his shoes in civilian life. After a short interlude, having proved himself a capable leader, he is promoted from within the ranks, and receives a commission. In these texts, an Australian commanding officer is a fighting man's mate, never an officious authority, as among the English rank and file. Typically, officers remain with their men on the firing line rather than retreating to safety, as British officers are wont to do. In *The Scarlet Cape*, Rixon's officer (a colonel, of course), works alongside his men "manning" a shovel in mud, and surrenders his uniform on the battlefield for bandages.[52] This democratic system, which negates the division between soldier and officer, makes for happy troops. An egalitarian philosophy is also part of the mateship credo; it is customary, Bean pronounced, for well-qualified men to turn down promotions because they do not want to desert their mates. In Brookes' *Broken Idols*, an officer asks a private why he does not try for a commission. The private's response, that he does not want to desert his mates just for the sake of promotion,[53] bounces directly off of Bean's philosophy. The one law that Bean decreed the good Australian [man] must never break was that a man should at all times and at any cost stand by his mate, especially when that mate is wounded.[54] No matter what transpires on the battlefield in these texts, men stay with their mates. In *The Scarlet Cape*, Rixon exaggerates the compelling power of mateship, and combines it with the principle of egalitarianism. A colonel and his dresser are tending the wounded at Gallipoli when a bomb falls at his dresser's feet. Without hesitating, the dresser kicks the bomb several feet away, and then deliberately throws his body on it. His wounds are terrible beyond description. In spite of the obvious danger to himself, the colonel stays by his subaltern's side, leaving him only temporarily to ascertain the whereabouts of reinforcements. While the colonel is absent, the young man rips the bandages from his wounds in order to make the blood flow faster and shorten his life; then the colonel can be released from the responsibility of caring for him and can escape.[55]

Another aspect of Bean's mateship held that Anzacs would, with disregard for their own safety, stay by their wounded friends until they could be carried off the battlefield.[56] The credo extended to stretcher-bearers who, according to Paterson's dispatches, exhibited extreme selflessness for the wounded. Rixon's Anzac, functioning temporarily as a stretcher-bearer, testifies to the endurance of these medical men by working dozens of hours without relief.[57] Here, Rixon reflects Bean's declaration that Australian bushmen were accustomed to working sixty to seventy hours without closing their eyes, especially when putting out raging bushfires.[58] Rixon's narrator implies that only Anzacs would have sufficient stamina

---

52   Rixon, *The Scarlet Cape*, 158.
53   Brookes, *Broken Idols*, 280.
54   Bean, *Official*, 6.
55   Rixon, *The Scarlet Cape*, 154–5.
56   Bean, *Official*, 7.
57   Rixon, *The Scarlet Cape*, 158.

to sustain wartime duties. The narrator overlooks, however, the fact that if stretcher-bearers were required for extensive periods of time, they would be conveying staggering numbers of wounded. But the waste of human life in these texts is never as significant as the intrepid feats Anzacs perform on the battlefield.

Women writers took their assessment of the fighting man's character from Paterson and Bean and gleaned their knowledge of trench life and combat from Bean, too. Most instructive in their literary training was the immensely popular *The Anzac Book*, written by the men at Gallipoli, which Bean edited.[59] According to Gerster, the collection was "something of a manifesto which sets out a thesis of Australian heroism. It is the first real unveiling of the 'official' literary portrait of the Digger".[60] David Kent writes that Bean wished above all to preserve the good name of the Anzac, and thus rejected any submission which might tarnish the soldier's reputation. His editorial pen toned down much of the danger and allowed the spirit of adventure to predominate; he removed references to "death-dealing bullets" to savage shellfire and snipers.[61] Further, Bean rejected any notice of cowardice or malingering, and refused any writing which adopted a cynical view of war. Correspondingly, no writer in *The Anzac Book* makes anti-war statements; none questions the Gallipoli operation; none recounts the savagery and brutality the men experienced, and none depicts the landing as the heinous, bloody slaughter it was. What Bean did include led to a facile and misleading account of war, for the overall impression that emerges is that war is a slightly dangerous but exhilarating adventure. To be sure, there are minor discomforts like flies and fleas, but the soldiers recount these annoyances with ironic detachment. After reading *The Anzac Book*, I find it difficult to be critical of the way women portrayed war, for in their texts, they were merely mimicking what they believed were first-hand versions of combat. They had no way of knowing what Bean rejected, or how much editing and revising he had to do to make the war seem like a sporting event.

The landing at Anzac Cove is a crucial event that several women writers recreate in their texts. A.R. Perry's account which opens *The Anzac Book* (and which Bean carefully sanitised), sets the tone the correspondent desired. Perry emphasises the importance of a hearty meal before battle; he gives a breezy testament to the high spirits of the men who, before disembarking, laugh and joke as though "picnicking"; he makes their wounds trifling (one Anzac receives a "bruising blow on the wrist"[62]) and insists that the landing was a "great adventure" that he "would not have missed for all the money in the world".[63] In *The White*

---

58 Bean, *Official*, 46.
59 C.E.W. Bean, *The Anzac Book: Written and Illustrated in Gallipoli by the Men of Anzac* (Melbourne: Cassell, 1916).
60 Gerster, *Big-Noting*, 28.
61 David Kent, "The Anzac Book and the Anzac Legend: C.E.W. Bean as Editor and Image-Maker," *Historical Studies* 21 (1985), 386.
62 Bean, *The Anzac Book*, 3.
63 Bean, *The Anzac Book*, 4.

Feather (which might have been more aptly titled *It's a Wonderful Life*), Phillips apparently secures her depiction of the landing from Perry. Her Digger perceives the landing as a "wonderful business," and observes that it's "wonderful" to see all the ships. In a letter to his sweetheart, he describes the spirit of the men as follows:

> It is wonderful to think that our infantry-men cleared the cliffs and hills as they did – and got so far inland. The Turks were waiting for us on the beach. Nearly all the men in the first boat were killed. The men in the other boats were fearfully angry at that, and as soon as they could they jumped out of the water, and rushed at them, yelling "Australia! Australia!" for all they were worth.[64]

The Anzac does not say that he would not have missed the landing for all the world, but he implies it. The exact phrase appears, though, in Stirling's *Soldiers Two*[65] and in Brookes' *Broken Idols*.[66] No women writers avouch to the soldiers' fears or confusion, or to serious wounds. Reproducing the depiction of combat faithfully from *The Anzac Book*, women writers make of it a "game" which their fighting men tackled with great spirits.

Although admittedly writing for a juvenile audience, Grant Bruce was obviously influenced by *The Anzac Book*, describing war, especially in *Jim and Wally*, as if it were a "lark." While in the trenches, her two soldier-figures engage in much discussion about the type of food they should consume before heading into battle. When not flashing their bayonets, the mates sit around the campfire telling bush yarns, playing board games, and recounting anecdotes about the Huns' stupidity. Throughout the trilogy, Grant Bruce euphemises combat, describing it as "jolly good work" or "business," and fighting against the Huns as "hating".[67] Taking their cues from Paterson, Dennis, and Bean, Australian women writers unfailingly obscure what the purpose behind war is – injuring and killing opponents,[68] for there is little notice of serious affliction or death in these texts. Anzacs endure childish ailments like measles and mumps, or suffer the heartache of calloused hands and sore throats. Should they lose limbs, they are never downhearted, consistently maintaining their sunny dispositions. Occasionally soldiers refer to "inconveniences" such as being bombed – "Goodness me there was a mess",[69] says Stirling's Anzac – but serious complaints of any nature are rare. More routinely, soldiers gripe about the weather, or about "attacks" from flies and fleas.

---

64 Ray Phillips, *The White Feather* (Melbourne: Melville and Mullen, 1917), 276–7.
65 Stirling, *Soldiers Two*, 120.
66 Brookes, *Broken Idols*, 97.
67 Grant Bruce, *Captain Jim*, 23.
68 In *The Body in Pain: The Making and Unmaking of the World* (New York: Oxford UP, 1985), Elaine Scarry argues that "the central activity of war is injuring, and the central goal is to out-injure the opponent. The fact of injuring tends to be absent from ... descriptions of war" (12); so, too, does the object of war, which is "to kill people" (61).
69 Stirling, *Soldiers Two*, 92.

On the rare instances in which Australian soldiers are seriously wounded, none yearns for a "Blighty"; all want to get well enough to return to battle, to take another crack at the bestial Boche. Australian women's novels are full of stories of men who won't give up fighting, no matter how serious their wounds are. Phillips' hero recounts an Anzac's tenacity at the Gallipoli landing as follows: "Shot in one hand – he kept on! Shot in the other – he kept on! His leg shattered – he kept on; till he fell from a crack on the head.[70] Additionally, one of Rixon's enlisted men refuses point blank to go home when he loses an arm, and on account of his commission, cannot be forced to do so. Previously an extremely accurate but right-handed marksman, he teaches himself to shoot left-handed, and becomes almost as good as formerly.[71] Throughout women writers' texts runs the notice that Australian men like to fight. Several overcome staggering obstacles just to get into battle. One of Rixon's soldiers travels eight hundred miles (traversing the last two hundred on foot) to enlist.[72] Rixon is likely parroting *The Anzac Book*, for in "Anzac Types," Wallaby Joe rides a thousand miles over sun-scorched, drought-stricken plains to enlist.[73] Once at the front, Anzacs eschew contemplation, preferring action to inaction. So anxious are Diggers to fight the Hun that they reject the opportunity to retreat to safety.

Aside from taking the character of the Australian male directly from *The Official Story* and the casual AIF slang and accounts of trench warfare from *The Anzac Book*, women writers also reproduce phrases and incidents from Bean's writings and from C.J. Dennis' *The Moods of Ginger Mick*. One of the most faithful mimics is Mabel Brookes. In *Broken Idols*, Brookes' heroine argues that the men who enlisted in the first contingent possessed special qualities which set them apart from other recruits. Listen, now, to Bean: "The first fine rush to enlistment brought to the 1st Australian Division a class of men not quite the same as that which answered to any later call".[74] Further, in his Introduction to *The Official History*, Bean contends that "to the Allies, and to our own country among them, the war was of the nature of a crusade. Not merely was their independence threatened or invaded; a new creed was being thrust upon the world, a creed utterly repugnant to the humanity of Christian civilization".[75] Now hear Brookes' character: "They [Anzacs] should look upon this war in the light of a Crusade. They are modern Crusaders fighting for the Christian ideals of the world".[76] This is the only time the subject of religion comes up in these texts. Bean declared in *The Official History* that the Australian was "seldom religious in the sense in which the word is generally

---

70 Phillips, *The White Feather*, 276–7.
71 Rixon, *The Scarlet Cape*, 205–6.
72 Rixon, *The Scarlet Cape*, 141.
73 Bean, *The Anzac Book*, 45.
74 Bean, *Official*, 43.
75 Bean, *Official*, xlvi.
76 Brookes, *Broken* Idols, 189.

used".[77] Bean and his writing were the Bible: all women's texts follow his sermons. He leaves religion off the agenda; so do they.

A careful reader, Brookes cribs an event directly from *The Anzac Book*. In "The Raid on London: A Modern Chronicle," Private Pat Riot records that a wounded Anzac attends a London theatrical production. Before anyone else, he hears Zeppelins and, anticipating a panic, rises to his feet, and shouts to the patrons to keep their seats. Riot thereby prevents a riot.[78] Brookes' Anzac performs an identical feat,[79] but with an added gibe at an English Tommy, who cowers in fright while the intrepid Australian calms the audience.

Brookes also plagiarises from Dennis' *The Moods of Ginger Mick*. The account of the fugitive-turned-hero in *On the Knees of the Gods* echoes the storyline in Dennis' extremely popular verse narrative. She shortens the episode considerably, but the similarities – both outlaws are reformed by the sensitive poets they meet in the trenches, and both die gloriously on the battlefield – are too marked to be coincidental. Brookes, reading Bean's and Dennis' prose hot off the press, wasted no time in replicating the incidents quickly in her texts. This emulation comes out of these writers' adulation, their lack of critical thought for their male heroes, real or fictional. The desire to replicate, to enact a pseudo-male position, is a real mark of insecurity, of self-doubt, and speaks to the extent to which these writers had internalised the expectations that Australia and her heroes had of them.

Further evidence of women writers' timidity about their subject matter arises in the number of times authority figures turn up in their texts. Brookes' central character visits Egypt in *Broken Idols*, and is taken to meet "a famous Australian poet," obviously Banjo Paterson, who crows that the Australian Light Horse performed an unprecedented feat in "droving" four hundred horses through the crowded streets of Cairo.[80] Paterson's proficiency with animals is greeted with "polite incredulity" by the British.[81] If Paterson tells the story himself, it is "true," believable; if Brookes transfers it into her woman character's voice, the story lacks authenticity. Thus the appearance of Paterson adds weight and authority to her text. Moreover, Paterson is a man of the bush; Brookes contributes to the blurring of bush legend into Anzac legend by injecting him into her text. In *The Scarlet Cape*, Rixon has Bean as his historical self visit the trenches and observe the men trying to relieve their monotony. He writes a letter describing the soldiers' activities, ultimately eulogising Rixon's hero. But the inclusion of Bean himself represents the extent to which she wishes to validate her version of the trenches with the man who has validated his version of the trenches. By using him to authenticate her reading/writing, she reveals the extent to which women writers were actually replicating

---

77   Bean, *Official*, 6.
78   Bean, *The Anzac Book*, 145.
79   Brookes, *On the Knees of the Gods*, 109–13.
80   Brookes, *Broken Idols*, 106.
81   Brookes, *Broken Idols*, 107.

a male story. Bean's presence in the novel is an act of mimicry, an attempt to substantiate the female-created story.

In making Anzacs super-heroes, tenacious and indefatigable good "mates" and savage fighters, Australian women writers were repeating the master narrative, retelling Bean's "official" story. But their worship of the Anzac estranged women from their own experiences, for they could not reflect them while mimicking a man's view. Women writers, forced to celebrate an event they could not attend, were unable to use their writing to record their frustration at being handed passive and trivial roles on the home front; unable to be the stars of their own home-front wars, they could only shoot blanks at patriarchy. In foregrounding male adventure, disseminating values they did not help formulate, they produced inauthentic art, and wrote dangerous and distorted views of war. More seriously, their writing reinforced traditional perceptions that women's experiences are unworthy material for a national tradition, and ironically, in their adulation of the Anzac, they bolstered the power of the patriarchal culture which denounced them as other.

In loyally promoting the Anzac in their texts, Australian women writers lost the home-front war, the battle between the sexes, for as Patrocinio P. Schweickart asserts, women writers who tell men's stories do not gain virile power; on the contrary, they double their oppression, for they continue to equate maleness with universality:

> Androcentric literature is all the more efficient as an instrument of sexual politics because it does not allow the woman reader to seek refuge in her difference. Instead, it draws her into a process that uses her against herself. It solicits her complicity in the elevation of male universality and, accordingly, the denigration of female difference in otherness without reciprocity.[82]

In extreme cases, as in the texts by Hain, Rixon and Burge, they allowed their narratives to be completely usurped. Thus they fell prey to what Mark Schorer terms women's ultimate anonymity, to be "storyless".[83] Elaine Showalter, analysing women writers who tell men's stories, puts the case even more strongly: "to deny that they are affected by being women at all is self-delusion or self-hatred, the legacy of centuries of denigration of women's art".[84] In succumbing to what Sharon O'Brien terms "combat envy",[85] Australian women writers facilitated their own domination, and left no path for future women (writers) to follow.

---

82 Patrocinio Schweickart, "Reading Ourselves: Toward a Feminist Theory of Reading," in *Speaking of Gender*, ed. Elaine Showalter (New York: Routledge, 1989), 27.

83 Cited in Carolyn Heilbrun, *Writing a Woman's Life* (New York: Ballantine, 1988), 12.

84 Elaine Showalter, ed., *Speaking of Gender*, (New York: Routledge, 1989), 14.

85 Sharon O'Brien, "Combat Envy and Survival Guilt: Willa Cather's 'Manly Battle Yarn'", in *Arms and the Women: War, Gender and Literary Representation*, eds. Helen M. Cooper, Adrienne Auslander Munich and Susan Merrill Squier (Chapel Hill: University of North Carolina Press, 1989), 188.

That so many Australian women writers meticulously replicate the narratives of the dominant patriarchal discourse is singular, and for this reason, I would argue that their writing is of unique literary interest. In making this claim, I differ from Jan Bassett, who contends that "[p]oetry and verse, personal narratives, and popular novels written by Australian women about the Great War are generally of much greater historical interest than literary significance".[86] But no other sources inform readers of the extent to which women were oppressed in Australia during the war. Historians like McKernan document that Australian women failed to hunt up paying jobs; social historians like Patsy Adam-Smith apprise the fervour with which women threw themselves into volunteer work. Only women fiction writers, especially those who efface their own stories, confirm how insignificant the dominant culture considered women to be. Only Australian women writers' texts, which reveal women's intense and cloying adulation of the Anzac, inform us how easy it was for the bastards to win the home-front war.

---

86   Jan Bassett, "'Preserving the White Race': Some Australian Women's Literary Responses to the Great War", *Australian Literary Studies* no. 12 (1985), 223. Bassett did not apparently notice the dominance of Anzacs in women writers' texts, for she does not mention it in her article.

2

"Guns 'n' Roses"

Mollie Skinner's Intrepid Great War Fictions

In spite of the fact that the West Australian writer M.L. (Mollie) Skinner wrote newspaper articles, radio dramas, gave several talks for the ABC, published a book on midwifery, a collection of short stories about Indigenous Australians, six novels and left a series of unpublished manuscripts, her literary reputation rests almost entirely upon her unlikely association with D.H. Lawrence. I say "unlikely" because Skinner was a middle-aged Quaker and avowed celibate when she met the writer of *Lady Chatterley's Lover* in 1922. She was running a boarding house outside of Perth; Lawrence and Frieda came to stay. When Lawrence learned she was a writer, he asked to see a copy of her first novel, *Letters of a V.A.D.* (1918), praised it highly, and then suggested she write another based upon her brother Jack's adventures in the Australian bush. Skinner produced a draft which Lawrence offered to improve, and even though Skinner did not approve of Lawrence's alterations to the ending, the book appeared as jointly authored in 1924, under Lawrence's title, *The Boy in the Bush*. British reviewers, most of whom assumed M.L. Skinner was a man, largely ignored her contribution. One eclipse followed another, as Australian book reviewers and critics either disregarded Skinner's subsequent works altogether or discussed them solely in light of her collaboration with Lawrence.

Even the reviewers of her posthumous autobiography *The Fifth Sparrow* (1972) overlook Skinner's fascinating life as a journalist, nurse, and midwife in several countries; her perpetual struggle with physical disabilities (she was born with a cleft palate and suffered partial blindness at eleven and poor eyesight thereafter); her physical unattractiveness during a time when women were expected to attract men, marry, and produce sons; and her desperate financial struggles. Most significantly, they ignore her valuable contribution to Australian writing and concentrate instead upon the Lawrence connection.[1] This chapter argues that Skinner's writing – in

---

1   See Maurice Dunlevy, "A Lawrencean Coupling That Set a Puzzle", *Canberra Times*, 6 January 1973, 8; J.H. Laurence, "He Seared My Spirit", *West Australian*, 2 December 1972, 27; A.A. Philips, "Followers of the Inner Light", *Nation Review*, 16–22 December 1972, 295; Olaf Ruben,

particular her two unique wartime novels – *Letters of a V.A.D.* and *Tucker Sees India* (1937) – has been unjustly neglected and deserves a prominent place in Australian war writing.

Although I hesitate to evoke Lawrence's words in a feminist article, I will acknowledge his discernment in praising *Letters of a V.A.D.* for its "vitality, freshness, and originality."[2] Lawrence's regard for the book's literary qualities is without question, but what I want to emphasise here is that he could not have comprehended how original a wartime novel it was, for presumably he would not have read the other eighteen or so women's Great War fictions that had already appeared,[3] and thus could scarcely have recognised that Skinner's text violated all the rules of the Australian Great War literary campaign. Since it is equally doubtful that contemporary readers will have read Australian women's World War I fictions, and in order to demonstrate how original Skinner's texts were, I will describe the other wartime fictions and outline briefly the context out of which they arose.

It is important to stress at the outset that Australian women who wished to write about the war faced a more daunting task than their American, British or Canadian counterparts, as several important factors worked against women attaining a strong voice. Prior to the war, the workplace had been a "forbidden zone" for women, which the hostilities did nothing to change. No serious disruption of the workplace occurred, for there was no large-scale munitions industry in Australia, no labour shortage, and no wide-scale mobilisation of the civilian population which would have stimulated women to take up new occupations or engage in previously unacceptable activities.[4] Thus the war did little to facilitate Australian women's movement into the public sphere. But most significantly, the persistent glorification of the Anzac and his fighting prowess overshadowed women's concerns and made it difficult for them to compete for a space within the discourse of war. As I have argued in Chapter 1, Australian women did not write their own stories; they had them written for them by the dominant ideology that permitted only one voice, a single interpretation of the war that eulogised the Anzacs' participation in the hostilities.

According to Robin Gerster, Australian war writing was "propagandist in its promotion of nationalistic sentiment and ideals",[5] and based on the "fundamental

---

"Memoirs of a Humble Sparrow", *Australian*, 9 December 1972, 22; Maslyn Williams, "The Quaker Spinster's Story", *Sydney Morning Herald*, 3 March 1973, 25. Judah Waten in "The Writer and the Nurse", *Age*, 20 January 1973, 19, is the only reviewer who insists that the credit for the writing of *The Boy in the Bush* should go primarily to Skinner. Waten also offers a more detailed analysis of Skinner's autobiography than other reviewers.

2   Cited in Mary Durack, "Foreword", in *The Fifth Sparrow: An Autobiography*, M.L. Skinner (Sydney: Sydney University Press, 1972), x.

3   In Canada, for example, a country with a much larger population, women writers produced only seven novels.

4   See Anne Summers, *Damned Whores and God's Police: The Colonization of Women in Australia* (Ringwood, Vic: Penguin, 1975),65–66; and Michael McKernan, *The Australian People and the Great War* (Melbourne: Nelson, 1980), 380.

premise that Australians excel, even revel, in battle".[6] Most prominent among the myth-shapers was war correspondent and historian C.E.W. Bean who, like his literary predecessors of the 1890s, worshipped the noble bushman, his physical appearance, temperament, and democratic values, and bestowed his veneration onto Anzacs. Although critics like Gerster have overlooked women writers' valuable contribution to the genre, it is indisputable that Great War writers Gladys Hain, Linda Webb Burge, Ray Phillips, Annie Rixon, Mabel Brookes, Ethel Turner, Mary Grant Bruce, and Chrystal Stirling read and absorbed Bean's writing, for their texts replicate his depictions of the Australian warriors' appearance, personality, egalitarian philosophy, mateship, and love of combat. In their fictions, the figure of the Anzac looms large, his dominating presence firmly establishing that women writers were as anxious as their male counterparts to back the attack and stand by their men. Indeed, several writers are so obsessed by the Anzac and his fighting prowess that they reproduce the master narrative of the soldier in the trenches, nullifying women characters, to whom they hand speaking parts or walk-on roles. Other writers nullify women's experience on the home front and tell pro-war soldiers' stories, which reinforce traditional assumptions that war is none of women's business. They leave their female characters waiting, silently and passively, for news from the trenches of France or the cliffs of Gallipoli, or for their men to return home. In short, women who wished to write about the war had to conform to the standards and preoccupations that patriarchal society had defined for them.[7]

But not all women writers were content with the designated feminine role of powerlessness, resignation, and denial. Several who were able to travel overseas during the war were quick off the mark and wrote novels transporting their protagonists away from the all-restrictive homeland and focusing more specifically, although not entirely, on women's experience of war. As the titles of the Australian novels indicate, the figure of the Anzac continues to dominate. Mary Grant Bruce's wartime trilogy – *From Billabong to London* (1915), *Jim and Wally* (1916) and *Captain Jim* (1919) – takes her characters to England and Ireland. Mabel Brookes' three novels – *Broken Idols* (1917), *On the Knees of the Gods* (1918) and *Old Desires* (1922) – situate women in England, France, and Egypt. Although Ethel Turner remained on the home front during the war, she sends her heroine to Belgium and France in *The Cub* (1915), *Captain Cub* (1917), and *Brigid and the Cub* (1918). In *A Marked Soul* (1923), Doris Manners-Sutton's character waves goodbye and makes her way to France. But even though these characters journey away from the familiar, they effect only flights of escape, not acts of rebellion. Rather than moving towards emancipation or autonomy, they tread water, and hence cause merely a

---

5   Robin Gerster, "Preface", *Big-Noting: The Heroic Theme in Australian War Writing* (Melbourne: Melbourne University Press, 1987), ix.

6   Gerster, *Big-Noting*, 2.

7   That writers like Linda Webb Burge and Annie Rixon continued to produce Great War fictions as late as 1944 indicates women's slavish devotion to hegemonic tradition.

ripple in the surface of the patriarchal structures which keep them submerged as subalterns in the war effort.

The novels by Grant Bruce, Brookes and Turner begin optimistically though, for long sea voyages provide much scope for action and adventure. En route to England, France, or Egypt, women thrill to shipboard romances, visit shops agleam with precious stones and metals in exotic ports-of-call like Colombo and Durban, and observe foreign cultures which invariably pale in comparison to the Australian way of life. In these novels, women face peril on the sea, too; at any moment, submarine attacks threaten to blow their ships sky high or sink them fathoms deep, and German spies infiltrate their vessels and threaten to take passengers as prisoners of war. Overall, women's voyages are marred only in that they are made to feel nuisances who ought not to be "allowed" to travel because they require men to be their protectors.

When these protagonists reach their destinations in England, France, or Egypt, the excitement of travel begins to wane, for they find it difficult to get meaningful jobs and, like their counterparts on the home front, are often forced to take up "waiting" as their major activity. In the case of the adolescent heroines who are plucky and eager to serve, their male guardians eventually select volunteer jobs for them which amount to little more than apprenticeships for their future roles as wives and mothers. Turner's Brigid works at a home for refugee children, but since she spends her time digging up cabbages (her job does not make her a Digger, though), it is ultimately unsatisfying. Grant Bruce's Norah runs a domestic establishment she calls a "Home For Tired People", but the establishment is already well staffed with servants and lacks nothing in the way of facilities and amenities, so Norah really has nothing to do but smile, smile, smile. Brookes' protagonists take up untaxing duties serving in canteens or singing for the troops, but the writer uses these encounters to boast about the Anzac's resilience and stamina in the trenches, not to suggest that women can contribute to the war effort in any significant way. Volunteer work is essentially diversionary, something to fill in the time between sightseeing excursions. Obviously uncomfortable describing trench warfare and uncertain what to do with their female characters over long stretches, these writers turn their protagonists into tourists, so that there is a blurring of genres; the texts read at times more like travel books than war novels. By taking their characters travelling, writers use the war as a temporal setting only; they write during the war, but avoid writing about it.

One of the other factors which inhibits these women characters' active participation in the war is that they do not travel unencumbered: a large part of their baggage is their identification with men. They go to war not as independent women, but as wives, daughters, sisters, or sweethearts, and are constantly reminded that their needs are subordinate to men's. As well as being male-identified, these protagonists are also isolated from other women. Although Nina Auerbach argues that "friendships among women ... are one of the acknowledged fruits of war",[8] she has clearly not read Australian women's wartime fiction, where women are one another's foes. In Australian texts, women's confidantes are routinely men, each writer thereby reinforcing the negative value women have been conditioned to place upon their own sex. Congenial relationships between women do materialise, but commonly an older woman, often a God's Police or mother-figure, wise in the ways of the world, instructs a younger in the domestic arts, or restores an errant woman to her proper station in life – as wife. Brookes in particular severely punishes any woman who dares violate the social codes: in *Old Desires*, she subjects a transgressor – a spy who uses her sexual power to persuade men to give up official secrets – to disfigurement and finally death. Lacking camaraderie, the women in these texts are unable to call into serious question the social constraints that confine them, or to gain any insight into the asymmetrical power structures that govern relationships between women and men. As Rita Felski argues, women need supportive communities because "the exploration of subjectivity within a dimension of group solidarity inspires activism and resistance rather than private resignation, and makes it possible to project a visionary hope of future change."[9] But the women in these texts remain isolated from one another, always travelling in the company of, and for the comfort of, men.

Moreover, because they are situated well behind enemy lines, women are protected from the harsh realities of war. Indeed, the young women in Grant Bruce's and Turner's novels are only "allowed" to journey overseas because they might be needed to nurse their loved ones well behind enemy lines. Brookes' more mature heroines travel for ostensibly the same reasons – to nurse sick husbands. But rarely do these characters come into contact with severely wounded or maimed men, so their nursing skills are never called into play. Brookes' Anzacs who serve in Egypt suffer from childish ailments like measles and mumps, or minor afflictions like sore throats and skin rashes. In *Broken Idols*, her heroine travels to Cairo to nurse her husband who suffers from para- typhoid, but we should all be so lucky to get his disease. By the time she arrives, he is sufficiently fit to tango and fox-trot the nights away at the luxurious hotel where they reside for the duration of her stay, but not well enough to resume his duties as a soldier. Grant Bruce's heroes are victims of gas attacks, but they recover nicely under expert medical care in the best London hospitals; unfit to fight in the trenches, they are nonetheless sufficiently healthy to spend six weeks' touring Ireland. Convalescing at Norah's rest home, too, are Diggers who have lost limbs but are nonetheless remarkably adroit, able to drive cars and play polo. For the most part, the war takes on the flavour of dangerous sport, so none of the heroines revises her feelings about war: each has set sail from Australia convinced that her country's allegiance to Great Britain is sound, and nothing she sees or hears causes her to view war as brutal and barbarous. She

---

8   Nina Auerbach, *Communities of Women: An Idea in Fiction* (Cambridge, MA: Harvard University Press, 1978), 187.

9   Rita Felski, *Beyond Feminist Aesthetics: Feminist Literature and Social Change* (Cambridge, MA: Harvard University Press, 1989), 129.

is seemingly unaware that Gallipoli, meant to be a glorious conquest, ended in a disastrous stalemate, and therefore should only be regarded as a vast and tragic blunder. No heroine feels the need to denounce those responsible for the ruin and desolation of war, or to make passionate appeals for its end. Each continues to glorify war, and the Anzac remains her hero, a demigod in khaki.

Do these heroines' excellent adventures serve any purpose at all, then? Minimally, yes. For the young women in Grant Bruce's and Turner's novels, the advent of war acts as a rude awakening, for they are suddenly brought to the realisation that their gender is a liability in wartime. More at home in the paddock than the pantry, these protagonists have been, until the war, unaware of gender imbalances. But while their male counterparts get to go into "action", to test their mettle through the metal of the bayonet, the best these young women can do is reach for their knitting needles or fountain pens. Brookes' more mature heroines also suffer from combat envy, but the best they can do is travel to escape meaningless lives. The conflict serves, then, to bring women to an awareness of the circumscribed nature of their roles and encourages them to seek alternatives to entrapment and enclosure. But in the end, the war strengthens, not relaxes, cultural definitions of gender, for the protagonists retreat willingly from Mother England to the fatherland, that unhomely place, when the war is over. Cheerfully picking up their brooms and dustpans, they sink back into their prewar existences, grateful to have had any experiences at all; their not-so-bold journeys into war will have to last them a lifetime. Turner's and Grant Bruce's adolescents will marry their Anzac sweethearts, the war having only temporarily interrupted their limited trajectory from parental to marital home, or from (t)here to maternity. Mollie Skinner, then, I will demonstrate, was the only Australian woman wartime writer who wished to bring an end to female passivity, dependence, and subordination.[10] Her *Letters of a V.A.D.* is an exceptional text because, true to the feminist agenda, it resists reigning ideologies, and on a variety of fronts. According to Mary Durack, Skinner had always been an avowed champion of women's rights; she possessed a "spirit of unusual courage and independence that led her, against all the conventions of her age and class, to complete nursing training" prior to 1900; and she routinely

---

10 One unusual text deserves brief mention because it shows a woman who takes up an unequivocally aggressive role in wartime. She's Catherine, a minor character in Doris Manners-Sutton's [C. Gentile] novel *A Marked Soul* (Melbourne: McCubbin, 1923). Catherine receives news that her husband is missing: she immediately travels to France to find him, and while she searches, supports herself by working as a ward attendant at a small hospital close to the front. By accident, she discovers that the Germans have crucified her husband for interfering in the rape (referred to in the novel as an "old tale", 181) of a French woman. Without hesitation, Catherine takes revenge by stabbing fourteen German prisoners of war in her hospital – one for every nail driven into her husband's body. The bloody butchering completed, she takes one last look at her "hideous handiwork" and declares "I have been just" (181). When the commanding officer hears of the slaughter, he calls her "a deuced fine woman" (187). For obvious reasons, Manners-Sutton's text is not one that I advocate as emancipatory reading.

asserted that "women no less than men, should use to its fullest extent any talent given them".[11]

Like her creator, Skinner's protagonist, R.X., is a talented and dedicated nurse, a member of the Voluntary Aid Detachment (VAD) who is in uniform, but is not a uniform heroine.[12] She's a woman who writes, not a woman who waits. Using what Linda S. Kaufman would term an "amorous epistolary discourse": a discourse which combines "writing and revolt, defiance and desire",[13] Skinner's R.X. tells the story of war from the inside, detailing for her readers what we are not supposed to know about the nature of war; for example, she describes the endless procession of mangled bodies across operating tables, and speaks of the suffering and death of its victims. Although she does not dwell excessively on graphic descriptions of wounded men, she does acknowledge that, more than once, both she and the male orderlies faint at the horrific sight of men's mutilated bodies, and thanks God that morphine and chloroform are available to alleviate suffering. In permitting us to enter the forbidden zone with her, R.X. is a dangerous woman, for she breaks the codes of silence and invisibility war offices counted upon women to obey in wartime. She and the other nurses single-handedly save the lives of several men, yet according to the rules of the war game, their actions must pass unacknowledged and uncommemorated. *Letters of a V.A.D.* records the nurses' courageous deeds for which they will receive no medals.

Since cleaning up the blood and muck of the battlefield is traditionally a woman's chore, *Letters of a V.A.D.* may seem initially to offer limited scope for women. As well, R.X. frequently refers to "mothering"[14] the soldiers under her care, a stance patriarchal authorities find acceptable. According to Nosheen Khan, "portrayal of the nursing profession as an extension of mother-love allows patriarchy to exploit women-power for its own purposes – the patching, mending and caring of wounded heroes – while ensuring that women remain firmly tethered to their time-honoured roles of carers and nurturers."[15] But Skinner only partially embraces the analogy between nurse and mother Khan describes so disparagingly: Skinner places the word "mothering" in quotation marks, indicating that she uses the term self-consciously, in full knowledge of the patriarchal approbation it carries. Further, one of the Red Cross sergeants R.X. works with, a gentle healing man, also refers to the men as his "sons" (205); like R.X., he uses these terms of endearment to

---

11   Durack, "Foreword" *The Fifth Sparrow*, ix–x.
12   While many of the events and circumstances in *Letters of a V.A.D.* can be traced to Skinner's own experiences as a nurse in India and Burma, it is erroneous to assume, as have several reviewers, that the text is either wholly autobiographic or a "wartime reminiscence" (Williams, "The Quaker Spinster's Story", 25).
13   Linda S. Kaufman, *Discourses of Design: Gender, Genre, and Epistolary Fictions* (Ithaca. NY: Cornell University Press, 1986), 20.
14   Mollie Skinner, *Letters of a V.A.D.* (London: Melrose, 1918), 80, 139. All subsequent references are to this edition and appear in parentheses in the text.
15   Nosheen Khan, *Women's Poetry of the First World War* (Lexington: University of Kentucky, 1988), 117.

facilitate the healer/patient relationship. Nor is R.X. merely a ministering angel who provides pills and injections to wounded men: she has an easygoing camaraderie with the soldiers and, recognising their need to talk about their experiences in the trenches, becomes their willing confidante. She is also the men's intellectual equal, carrying on heated debates with them over issues such as the merits of faith in wartime. Placed in charge of her unit, R.X. refers to the men somewhat cavalierly as the "puppets in my little show" (247), indicating that she does not see herself in a subordinate position. R.X. also claims that she felt God's guiding hand on her shoulder, and believes he called her to play a vital role in the war as a healer; she nurses, then, not out of the presumed "woman's natural inclination" to self-sacrifice and nurturing, but regards nursing as a skilled vocation which brings her not only happiness but an "intense sense of joyfulness" (230).

In several other respects, R.X. is an unusual heroine. Unlike the protagonists in the aforementioned novels who view the war from the perspective of tourists and accept unquestioningly their country's commitment to it, R.X. is ever mindful of the "ineffable sadness and sin and pain of the world" (19) and never fails to question the meaning of war. Her beliefs, with their strong Christian overtones, provide moral frameworks for justifying the war and proffering comfort to those who participate in it. R.X. locates virtue in pain and suffering, believing ultimately that men's sacrifice is redemptive, and will purge society of its complacencies. While these values may not sit well today, they did hold currency during World War I.

Additionally, although Skinner begins her novel with an epigraph by Billy Hughes which pays tribute to the Anzacs' "glorious valour", her protagonist does not expend her energies shoring up the Anzac myth, an undertaking which I have observed marginalises and ultimately defeats women in the other texts. R.X. does express affection for the Diggers, but she admires their fun-loving natures and mateship practices, not their wartime bellicosity, as other women writers do. And unlike other writers who routinely depict English soldiers as weaklings or cowards, Skinner's R.X. praises Tommies and Anzacs equally. Although I hesitate to introduce biographical material, I need to mention that Skinner remarks in her autobiography, *The Fifth Sparrow*, that because she was living in India, she did not hear of the outbreak of war until April 1915.[16] Thus she would have missed the exemplary reports on the Anzacs' fighting prowess emanating from overseas by correspondents C.E.W. Bean, Ellis Ashmead-Bartlett and John Masefield. Without male views of war to mimic, Skinner was free to devise her own impressions of the conflict and the composition of the soldiers.

The major difference between Skinner's text and those by Grant Bruce, Turner and Brookes, however, is that her protagonist goes to war as an independent woman who claims the right to an identity not determined by sexual or maternal roles. R.X. openly confesses that the desire for adventure in the "uttermost parts of the earth"

---

16   Mollie Skinner, *Fifth Sparrow*, 95.

(255) is part of her incentive to go to war, and her brother and fiancé having been killed in the trenches, she is free to carve out her future as she sees fit. But because she is both attractive and capable, R.X. receives several proposals of marriage. The women of her outfit, most of whom have enlisted in the war as nurses to find husbands, regard her as a threat, and have her removed from her position out of jealousy and spite, even though she rejects the offers.

Making the decision to remain single does not come easily to R.X. She claims to love one of her suitors, a colonel, but because he is divorced and she is in training to become a Catholic, she cannot marry him. But R.X. has other, more deep-seated reasons for rejecting the colonel's offer. She wants children, but autonomy more. R.X. takes a cynical view of wedded bliss, arguing that while women are conditioned to think they want marriage, children and men to protect them, they are inevitably disappointed by the outcome. She draws upon images of caged birds and trapped rats to signal her awareness of the circumscribed nature of women's situation within marriage, and in the end recognises that she can maintain her identity best through her uncomplicated relationship with her "little sister" (11), the Catholic nurse who trained her, and for whom she professes in her letters a deep and abiding love. Skinner is not, I believe, writing of lesbian love; rather, she places her faith in women's support and encouragement of one another. Accordingly, R.X.'s friend does not ask her to relinquish her identity, or to subordinate her needs. Instead, she functions as R.X.'s mentor, teaching her to behave charitably, to take pride in her profession, and guiding her along the "difficult path" to independence (274). In suggesting that women should think well enough of femaleness to care for other women, Skinner was offering a unique view.

Throughout the novel, R.X. is constantly on the move, but never as a tourist. Her sea crossing to the front is brief and uneventful; she does not engage in a shipboard romance but gets seasick instead. And when the ship calls in at exotic ports, R.X. delights in cultural difference, and makes no racist comments, as the characters in the fictions by Grant Bruce and Brookes do so freely.[17] Arriving at base camp, she tends soldiers who are leaving for Blighty, but is soon transferred to the hospital nearest the front, well within the range of shot and shell. At the end of the novel, she is asked to go with the head of the VAD to "an uncertain indefinite place", where the work will be "hard", and the life "trying" (273–74); undaunted, R.X. continues to swim against the tide, and moves full steam ahead into uncharted waters.

In writing this novel, Skinner utilised some curious "camouflage" techniques. In her autobiography, she confesses that she published *Letters of a V.A.D.* under a pseudonym because she "could not bear to be unloved by those about [her];

---

17   Skinner herself seemingly had few prejudices. In *My Place* (London: Virago, 1988), Sally
     Morgan recounts that Molly [sic] Skinner was "very sympathetic to Aboriginal people and
     treated them kindly" (275). She gave Morgan's grandmother and mother a place to live and
     treated them with dignity and respect.

that everything [she] wrote made them scoff ... that [she] was scared of writing what went on about [her]".[18] Since her parents regarded both her writing and nursing careers as "common", she perhaps wished to protect them from being identified with a novel based loosely on their daughter's nursing experiences. That she selected "Leake" is curious, for it was her mother's birth name, and also the name of her uncle, a West Australian premier, so her choice could also have been a public disavowal of her family's social values. Whatever her motivations, the novel is replete with maddening omissions and ambiguities, perhaps signalling Skinner's unease at writing a novel "which kicks against the pricks".[19] Among the gaps are details of what country R.X. nurses in, what years she serves, or even what nationality she is.

Nonetheless, Skinner's novel is a triumph of inventiveness, for while Grant Bruce, Turner and Brookes dimly recognised that women were oppressed within male-defined environments, they were unable to articulate the possibility of even partial liberation from those social and ideological constraints. Skinner's *Letters of a V.A.D.* is the only wartime novel I have found which disrupts the traditional heterosexual romance plot. Her R.X. is the only heroine in Australian women's fiction written and published during or immediately after the war to reject psychological and emotional dependence upon a man, the only one who can see herself in terms other than nurturing and supportive.[20] As the only writer to "call the shots" in wartime, the only one not at a "loss" for words in defence of her gender, Mollie Skinner is the only writer to attempt to score a literary victory for women during World War I.

Regrettably, Skinner's first novel sank immediately into oblivion, as Katharine Susannah Prichard discovered when she was unable to locate a copy in Perth in 1924.[21] I have only been able to locate two reviews of this text: the first, a favourable, but unsigned commentary titled *"Letters of a V.A.D."*, states that the "letters from first to last ring true", and that "[t]he book bears the obvious imprint of actual experience"; after providing a lengthy quotation from the novel, the reviewer "heartily recommend[s]" it,[22] but does not suggest that the book differs from other Australian women's wartime fictions. Another reviewer, "Norbar", commenting upon both *Letters of a V.A.D.* and *Tucker Sees India*, another delightful novel, comes closer to the mark by offering that Skinner is "strangely different" from other West Australian authors. Norbar adds that Skinner's work has "an elusive character which

---

18 Skinner, *The Fifth Sparrow*, 115.
19 Skinner, *The Fifth Sparrow*, 312.
20 Lesbia Harford's *The Invaluable Mystery* (Fitzroy: McPhee Gribble/Penguin, 1987) is another rare text that suggests that women could lead independent lives. For an analysis of this unusual text, see Chapter 4.
21 Katharine Susannah Prichard, "M.L. Skinner: The West Australian Writer Who Collaborated with D.H. Lawrence in His Latest Book 'The Boy in the Bush'", *Women's World*, 1 December 1924, 18, 41.
22 Unsigned review, *"Letters of a V.A.D."*, *West Australian*, 18 April 1919, 6.

is difficult to grasp"; and further remarks that in none of her books does she "fall into the facile pattern of stock character and situation".[23] In the end, however, Norbar damns with faint praise, declaring that Skinner's writing is naïve, lacks discipline, and that she is "neglectful of construction". Norbar clearly did not see the literary qualities Lawrence identified.

In *Tucker Sees India*, Skinner makes another bold attempt to shatter, not shore up, reigning ideologies and debunk national sentiments,[24] this time utilising humour as a weapon. She also writes under her own name and sets the novel clearly in India. Like other women writers, she foregrounds the story of the Anzac, but C.E.W. Bean would not approve of her Digger, for Tucker is, atypically, no perfect specimen of Australian manhood. Rather, he's a self-confessed "waster" who's enlisted reluctantly and for non-military reasons – he's "attracted by war songs and the idea of pleasing his mother", to whom he refers frequently. Initially, Tucker signs up for the infantry, then changes his mind and tries to get out of the war altogether by marrying, but he's "shoved" into the Australian Light Horse against his will.[25] Moreover, unlike other fictional Anzacs who like to fight so much they won't give up even when wounded, Skinner's Tucker is bored by military talk, faints at the sight of blood, freely admits he's a coward, and doesn't see the point in killing anyone. And while other Anzacs are often oblivious to the carnage around them, Tucker laments the loss of life wrought by war. Because he doesn't want to participate actively in the carnage, Tucker drinks too much and, hungover, he literally "misses the boat", the troopship that sails from Bombay to Egypt; thus he inadvertently misses the Gallipoli disaster altogether. By presenting Tucker as a larrikin, Skinner suggests that the ruffian reputation which persistently dogged Anzacs abroad, but which other women writers routinely downplayed, was perhaps well deserved.

Unlike other women writers who label men who do not want to fight "womanly", Skinner permits her military man, Tucker, to "serve" out the war, in true egalitarian fashion, by picking up the kinds of subservient jobs often "reserved" for women. When he misses the troopship, he turns to a woman, his nursing sister Penny, not his mates, for advice. She refers him to a military officer who sends Tucker travelling throughout the country carrying out various military assignments. Like a rogue in a picaresque novel, only in this instance "on the train", Tucker conveys the dispatches by passing himself off as an expert on foodstuffs. But he also consistently behaves in a "womanly" fashion, for he is called upon to nurse the sick and perform as a midwife (he delivers twins!); in his spare time, Tucker pursues his favourite hobby, flower-arranging.[26] Whereas the women in the

---

23 Norbar, "Novelist and Nurse: Work of Miss M. Skinner", *West Australian*, 23 July 1938, 6.

24 Angela Thirkell's *Trooper to the Southern Cross* (London: Faber and Faber, 1934; London: Virago, 1985), which she wrote under the pseudonym Leslie Parker, also denounces the Anzac myth. See Chapter 3 for more details.

25 M.L. Skinner, *Tucker Sees India* (London: Secker & Warburg, 1937), 13. All subsequent references are to this edition and appear in parentheses in the text.

texts by Grant Bruce, Turner, and Brookes travel in the company of men and for their comfort, Tucker tours about in the company of women, a British mother and daughter he meets along the way. In a nice turn of the tables, the mother saves Tucker's life. When she asks why he hasn't used his revolver to save himself, he replies that he doesn't want to "hurt" anyone (43). Yet in spite of his reluctance to enter the fray, Tucker often behaves in a manner befitting a "gallant" hero: he rescues a woman who's been taken hostage and he exposes gun-smuggling Huns, but he never distinguishes himself through the skilful use of a deadly weapon. Rather, in one instance, he tests his mettle by wielding a pair of wire-cutters which halt a train and enable the authorities to capture seditious hillmen. Unlike his fictional counterparts who routinely boast that they are winning the war single-handedly, Tucker remains modest, never once big-noting his war efforts, even when awarded a medal for bravery (325).

In other respects, Tucker is an unusual hero. While the other texts produce handsome, physically fit men who are so identical that they appear to have been fashioned on an assembly line or spewed out of a photocopying machine with perfect "Anzactitude" – they are all of herculean looks and stature – Tucker is often chided about how old he looks. To compensate, he dyes his grey hair black, wears false teeth, and takes comfort in his own belief that he resembles Rudolph Valentino. Nor does Tucker give a fig about maintaining a fiercely masculine identity: in one instance, in order to protect himself from enemy attack, he darkens his skin and cross-dresses as an ayah; in another, he sports a wig and wears a choti (split skirt). He's also not above disguising himself as a visible minority; he informs one of his would-be attackers that he's Māori, and thereby saves his hide.

Another of Tucker's unique features is that, like Skinner herself and her fictional R.X., he embraces cultural differences. He tries to learn Urdu, never makes disparaging remarks about "The Other", and early on in the novel, acquires a "holy mark" on his forehead after offering his warm overcoat to a needy Indian man. No coloniser himself, Tucker is always keen to learn about local customs, history, architectural practice, (185) and presciently questions imperialism, the role of the white man in India (181). Unlike the other women writers who take their characters sightseeing in order to avoid writing about combat, Skinner sends Tucker travelling to stress that he has a genuine and open desire to see the people and to comprehend their way of life. Over the space of three months in early 1915, Tucker "sees" Bombay, Lahore, Peshawar, Delhi and the Khyber Pass. The last words of the novel – "Tucker had seen India" (326) – indicate that he emerges victorious in his war effort.

But how might we account for the singularity of *Tucker Sees India*? One clue may lie in the name Skinner selects for her hero – Richard Smith. She may have been mimicking other women writers whose work she had undoubtedly read,

---

26 Judging by the description of her brothers that appears in *The Fifth Sparrow*, Skinner's Tucker appears to be a composite of Bob and Jack.

for many of them called their Anzacs "Dick". Skinner may also have utilised the surname "Smith" (or, for that matter, the nickname "Tucker") to indicate that there were many ordinary Australian men who did not want to fight, who were frightened in battle, who were not "good" at combat, and who may even have enlisted, as Richard White has suggested, out of a desire to see the world,[27] a notion other women writers tended to gloss over. Skinner may also have wished to minimise, even eradicate, the ubiquitous notion that all Anzacs were bloodthirsty sharpshooters or vicious sabre-wielding killers. She may have wanted to emphasise that many Australian women and men were appalled by the violence, the bloodshed, the utter waste of human life; sentiments rarely, if ever, uttered by other women writers. Her feelings about war may have arisen because Skinner herself was all too familiar with these follies of war, for not only had she nursed wounded soldiers herself, one of her brothers, Bob, had been killed during the war. The other, her beloved brother Jack, was wounded in Egypt, but according to notes in Paul Eggert's scholarly edition, was forced to fight at Gallipoli nonetheless, and often brutally told, when he complained, that he was malingering.[28] Jack never recovered from his injuries and died prematurely in 1925.

Whatever her motives, it is indisputable that Skinner was the only Australian woman wartime writer who refused to be a dutiful myrmidon and conform to the standards and preoccupations that patriarchal society had defined for her. In writing these atypical wartime fictions, she displayed a great deal of courage, a kind of bravery reviewers did not often recognise, although one or two dimly perceived that Tucker was a unique Digger figure. In an untitled review in the *West Australian*, an anonymous evaluator who notes that it may be a "misnomer" to consider *Tucker Sees India* an "Australian tale" since it takes place in India, nonetheless concludes that the novel makes "highly entertaining reading", and hopes to see more of Tucker's adventures in print in the future.[29] Another unsigned review declares that *Tucker Sees India* is "unusual", and observes that "it defies classification", for it is "not a thriller, or traveller's tale, or satire, or Novel With a Mission", but a "plain story of the adventures and misadventures of a happy-go-lucky, irresponsible, supremely casual Aussie in India." Correctly, the reviewer, who concludes that *Tucker Sees India* is a "darn good book", reaches his conclusion by observing that Tucker is "something quite new in heroes. Like the book itself, he can't be classified".[30] "Norbar", however, while agreeing that the novel is "an exciting unusual piece of work" displaying "considerable originality, spiritual perception and feeling", further suggests that these positive attributes are "circumscribed at every turn by almost school-girl conceptions of situation and character, probably an unconscious legacy

---

27   Richard White, "The Soldier as Tourist: The Australian Experience of the Great War", *Kunapipi*, nos 18.2. and 3 (1996): 117–29.

28   D.H. Lawrence, "Note on Miss M.L.Skinner", in *The Boy in the Bush*, D.H. Lawrence and M.L. Skinner, ([1924]; Cambridge: Cambridge University Press, 1990), 373.

29   Unsigned review, *West Australian*, 18 Sept. 1937, 4.

30   Unsigned review, "Books", *Daily News*, 10 September 1937, 5.

from a mid-Victorian middle-class sensibility which has lingered among the old families of Australia long after its wane in England." But "Norbar" completely misses the point by suggesting that Skinner's work bore the "mark of isolation", and that she would have benefited from "early introduction into a circle invigorated by the new realism inspired from Scandinavia and France." Without such an infusion, s/he posits, Skinner has been left "high and dry".[31] But it is "Norbar", I suggest, whose review bears the mark of isolation, for s/he has not read the other works by Australian women writers that would enable her/him to comprehend how truly original Skinner's work was. As contemporary critics, our own salute to Mollie Skinner's intrepid, unduly neglected, wartime fiction, is long overdue.

---

31   Norbar, "Novelist and Nurse", 6.

3

(Not) Talking Back

Australian Women Novelists Lose the Great (Linguistic) War

That so many Australian women writers meticulously replicated the narratives of the dominant patriarchal discourse during and after World War I is singular and of unique literary interest.[1] In Canadian women's fictional responses to the Great War, for example, writers recognise that language is an important site of political struggle, and they use men's language, not to reproduce the same history, not to underscore their own subordination, but to convert marginalisation into affirmation, and to speak from a position of power. By contrast, Australian women writers re-inscribe their own marginality by using militaristic language as a means of keeping women firmly on the boundaries of war. Thus they send a clear signal that they feel themselves to be but interlopers in a man's game, replicating stories already written by the dominant ideology. They employ martial language to underscore that any woman who refuses to bear cannon fodder for future wars or who shirks her duty as a mother will find herself engaged in a home-front war she cannot possibly win. With the dominant ideology's insistence that women take on solely maternal and caretaking roles, there is no destabilising which would lead women to an awareness of the way the sexual territory is mapped; instead, the texts reinforce women's oppression by speaking the same language as their oppressors. In their texts, it is the narrative voice of the dominant ideology that uses militaristic language to defeat wayward women: female characters who dare to claim the right to independent thought and action do not employ fighting words. Australian women writers thus indicate that they can mime male discourse, but they remain parasites of the language, engulfed and silenced by its power. In sum, Australian women writers lost the linguistic war. Their readers, future generations, suffered the losses.

---

1   This chapter was written with support of a Killam resident Fellowship.

No, I dont [sic] see whats [sic] [to] be done about war. Its [sic] manliness; and manliness breeds womanliness–both so hateful.[2]

The feminist critic who asserts that "the voices of women's narratives are never those of the dominant patriarchal discourse, because women's relationship to that discourse is different from men's",[3] has clearly never read Australian women's Great War writing, which is, with rare exception,[4] an almost verbatim re-inscription of the way Australian and British war correspondents, poets, and journalists C.E.W. Bean, C.J. Dennis, Banjo Paterson, John Masefield, Ellis Ashmead-Barlett and Compton MacKenzie depicted the Anzacs' participation in combat. Fictions by Mary Grant Bruce, Ethel Turner, Gladys Hain, Mabel Brookes, Linda Webb Burge, Kathleen Pearson, Ray Phillips, Annie Rixon, Chrystal Stirling, and Mary Marlowe[5] are, for the most part, a working out in fiction of these men's models of the Anzacs' physical appearance, his fighting prowess, and his insistence upon egalitarianism and mateship. These women writers dutifully set their novels on the battlefield, boast about the Anzacs' fighting prowess, tally up his courageous assaults, record his victories against the Boche, but mute women's voices. In placing themselves firmly in the war zone, they emasculate themselves, and make their only entry into the discourse of war through submission to phallocentricity. Sadly, their shoring up of soldiers' stories went for naught, for with the exception of the works by the popular children's writers Mary Grant Bruce and Ethel Turner, the remainder disappeared into obscurity.

The idea that so many Australian wartime women writers meticulously replicate the narratives of the dominant patriarchal discourse is singular and hence of unique literary interest. In Canada, for example, the absence of men brings about positive results.[6] While none of the Canadian writers' texts expresses the kind of "invigorating sense of revolution, release, reunion, and revision" which Sandra Gilbert identifies in her study of British and American Great War women writers,[7] it could be argued that Canadian women writers are war profiteers, seizing the chaos occasioned by war to vanquish women's subordinate status. In their

---

2   Virginia Woolf, *The Letters of Virginia Woolf*, ed. Nigel Nicolson and Joanne Trautmann. 6 vols. (New York: Harcourt, 1975–80), 464.

3   Tunde Nemeth, "Taboo, Silence and Voice in Women's Writing: Intertidal Life as Case in Point", *Canadian Research Institute for the Advancement of Women (Ottawa)*, no. 23 (1989), 3.

4   Mollie Skinner tells *Tucker Sees India* (London: Martin, 1937) from a male point of view, but Skinner derides the Anzac myth by creating an atypical Digger who does not want to fight, see Chapter 2.

5   Mary Marlowe's *The Women Who Wait* is set in London, but I include it here because Marlowe, a prolific writer, was born in Australia and spent the bulk of her life there.

6   For a further analysis of Canadian women's Great War writing, see my "The Best Soldiers of All: Unsung Heroines in Canadian Women's Great War Fictions", *Canadian literature*, 151 (Winter 1996): 66–99.

7   Sandra M. Gilbert, "Soldier's Heart: Literary Men, Literary Women and the Great War," in *Behind the Lines: Gender and the Two World Wars*, eds. Margaret Higonnet, Jane Jenson, Sonya Michel, and Margaret Collins Weitz (New Haven, CT: Yale University Press, 1987): 197–226.

women-centred texts, they insist upon bringing an end to the image of women as caregivers and nurturers, and forcefully reiterate that women deserve a place in society alongside men, not as their subalterns. Canadian writers express their anger that women have been denied access to public and political realms, caution that they can no longer afford to be onlookers in a man's world and beseech their characters to make their presence felt during the war. With women's voices and values part of the discourse, they argue, Canada will be a better place for all. Although New Zealand women writers produced only a handful of Great War texts, none of them nearly as exuberant or exhilarating as those published in Canada, like their Canadian counterparts, they clearly did not feel they had to adhere to a single myth, a prescribed set of values, or act as magnifying mirrors to bolster male ego and fighting prowess.[8] British women writers, too, according to a recent anthology, found themselves "charting the new social roles" that the war evoked and taking up "new positions in relation to the war".[9] Moreover, most impressive "is the commitment with which women recorded their experience, painful or otherwise, their self-awareness and confidence in being alert chroniclers of their part in the conflict".[10] But in Australia, aside from the aforementioned Mollie Skinner, only Lesbia Harford was sufficiently brave enough to violate all the rules of the Australian Great War literary campaign in her novel *The Invaluable Mystery*. She set her novel in Sydney, ignored entirely the almighty Anzac, and featured a feisty woman who was determined to get by on her own. Ironically, once she found her voice, patriarchal publishers prevented her from speaking to contemporary readers, for they refused to publish the manuscript. It appeared in print only after researchers accidentally discovered it in the National Archives of Australia in Canberra in 1987. The publishers' rejection of such an emancipatory text reinforces the possibility that other brave new works were obscured, but how many, we may only speculate.[11]

But why were Australian women writers the only ones not able to stick to their guns, the only ones not able to shoot anything but blanks at the patriarchy? Anne Summers asserts that "where women have participated in Australian culture it has had to be with due acquiescence to a game whose rules were drawn up without their consent. They have had to conform to what men assured them was important".[12] Male writers like Henry Lawson, Joseph Furphy, Banjo Paterson and Steele Rudd assured women that the Anzacs were superb fighters and that their prowess in

---

8 For an analysis of New Zealand women's Great War writing, see my "Myrmidons to Insubordinates: Australian, New Zealand and Canadian Women's Fictional Responses to the Great War" in *The Literature of the Great War Reconsidered: Beyond Modern Memory*, eds. Patrick J. Quinn and Steven Trout (New York: Palgrave, 2001): 113–42.

9 Agnes Cardinal, Dorothy Goldman and Judith Hattaway, eds., "Introduction" in *Women's Writing on the First World War* (Oxford: Oxford University Press, 1999), 1–2.

10 Cardinal et al., "Introduction", 2.

11 For an analysis of this fascinating text, see Chapter 4.

12 Anne Summers, *Damned Whores and God's Police: The Colonization of Women in Australia* (Ringwood, Vic: Penguin, 1975), 33–34.

combat brought Australia nationhood. Lacking a strong tradition of their own to identify with, and not brave enough to be refractory, they adapted their writing to identify with and emulate men's preoccupations in war.

Australian women were prevented from achieving even limited liberation, in spite of the fact that they were eager to fight for their country in any way they could. They haggled for men's jobs and tried to enlist in military service, but were prevented from taking "active" roles by the military and government, which resolutely spurned their offers as there was no wholesale shortage of labour to oblige them to take men's jobs. Another factor that robbed women writers of ammunition was that they had earned the right to vote at Federation in 1901. Lacking a particular feminist cause to rally around prior to the war, they were not well organised to fight for their rights at the outbreak. Their distance from European feminist organisations hampered their emancipation, as well. Canadian women were in part successful in their struggle for enfranchisement because politicians were aware of the revitalised feminist movement that was making gains in Europe and America. At such a remote distance, pressure from women's organisations would not have been felt in Australia. Denied paid employment, rebuffed by the military and the government, Australian women had little choice but to back the attack indirectly: they faced little opposition as long as they confined their activities to the ones patriarchal society sanctioned. Making soldier comforts posed no threats; thus Australian women developed a plethora of voluntary aid organisations, all for the sake of the soldier. In Canada, by contrast, although women also undertook a wide variety of volunteer duties, they were quick to spot societal needs, to rectify them, and to eradicate a number of gender inequalities. Unlike their Australian counterparts, Canadian women were also encouraged to enter non-traditional areas of work; they were, for example, actively recruited to produce shot and shell for the munitions industry.[13]

Given the circumscribed nature of women's lives on the Australian home front, it is surprising that so many writers took up the challenge of documenting women's experiences in fiction during World War I. But in the end, most were merely passive receivers of the dictates of the dominant ideology. They reproduced word for word the discourse of the master, espoused his patriarchal ideals, and took up the masculine language of war in order to become a man's mouthpiece. In so doing, they misappropriated language, silenced their own voices and their own stories; wartime vernacular defeated them, rendered them powerless.[14]

---

13   For an examination of the myriad ways the war had a beneficial and liberating effect on Canadian women, see Alison Prentice et al.'s *Canadian Women: A History* (Toronto: Harcourt, 1988).

14   By contrast, Canadian women writers recognise that language is an important site of political struggle, and they use men's language, use sameness, not to reproduce the same history, not to underscore their own subordination, but to convert marginalisation into affirmation, and to speak from a position of power.

The simple formula that patriarchy constructs for literary women, and which these writers embrace, is stifling and repressive. Female characters must find fulfilment through marriage and motherhood, assume pro-war stances, and cheerfully send their loved ones off into combat; in the absence of men, they may occupy themselves only in the bearing and rearing of children. The rules of the wartime "game" for Australian fictional women are inflexible and unyielding: any woman who shows signs of straying from the status quo must either be quickly restored to her proper place, severely punished, or destroyed.

The plots of both Ray Phillips' *The White Feather* (1917) and Mary Marlowe's *The Women Who Wait* (1918) are similar. Both feature two types of women – those who adhere to societal prescriptions, and those who rail against them. In each text, the conformer, either a cheerful and happy mother or an aspirant to the role, defeats the non-compliant. In *The White Feather*, set in Melbourne, Phillips' unconventional woman is the frail Jessie who does, at least initially, stick closely to the demands of the marriage plot by snaring a husband. But in order to procure her wedding band, Jessie must resort to manipulation: she seduces a man (he is only doing her a favour by succumbing to her "advances"), gets pregnant, and then married. Her timing and selection are poor, however: she becomes pregnant at the outbreak of war by Dick, a man who has wanted from childhood to be a soldier. She tries to prevent Dick from enlisting, not because she is a pacifist, but because she fears childbirth,[15] dislikes children, and does not want to raise one on her own. Phillips' hero, sufficiently decent not to desert his wife, is nonetheless able to effect an escape when his ex-sweetheart, Neville, comes to his rescue. So eager is Neville to see Dick enlist that she springs into action "like a soldier when the reveille sounded".[16] Neville is the feminine type Phillips most admires. Unlike Jessie, who prefers to remain indoors, Neville loves to be outside in the "wild'ness" on her vast urban property. In creating Neville as the outdoorsy type with a suitably tomboyish name, Phillips, like the majority of other women (and men) writers, was romancing life in the bush, and upholding bush mythology. (Charles Bean would have approved.) Moreover, Neville is intensely pro-war, having eagerly relinquished three brothers and a father to war, yet she is totally dedicated to home and hearth. While Phillips censures Jessie's strategies for inveigling a husband, she commends the underhanded tactics Neville uses to pry her loved one from Jessie's clutches so that he can fulfil his ambition and get away to war.

When the antagonists Jessie and Neville first meet, they size one another up "as if measuring weapons" (205), but as defender of the status quo, Neville is the fiercest aggressor, determined to destroy her home-front enemy, a woman

---

15 In "Inside the Deserted Hut: The Representation of Motherhood in Bush Mythology", *Westerly*, no. 34.3 (1989): 76–96, Sue Rowley points out that Australian women had good reason to fear pregnancy; around the turn of the century, about one in thirty women could die in childbirth (96).

16 Ray Phillips, *The White Feather* (Melbourne: Melville, 1917), 34. All subsequent references are to this edition and appear in parentheses in the text.

who refuses to play the game of war by patriarchal rules. In doing battle with Jessie, Neville recognises that she has ventured into a "remarkably antagonistic atmosphere", but undaunted, knows that her "adversary" is "worth fighting" (205). Neville also comprehends that she needs "a mighty weapon to pierce such smothering armour" (206), so she plans her "advances" slowly (208). Like a ruthless bayonet-wielding soldier in the trenches, Neville, too, fights to the finish: the narrator states that "she meant to have no mercy. She meant to return to the attack again and again, till she forced a way through Jessie's defences" (221–22). Not surprisingly, Jessie proves to be powerless against Neville's ferocity. She survives only long enough to give birth to a son (of course); learning from Neville that Dick will never love her, and hating her child, Jessie conveniently expires. The spoils of war go to Neville, who zealously claims the son and the soldier, the latter having returned from war with a barely perceptible limp (of course). In her novel, then, Phillips draws upon military discourse to issue a warning to any woman who stands not by her man but in his way. Moreover, should she not wish to have children, she is useless to society, and might as well die. Jessie's death does not function as a critique of the societal restrictions that confine her. No one mourns her demise in this text.

Mary Marlowe's central character, Clare, like Phillips' Jessie, dislikes children and fears childbirth. A "new woman",[17] she logically reasons that not every female need procreate. But because Clare is also a fashionable London socialite anxious not to lose her physical attractiveness, her motivations are not entirely feminist. Clare's rejection of children causes a serious rift in her marriage, but the tension escalates when the war breaks out. Her husband, another Dick (!), enlists, and "orders" Clare to become pregnant before he leaves; he wants a son to carry on his name, and a child to bequeath to his country's depleted population,[18] but Clare refuses his sexual advances. On the night before he departs for war, Dick cruelly informs his wife that, in refusing motherhood, she is "shirking" her wartime duties, but Clare sits calmly knitting khaki socks, not booties for babies, and sticks to her guns. Even before he departs for war, Dick has already lost "his first battle", the "attack on his manhood" (120); he has fought, yet failed, to bring his wife to heel. Later, licking his wounds, Dick finds cold comfort in the thought that "the only commanding officer he had to report to was his own self-respect" (120). In the trenches, he recalls the sharp, glinting points of Clare's knitting needles, which he now perceives as more piercing than "the raw steel of bayonets on the battlefield" (117). Marlowe's analogy is clear: a woman who refuses to bear children wields powerful weapons that are more destructive to her society than any wielded by a combatant on the battlefield.

---

17 "New woman" was the term used from the end of the nineteenth century to describe women who pushed against societal limits and wanted more than to be just a wife and mother.

18 Mary Marlowe, *The Women Who Wait* (London: Simpkin, 1918), 119. All subsequent references are to this edition and appear in parentheses in the text.

According to Marlowe, women have two types of "weapons" at their command: their natural weapon, "woman's greatest asset through the ages" is their "capacity for tears" (144) and "the noble and advanced weapon of birth control, unnatural because it depends entirely upon female discretion" (123). Only the socially deviant, she avows, take up the latter. Marshalling her forces, Marlowe demonstrates what fate will befall a woman who denies the maternal role. She will not be able to locate allies. Everyone Clare encounters, from housemaids to aristocrats, insist that it is a woman's duty to bear children. Increasingly isolated, Clare nearly succumbs to the outstretched arms of an unarmed man, a "shirker", a lady-killer who has not even "the glamour of khaki" about him (250). Marlowe makes her protagonist resourceless, too: once Clare rejects motherhood, she can only fill her days playing bridge, or "playing" at the "game of hospitals," where her limited skills (according to her husband), make her merely a "dilettante in the arena of heroism" (121). Ultimately, Clare becomes a rebel without a cause. By the novel's end, recognising that she fights a losing battle, she capitulates to patriarchal ideologies, finally realising that, were she a good woman, she would have "burnished her man's sword and sent him into battle" (157), and willingly borne his child. Unlike Phillips' Jessie, Clare gets a chance to reform, to become "the woman who loves children". Dick returns from the war blind, but still able to father a child, and sufficiently fit to "commandeer her every thought and every desire" (272). Like Phillips, through martial discourse, Marlowe rigorously upholds that in wartime, women must adhere to their maternal role and breed.[19]

In her Foreword to *The Women Who Wait*, Marlowe informs her readers that there is no "official heroine"(i) in the book, but that should "the real heroic spirit of the book be sought, she may be found under the guise of the French girl whose life-purpose is expressed thus ... 'I can give back to France what they take from her now.'"[20] This French "girl", Clare's maid, leaves her service to rush back to France to nurse her wounded soldier-husband. A "remnant" of a man, he can still sire children, none of whom will be born with disabilities. (126) Marlowe's French maid is the "official" heroine because her desire to have children is one that patriarchy, the "official" keeper of social codes, sanctions. In refusing to give her readers any "heroines", Marlowe re-inscribes traditional assumptions that women's contribution to the war effort – even providing cannon fodder – can only be secondary to men's.

---

19 Marlowe's insistence that women's only role in wartime is to produce cannon fodder seems extreme to contemporary readers, but according to Mary Sargant Florence, Catherine Marshall, and C.K. Ogden in *Militarism Versus Feminism: Writings on Women and War*, European, especially British, governments encouraged soldiers leaving for the front to "beget" children. That women were urged to become "breeders" was strongly protested by anti-militarists (31).

20 Mary Marlowe's *That Fragile Hour: An Autobiography*, published posthumously in 1990, includes a photograph of the cover of Marlowe's *The Women Who Wait* with a caption explaining that the book was published in London during the war: "It was intended to impress British women with the need to produce children. Posters advertising it were plastered in every London tube station for a month" (143).

Australian women writers, then, internalised patriarchal visions of women's maternal roles in wartime, and surrendered to the occupying language, seemingly unable to convert marginalisation into affirmation. They draw upon military language to reinforce women's subordinate position and to keep them complicit with the war effort. In these texts, it is the narrative voice of the dominant ideology that uses militaristic language to defeat wayward women; female characters like Jessie and Clare who dare to claim the right to independent thought and action do not employ fighting words. In several other novels, Australian women writers deploy military language, but only to demean their female characters' commitment to volunteer war work. In *The Cub*, Ethel Turner's Mrs Calthrop takes up Red Cross duties because she relishes the power they give her. Martialling the forces in her large living room, she enjoys being a "general for the Empire, a general with a large army to be organised and directed" more than she does the actual duties.[21] Likewise, Phillips' Neville takes up war work because she fancies being part of the military machine. A "pie girl" in a hospital, Neville takes her "orders" from her supervisor, a woman she refers to as the "O.C." (291). In neither instance, however, do the characters feel as if they are helping to win the war. In sum, these Australian writers show that they can mime male discourse, but they remain parasites of the language, engulfed and silenced by its power.

In what seems a peculiar omission, given that Australia has a culture that stresses the maternal role in wartime, there are few mothers analysing what it means to send a son to war. In these texts, there are only two mothers of sons old enough to go to war, and neither provides much insight into how she feels at her son's departure. In *The Cub*, Ethel Turner puts forth a strange mother-son relationship that she never explains. At the outbreak of war, Mrs Calthrop, a Sydney society woman, is dismayed that her oldest son Alec is keen to enlist and immediately pictures him as a child (134). Then she denies her son permission, not because she fears for his life, but because she feels Australia should not fight in England's war. When he persists, in a cavalier display of favouritism, she tries to convince her younger son, the Cub (too young to enlist), that he should go in his brother's place! Understandably, the Cub is shocked to learn that his mother regards him as expendable and refuses to comply. Eventually, both sons go to war, but in neither instance does Turner give us a farewell scene between mother and son, or any indication of how Mrs Calthrop feels about her sons' absence, although the Cub is "touched" that his mother minds his going after all (248). When Mrs Calthrop's favourite son is killed, we learn only that she dresses in black; Turner obliterates the mother's emotional response, perhaps because, as Berit Ås argues, making mothers invisible in the war narrative promotes war and hinders peace.[22]

---

21   Ethel Turner, *The Cub* (Melbourne: Ward, 1915), 95. All subsequent references are to this
      edition and appear in parentheses in the text.
22   Ås, Berit, "A Materialistic View of Men's and Women's Attitudes Towards War", *Women's Studies
      International Forum*, 5 (1982), 360.

Turner was pro-conscription, intensely pro-war, and in expunging the tragic side of war, she was aiding the war effort.

Linda Webb Burge's *Wings Above the Storm* offers a more extended view of a mother's response to her son's enlistment. The writer does not tell us how Mary Webster feels when she learns of her son's signing up, but she does show Mary thinking of her son as a child, a common trope in Canadian women's Great War fictions. But Mary reflects not on how she cared for her child (as Canadian writers do), but of his desire to fight, which she purports is born in most men: "From the time they can walk they prefer a toy gun or a sword to anything else, and war after war ... has been caused by the lust and wickedness and unlimited ambition of some ruler or another already possessed of great position and power".[23] She follows these essentialist remarks with her belief that if women had power, mothers would never give up their sons: "one does not destroy what is dearly bought and difficult to keep" (64). The mother's position is inconsistent, however, for she follows those remarks with an expression of "pride" at her boy's immediate response to the call up (65). Throughout the novel, Mary contradicts herself, positing at one point that wars are "inevitable" (127), at another that "man is half animal" (210), and at another, that women, should they achieve power, would not usher in a reign of peace, but would be as bitter and reviling in hatred as men (207–08). Additionally, the leave-taking scene occurs between Mary's son and his sweetheart, so that Burge never examines how a mother feels about the loss of her son.

Few fathers see their sons off to war in these novels, either. At the notice of his offspring's desire to join up, Mary Grant Bruce's David Linton uncharacteristically reverts to the memory of his son as a small boy.[24] His wife having died, Linton has raised his son and daughter with the help of a housekeeper. When he thinks of his son as a child, he does not recall nurturing him, only that his son has always been a good "mate" (25). Typically, he expresses pride in his son's desire to fight and wholeheartedly supports his decision to enlist, telling him that, "This thing is bigger than we are. I wouldn't have you not want to go" (38). When the leave-taking scene occurs, the family has relocated from Billabong to London, and it takes place between brother and sister, not father and son. Strained, it is nonetheless jovial, with Jim telling his sister he will bring her back German scalps, and she cautioning him to keep his socks dry (319). Later, David Linton tells his daughter that he is gratified his son wants to fight (320). Throughout the trilogy, Mr Linton refers to the war as "a show" and a big "job" which the Empire has to tackle, but those remarks constitute the extent of his analysis of the war and his son's participation in it (31).

---

23 Linda Webb Burge, *Wings Above the Storm* (Melbourne: The National Press, 1944), 64. All subsequent references are to this edition and appear in parentheses in the text.

24 Mary Grant Bruce, *From Billabong to London* (Melbourne: Ward, 1915), 27. All subsequent references are to this edition and appear in parentheses in the text.

Only one other novel features a father seeing a son off to war, but it is equally unsatisfying. In the Foreword to Hain's *The Coo-ee Contingent*, a father, Captain H. (in real life, J.D. Burns, a Melbourne poet killed in 1915), tells why his son enlisted: "The bugles of England called him, and how could he stay?"[25] Hain repeats the Anzac's famous poem, "For England", which "drew [soldiers] as a magnet towards the Motherland's wars" (3). But that she used material not of her own making underscores her hesitancy, or lack of confidence, as a wartime writer.[26] Burns follows this "reason" with a brief account of the excitement surrounding his son's farewell. But Hain does not tell us how the father feels, other than proud. The leave-taking scene seems detached and distanced, and we learn at the end of the story that the departure took place two years earlier. What a son's enlistment means to his parents, mother or father, Australian women writers rarely diagnose.

Why women writers should provide so little comment on the subject of parenthood in wartime bears its own analysis. As I suggested earlier, Australian women writers were myrmidons, taking their orders from the dominant ideology, which permitted only one view of war. Anyone who took up the wartime pen had to big-note the Anzacs' fighting prowess and consign women to the sidelines as bearers, not of arms, but armies. Given women's marginalised roles, few writers were prepared to investigate motherhood as a central social and political issue that affects all aspects of women's lives. Writing about motherhood in general, Adrienne Rich suggests:

> when we begin to describe motherhood, so-called instinctual or natural behaviour as part of the public world "out there" – that is, affected by power politics, rights, property, the institutionalized ownership by men of women and children – we encounter acute anxiety on the part of most men and many women. The suggestion that motherhood is not only a core human relationship but a political institution, a keystone to the domination of every sphere of women by men, evokes outcries of distress, or of vituperative denial, from people with a heavy emotional and practical investment in leaving unexamined this "sacred calling". It is immediately assumed that the experience of maternity itself is under fire, that the maternal emotions will be invalidated if we look closely at the politics of motherhood.[27]

---

25 Hain, *The Coo-ee Contingent*, (London: Cassell, 1917), 4. All subsequent references are to this edition and appear in parentheses in the text.

26 Hain's novel was briefly lauded because its title and lack of authorship led male critics and reviewers such as H.M. Green to believe that a man had written it. When these critics and reviewers discovered that Hain was a woman, they quickly dismissed her book as a series of brief and trivial sketches. "Australian Authors", *Graphic of Australia*, 5 October 1917, 32.

27 Adrienne Rich, *On Lies, Secrets, and Silence: Selected Prose 1966–1978* (New York: Norton, 1979), 216.

During the Great War, motherhood achieved a revered status, offering Australian women a chance to attach value to an activity unique to their sex and to a role which they could wear with pride. Denied any other function, it was unlikely they would question the confinement of confinement. Further, these women writers held pro-war stances; any examination of motherhood would, as military authorities recognised, promote peace and hinder war.[28] Sara Ruddick supports this assessment, writing that maternal militarism arises from women's confinement and powerlessness.[29] Thus propagandist texts like Marlowe's and Phillips', which valourise marriage and motherhood, support the war effort and bolster Australian society's patriotic commitment to the conflict.

One of the most prevalent features of these novels is located in their reiteration that women do not need a voice. Taking their cue from patriarchy, Australian writers maintain that women's feelings and reactions to war are invalid, do not count. Their texts re-inscribe "official" stories of invasions and conquests and, because women write for male approval, they are acutely conscious of being overheard, of saying what will earn them praise. Rich comments that being muzzled poses severe restrictions on a woman writer:

> No male writer has written primarily or even largely for women, or with the sense of women's criticism as a consideration when he chooses his materials, his theme, his language. But to a lesser or greater extent, every woman has written for men even when ... she was supposed to be addressing women.[30]

Australian women writers wanted to avoid criticism by making their writing universal (about men). To that end, a number of women writers reinforce the patriarchal assumption that women have no place in war stories, and no stories of their own worth telling. Several give women literally no speaking parts at all. In *The Coo-ee Contingent*, Gladys Hain narrates her tales exclusively from a male point of view, a regrettable omission since she was herself a volunteer for the war effort in London and would therefore have had her own stories to render.[31] Hain further

---

28   Ås, "A Materialistic View", 360.
29   Sara Ruddick, "Preservative Love and Military Destruction: Some Reflections on Mothering and Peace", In *Mothering: Essays in Feminist Theory*, Joyce Trebilcot, ed. (Totowa, NJ: Rowman, 1984), 257.
30   Rich, *On Lies, Secrets, and Silence*, 37–8.
31   According to the *Australian Dictionary of Biography*, Gladys Hain married in 1915; a week after her marriage, her husband embarked as a lieutenant in the AIF, serving in Gallipoli and in France before being invalided to England. Hain sailed for England in 1916, where she did voluntary war work and began writing for a living. The stories she told were her husband's, however, not her own. That she silenced her experience of war is lamentable because, according to the *ADB*, Hain was a spirited woman: prior to the war, she had given papers on the legal status of women to the National Council of women and campaigned for the standardisation of divorce laws in Australia. She had also trained as a lawyer, but forfeited her practice after the war because her husband disapproved of her career. Hain continued to write after the couple returned to Australia, but as "social editress" of several Melbourne papers. When her husband

contributes to the silencing of women's voices by publishing *The Coo-ee Contingent* anonymously. Because she concentrates on big-noting the Anzac, we learn nothing from her novel about what it was like to be a woman during the war.

In *Trooper to the Southern Cross*, Angela Thirkell (Leslie Parker) also utilises a male perspective. Thirkell's central character is an Australian army doctor who returns to Australia on a troop ship with his English bride. In the Introduction to the Virago edition of the novel, Tony Gould tries to pin down why Thirkell chose to write under the pseudonym Leslie Parker. He speculates that she may have wished to foster the illusion that the book was written by an Australian officer of the very type of the narrator; she might also have used a male voice to find a publisher for, thoroughly versed in Australian literature and history, Thirkell takes great delight in creating a wickedly funny satire which debunks the myth of the Anzac soldier. Her book would almost certainly have been dismissed were it known that a *woman* was spoofing the almighty Digger! Gould further suggests that *Trooper to the Southern Cross* is based on Thirkell's personal experiences, for her hero closely resembles her husband George; he speculates, too, that Thirkell herself appears as Mrs Jerry Fairchild, a minor character who makes shrewd observations about Australian life and customs. Gould claims that "the satire gets its bite from the fact that while Major Bowen, with his amateurishly prolix remembrances, is the ostensible author of the book, the informing intelligence is Mrs Jerry's".[32] Thirkell's son, Colin McInnes, also a writer, found that this was the only book of his mother's that he admired, "because it was the only book of hers in which she had been true to her own experience".[33]

Both err in these assessments for, in choosing to adopt a male point of view, Thirkell was obviously not being completely true to her own experience. Further, Mrs Jerry cannot provide the "informing intelligence" because she appears too infrequently. One aspect of Thirkell's narrative stance is certain, however; in privileging a male story, Thirkell, like Hain, denies her readers a story that validates women's experiences in war. Kathleen Pearson, in *Hugh Royston*, and Annie Rixon, *Yesterday and Today*, also valourise soldiers' stories, and hand their female characters peripheral, walk-on roles. In *Hugh Royston*, a novel set in England, the bulk of the story goes to Hugh, the central character, a stretcher-bearer who is severely wounded (paralysed from the waist down) at the front. Hugh's attempt to live a dignified life forms the basis of the story, but Pearson writes two sisters into

---

died in 1947, Hain resumed her law career and her interest in women's organisations, acting as legal adviser to women's groups on such subjects as the adoption of children, prostitution, and the problems of venereal disease. She had forthright opinions. I have provided this brief biographical sketch of Hain to show that, as a woman who possessed both writing and legal skills, she would have had fascinating stories to tell about women had she felt free to exercise that option.

32 Tony Gould, "Introduction", in Angela Thirkell, *Trooper to the Southern Cross* (London: Virago, 1985), xii.
33 Gould, Introduction, *Trooper to the Southern Cross*, x.

the text. The younger spends the war years as a member of the VAD, although what her duties amount to or how she feels about working with the sick and wounded, Pearson never reveals. The older sister, with time on her hands when several of her brothers are away at war, fills the empty hours by adopting two Belgian orphan girls (neither of whom ever refers to her trauma), and then cares for Hugh. But while Hugh is an invalid, she is invalid. Like her younger sister, she expresses no opinions on the rightness or wrongness of war and rarely speaks of matters not domestic; she is pleased, in fact, when Hugh praises her for her silence.[34] The end of the war finds the sisters marrying returned veterans, one with a "funny" heart, the other missing a leg. Neither speaks about the sacrifices she will be required to make; nor does the elder of the two Belgian orphans, who vows to marry Hugh when she grows up. The women in this text are ciphers who wait, weep, and nurse. Australian women writers allow only men to speak.

In *Yesterday and Today*, Annie Rixon (like Hain, Thirkell and Pearson) permits a soldier's experiences to dominate the novel. Rixon sets her story in the bush, and her major figure, David Grant, enlists shortly after his sons. Both sons are killed immediately prior to the Armistice, so Grant returns home a saddened man. In his absence, his wife and daughter have turned hedonist; both crave jazz and excitement. Margaret Grant does not leave off her pleasure-seeking activities when her husband comes home, and says, in fact, farewell to her husband's arms. As a result, Grant finds comfort in a platonic relationship with Eva Hardy, an exemplary woman who possesses the "mother instinct"[35] and is willing to nurse the returned soldier. Normally a quiet, submissive woman, Eva assumes the God's Police role to warn Margaret that if she is not careful, she will lose her husband:

> [H]e came home from the war starving for affection. He was hungry, passionate, savage almost. You always had an ailment – were always tired. You wailed to a soldier, who for three years endured the heat and the dust and the torments of Egypt, the frost, the intense cold, and the mud of the Somme; the maddening din, the smell and the agony. You always manage to choke him off with your petty ailments and your everlasting tiredness. He can sacrifice to any extent for you. Would you sacrifice for him? (151)

Eva's harsh words indicate the fervour with which women policed their own gender, and the extent to which other women were prepared to discredit women's experiences as trivial. No matter how Margaret might have occupied herself on the home front, nothing she does or says can equal the soldier's sacrifices. Eva, adopting a male point of view, tells Margaret that her husband renounced his own safety for hers. If a husband is willing to give up his life for his wife, her complaints

---

34 Kathleen Pearson, *Hugh Royston* (Sydney: Cornstalk, 1924), 8.
35 Annie Rixon, *Yesterday and Today* (Sydney: Criterion, 1940), 27. All subsequent references are to this edition and appear in parentheses in the text.

must be picayune; nothing can compare to the potential loss of life. That the war might affect women is not a subject these Australian writers take up; that they might change in the absence of men, that they might even have a good time with their "keepers" removed, or that it might be difficult to return to "normal" life after a lengthy separation, they do not address. This passage underscores that only soldiers' sacrifices counted and demonstrates the extent to which women writers internalised the importance of the fighting man. Eva's brutal remarks hit home. Shamed by her shallowness, Margaret adopts two orphans (boys, of course) to replace the sons she lost at war, and recommits to caring for her husband. At the same time, her daughter marries a returned soldier missing a leg. All ends well. But how any of these selfish hedonists or selfless angels feels about war, or about women's place in it, Rixon never tells us. Her subject is soldiers.

Several novels, Rixon's *The Scarlet Cape* and Chrystal Stirling's *Soldiers Two*, appear to be about women in war. At the outset, both writers create strong central female characters, but both allow their women's voices to disappear almost completely once the war breaks out, underscoring that a soldier's story is more worthy of the telling than a woman's. *The Scarlet Cape* opens with a resilient woman who survives a number of hardships in the Australian bush. Pearl Stephenson becomes a nurse and speaks candidly about the way women are demeaned in her profession. She claims that nurses are overworked, underpaid, and exploited by doctors who bully and sexually harass them.[36] For the first third of the novel, the title *The Scarlet Cape* seems appropriate, for Rixon's Pearl offers a rigorous critique of the nursing profession. And early in the novel, Rixon makes an analogy between women who nurse and men who soldier. One of the nurses, asked why she puts up with rotten conditions, replies: "For the same reason that a soldier sticks to his jobs. Once let him enlist, and he won't let down his pals. Though mark you, there is a great fascination about it all" (25). Rixon's "great fascination" ultimately lies with the Anzac, however, for when she turns to writing about war, without any advance warning to her readers, she drops the nurse's story and takes up the soldier's, even though he has heretofore been only a minor character in the novel. Her story becomes history.

The switch in point of view is disconcerting and annoying, especially since Rixon also sends Pearl Stephenson overseas to nurse. But once Pearl becomes the ex-protagonist Rixon tells us nothing about her journey, what her living conditions are like, what kinds of duties she performs, or most significantly, how she responds to the death and destruction of the battlefield. In failing to narrate Pearl's experiences, Rixon adopts a traditional patriarch's view of nurse's work – that it is a woman's job to patch up the sick and wounded in silent submission (in textual absentia?). Through her Anzac, Rixon makes this point overtly. At great personal risk, Pearl saves her lover's life. But when the Anzac learns of her sacrifice, he

---

36 Annie Rixon, *The Scarlet Cape* (Sydney: Criterion, 1939), 31. All subsequent references are to this edition and appear in parentheses in the text.

registers neither surprise nor gratitude; rather, he states insensitively that it is the duty of any nursing sister to relinquish her life for a soldier's (149). And one of his mates asks him if he doesn't feel "queer" having a nurse's blood running around in his veins! Caring for a soldier, then, is a nurse's duty; his sacrifices on the battlefront "count", whereas hers as a nurse do not. Rixon demeans a woman's experiences on, or near, the battlefront; even if a woman is near the forbidden zone, working alongside men to defeat the enemy, her experiences are still insignificant.

Rixon does give Pearl some harrowing ordeals of her own: the hospital is bombed and she is taken prisoner of war, but the heroism and bravery nurses like Pearl display in carrying out their duties amidst air-attacks and shelling is not fictionalised, nor is the nurses' courage and spirit of endurance. At one point, Pearl saves her own life by stabbing her captor with a syringe (always "prepared," Pearl has one tucked in her bosom) (193). Her ploy to save her life works, but Rixon refuses to allow Pearl to be a heroine; she does not give credit to the nurse for having foresight and being brave, but comments that it is demeaning for a man to be felled by a woman! Throughout Pearl's exciting adventure, what concerns Rixon is not how the nurse feels about her injuries, her narrow brush with death, or her escape from the enemy camp. More important is the Anzac's view of these events; he fears that his loved one might be captured and tortured (read raped) as one of the spoils of war. His vicarious "wounds" are more important than Pearl's.

By allowing her nurse's voice to evaporate, Rixon reaffirms the central importance of the soldier's story in Australian fiction, a move which apparently pleased her publisher. George M. Dash, in his Publisher's Foreword seems satisfied with the percentage of the story that a woman tells, stating: "The author ... has shown us something of the magnificence of our women, our Anzac nurses in their great struggle to keep the Five-Starred Banner Flying ... *The Scarlet Cape* is a brief glimpse of men and women in action".[37]

This statement is only partially accurate; Rixon gives her readers a brief glimpse of a nurse in action, but she provides a sustained view of a soldier at war. More than two-thirds of *The Scarlet Cape* is taken up with descriptions of the heroic exploits of the Australian warrior, his recuperation from war wounds, and his unsatisfactory re-assimilation into life in Sydney as a veteran, all told from his point of view.

Yet another case of the vanishing female voice occurs in Stirling's *Soldiers Two*. If a woman writer chose not to parrot a soldier's story, she had to select silence. Although Stirling calls her novel *Soldiers Two*, she, like Rixon, misleads her readers, for we believe that the epistolary format she adopts will consist of an equal exchange of letters between Arthur and Emily. In her Foreword, Stirling refers to both Arthur and Emily as "ordinary" citizens, but she also serves notice that some citizens are more ordinary than others, for Emily's letters are merely "inserted"[38] into the main

---

37   George M. Dash, "Foreword", in Annie Rixon, *The Scarlet Cape* (Sydney: Criterion, 1939), n.p.
38   Chrystal Stirling, *Soldiers Two* (Sydney: Bookstall, 1918), n.p. All subsequent references are to this edition and appear in parentheses in the text.

story, which is ultimately Arthur's. Arthur is presumably "soldier one", a man who enlists meritoriously, whereas Emily, as "soldier two", is relegated to a secondary, or subordinate position. While Arthur is *in* uniform, Emily *is* uniform. "Like thousands of others", Arthur goes to war because "he thought he ought to", whereas Emily lives "like thousands of other women" and acts "the brave soldier" at home. Stirling's Foreword leads her readers in the wrong direction; Emily does not truly "live" on the home front, nor does she ever fulfil her role as a brave soldier. Once Arthur leaves for war, Emily is so bereft that she cannot keep up a good "front"; hers is a death-in-life existence.

Like Rixon, Stirling begins her novel with a woman's point of view and, for the first few chapters, makes Emily's letters equal in length and subject matter to Arthur's. Emily stays at home to care for the couple's two children, while Arthur assumes responsibility for another type of home-front family – the men under his command. The Anzacs, like a group of children, are unruly and undisciplined, and Arthur endeavours to keep them in check. Both Emily and Arthur write of the sorrow of their parting, and at the beginning of their correspondence, Arthur professes to miss Emily as much as she misses him. In going to war, he loses everything that matters to him: "Truly, you three are all my world", he writes (3). But once Arthur departs, his world expands; he thrills to overseas travel, delights in the "spectacle" of war, takes joy in sightseeing, and recognises that he fights the Great War with "great" men, his fellow Anzacs. Rapidly, his letters, brimming with exploit and adventure, dominate the correspondence. Emily's, by contrast, dwindle, and become less an account of her domestic routine than a lament for Arthur's absence. The "lack" of Arthur constricts Emily's world.

In *Wings Above the Storm*, Burge, like Stirling, also contends that men's lives are enhanced by their participation in war, whereas women's are diminished because they have little to do but wait passively on the home front. Burge sets up a sharp dichotomy between the sexes at war:

> In the wild charge of the battle, the exultation and storm of sound, the flares of light and booming of the guns, he had thrilled to triumph and the anticipation of glorious victory, and, passing on in the excitement of the hand to hand fighting, had found peace (93).

Not so easy was the future lot of the women bereaved – the women whose husbands, sons and brothers' names figured in the long casualty lists; for them there was only the agony and sorrow of war; the loneliness of widowhood; the wails of fatherless children; tears and desolated homes (93–4). Rather than attempting to deconstruct the gendered polarities she identifies, Burge reaffirms the notion that war is none of women's business. Women are charged with enduring the war years in silence, their only task to "keep the home fires burning" (124). A mother who has recently seen her son off to war delineates for his sweetheart what shape the young woman's life will assume while her beloved is away at war. Nature will no longer flourish, all social activities will cease, and she will feel bereft and lonely: "then, indeed, will we women know the meaning of war" (65). The "meaning" of war, then, is that women without men have no meaning. In the absence of men, the animate world becomes inanimate. Without men on the home front, women have no reason to exist, and hence they enter a textual silence.

In *Soldiers Two*, Stirling makes a similar point. When Arthur goes to do the important "work" of soldiering, he leaves behind a broken woman who writes him of her loneliness, her tears, her existence where both pleasure and purpose have disappeared. Emily cannot overcome her feeling that Arthur's life has meaning; hers has none. She expresses this bleak sentiment in a letter to him: "a nation's work is a wonderful thing, and when you think of it at all, a woman's heart looks so small in the balance" (33). Arthur does indeed find purpose and satisfaction in his life as an Anzac, whereas Emily, with so little to do, finds it difficult to be "brave and steadfast", (25) to be a courageous home-front soldier. Stirling's Emily casts about for something "heroic" she can convey to Arthur, but she searches in vain (124). While Arthur serves "a supreme purpose", (19) Emily suffers only "dark, dreary days of waiting" (20).

Midway through the novel, in what seems a callous move, Emily begins to badger Arthur to earn promotions and to win medals, for as a woman on the home front, she can derive her identity only from his stature in war: if he gets his "stars", her status will improve (167). Ultimately, Emily feels that women need men to give them "orders":

> we are all the time waiting, waiting for some sound. Often I think of ourselves here as little children playing safely in the sun, and that our parents have gone out to face a terrible darkness and protect us from it, and if they should be lost and destroyed ... (66)

The ellipses signify Stirling's belief that women are nothing without men; if soldiers do not return from war to provide meaning and substance to women's lives, they will be nullified. Stirling's text upholds the common patriarchal assumption that women are but children: they can never be mature, never be adults. They can only "play in the sun", while their "parents" – soldiers – carry out the important "work" of the world. A woman is only a man's adjunct; once that parental guidance is removed, she, too, must disappear. She has no skills to survive autonomously. At the end of the novel, when Emily learns of Arthur's death, she writes, in her final letter, that she has expired: "my light has gone out" (192). She feels disoriented, outside herself, listening to others sympathise with her loss. But nothing can console her, for Arthur was her life (193). The novel ends in a void, a wordless, inarticulate cry, with Emily calling to Arthur, but "there is no answer" (193). Emily will never recover from Arthur's death. She cannot: death in war presages a barren existence for women like Emily, who are fit only to take their essences from the men they marry. Rita Felski comments on the harm done to women who must depend exclusively on their husbands for mental, physical, and spiritual survival:

> Women's confinement to the private sphere denies them the potential for public activity and independent self-fulfilment, while locking them into a relationship of psychological or economic dependence ... This sense of female identity as a lack, a problematic absence, offers no basis from which to challenge existing ideologies of gender as they are manifested at the level of commonsense assumptions and everyday practices ... [Protagonists] can experience restlessness, uneasiness, ennui, and nothing more.[39]

Once their men enlist, the women in these novels are resource-less, scarcely able to function, and silent.

In the texts set on the Australian home front, there are no women making their way into the public sphere for paid employment, no women achieving power through men's absence. With the dominant ideology's insistence that women take on solely maternal and caretaking roles, there is no disruption of the gendered division of labour, no destabilising which would lead women to an awareness of the way the sexual territory is mapped; the texts re-inscribe women's oppression, speak the same language as their oppressors. In Australia, women writers lost the linguistic war. Their readers, future generations, suffered the losses.

---

39 Rita Felski, *Beyond Feminist Aesthetics: Feminist Literature and Social Change* (Cambridge, MA: Harvard University Press, 1989), 129–30.

4

Lesbia Harford's Home Front Warrior and Women's World War I Writing

Sometime during the early 1920s, Lesbia Harford wrote *The Invaluable Mystery*, a novel which concerns Sally, an urban working-class woman, and her struggle to survive on her own when her German-born father, Mr Putman, and brother, Max, are interned as enemy aliens during the Great War. To a contemporary reader, the plot seems conventional, but the novel failed to find a publisher until 1987, after it was accidentally discovered by researchers Richard Nile and Robert Darby in the National Archives of Australia in Canberra. In their Introduction, Nile and Darby provide a history of this delay and, along with Helen Garner, speculate on why it was suppressed. In her Foreword, Garner suggests that the book's radical subject matter, "the grotesque internment and maltreatment of foreign nationals in Australia during the First World War",[1] may have prevented its publication. But this is to misread the text, for the Germans (including the Putman men) who are imprisoned are not treated badly; their jailers are strict and intolerant, but never abusive or cruel, and several of the Australian officers who capture them are affable, even kindly.

Nile and Darby suggest a number of possibilities as to why the book did not get into print. They propose that English publishers, who dominated the industry, preferred bush, not urban novels (13), and that the Australian publishing enterprise was "controlled by conservative men" who gave little credence to women writers (9). They further surmise that Harford was "critical of Australian attitudes to the war effort and particularly government 'precautions' such as censorship and the removal of civil rights" (15), but this notion is unsubstantiated by the text. On the one hand, Harford makes it clear that the arrest of harmless and innocent foreign nationals like the Putman men is unwarranted, as one of the neighbours remarks that Mr Putman is an old chap who "wasn't doing no harm to anybody" (128). But on the other hand, Harford also establishes that the Putman

---

1 Helen Garner, Foreword in *The Invaluable Mystery* (Ringwood, Vic: Penguin, 1987), 1. All subsequent references are to this edition and appear in parentheses in the text.

men occasionally behave unwisely, taking risks in what they know to be a volatile political climate. Both are outspoken in their hatred of the English and get into public rows over issues of nationality, thereby drawing attention to themselves unnecessarily. Harford thus captures the tenor of the paranoia and prejudice that existed on the Australian home front during the early days of the war, but she does not take sides.

Reviewers of *The Invaluable Mystery* were also curious about the book's failure to find a publisher but, like Garner and Nile and Darby, they lay the blame either on Harford's supposedly unsympathetic subject matter, or on conservative publishing practices. In addition, both Myfanwy Gollan[2] and Helen Thomson[3] argue that it was the author's own radicalism as a member of the Industrial Workers of the World that may have caused her work to be rejected, a valid argument given that, as Nile and Darby point out, patriarchal publishers were "conspicuously reluctant to market socially conscious Australian fiction" (8–9).

A number of reviews and reviewers[4] echo Nile and Darby's comments that the novel contains "dangerous ideas" (5) and "threatens dominant values" (6), but it is Drusilla Modjeska who perhaps comes closest to identifying the reason the text remained out of print. Although Modjeska refers to Harford's poetry, her statement, that "[Harford's] writing does not fit comfortably into perceived traditions and discourses" (cited in "Introduction" 10), is equally applicable to her fiction. What these "dangerous ideas" and discourses are, however, critics do not specify because this requires a detailed knowledge of the context of the large numbers of texts by Australian women writers published either during the war or after.[5]

At the outset, Harford's text violated all the rules of the Australian Great War literary campaign. Although Nile and Darby are aware that during the postwar years "the image of the Anzac ... was extolled as a desirable national type" (15), they fail to point out that in Harford's novel Anzacs are "missing": there are no soldiers jockeying for star position in the narrative, and no allusions to the Digger's fighting prowess. Furthermore, the young men in Harford's novel do not believe in the imperial cause and have no intention of enlisting. Instead of writing about Australian men from the bush who like to fight and excel at it, Harford creates male characters – Russians, Scots, Danes, Italians, the French – who appreciate urban pleasures. They applaud enthusiastically at theatres, kick up their heels at dance balls, stroll through public parks, linger over ice cream in restaurants. Most of the characters, female and male, are cosmopolitan, cultured and erudite; they listen to

---

2   Myfanwy Gollan, "A Radical of the '20s Has Her Day At Last" *Sydney Morning Herald* 19 Sept. 1987: 47.

3   Helen Thomson, "Of Charm and Politics: Two Novels Reclaimed" *Australian Book Review* no. 94 (1987), 16.

4   See David Latta, "Out of the Box." *The Book Magazine* no. 1.2 (Aug–Sept. 1987): 39–40; *Mercury*, 4 July 1987: n.p.; Thomson, "Of Charm and Politics".

5   See also Reba Gostand, "Penguins New and Revisited", and Myfanwy Gollan's untitled review in *The Good Reading Guide* (1989).

classical music on the gramophone, play musical instruments, sing opera, recite Shakespeare and Banjo Paterson and debate cultural matters. They discuss the war, but focus primarily on issues of censorship and treason, and display no interest whatsoever in the Digger in the trenches. Thus Harford's text was entirely different from those published by other women writers whose works "fit comfortably into perceived discourses". These discourses held that writers had to privilege soldiers' stories, praise the Digger's fighting prowess, glorify men's participation in war, and assume pro-war stances. In making the bold decision to dismiss the almighty Anzac, Harford did not stand a likely chance of seeing her book published.

Equally contributing to the book's failure to find a publisher would have been Harford's insistence that women could benefit from male absence, that the home front could be a site of radical change for women. Women writers such as Mabel Brookes, Gladys Hain, Mary Grant Bruce, Ethel Turner, Linda Webb Burge, Ray Phillips, Annie Rixon and Chrystal Stirling do not go on the warpath to overcome women's oppression, do not deploy their words as artillery to help overcome their marginalisation, but commit themselves instead to Anzac aggrandisement. Moreover, these writers uphold conventional pursuits for women: rarely do they argue that women's emancipation from marriage and motherhood is possible, or even desirable.[6] Consistently missing from their texts is a candid confession of women's desire for power and control over their lives, female characters remain male-identified as wives, sweethearts, or sisters. Thus the majority of women writers accepted the script assigned to them: their female characters complain of loneliness, have a difficult time functioning without men to give them orders, or die from lack of love. While several reviewers proclaim Harford's novel as feminist,[7] it is difficult to grasp how revolutionary it must have appeared to patriarchal publishers. Probably it was her militant recommendation that women were talented and intelligent, deserving of an equal place in society, which a conservative publishing industry would not tolerate. White fathers would publish only white f(e)ather texts that were ideologically complicit and reinforced women's status as men's inferiors.

Yet when the novel opens, Sally Putman is as oppressed as the other fictional women I have already discussed. She keeps house for her father and brother, and voluntarily runs her father's confectionery shop in his absence. The text depicts a clear separation between women's and men's realms of activity, for Sally's brother Max, an apprentice engineer, travels daily from the Putman suburban Mosman

---

6   I. M[ay] Howson's *Love's Sacrifices (Founded on Facts): A Book From the Trenches Depicting Undying Love* (Melbourne: Imperial, 1917) and Catherine Scott's [G.I. Ehrenberg] *"Adieu, Beloved"* (London: Hutchinson, 1927) tentatively broach the view that women might be other than wives and mothers. Only Mollie Skinner's [R.E. Leake] *Letters of a V.A.D.* (London: A. Melrose, 1918) brazenly asserts women's right to autonomy and independence. See Chapter 2 for a discussion of Skinner's exceptional text..

7   Andrew Gurr, Untitled Review, *Australian Studies* (UK) no. 4 (1990), 128; Thomson, "Of Charm and Politics", 16; Nile in Latta, "Out of the Box", 39)

home into Sydney to work or socialise, and her father frequently visits the city either on business or to fraternise at a social club. The men return from the public arena of male competition and camaraderie to a tidy, welcoming hearth replete with food prepared in their absence. But Sally, burdened by domestic and business chores, is imprisoned in a claustrophobic environment. Her world is so constricted that even an outing to mail a letter takes on the proportions of an exciting adventure. Harford frequently depicts Sally standing at windows or in doorways gazing out at life, with curtains and blinds obscuring her perspective. She is a spectator, too burdened by serving male needs to be a participant in life.

Moreover, because she lacks a supportive community, Sally spends her leisure time alone. Her mother is dead, her sister lives far away. Sally is a stranger in her neighbourhood; recently having moved from Melbourne, she is not even on speaking terms with the shopkeepers next door. In order to have any friends or relationships, she must find them in books that her father selects for her from the Sydney library; although Sally does not specifically articulate a fondness for fiction by women writers, she prefers *Jane Eyre* and *The Mill on the Floss* to works by men, which she finds disagreeable.

Sally is also locked into silence. The men in her family validate only male experience and shun topics Sally broaches; thus she has learned to guard carefully what she says (30). A good listener (albeit forced to be), she hears conversations only in snatches, missing much of the dinner-table talk on current affairs while waiting on her keepers. Lacking friends or relatives with whom she can discuss ideas and share opinions, she has no opportunity to cultivate introspection. As a result, Sally remains isolated from herself.

The following passage, which finds Sally rearranging rooms and furniture in order to accommodate a boarder, illustrates her selflessness, her tendency to put her family's needs and pleasures ahead of her own. The "outer room" she refers to is the one she will occupy:

> Sally did not spend so much time over the work in the outer room. She made up the bed and arranged the dresses in the hanging cupboard behind the door. The window curtains here would have to stay up till next week, when she would take them down, wash them and iron them and bang them up again. The window did not look over the Putman's own yard, but opened directly onto the muddy road on the side of the house nearest the harbour; so that it was necessary to have a small curtain gathered on two brass rods, as well as the two long curtains, if one wished to protect oneself from the casual glance of passers-by. Above the little curtain the cliffs on the other side of Middle Harbour loomed so near that unless one stood quite close to the window to look out only the fragment of a view was to be seen. (50–51)

Here, Harford stresses that Sally is conditioned to put the needs of her father and brother before her own. For the first third of the novel, there is no Sally; she is a character without a plot, a nonentity who exists only to serve others. The narrative voice, which dwindles from "she" to "one" and then to the passive voice, exemplifies Sally's self-abnegation. There is no possessive case here, either; none of the rooms is "hers". Sally foregoes the room with a view, suffers a lack of privacy, and outfits the boarder's room meticulously, making do with scraps and remnants in her own. She does not complain about the new arrangements; rather, she undertakes the task of switching rooms like an automaton. But she does not, as Garner declares, derive from her chores a sense of personal worth (2); isolated from other women, Sally simply has no role models, no means of envisioning another way of life. Further, Sally has no sense of her physical being. Because she lives with a family of men, the house lacks a full-length mirror, and she can obtain only fragmented views of herself in mirrors positioned to accommodate her father's and brother's height. Sally is, at this stage of the novel, merely an absence: she has no personality, no sense of self-worth, no idea of who she is, and only a segmented view of what she looks like.

When she receives a letter from her sister expressing concern about the future of their German-born father, and suggesting that Australian-born Sally encourage him to be naturalised, Sally is alarmed. Totally dependent upon her father and brother for survival, and only dimly aware that war rages, Sally has not considered that it can threaten her family's safety or jeopardise her future. Sheepishly, she asks her brother to tell her what might transpire. When Max suggests that Mr Putman might be interned, Sally's response that her father is harmless reveals her naivety about the threat of sedition in wartime (42). And when Max advises that the government might seize her father's property, Sally again reveals her ignorance by claiming that Mr Putman has no holdings, failing to recognise that the stock in the store is a liquid asset (43). The effect is not to make Sally out to be a silly young woman who ought to know more about the outside world, but to demonstrate how innocent women are when they are raised to be men's chattels. Harford asserts that encouraging women to assume such credulity does them a huge disservice, for when the arresting officers take Sally's father away, she is thrown into utter confusion. Sally's predicament must have been common, yet in all of the other Australian women's novels women have protectors and providers on hand; only Harford addresses the question of how a woman might respond when her support system vanishes in wartime.

Raised to be ingenuous, Sally is not ignorant, however; she possesses business acumen. Anticipating that the war might bring financial hardship, she urges her brother to bring home a boarder so that she can set aside extra money (48). Her wartime intuition inadvertently sets in motion a chain of events that brings her to recognise strengths and abilities that have lain dormant and incites her to recognise that she is imprisoned within conservative structures. The first important event occurs when Max plans a party to celebrate the arrival of his friend Bob, the Russian boarder (62). The gathering introduces Sally to a variety of young women, each professing independence in her own way. Among the party-goers is a friend of

Bob's, Fanya Rosenberg, a revolutionary who determines never to marry, but to dedicate her life to politics (76–77). Meeting a variety of young women, learning that they hold down jobs, hearing them talk intelligently about wartime issues, witnessing their freedom of movement (they take trams and ferries on their own), Sally sees the contrast between her life and theirs, and awakens to the notion that not all women are tied to their families as domestic drudges.

Because of the party, Sally receives other invitations to outings like theatrical productions and comic operas where she begins to perceive that there are ways of living more desirable than hers. And, having observed Sally's isolation, Fanya, in a show of sisterly solidarity, urges Max and Bob to take Sally to the Sunday afternoon political speeches in Sydney. Although Sally does not distinguish between the arguments the speakers of the various leftist parties advance, she is impressed by the orators' knowledge, reminded of her own intellectual ignorance, and brought to the realisation that words have power. Because the men in her family commonly demean her concerns, Sally has tended to regard words as tools that diminish relationships between people. Hearing and engaging in serious dialogue, she becomes aware that words can be ambiguous, that language is complicated, and can function (or fail to function) as an instrument of expression. On the journey home, Sally ponders the complexities of words like "ferry" (87), a response which might seem simplistic, but in light of the lack of introspection or self-analysis displayed by female characters in other women's wartime novels, Sally's inner meditation is a giant step forward. These excursions into the wider community further illustrate for Sally that women are women's best friends. At the political speeches, Sally learns that Fanya lives with an old woman whom she calls mother, but who is not a blood relation. Socialised to believe that women live either with their families or husbands, Sally is prepared to criticise the unusual living arrangement until she learns that Fanya lives with the old woman out of love and respect. An existence that does not centre around men is a new concept for Sally; she had never realised that women might live with other women out of choice. Sally also learns that Fanya has freely chosen her own identity, adopting the name Rosenberg because the Jews in Russia are poor and despised, and she wants to throw in her lot with the humblest (87).

About the time she learns of Fanya's affection for an older woman and her desire to help the oppressed, Sally is befriended by a neighbour, Mrs Kerrigan, whose sailor husband is currently away, leaving his wife to raise the couple's eight-year-old daughter. Sally's initial meeting with Mrs Kerrigan reveals to her that women who live without men need not be lonely, for Mrs Kerrigan is fully occupied; moreover, unlike Sally who slaves round the clock, Mrs Kerrigan organises her domestic chores so that she has leisure time. In meeting women who exist well without men, Sally is developing an "air of preparedness", arming herself to take aim at her own narrow existence.

At this point, Sally is forewarned, but insufficiently armed. When the authorities arrive, take her father to headquarters and confine her to the house, she appears to have forgotten everything she has learned. Desperate to prevent her brother from being arrested (she will be left entirely on her own if he is), yet severely hampered because she has no money, she is unable to devise any workable schemes. She spends most of the day in tears, frustrated by her resourcelessness and inability to take action. Immensely relieved when Bob arrives, Sally abandons all planning to him. He orders the authorities to leave the house.

When Bob departs in order to warn Max not to return home, Sally is released from all domestic demands. With no one to prepare meals for, she dines out at a nearby restaurant (Bob arranges to pay for her meals), where she encounters a waitress who, having witnessed her mother's continual child-bearing/rearing, takes a dim view of marriage (129) and openly declares that she intends to remain single. Until the war, Sally has not realised that women can refuse to be wives and mothers; because of the conflict, she comes into contact with several women who shun marriage, either because they reject domestic slavery or wish to devote their energies to politics. She learns that young girls, too, are being conditioned to take up non-traditional roles. Mrs Kerrigan takes her daughter to political speeches, and, during Sally's incarceration the previous day, had encouraged her daughter to dodge the soldiers and to run messages for Sally. Sally feels shame that a child should be able to perform courageously in the face of danger when she is not.

When the Australian officers come to arrest her brother, Sally gets a second chance to test her mettle, and this time does not succumb to tears or acquiesce to male authority, but springs into "action". In defence of her brother, she takes up arms – the ones she was born with – and "attacks" a lawman (136). Flinging herself onto the floor, she grabs the officer around the knees, trying to impede his movements (136–37). Sally does not succeed in preventing her brother's capture, but only because Max is too drunk to resist arrest.

At first, feeling that the struggle with the officer makes her look ridiculous, Sally does not "big-note" her bravery. But one of her acquaintances hears about her pluck and daring, and openly expresses admiration that her friend is a home-front woman warrior (147). Sally is gratified that another woman identifies the kind of courage needed to oppose the forces of the law and realises that she should take pride in her fearlessness, her fighting prowess and her physical strength. As readers, we are meant to salute Harford for creating a home-front heroine. And, since Bob's plan fails and Max gets himself arrested, Harford stresses that there are no heroes, but heroines: only Mrs Kerrigan, her daughter Justine, and Sally perform effectively "in action".

When the men in Sally's family vanish, everything in her world changes. At first, Sally is not quite ready to take charge of her future alone, and nearly jumps at Bob's marriage proposal: taking care of a man is a "career" she knows. But ultimately, Sally finds Bob's behaviour offensive: he asks her to forego a church wedding, thus compromising her moral and religious beliefs; he has a propensity to issue commands and to speak for her, labouring under the assumption that, like her father, he knows best (168); and he displays no interest in having a physical relationship with her. Although Sally is naïve about sexuality (she has failed to comprehend the rape scene in *Tess of the d'Urbervilles*), the text shows her increasing awareness of herself as a sexual being, her bold desire to have a lover. And when Bob takes Sally to a dance, she learns that she is physically attractive. Being sought after is a novel experience for Sally; she comprehends that Bob will not be the last of her suitors. The final scenes of the novel find Sally determined not to marry anyone, at least for the present. She proposes to earn her living by running her father's confectionery shop, his absence giving her a chance to put into practice the innovative ideas she dared not implement earlier.

Throughout the novel, the verb Harford most commonly associates with Sally is "wonder",[8] a word that routinely underscores her confusion about the world, the war, and its impact on her. In the final reference, Sally thinks like a businesswoman, "wonder[ing]" how many cups and saucers she will sell (182) and conceives a clever plan to dispose of the unpopular items. As she takes stock of the goods in the shop, she simultaneously takes stock of her future; for once, no longer "occupied" by men, her thoughts are characterised by neither apprehension nor uncertainty. At the same time as she declares her desire for autonomy, she draws attention to her physical appearance, commenting specifically on the shape of her lips. In referring to her mouth, Sally draws attention to both her physical presence (previously ignored) and to herself as speaking subject (183). In giving Sally a voice, Harford is asserting that women should not simply be dutiful mouthpieces for the dominant ideology, but should articulate their own feelings about war and how it affects them. Towards the end of *The Invaluable Mystery*, Sally issues orders to Bob: "*Stop* doing this ... *Take* Carlo for a walk before dinner ... *Move* the little table" (185, emphasis added), and stresses her desire to be independent: "I want to see how I get on by myself" (184). The first-person pronouns indicate that Sally has gained a sense of self-worth and a passion to take charge of her own destiny: neither asking for permission nor seeking approval from Bob, she cares not whether her words are heard or welcomed.

While Sally is eagerly embracing her entry into the male world of privilege and power, the Putman men simultaneously discover what it is to be oppressed. One of the family's friends remarks that he finds the men's incarceration harsh, for as he tells Sally, they must endure "loss of freedom," "want of privacy," and the company of "degrading people" (177). But Sally's response, that the camp is not such a bad place, is ironic (174), for the Putman men's lives now resemble Sally's before the war sprang her from domestic prison: the men must speak guardedly; they cannot come and go at will; and they are dependent for their survival upon the goodwill of their keepers. It is pointless for them to complain, for their grumblings fall on the deaf ears of their jailers. That the Putman men are guiltless victims of male tyranny will not lead naturally to their emancipation. And in a nice turn of the tables, when

---

8   See, for example, pages 24, 34, 94, 101, 103, 111, 135, 138, 158.

Sally's father complains that he is too idle, that he has no "occupation", Sally offers to choose library books for him. Perhaps she will bring him Mollie Skinner's *Letters of a V.A.D.*

In her Foreword, Garner suggests that Sally is "left behind by the externally active world of men. Harford gives no hint of what her future might be ... [S]he leaves Sally floating, intellectually unmoved by the political passions that stir the men" (3). Garner is mistaken, however, for Harford points directly to Sally's bright prospects: she is not left behind, she is left *alone*; now immersed in the "externally active world", she is free to determine what shape her future will take. Throughout the novel, contrary to Virginia Woolf's theory of female emancipation, Sally has had neither a room of her own nor money. By the conclusion, she has appropriated her father's shop and the "master" bedroom, both spaces of male authority. And while Sally may not be moved by men's political passions, as Garner suggests, she has her own obsessions – work, friendship, freedom of thought and movement – all of which become political when they engage women's energies. For Harford to leave Sally "floating" is more hopeful than Garner knows, for in the texts by other women wartime writers (with the exception of Skinner's novel) the female characters are static, not in flux. In writing about a female character whose life is amplified by the war while men's are curtailed, Harford was offering an original view. By insisting that her central character should speak her own thoughts in her own voice and redefine the nature of authority so that she could depend upon benign, not dictatorial sisters, Harford was writing against the grain. Unlike other women writers, Harford recognised the power women could harness if they spoke with other women, shared their secrets, and compared their wounds. By joining forces, "new women" could utilise their talents and employ them in the public sphere and would not have to depend upon men for their livelihood. Given that *The Invaluable Mystery* ends in the spring of 1915, with the Putman men unlikely to be released "for the duration" and Bob having moved out of Sally's house, Harford gives Sally fictional time to gather her strength in a woman-dominated environment. She utilises the war to women's advantage, writing a novel which features a woman who has her own story and does not need to mimic the almighty Digger's.

Although several reviewers like Gollan appreciate Harford's depiction of "social and domestic detail",[9] or reflect, like Nicolette Stasko, that the "novel... is a valuable contribution to our knowledge about ourselves, our society and our past",[10] they are unaware, I suspect, that Harford's is the only woman's wartime text to give any impression of what it was like to be a working-class woman on the Australian home front during the Great War. Readers learn, for the first time, about the type of confining clothing women wore during the war (109) and about the small customs of the day – that it is inappropriate for women to ride on trams unless they are wearing hats, for example. Only *The Invaluable Mystery* depicts a woman carrying

---

9   Gollan, "Radical", 47.
10   Nicolette Stasko, "Notes on Fiction", *The Phoenix Review* no. 2 (1987–88): 120.

out daily routines. Sally feeds chooks, cooks lamb roasts in spite of the sizzling climate, stews over the price of foodstuffs, struggles to make a comfortable home on a limited budget, frets over her paltry wardrobe. Harford's is the only wartime text that gives us a woman's presence: the other novels, which read like conventional history texts which concentrate on battles, dates, a soldier's life in the trenches, descriptions of artillery, absent women and their concerns almost entirely.

Nile and Darby suggest that *The Invaluable Mystery* "draws attention to the possibility of other unpublished or published and obscured Australian writing" (6). We can only speculate about but never know how many other women's wartime fictions did not fit comfortably into perceived hegemonic traditions and discourses and hence were not published.

5

Sleeping with the Enemy

Patriot Games in Fictions by Lesbia Harford, Gwen Kelly
and Joan Dugdale

In her Preface to *Struggle of Memory*, Joan Dugdale notes with some irony that she is completing her novel just as Australia is celebrating the seventy-fifth anniversary of the first AIF's landing at Gallipoli, "an event which, according to the overwhelmingly masculine anthology of this nation, symbolises Australia's coming of age";[1] by contrast, the kind of war story she tells, which shifts the focus from the battlefront to the home front, has also been instrumental in shaping Australian society, but it has been "almost completely repressed" (xi). Lest readers have forgotten the shocking details of her story, Dugdale provides a brief synopsis:

> During the First World War, 6890 people were interned in concentration camps. Of these, 4500 male civilians had been arrested and detained without trial on mere suspicion of disloyalty. These civilians were all residents of Australia, most were of German origin, and among them were 700 Australian citizens. The suffering of their wives and children was commensurate with theirs. (xi)

Although Dugdale bases her fiction on the "life and fate" of the Brisbane merchant Carl Zoeller (xi) (whom she re-names Otto Gluck in the novel), she has nonetheless chosen to tell her story from the point of view of Miriam Wemyss, the woman who eventually becomes Otto's wife.

That Dugdale writes her fiction from a woman's perspective is significant, for while historians have continued to document experiences of male internees,[2] they have unduly neglected those of women and children who were left to cope on their

---

1   Joan Dugdale, *Struggle of Memory* (St. Lucia: University of Queensland Press, 1991), xi. Subsequent references are to these editions and appear in parentheses in the text.
2   See Josef Vondra's *German Speaking Settlers in Australia* (Melbourne: Cavalier Press, 1981); and Ian Harmstorf and Michael Ciglar's *The Germans in Australia* (Melbourne: AE Press, 1985). In *Enemy Aliens: Internment and the Homefront Experience in Australia 1914–1920* (St. Lucia: University of Queensland Press, 1989), however, Gerhard Fischer devotes a few pages of one chapter and an appendix to the plight of women and children.

own in a hostile environment when their husbands were interned.[3] In order to gain insight into women's experiences, it is to the fiction writers Lesbia Harford, Gwen Kelly and Joan Dugdale we must turn. Their novels, *The Invaluable Mystery*, *Always Afternoon*[4] and *Struggle of Memory* respectively, challenge the assumptions about both war and gender that have informed the aesthetics of the prevailing canon of Great War literature in Australia.

One of the distinguishing features of Harford's text, *The Invaluable Mystery*, is that it neither dwells upon what happens to interned German-born men or rails against an unjust system that incarcerates the innocent.[5] Harford does acknowledge that there is a dark side to confinement, but the aspects that her male characters most resent – isolation, cloistered environments, the lack of privacy and suitable companions, uncertain futures, and monotony which leads to depression – are the sorts of afflictions that have figured prominently in women's writing: Charlotte Perkins Gilman's "The Yellow Wallpaper," Jean Rhys' *Wide Sargasso Sea* and Kate Chopin's *The Awakening* come immediately to mind. The persistent omissions that do such damage to a female literary tradition are impossible to estimate, but as Elaine Showalter points out about *The Awakening*, Kate Chopin's revolutionary novel that dropped out of sight after its publication in 1899,

[l]iterature depends upon a tradition, on shared forms and representations of experience. Literary genres ... evolve because of significant innovations by individuals that survive through imitation and revision. Thus it can be a very serious blow to a developing genre when a revolutionary work is taken out of circulation [or in this instance, never put into circulation]. Experimentation is retarded and repressed, and it may be several generations before the evolution of the literary genre catches up.[6]

---

3   Although I do not examine here the experiences of women and children who were interned, it is worth noting that eighty-four women and sixty-seven children were sent to Bourke, a sweltering, isolated spot some 800 kilometres to the west of Sydney, a situation one of Kelly's male internees terms "deplorable" (31). Conditions were also harsh for those who remained at home for, as Dugdale's narrator points out, the government inflicted "needless anguish" on women who had no income to feed their children once their husbands were interned, allotting them only a weekly pittance. Many "loyal Britishers" felt that the government was too generous, however; they believed that prisoners' wives should suffer worse privation than Australian war widows and orphans because the Germans were to blame for the war in the first place (231).

4   Lesbia Harford, *The Invaluable Mystery* (Ringwood, Vic: Penguin, 1987); Gwen Kelly, *Always Afternoon* (Sydney: Collins, 1981). Subsequent references are to these editions and appear in parentheses in the text.

5   The novel ends in 1915, with the Putman men unlikely to be released "for the duration", thereby giving Harford's Sally fictional time to gather her strength in a woman-dominated environment.

6   Elaine Showalter, "Tradition and the Female Talent: *The Awakening* as a Solitary Book", *The Awakening: Case Studies in Contemporary Criticism*, ed. Nancy A. Walker, Boston: Bedford, 1993, pp. 169–70.

Showalter's comments ring true in this context, for very few innovative Australian women's Great War fictions have emerged since that time.[7] That Dugdale's and Kelly's texts should reflect so many of the same concerns as Harford's reinforces the notion that *The Invaluable Mystery* was indeed a revolutionary work.

Like Harford, both Dugdale and Kelly also challenge their predecessors' depiction of the Almighty Antipodean, a "uniformly" larger-than-life figure who liked to fight and was good at it. Although Harford renders the Anzacs "missing" in her text, the soldiers in Dugdale's and Kelly's have overwhelmingly negative experiences at war, which they convey primarily through the device of letters. In *Struggle of Memory*, several are reluctant to enlist and then almost immediately become "scared sick" in combat; one suffers from shell shock, a "weakness" reserved in the earlier texts solely for the "Tommies". Horrified by the "the stink of death" (229), these Anzacs denounce their officers as "bloody fools" and consider the war a "madman's nightmare" (259).[8] Although Kelly's are initially eager recruits who believe they are enlisting in a "Great Adventure" (182), they soon find that their country has betrayed them, for their war is so "awful, bloody awful" (36) that they are driven to commiserate with their enemies about their common fate (103). One writes that their fighting prowess (which invariably made them heroes in the earlier texts) renders them "permanent shock troops" (240), and another undercuts the much-lauded principal of mateship by confessing that he laughs when a shell kills a "mate" but misses him. With rare exception, Kelly's survivors are confused and frightened men who drink to excess, weep in private, and secretly wonder what they have been fighting for. When their government threatens to renege on its prewar promises of war pensions, soldier settlements and preferential employment (141), the returned men take out their vitriol on the internees, whom they believe live in the "lap of luxury" at the Trial Bay camp, by destroying the monument the Germans have erected to commemorate their dead.[9]

Besides challenging the depiction of the Anzac, both Kelly and Dugdale also stress, as does Harford, that women on the home front are as confined as the German men locked away in camps. But whereas Harford uses the absence of the German-born men in her novel to bring her heroine to freedom and independence, Kelly and Dugdale posit that the emancipation of women on the home front comes about because of the *presence* of German men. In their novels, it is women's association with their "lovely enemies" that enables them to achieve autonomy and selfhood.

---

7   I argue in Chapter 2 that reviewers dismissed Skinner's *Letters of a V.A.D.* (1918) and *Tucker Sees India* (1937) because they failed to identify the extent to which she was writing against the grain.

8   As Paul Fussell demonstrates in *The Great War and Modern Memory* (London: Oxford University Press, 1975), letters depicting such graphic views of war would not likely have reached the home front (179–87).

9   In "The Monument at Trial Bay", *The Newcastle Herald*, 18 March 1983, Kelly writes that in 1960, the Returned Soldiers League agreed to allow the Germans to pay for the rebuilding of the monument the soldiers wrecked in 1919, and that the Arakoon townspeople helped clear rubble from the site (p. 7).

Kelly's *Always Afternoon* tells the story of the Kennons, a family that lives, prior to the war, an idyllic existence in an isolated community near Arakoon, on the breathtakingly beautiful north coast of New South Wales. But life in the peaceful backwater is shattered when war is declared: the family's two sons enlist and are now fighting with the Australian Infantry Forces at Gallipoli, while the parents and three daughters are keeping the home fires burning. The Kennons' lives are further disrupted when the abandoned old jail at Trial Bay near their Arakoon home becomes an internment camp, and the community splits into two contingents: those who perceive of the Germans as menaces to society or natural-born killers, and those who regard them as civilised human beings caught up in events beyond their control. Kelly's protagonist, sixteen-year-old Freda, joins forces with the latter when she falls in love with Franz Muller, a Hong Kong-born concert violinist who is captured while returning home from study in Salzburg.

Kelly emphasises that Franz' arrest is unnecessary: raised by a German father and half-Welsh mother in the British colony of Hong Kong, Franz has never set foot in Germany, so he feels little allegiance for the fatherland. The majority of the other internees, an elite mix of 500 professors, doctors, bankers, planters, merchants, consuls, naval heroes, Buddhist priests and Christian missionaries, rounded up from German territories throughout South-East Asia and the South-West Pacific, have similarly tenuous connections to Germany. But in spite of his incarceration, justified or not, Franz has considerably more intellectual stimulation and freedom than Freda. In fact, readers may find it difficult to sympathise with internees like Franz, for with their plentiful supplies of gourmet food, bootlegged booze, ready access to outdoor cafes, sports facilities, medical supplies and a full range of services such as banks and specialty shops, they appear to be inhabiting a fashionable seaside resort – a sort of Club Med – rather than an internment camp. Moreover, these men of rank and substance have established a remarkably rich cultural life: they have organised a library with 2,500 volumes, a weekly newspaper, a choral society, an orchestral and drama group and a lecture series on highly esoteric and scholarly topics. The conditions of internment are equally generous: the men are free to walk about the sunny peninsula during the day and to earn small sums for bush clearing.[10]

Although the prisoners struggle to stave off boredom and feelings of idleness by keeping their minds and bodies fit, many nonetheless chafe under the restrictions: they rail against the obligatory subservience to Australian guards (whose indolence and laxity they disparage); they bemoan their inability to protect their families; and they resent the imposed celibacy that reduces them to "masturbation or meditation" (66). The aspect of camp life Franz most deplores, however, is his "exclusion from the real business of living" (88), for, as the epigraph from Tennyson's "The Lotus-Eaters" suggests, the prisoners at Trial Bay inhabit a land

---

10   The conditions at Trial Bay were even more agreeable than Kelly allows. See Fischer's "Beethoven's Fifth in Trial Bay: Culture and Everyday Life in an Australian Internment Camp", *Journal of the Royal Australian Historical Society no. 69.1 (1983)*: 48–62.

"in which it seemed always afternoon". So intense are Franz' feelings that, captured while trying to escape, he chooses, like the jolly swagman in Waltzing Matilda, to kill himself rather than return to "the everlasting monotony" of captivity.

Because of their equally narrow range of options, the Kennon sisters in *Always Afternoon* also feel removed from the "real business of living", an exclusion the war helps overcome. The male-identified Ailsa, jealous of her attractive siblings and suffering from an acute case of what Sharon O'Brien has termed (in another context) "combat envy",[11] longs to join her brothers and sail away to war. Since she cannot, she follows her older and more conservative sister to Sydney; Mary nurses convalescents with the VAD in Sydney, whereas Ailsa volunteers for non-traditional occupations such as driving ambulances and helping returned soldiers clear land and build houses. The sisters' absences leave the youngest daughter, sixteen-year-old Freda to "serve out" the war as her mother's domestic helpmate. Although Nancy is a kindly warden, Freda cannot enjoy even a rare afternoon at the beach, for according to Richard White, women's surf bathing was considered a "threat to national purity",[12] so she can only cool her heels (and ankles) at the edge of the seaside. And in the same way as Franz' incarceration squanders his talents, so, too, are Freda's wasted; her father, a God-fearing Methodist who deems the Bible the only book worth reading and the domestic arts the only ones worth learning, has forced her to quit school at fourteen. In spite of her youth, Freda knows her horizon is limited: declaring there are "no princes" in Australia (52), she reluctantly agrees to marry Bob, a taciturn Anzac, when he returns from war, thereby making the traditional female trajectory from father's house to husband's.

Thanks to the war, however, a handsome "prince" miraculously materialises in the form of the internee Franz Muller. The talented musician, recognising (as few Australian men at the time might have) how confined Freda is, refers to her as "Andromeda," the legendary Greek figure chained to a rock by the seashore as a sacrifice to a sea monster (read Anzac). Of course, Franz sees himself as Perseus, the figure who overcomes the forces of evil (read patriarchy) in order to free her, which he does (51). Making literary allusions Freda cannot identify, Franz re-awakens her love of learning and then further expands her universe by using Rilke's love poetry to teach her German. (In exchange, Freda teaches Franz "Botany Bay" and recites passages from C.J. Dennis's *The Sentimental Bloke*. Franz delights thereafter in calling her "Doreen.")

As part of her "getting of wisdom", Freda also learns, during the secretive midnight trysts she arranges with Franz, that she is ignorant about history and

---

11   Sharon O'Brien, "Willa Cather's 'Manly Battle Yarn'", *Arms and the Woman: War, Gender, and Literary Representation*, eds. Helen M. Cooper, Adrienne Auslander Munich and Susan Merrill Squier (Chapel Hill: University of North Carolina Press, 1989), 192.
12   Richard White, *Inventing Australia: Images and Identity 1788–1980* (Sydney: Allen & Unwin, 1981), 127.

the intricacies of European politics, particularly as they pertain to the war. Prior to her relationship with Franz (which begins in 1916), she had naively assumed that there was only one side to the war story: rapacious Germany invaded "gallant Belgium" and "poor little Serbia" (105). By presenting compelling evidence that Germany may have been justified in taking strong measures and cautioning Freda not to place all of the blame for the atrocities on the Germans, Franz teaches her to recognise that the story of war is multifaceted, that there are "Other" sides from which to view events. Stimulated by the excitement Franz' instruction generates in her, but dissatisfied with the infrequency of their meetings, Freda resolves to educate herself: she reads voraciously, befriends a school teacher,[13] investigates the pros and cons of conscription, but arrives at her own conclusions, no longer content to rely upon the opinions of others.

As Freda wrestles with the complexities of the battlefront, she simultaneously begins to challenge the construction of the home-front enemy. If it is wrong to love a German, then why does she? If the Germans are all reputedly bestial Boches or brutal, sex-starved prisoners, how is it that Franz is such a loving and gentle man? Her feelings about the enemy become even more confused when several members of her family behave as if they are her enemies. Her recently repatriated and fiercely pro-conscription brother John, for example, has ostensibly gone to war to protect women, yet he strikes Freda when she breaks the news that the people of Australia have voted against conscription (154); and her father, who has ordered her to leave all political decisions to men, makes threats when he discovers she has attended an anti-conscription rally (126) and then hits her when she proposes that his prayers for the cessation of slaughter should include Germans (143). Thus it appears that those whom Freda has most to fear, as Charlotte Perkins Gilman once remarked (in another context), are her "natural protectors".

Ultimately, it is the needless imprisonment of men such as the old dairy farmer Kurt Schreiber, whose two sons are fighting with the AIF,[14] and the distinguished Brisbane orthopaedic surgeon Dr Pieter Stein, which leads Freda to recognise that the government is manufacturing enemies in order to persuade young men to enlist. In reaching these conclusions, Kelly's youthful heroine echoes the words of historian Michael McKernan, who writes that Australians were so distanced from the battlefields they "needed to generate threats and crises in order to make the war seem real and immediate", and adds that "German-Australians were obvious

---

13 In *Communities of Women: An Idea in Fiction* (Cambridge, MA: Harvard University Press, 1978), Nina Auerbach suggests that female friendships are one of the fruits of war, a statement that applies to Kelly's and Harford's texts, but not to Dugdale's or to the women's fictions that emerged during the war.

14 A young man in Dugdale's novel enlists with the AIF because he believes he will save his father from internment, but the latter is rounded up nonetheless. This situation was not particularly unusual, for as Stuart Macintyre observes in "1901–1942: The Succeeding Age", *The Oxford History of Australia* (Melbourne: Oxford University Press, 1986), vol. 4: 156, when the troopships departed for war, on board were "German-speakers wearing the King's uniform".

targets".[15] Yet prior to the war, as Gerhard Fischer attests,[16] Australians had considered those of German extraction model settlers and freely acknowledged their many contributions to pioneering life. Moreover, as Dugdale points out, these German immigrants always intended to "maintain allegiance to the state to which they [were] subject," and accordingly professed "unswerving loyalty to the King and Australia" (189), a point Fischer echoes. But the government needed scapegoats, as Kelly's Ailsa points out, "to prove they have a war effort" (56). Both Kelly and Dugdale note, too, that the churches fuelled anti-German sentiment: Kelly's Methodist pastor proposes that "the Huns [are] barbarians of modern Europe" (35), and Dugdale's Anglican priest, who "revil[es] all things German", preaches "militant sermons" (232). Given the kind of hysteria the government generates to perpetuate the war, Freda's cynical remark, that the townspeople are keeping the home fires burning in order "to cremate the enemy" (74), seems disconcertingly apt.

That Freda is one of the few who remains immune from the bitterness of the war campaign can be attributed in part to her mother Nancy's "humanitarianism and the underlying pacifism of the family religion" (106). Nancy's goodness – she is one of the few who consistently challenge racist and propagandistic remarks – stems from her deep faith in Methodism, specifically in the three little words "GOD IS LOVE". For much of the war, Nancy does not waver from this simple philosophy, for she believes that "the faithful do not doubt" (38). Full of good words, Nancy is also full of good deeds, for in spite of the added domestic burden, she welcomes into her home the wives and children of enlisted men in need of a holiday. While Freda applauds her mother's generosity and compassion for others, she nevertheless begins to see that Nancy lacks the courage to confront the larger institutions – government, religion, marriage – that govern her existence. Freda knows, for example, that her mother is by "nature and religion, a pacifist", yet she supports the war effort because her sons are fighting and she would never undermine the efforts of the Australian troops (36). Freda nonetheless scorns her mother's endorsement, telling her that it is her "eternal tolerance" that "keeps the war going" and "enables the war mongers to get away with it" (73). Although Nancy chastises her pastor for switching his allegiances from God to the "Little Digger" Prime Minister Billy Hughes, she remains silent when he insinuates that the war is none of her business, that she must make prayer her only contribution to the war effort.[17] Prior to the war, Nancy also acquiesced when her husband Bill decided that *his* offspring should

---

15   Michael McKernan, "Manufacturing the War: Enemy Subjects in Australia", *The Australian People and the Great War* (Melbourne: Nelson, 1980), 150.

16   Gerhard Fischer, "Integration, 'Negative Integration,' Disintegration: The Destruction of the German-Australian Community during the First World War," *Alien Justice: Wartime Internment in Australia and North America*, eds. Kay Saunders and Roger Daniels (St. Lucia: University of Queensland Press, 2000), 6–7.

17   Although Nancy clings blindly to her faith in God, others all around her – the soldiers in the trenches (123) and Kurt Schrieber, whose Australian son is killed by his father's people (180) – are losing theirs.

forfeit their education to help run *his* bakery and *his* home, although she knew that her son Greg wanted to teach and Freda loved school. During the war, she also lets pass his demeaning comment that women are "too emotional" to comprehend political issues (121).

Because Freda longs to have a sexual relationship with Franz, she further questions whether her parents' teaching that sex before marriage is a sin (although not for soldiers) is sufficient in a complex wartime climate and rapidly changing world, and she becomes increasingly frustrated when her requests for birth-control information evoke only shock and outrage from her sisters and friends. Gleaning from her brother's biology books that she can determine her fertility by "watch[ing] the moon" (176), Freda bravely decides to "sleep with the enemy", her resolution to allow a traditional female principle to help her avoid pregnancy thereby signalling a fundamental departure from her mother and sister Mary, both of whom follow the biblical proclamation that "the man is the head of the woman" (156). Freda derives her courage from the suffragettes, who insist that all women, single or married, should know the facts about birth control (146); and she concurs that it is foolish to keep women ignorant and then blame them when something goes wrong (145).

Kelly's emphasis on the suffragette movement is fitting for, as Jane Marcus argues, historians have tended to overlook the importance of the suffrage campaign: "bravery, physical courage, chivalry, group solidarity, strategic planning, honour – these things women had learned in the streets and jails of London, the *first* 'forbidden zone' they had entered".[18] That Freda should take her wisdom from the militant suffrag*ettes*, not the peaceful suffrag*ists*, may seem puzzling in a novel that places so much value on pacifism.[19] Yet like the suffragettes, Freda believes that actions speak louder than words, and thus openly defies patriarchal conventions on a number of fronts. She learns to swim, refuses to teach Sunday school because there's no "truth" there, campaigns against conscription and gives Franz her brother's Anzac uniform to aid his escape.

Although Freda laments that her relationship with Franz erodes the values and teachings of her home, she does not relent when her mother, worried that her daughter is becoming a "strident feminist", tells Freda that women are "by nature" (142) nurturers and caregivers, always ready to comfort anyone who needs it and advises Freda to adopt these respectable roles, for women will win "more new rights through their dedicated war service than all the noisy protests of their

---

18 Jane Marcus, "Corpus/Corps/Corpse: Writing the Body in/at War", *Arms and the Woman: War, Gender, and Literary Representation*, eds. Helen M. Cooper, Adrienne Auslander Munich and Susan Merrill Squier, (Chapel Hill, London: University of North Carolina Press, 1989), 135.

19 Franz' encounter with the hermit Matt Dene also raises the subject of pacifism, for Dene views war as a waste of human potential and insists that Franz relinquish the gun he has stolen from the Australian guards. Dene, a vegetarian, lives in harmony with nature, so Kelly may be drawing readers' attention to the links feminists have made between vegetarianism and pacifism. See Carol J. Adams, "Feminism, the Great War, and Modern Vegetarianism", *Arms and the Woman*, 244–67.

belligerent sisters, who simply antagonised respectable men and women". Freda's response, that were it not for the suffragettes, men would simply thank women nicely, "write a poem or two on the glory of women and then forget us, not even imagining we might like a few rights of our own" (142), indicates that she has attained a fully raised feminist consciousness. Moreover, Nancy's accusation that Freda is becoming bellicose is wide of the mark, for although Freda has abandoned the church, she has not abandoned its teachings, many of which Franz' instruction has reinforced: she consistently reminds others of the Golden Rule and by obeying the commandment to "love thine enemy" becomes one of the few who ensures it is not merely an "empty phrase" (243).

The text further suggests that women like Nancy pay a heavy price for their passivity. Her exhaustion from volunteer war work, anxiety over John's inability to adjust to civilian life (he has lost an arm in combat) and apprehension that her favourite son Greg may not survive the war, manifest themselves in a facial "twitch". When she receives the news that Greg has indeed been killed in action, in what has become a familiar woman's wartime trope, Nancy obsessively recounts stories of his childhood, the details acting as the "substance of personal immortality" (242). The simmering resentment she has felt towards Bill for taking Greg out of school re-surfaces, so that when she is laid low first by grief and then pneumonia, she either cannot or will not comfort Bill. (So disconcerted is Bill by this withholding that he turns, "like a small boy" [241] to Freda, not recognising that she, too, is in mourning over Franz' suicide. Freda is thus caught up in another familiar women's wartime trope – the plight of the woman deprived of the right to grieve publicly or to receive solace because she has been involved in a relationship society has not sanctioned.) The phrase "no one wins in a war" appears twice in the novel (80, 93), but it could be argued that both Ailsa and Freda emerge victorious at war's end. Although Freda initially succumbs to pressures to marry Bob when he returns from war, she decides against it after speaking with the returned soldier Tom Schreiber (he is one of the few who returns mentally and physically intact, perhaps because he has fought in Palestine with the Light Horse and thus has escaped the horrors of the Western Front), who informs her that she will only make Bob miserable if she does not love him; moreover, Tom points out what seems obvious to everyone but Freda – that Bob and Ailsa have a great deal in common. (Since Tom is of German origin, Kelly may also be signalling his difference from the Australian "blokes" who seem so inured to women's subaltern status.) Ailsa, whose work with returned soldiers helps her understand the pain Bob is experiencing, combined with her interest in male pursuits, will make him run his carpentry business. When Bob proposes, Ailsa eagerly accepts. Freda, meanwhile, although saddened by Franz' death, vows to honour his teachings – that knowledge, not ignorance, will build a better world (146). Recognising that the rock she once believed chained her to Arakoon is just a rock, she plunges into the water and emerges from the sea reborn as Aphrodite (262), not Andromeda. Soon after, she escapes a lifetime sentence of boredom and wasted talents by making her way to the city, where jazz, short hair and rising hemlines signify the emergence of a "brave new world" for women.

Although *Always Afternoon* concerns only the war years 1915–18, *Struggle of Memory* spans a much longer time frame, beginning in the 1870s and ending at the outbreak of World War II. The specific events of the novel, however, take place on "the one day of the year",[20] when the announcement of the National Securities Bill reminds the sixty-five-year-old Miriam of the *War Precautions Act* that destroyed her marriage. Distressed that history threatens to repeat itself, Miriam sets out on a long walk through Brisbane, the city whose citizens tormented her family during World War I. At the same time, she "walks through her life", the long-buried anger she has repressed evoking a "struggle of memory" (the phrase, which appears in the epigraph, comes from Milan Kundera) that is both a painful exorcism of the events that have given her life meaning and a critical examination of the "nature of the society" that "g[a]ve[] rise" to them (xii).

The story begins with an account of Miriam's childhood in the Queensland bush, where her father, Josh Wemyss, owns a thriving sawmill. At the outset, Miriam is an intelligent and high-spirited child who plays boisterously with an Aboriginal girl and longs for a governess who can help satisfy her boundless curiosity about the natural world. But a number of traumatic events destroy Miriam's trust in others: her mother abandons her to care for a new granddaughter; her father prevents Edward, her beloved brother, from playing with her on the grounds that he is behaving like a "sissy";[21] the governess, a prissy British school-marm, finds life in the colony and especially the bush dirty and disgusting; and Miriam herself inadvertently contributes to the death of one of her father's hired hands. Miriam never learns to deal with disappointment or sorrow or rage, however, because her mother immediately administers heavy doses of opium or morphine to pacify her, a solution that becomes habit-forming thereafter. Moreover, as she matures, Miriam becomes increasingly aware of her father's racist, sexist and homophobic views. She is appalled by his ruthless exploitation of his workers, outraged at his condoning of the rape of Aboriginal women and frustrated by his blatant contempt for women. While he does not believe in formal education for his daughters, insuring only that they are "schooled" in how to be conventional wives and mothers, he sees that his sons are educated at the best private institutions. In addition, he himself carefully constructs his sons' masculinity, teaching them to distrust, even despise women, and to prove their manhood through "physical prowess and deliberate distance from the cloying ties of women and children" (35). When he moves his family to Brisbane so that he can run for political office, Miriam realises that he seeks power solely for personal gain, not "his country's good".

---

20 This phrase comes from Alan Seymour's 1960 anti-war play, *The One Day of the Year* (Sydney: Angus & Robertson, 1976).

21 The text implies that because Edward is forced to deny his homosexual urges, he becomes a bitter alcoholic.

Unlike her four older siblings, Miriam stoically refuses to accept her father's conservative values, yet unlike Freda, she does not have the benefit of subscribing to her mother's more liberal beliefs because they have been, as she realises later in life, eclipsed by her father's: "[I]t was as though [her mother's story] was a minor theme suppressed by the strident brass of her father's work" (21). As a result, Miriam becomes insecure and withdrawn, uncertain of her place in the world, permanently scarred by an "incapacity for love" (159). Yet Miriam knows that, like Freda, because she lacks skills and training, she must make marriage her "brilliant career". Swiftly rejecting potential suitors whose values resemble her father's, Miriam is rescued (like Freda) from a grim future by another German "prince", Otto Gluck. Similar to Kelly's Franz, Otto has no firm ties to Germany; he was born in the Rhineland, an area Prussia took over before he was born, but he left Prussia when he was 17, before he could legally declare citizenship (84). Thus when Miriam meets Otto, he is technically a citizen of no country. Miriam is attracted to Otto because he is both similar to and antithetical to the men in her family: he possesses the energy, urbanity and prosperity of the Wemyss men, but lacks their "corruption to weakness" (65).

From the outset, Otto distinguishes himself from the others because he is a "man who loves children" and women, displaying his understanding of their needs by handing Miriam the deed to their home, attempting to involve her in the running of his business, setting aside money for his daughters' education and travel, supporting his mother-in-law's Catholicism, which she had been forced to relinquish when she married into the Quaker family; he also once rescued an Aboriginal woman from rape. Most significantly, Otto is a gentle man who rarely raises his voice in anger and never strikes a child. Unlike his father-in-law, who assumes a militant stance at the outbreak of World War I (often the prerogative of those too old to fight), advocating that all "young blokes" should enlist to "prove Australia's manhood" (202), Otto replies, when asked whose side he is on, that he is "on the side of peace" (187).

Ironically, although Miriam is initially drawn to Otto because of his alterity, she does not realise the extent to which he is more Australian than the Australians, but Otto, having emigrated to Australia during the 1890s, during the time that the much-lauded tenets so central to the formation of Australian national identity were taking shape – egalitarianism, mateship, anti-authoritarianism, ready initiative in a hostile environment, irreverence – has clearly studied these principles:[22] he masters the lingo, calling his red-haired son "Bluey", and in true egalitarian fashion, practices the Australian edict that "Jack is as good as his master" (115) by treating his employees as if they are family members, not workers ripe for exploitation.

---

22 For an examination of these principles, see Russel Ward, *The Australian Legend* (Melbourne: Oxford University Press, 1958); for a feminist analysis of these much-praised doctrines, see Beryl Donaldson Langer, "Women and Literary Production: Canada and Australia", *Australian-Canadian Studies: An Interdisciplinary Social Science Review*, no. 2 (1984): 70–83.

His prescient conviction that the country will only grow strong if populated with people from many countries is another indication of his conformity to egalitarian principles (132). Moreover, Otto is also a good "mate", ever ready to lend a hand or money to those who need it, and he fervently believes that whatever he does to develop Australia must benefit all. To that end, he criticises the country's reluctance to spend money on research and experimentation and accordingly finances his own technological innovations and contributions to agriculture. Otto also pursues Asian markets for Australian products, believing, with foresight, that Australians are too "Europe-centered" (172). Otto also conforms to the Australian (male) principle of anti-authoritarianism. He ignores warnings that his commitment to *Deutschtum* may be ill-timed; flaunts his presidency of the Brisbane German Club; and attempts to defend himself against the charge that he has traded with the enemy by writing letters to the newspaper, all foolhardy gestures which succeed only in drawing attention to his nationality. But Otto demonstrates that he is not merely a blind follower of all of the principles: he refuses to adhere to the noble bushman's values of rugged manliness and ignores the commonly held belief that women were agents of restriction and restraint, inhibitors of male pleasure, and overly concerned with manners and fashion. Moreover, Otto consistently challenges the "cultural cringers" who believe that the only educated elite in Australia come from Europe.

But in spite of his fervent desire and strenuous efforts to fit in, Otto recognises that he is never able to "strike the right note" that the country will "recognize and answer" (179). He is confounded by the gap between myth and reality because he has failed to realise that he attempts to adapt himself to a country that never made room for women, Aboriginal people, homosexuals, or those "Others" like himself who are, as Miriam's uncle informs him, "better than the British" at ruling this new land (88). Unable to satisfy his "hunger for home" (112), Otto becomes restless, succumbs to wanderlust, and ultimately devises a philosophy he terms "world citizenship" (180). Reminiscent of (or in this case, anticipating) Virginia Woolf, who remarks in *Three Guineas*, "as a woman I have no country, as a woman I want no country, my country is the whole world",[23] Otto, too, believes that "if all the people of the world were one, no one need feel restricted to part of himself [sic] only, but could live in his whole being" (180).

Prior to the war, Miriam is happily married to this "larger than life" paragon (70), her appreciation of Otto's sensitivity to her closed emotional state marred only slightly by his frequent association with the outgoing Germans and Austrians – both women and men – whose open displays of affection and forthright conversations on politics initially shock her; and by her family's repeated execration of her husband as a "foreign nancy". Dugdale hints, though, that under Otto's careful tutelage, Miriam might have regained her former vivacity had it not been for the advent of war. Once the fighting begins, Miriam becomes caught up in what Fischer terms a "re-definition of White

23   Virginia Woolf, *Three Guineas* (New York: Harcourt Brace Jovanovich, 1966), 180.

Australia" that designated it the "exclusive home for those of the British race", and he points specifically to the anti-German propaganda posters that "united Australians of British birth or descent".[24] When Miriam accidentally stumbles across one of these garish posters, with the "Hun's monstrous face smeared with lust" (206), her confidence in Otto becomes badly shaken; she begs him to shave off his moustache, to cease speaking German, and ironically, to be "as Australian as possible" (190).

None of these measures prevents Otto from being interned, for as Fischer points out, the government wished to deprive the German-Australian community of its leaders (men like Otto) and to increase economic control of "Britishers" by ensuring the demise of "enemy firms" (of the sort Otto runs).[25] But Miriam, horrified by the attacks on her family, is relieved when Otto is imprisoned and, reverting to the kinds of upper-class values she had once firmly rejected, willing relinquishes all decision-making powers to her family. When they encourage her to expunge Otto from her life, she agrees, and encourages her children to do likewise: they visit him only once at the Holsworthy camp in Sydney, just before he is deported, so that throughout the war, Miriam is never aware of the extent to which Otto suffers because he never burdens her with an account of his life at the camp; he does, however, write a number of letters to her family expressing his concern for her wellbeing and encouraging them to help her.[26] In the meantime, when a German acquaintance asks Miriam to march and stage sit-ins with other wives so that the Brisbane authorities might be obliged to give prisoners fair trials, she refuses; recalling her family's dictums that women should play no role in politics and not wishing to draw attention to her husband's nationality, Miriam is unable to stand with the others for the common good (242–3).

Throughout the novel, Miriam is often an unsympathetic character, in many ways reminiscent of the many listless women who appear in the fictions Australian women writers produced either during or shortly after the Great War.[27] But she surprises readers by gathering the courage to take her children to join Otto, who has, ironically, been deported to Germany as a result of a policy that Fischer argues

---

24   Fischer, "Integration", 6.

25   Fischer, "Integration", 114.

26   Joseph Vondra writes that the Holsworthy camp, much larger than the one at Trial Bay, accommodated about 6,000 Germans, Austrians, Turks, Serbs, and a number of the crew of the German cruiser *Emden, German Speaking Settlers in Australia* (Melbourne: Cavalier Press, 1981), 71. In *Struggle of Memory*, Otto informs his mother-in-law and Miriam's faithful niece Isobel about the transfer of men who were beaten at the Torrens Island camp in Adelaide, which was eventually closed because of brutality, and further relays that he was "bashed by a gang of thugs who ran a protection racket" (269). He also complains that the camp is muddy in winter, that the huts are draughty, the food poor, and there is nothing to do (269).

27   My article, "The Best Soldiers of All: Unsung Heroines in Canadian Women's Great War Fictions", *Canadian Literature*, no. 151 (1996): 66–99, demonstrates, by contrast, the extent to which Australian women were uniquely powerless. For an examination of New Zealand women writers' fictions, see also my "Myrmidons to Insubordinates: Canadian, Australian, and New Zealand Women's Responses to the Great War" in *The Literature of the Great War Reconsidered: Beyond Modern Memory*, ed. Patrick Quinn and Steven Trout (London: Palgrave, 2001):150–94.

was "far more repressive than similar policies in other comparable countries".[28] The move comes too late, for by now fifty-something and unable to regain his former high spirits or to settle into a permanent job, Otto can no longer support his family. Nor can Miriam or her children adjust well to a life of deprivation in an occupied war-torn country where they do not speak the language and so with Otto's encouragement, the family returns to Australia without him.

Although Dugdale never overtly states that it is Miriam's well-connected family who ensure that Otto is never permitted to return to Australia, she implies it, for German-Australians whose behaviour had been more suspicious than Otto's gain re-entry when the Australian government lifts its ban on German immigration in 1925. (The only one who genuinely attempts to help the family is Alfred Borden, Miriam's brother-in-law.) After Otto's applications to return first to Australia and then to New Zealand are rejected, he makes his way to South Africa, a country he once admired because of its physical resemblance to Australia. Upon arrival, Otto changes his name from "Gluck", a word meaning, ironically, "luck", to his mother's name, "Klein", a word meaning "small". Recognising that he is a liability to his family and envisioning for them only an impoverished existence if he remains alive, Otto commits his one and only act of violence: he puts a revolver in his mouth and blows out his brains.

The text suggests that Miriam lives thereafter in silence and seclusion – a kind of "living death" – until the outbreak of World War II, but at its declaration, she, like Freda, emerges reborn and, performing several small acts of courage in the process, makes her way confidently towards "home", a destination she has never been able to reach. Miriam regains her former strength by rejecting once more her family's conservative values: she alerts a young German family they may be used as scapegoats in the war, briefly befriends an Aboriginal woman, admits for the first time that it was "her country" that killed Otto; moreover, she resolves to live by the truth, to no longer "contrive in its burial" (256).

It appears, however, that the kinds of conservative values Miriam is finally able to discard continue to hold sway in Australia, for in spite of the fact that Australian intelligence failed to uncover a single case of espionage during the war,[29] and thus falsely imprisoned all of these men, there has been no attempt at apology or redress for those families who still cannot, as Dugdale stresses, "wipe from their names the smear of shame" (xi). Lamentably, too, although the Australian publishing and television and film industries continue to churn out vast numbers of historical and literary works that laud the almighty Anzac, not one of the three outstanding literary works under discussion here remains in print today.[30]

---

28   Fischer, "Integration", 12–13.
29   McKernan, "Manufacturing the War", 169.
30   *Struggle of Memory* did, however, go into a second printing in 1992; and SBS television produced *Always Afternoon* as a two-part mini-series Bicentennial project. Screened in March 1988, this fine video is now unavailable.

6

Demilitarising a Military Culture

Brenda Walker's *The Wing of Night*

Brenda Walker's 2005 historical novel, *The Wing of Night*, about the Great War and its aftermath, begins with an epigraph by Henry James that states, "My own taste has always been for unwritten history, and my present business is with the reverse of the picture." While several reviewers such as Aviva Tuffield and Gillian Dooley suggest that Walker draws her style, structure, and method of characterisation from James, I believe they have overlooked the specific words of the epigraph – "unwritten history" and "the reverse of the picture" – which to me indicate Walker's desire to challenge the monolithic narratives in history and fiction by both men and women writers who have, as historian Dale Blair asserts, regarded "the Australian soldiers who waded ashore at Gallipoli on 25 April 1915" as the "apotheosis of Australia's national identity".[1] These writers imbued their male characters with unique characteristics – albeit "singularly masculine" ones – which asserted a "distinct national character and code of behaviour"[2] that rapidly became known as the Anzac legend.[3] According to historian Alistair Thomson, "Charles Bean is widely regarded as the most influential of those who contributed to the creation of Australia's Anzac legend",[4] which Thomson summarises as follows:

---

1   Dale James Blair, *Dinkum Diggers: An Australian Battalion at War* (Carlton, Vic: Melbourne University Press, 2001), 1.
2   Blair, *Dinkum Diggers*, 1.
3   Blair acknowledges that he examines only the 1st Australian Infantry Battalion, which fought at Gallipoli, France, and Belgium. He contends that this battalion is worthy of study not only because it "participated in key battles," but it was also one of the "best-represented units in the Australian War Memorial's collection of diaries and letters" (Blair, *Dinkum Diggers*, 6). Blair cautions, however, that because Bean accompanied the Battalion on several journeys, including the voyage to Anzac Cove, he may have "fostered a close relationship with the officers" … that was "tapped into during the collection of papers for the War Memorial" (Blair, *Dinkum Diggers*, 6).
4   Alistair Thomson, *Anzac Memories: Living with the Legend* (Melbourne: Oxford University Press, 1994), 46.

At Gallipoli, and then on the Western Front, the Anzacs proved the character of Australian manhood for all the world to see and, through their victories and sacrifices, established a nation in spirit as well as in name. The Australian soldier of the legend was enterprising and independent, loyal to his mates and to his country, bold in battle, but cheerfully undisciplined out of the line and contemptuous of military etiquette and the British officer class. The Australian army suited his egalitarian nature: relations between officers and other ranks were friendly and respectful, and any man with ability could gain promotion. According to the legend, these qualities, fostered in the Australian bush, discovered and immortalised in war, typified Australians and Australian society, a frontier land of equal opportunity in which enterprising people could make good. This was the nation that "came of age" at Gallipoli.[5]

According to Blair, Bean's narrow depiction of the Anzac has led to a "stereotyping" of that Digger figure that has "served to obscure much of the reality of the experience of Australian soldiers in the First World War. Its perpetuation deflects attention from the sometimes-horrific realities of individuals' variegated experiences, and thereby limits our understanding of Australian experience in the First World War".[6]

Blair's views also reflect those of the former Great War soldiers Thomson interviewed in the early 1990s, whose testimonies recorded a war experience that was "much more complex and multifaceted than the homogenous identity of the legend, and which sometimes even contradict[ed] the legend".[7] Blair, too, also sharply criticises the uniform nature of the legend by suggesting it is folly to believe that all Anzacs could possibly "assume the same identity in the khaki of the AIF" because these soldiers were "drawn from different age-groups, from different workplaces and social environments, religious denominations and national backgrounds" [all of which Bean conveniently overlooked] and hence would not "respond to their collective experience in exactly the same manner".[8] Martin Ball, another historian, further argues that while the legend has "enabled Australians to project onto the Anzacs a raft of values that satisfy nationalist desires and anxieties," such depictions "cannot be sustained under historical analysis".[9] Additionally, in the "Epilogue" to *Zombie Myths of Australian Military History: The 10 Myths That Will Not Die*,[10] Craig Stockings alleges that the "national myth" of Anzac may be "based on, but does not necessarily reflect, historical fact. Anzac involves fictionalised

---

5   Thomson, *Anzac Memories*, 26.
6   Blair, *Dinkum Diggers*, 3.
7   Blair, *Dinkum Diggers*, 26.
8   Blair, *Dinkum Diggers*, 3.
9   Rev. Martin Ball, "Of Dinkum Diggers: An Australian Battalion at War and John McQuilton's Rural Australian Battalion at War", *Australian Book Review* (July 2001): 36.
10   For further criticism of the legend, see also *ANZAC'S Dirty Dozen: 12 Myths of Australian Military History*, ed. Craig Stockings (Sydney: UNSW Press, 2012).

exaggerations of actual incidents, commonly disregards inconvenient, historical details, and in some ways subverts or reinvents the past to fit the legend".[11] The title of one of historian Peter Stanley's books – *Bad Characters: Sex, Crime, Mutiny, Murder and the Australian Imperial Force* – clearly stresses the highly selective nature of Bean's depiction of the Anzacs. Stanley asserts that while the AIF's story spanned "the good and the bad, the greatness and the smallness",[12] Bean emphasised only the "good." Accordingly, as Stanley observes, "hundreds of books have been written about the 'good' – the most distinguished battalions, the best commanders, the most outstanding men from a force acknowledged as being among the most effective of the war". He concludes that as "the diet that nourished the Anzac legend", Bean's writing "has led to a seriously skewed understanding of Australia's military history" because it ignored "the AIF's dark sides", such as "how war made men into criminals; how men let themselves and their mates down by going absent or wounding themselves". Stanley further asserts that mention of the "riots and protests, or of the toll exacted by venereal disease (VD), which afflicted so many", are missing.

While there are, then, a few legend-dissenting historians, Walker is one of the few female fiction writers in nearly one hundred years to undercut the heroic tradition and call attention to the "dark sides" of war.[13] Acutely aware of the distorting effects of the legend and of the significance of what lies outside the frame, she establishes that the war experiences of her Anzac figures Joe Tully and Louis Zettler (both of whom come from Western Australia, the state that suffered the most losses during the Great War), neither support nor preserve the key characteristics of the Digger stereotype; instead, she places the legend under scrutiny and identifies the junctures at which myth and reality diverge.[14] It is important to stress, however, that Walker does not set out to destroy the legend, but leaves some of it intact.[15] For example, her depiction of an Anzac who is so anxious to "do his bit" that he chops off his toes to make his feet fit into his army

---

11 Craig Stockings, "Epilogue," *Zombie Myths of Australian Military History: The 10 Myths That Will Not Die* (Sydney: UNSW Press, 2010): 236.

12 Peter Stanley, *Bad Characters: Sex, Crime, Mutiny, Murder and the Australian Imperial Force* (Miller's Point, NSW: Murdoch, 2010), 10.

13 In *Intimate Strangers* (Sydney: Angus & Robertson, 1937), Katharine Susannah Prichard writes about a World War I veteran, but she concentrates mainly on the disintegration of his marriage rather than on problems re-adjusting to post-war civilian life.

14 In "Building on Gendered Ground: Space and National Identity in Brenda Walker's *The Wing of Night*", *The Journal of Australian Writers and Writing* (2010): 4–14, Laura White is accurate in her assumption that "Australian women have not been silent bystanders to nationalist constructions" (White, "Building on Gendered Ground", 4), but not in the way she means. As I have argued in Part 1, Australian women writers meticulously followed Bean's dictates and used their words to shore up, not shatter, the Anzac legend.

15 In "Innovation Meets Tradition in Brenda Walker's *The Wing of Night*", Clare Rhoden argues that Walker's novel "diverg[es] from a number of Anzac features … while also complying with others" (Rhoden, "Innovation", 118), but her essay emphasises overall accordance with the legend.

boots[16] comes straight out of Bean, who insisted that many men were so intent on either getting into or staying in the fray that they went to extreme measures to do so. In another example that demonstrates Bean's influence, a wounded soldier wants his arm "fixed" in a "jiffy" so he can pick up his rifle again (36). Moreover, the "real-life" figure Lieutenant-Colonel Noel Brazier's frequent boasts – that "everyone knew there were no finer troops in the Commonwealth" (47, 69) – echo not only Bean's sentiments, but those of the English correspondents Ellis Ashmead-Bartlett and John Masefield, who also depicted the Anzacs as superb fighters.

Another aspect of the legend Walker partially retains lies in the officer-man relationship, which Bean insisted was friendly and respectful. The text suggests that those under his command respect Lieutenant-Colonel Brazier (they bring him firewood) and grumble mildly when ordered (foolishly) to forfeit their warm overcoats before the Battle of the Nek and (even more foolishly) to charge their machine-gun-armed enemies with bayonets, not rifles. But Brazier also has feelings of compassion and understanding for his men, reflected in two phrases that underscore his abiding concern for their wellbeing: in the first, he states from the home front, "You'll always have hills. You won't always have sons" (25), and in the second, he cites a worrying message from the easterner, his superior officer (and military enemy) Brigade Major, Colonel J.M. Anthill, who states "We are out there to stay. There is no coming back" (26). Prior to the war, Brazier had imagined himself as an explorer, as "Scott of the Light Horse," but once he witnesses the grim realities of combat, he fervently wishes he could "take all his soldiers" to a "whole city waiting cleanly in the ice," not the "filthy city like this encampment in the gunfire and the dirt" (20). At the Battle of the Nek, Brazier tries desperately but unsuccessfully to convince Anthill that it is futile to order his men – the third line of attack – to advance towards the enemy when almost all of those in the first two lines have been slaughtered. Walker also gently deflates Bean's dictum that war was the "great leveller": as Blair writes, "given the paternalistic and ambitious nature of many of the men who became officers, it is unlikely that their relationship with their men could ever become friendly" (60). Thus in Walker's text, although her narrator describes Brazier as a "steady old fellow who knew his men and his horses" (11), the officer neither recognises Tully nor does he know his name. Moreover, Brazier maintains a strictly hierarchical relationship with the men perhaps because he was not, as Bean insisted was common practice, a poor, uneducated man in command of the rich and educated, but the owner of a prosperous farm.[17] Walker's text also infers that some officers were needlessly cruel, as several

---

16 Brenda Walker, *The Wing of Night* (Camberwell, Vic: Viking, 2005), 47. All subsequent references are to this edition and appear in parentheses in the text.

17 Blair argues that "in reality, *class* was a factor in the shaping of the AIF and democracy *was not* a concept that particularly underpinned or informed martial control in the... Australian arm[y]" (Blair, *Dinkum Diggers*, 3). Monash's declaration – that "the officers (the great majority of whom [he had] promoted from the ranks) represent the cream of our professional and educated classes, young engineers, architects, medicals, accountants, pastoralists, public-school boys, and so on" (cited in

nurses at the hospital discuss a rumour that "the men were made to lie to attention when an officer walked through the wards" (36).

But in all other aspects, Walker overtly challenges the legend, beginning with the reasons men enlisted. On the opening page of the novel, her Anzacs are clearly in a holiday mood, scarcely able to contain their desire to get away to "the great adventure of war" (155), which they have been informed will take them first to England and then to Europe, with its "cool dark girls and snow" (71). She writes:

> The horsemen sailed at five o'clock when the day was almost over and although they were travelling to do the hard work of fighting England's enemies it felt like knock-off time on the last day of the harvest: a golden afternoon, full barns and a safe year ahead, all memory of strain and labour and injury gone from the mind. (3)

None of these Anzacs resemble Bean's "dutiful patriots and innocent adventurers," a depiction that persisted for so long that even the advertisement for the Anzac Seventy-Fifth Anniversary Commemorative Coin "eulogise[d]" the motivations of the Anzacs in the following terms:

> They fought for what they believed in. They fought for freedom. They fought for their country. They fought for us. They fought for our children.[18]

But none of Walker's Diggers utter any ennobling rhetoric about why they wish to sign up, either. The working-class Joe Tully, a yardman at the local pub, never mentions why he volunteers, but it seems likely that, similar to Thomson's veterans, he was "only too keen to leave [a] tedious, exhausting or unfulfilling working li[f]e" (28). Well-off station-owner Louis Zettler offers his wife Elizabeth no specific reason for enlisting, but simply says that he feels he "ought to go," that "the war will soon be over," and her reply – "and you don't want to miss out" (70–71) – indicates her recognition that he longs for the kind of excitement and adventure that stems from personal, not national, sentiments. (On the day of his departure, Elizabeth nevertheless tries to convince herself that it is duty, "[t]he crimson thread of British kinship [7], which lures Louis to war.) But like some of Thomson's "old soldiers" who confessed they had signed up because they were "seeking respite from domestic problems",[19] Louis signs on because Elizabeth has suffered two recent miscarriages, and as a result, he appears to have lost his sexual passion, perhaps even his love, for her. Shortly before enlisting, he is tempted to take out his frustration at her inability to provide him with a son (of course) by getting involved in a drunken brawl at a country dance (70), but he does not act upon his feelings.

Blair, *Dinkum Diggers*, 23) – underscores that this feature of the legend was far less pervasive than generally believed.

18   Cited in Thomson, *Anzac Memories*, 26.

19   Thomson, *Anzac Memories*, 29.

In making Zettler a man who loves children, though, Walker was further contesting the traditional depiction of the noble bushman, for as Linzi Murrie writes, most country "boys" valued their freedom and hence "seriously avoided marriage"[20] and familial responsibility.

Walker's narrator also indicates that there was another, perhaps even more disturbing reason men signed up – they were goaded into it by overzealous, patriotic women who behaved as if they were recruiting officers for the war office. In one instance, a woman who spots the bush woman Annie Crane's husband on the street regards him as a shirker and immediately tells him to "Join up" (104). He might have ignored her order had the "assaults" not continued even more forcibly, as "white feathers … begin turning up in folds of paper on his verandah," and then someone crept into his house "with vicious notes in envelopes" (104). Walker's novel thus reflects Patsy Adam-Smith's comment that "handing out white feathers was … [one] way women felt they were serving … They went forth as if they were 'going over the top', 'off for a hop-over' to defeat the enemy, and passed out white feathers to such a degree that every white chook in Australia must have trembled with the cold". Adam-Smith concludes that such behaviour "was a terrible thing",[21] as it proves to be in Walker's novel: Annie Crane's husband, father of two sons, is killed on the battlefields of France shortly after he reluctantly joins up.

Walker also calls into question Bean's tendency to emphasise the Anzacs' physical qualities and to overlook the damaging effects of war by spending little (fictional) time on the physical qualities of her Anzacs. While Bean's Diggers were all sun-bronzed, hatchet-faced athletes of a towering six feet in height – the British Anzac worshipper Compton MacKenzie went him one better by claiming that Diggers were all six-foot-four – in reality, Blair notes that "fewer than 2 per cent of the unit's soldiers exceeded the six foot mark";[22] in fact, seventy-two per cent were under five-foot nine, more or less the same size as the reputedly stunted English Tommies.[23] Walker's Anzacs are admittedly tall (Zettler describes Tully as "a long thin streak of a man" [19]), but neither is bronzed, hatchet-faced, vigorous, nor athletic. Although Bean insisted that the ideal Australian man was a "robust, resourceful individual engaged with the land, combating the perils of the bush as he carved out a living",[24] Walker's novel contains no fires, floods, or droughts, and thereby undercuts Bean's insistence that bush life provided "training" for the trenches. Nowhere in the novel does Walker indicate that life in the bush has imbued her Anzacs – neither of whom ever declares he likes to fight or is good at it – with natural-born martial qualities. Instead, her novel supports Stockings' argument that "ethnicity is no explanation of battlefield outcome".[25]

---

20 Linzi Murrie, "The Australian Legend: Writing Australian Masculinity/Writing 'Australian' Masculine", *Journal of Australian Studies* no. 22(56), 71.

21 Patsy Adam-Smith, *Australian Women at War* (Ringwood, Vic: Penguin, 1996), 78.

22 Blair, *Dinkum Diggers*, 70.

23 Blair, *Dinkum Diggers*, 28.

24 Blair, *Dinkum Diggers*, 20.

While Bean insisted that the good life could be enjoyed only in the bush, neither Zettler nor Tully adhere to his proclamation, although Zettler is educated in the city and, like Roo and Barney in Ray Lawler's 1978 well-known drama *The Summer of the Seventeenth Doll*, expresses disdain for any man who works indoors. But in the main, Zettler is a contemplative, constant reader more intent on stocking his bookshelves with literary works by Longfellow, Hugo, Zola, Poe and Hawthorne than he is with tending his stock of cattle. As well, after he proposes, Elizabeth notes that had she wanted, he could have put the farm under a manager and moved to town. Atypically, Zettler is not a laconic, taciturn Australian "bloke" who prefers the company of men: rather, he is an amorous, romantic man who reads poetry to Elizabeth on their honeymoon (he also recites Longfellow's "The Song of Hiawatha" to the Anzacs in the trenches [50]), and during Elizabeth's pregnancies, devotes so much of his time taking care of her that his workmen begin to "laugh at him" (60). Elizabeth herself regards Louis as a gentle man: when she hears a story about a man's violence towards his wife, she cannot "imagine Louis hurting a woman" (64). Similarly, like Zettler, Joe is a considerate, decent man: he deeply regrets that he has "failed" his sweetheart Bonnie (141), and Annie Crane remarks that Joe is not the kind of man who would arrive "unannounced" or "force" himself on anyone: to that end, postwar, Joe makes a point of introducing himself to the women living near the row of derelict houses where he intends to squat temporarily because he "doesn't want to frighten" them (142). And like Zettler, who lovingly tended to Elizabeth's needs, Joe tenderly washes her calloused feet (186), and before she is even aware that she is pregnant, experiences sympathetic symptoms (204). Similar to Zettler, Tully expresses no reverence for life in the bush; after the war, he tries to find work in Perth, but with the nation plunged into a depression, cannot.

While Bean paid scant attention to the harmful effects of war, Thomson's old soldiers spoke up. They emphasised the "appalling conditions of trench warfare," "their own feelings of vulnerability, confusion, and fear," and "the ordeal of constant shell and rifle fire [and] the stench of the unburied dead on Gallipoli".[26] Brazier also offers gruesome depictions of the blighted landscape: "The dead stayed on the ground, above the trenches, or they showed up within the trench walls. Layers of them. The earth was not big enough for all the dead" (19), and he has nothing good to say about the conditions the men were forced to endure: he complains that "the food was so rough up here that [his] teeth came loose in [his] mouth" (21). By comparison, Walker's Tully recalls neither "the faces of the men, not the conversations or the orders," but only "the black cold of Anzac Cove at night" (148). He also finds the persistent roar of the gunfire – "so loud it was like a perfect silence, like a blotting out of sound" – unbearable (129). And while Bean downplayed incidences of serious injuries – his Anzacs were plagued by fleas and

---

25   Craig Stockings (ed) "There is an idea the Australian is a natural born soldier," *Zombie Myths of Australian Military History*, (Sydney: UNSW Press, 2010), 93.
26   Thomson, *Anzac Memories*, 37.

flies – Tully mentions typhoid-infested trenches and describes the kinds of wounds men suffered in detail. While lying in a hospital troopship, he observes that some "had broken teeth from biting into the hard biscuits in their rations" (32); others had "shattered ribs, or the contents of their pockets had been blown into their bellies and their internal workings were mixed up with shreds of photographs and pencil scraps. Rib bones shifted among the spent ammunition on the ocean floor below the ship" (32). Clearly traumatised by his war experiences, Joe "lay within his own ribs like an insect trapped in stone" (34). Another of the nearby wounded – "the one whose voice had stopped working, the one whose arm held tight to an imaginary gun, the single catatonic," lies, like Joe, "curled up in a ball" (34). Other suffering men near Joe were "sobbing" or "blind" (34). Walker's novel thus documents the horrors of the trenches, the fear and dread men felt in battle, the pain and suffering they experienced, and thereby provides a less sanitised and more balanced perspective of combat than found in earlier fictions.

Additionally, while Bean's stalwart Anzacs rarely admitted to feelings of confusion or disorientation, Blair's front line infantryman "lived in an extremely volatile environment and his immediate opinions and perceptions often reflected his anger and suspicion".[27] The historian then cites the words of Lieutenant A.W. Edwards, who observed that "we often went into and came out of the front line with our horizon[s] and objective[s] obscure. We were too close to events to see them in perspective".[28] Blair concludes that foot soldiers "lived a confused and fragmented existence … It was through this myopic and distorted prism that [they] experienced the war".[29] Hence when the widowed Elizabeth asks Tully to tell her what happened at Anzac Cove because Louis's letters had recounted nothing except that the food was delicious, the weather fine (46), and that the Anzacs were "giving as good as they got" (49), Tully replies in the only way he can: "You'd have to be God to know what happened. Even those who were there don't know what happened" (174). That Joe is unable to convey the experience of trench warfare does not stem from the "inadequacy of language" that, according to Paul Fussell, became "one of the motifs of all who wrote about war";[30] rather, it is the mayhem and chaos of war that prevent lucidity. Significantly, when Joe is sent to fight in the Middle East, he does so with more assurance because this is the kind of war he signed up for – that is, a "quick and fast" one mounted on his horse. Nonetheless, he picks up some ancient tiles to prove "that what he had seen actually existed" (132).

In addition, unlike her predecessors who demonstrated their veneration for Bean by occasionally giving him a flattering cameo role or mimicking his words in their fictions, Walker takes a swipe at an unnamed newspaperman (presumably Bean) who talked to some troops on the ridge, and then wrote that "they were all

---

27   Blair, *Dinkum Diggers*, 8.
28   Blair, *Dinkum Diggers*, 9.
29   Blair, *Dinkum Diggers*, 8.
30   Paul Fussell, *The Great War and Modern Memory* (Oxford: Oxford University Press, 1975), 170.

longing for the coming fight" and were "homesick for the open country behind the Turkish trenches" (23). The narrator points out that the men were indeed homesick, but not for the space behind enemy lines: "as the pressure of the sound of gunfire and explosions rose, each man sens[ed] that he was adrift and struggling and hoping for a sailboat, a rowboat, anything to take him home" (16). Brazier, too, reflects that there are no words to express the "sick excitement" (23) war engenders, which "had nothing to do with home" (24). Moreover, while Bean depicted his Anzacs as consistently cheerful, never downhearted, never willing to abandon the fight, one of Walker's Anzacs is so full of despair that he pours "cordite into his own eyes in the hope of being led off home, blind" (236).

None of Walker's Anzacs find release from the pressures of war by behaving as larrikins, either; hers spend their spare time sitting around the campfire talking about their wives and describing what improvements they will make to their land once they return home.[31] Although Blair writes that "the positioning of the camps and restrictions placed on the movements of the troops ensured that Australian contact was limited to one section of Egyptian society, the donkey-boys, hawkers, various traders and prostitutes",[32] and Tully does mention visits to prostitutes on Sister Streets in Cairo and Constantinople, his comments, which describe the soft moaning sounds women make during fleeting moments of intimacy, are not those of a "wild colonial boy" intent on having the time of his life, but instead reflect the mournful feelings of a despondent man eager to escape the stark, abnormal, male-dominated world of the trenches. Once back on the home front, when Tully recalls the harsh, injurious conditions of soldiering, he "allow[s] himself to cry" (148), an emotional outpouring of the kind utterly unthinkable in Bean's world.

But if none of Bean's stalwart Anzacs were ever reduced to tears, none would admit to being inadequate fighters, either. According to Blair, the Anzac legend "tended to be extremely chauvinistic in its portrayal of the Australian soldier. The 'digger' has been depicted as a superior soldier when matched against the men of other nations, enemy and Allies alike. Two types that have been particularly vilified in this respect are the British officer and the English soldier or 'Tommy'". But as Blair rightly insists, "if our degree of self-worth is still predicated, in part, by the denigration of others, then it is surely desirable to jettison such mean-spirited vanity in favour of a more equitable and honourable appreciation of the Australian experience".[33] *The Wing of Night* identifies no Anzacs who were more courageous or better warriors than others on the battlefield; nor does it suggest that the British were weak or cowardly. When Tully thinks of his allies, he reflects upon the dying words of the wounded/dying British; their longing for the "countryside, the

---

31 Zettler tells the other soldiers he intends to clear the bracken from his property when he returns home. Here he seems to be channelling Elizabeth, since she spends much of her time (uselessly) scraping at the bracken with a hair pin.

32 Blair, *Dinkum Diggers*, 47.

33 Blair, *Dinkum Diggers*, 4.

hawthorn and the hedges of England, or their mothers" (161). Dying Anzacs would replicate those sentiments, with wattle and gum tree to replace the hedges. Walker's depiction of the Anzac experience may, then, be closer to reality than Bean's: like Thomson's "old soldiers," neither Zettler nor Tully makes fighting ability "the dominant feature" of their war memories (37). Neither is the type of man whose "worth revolves around acts of physical endeavour or violence ... peculiar to an extraordinary male world".[34] In fact when Joe stumbles upon "a small hand" that appears to belong to either a Turkish woman or a boy, he feels no sense of victory, but is "sorry, so sorry" (37).

Moreover, Walker also appears to ignore Suzanne Brugger's assessment that "Australians, imbued with an air of racial superiority – evident in their adherence to the White Australia policy – unquestioningly applied their pre-existing prejudices towards Aborigines and minority racial groups in Australia to the native population in Egypt",[35] since none of Walker's Anzacs utter racist comments. Although Tully fights alongside both Māoris and Indians, he never disparages them (or the Turks) as inferior fighters (261–62) and is even angered that he has been misled about the physical appearance of the Turks, who "do not wear sashes or brandish great curved sword[s]" (238), but in fact resemble young Australians, with their "very white teeth," their "smooth skins" and their "lithe and young and pale" bodies (238). Joe also identifies common cause with the Turks who are, he realises, fighting "hard" for their country and for their cities because "[n]o man likes to be put out of his home" (36).

Walker's novel also questions Bean's insistence that all Australian soldiers were "rugged individuals" who displayed both ready initiative and tactical knowledge on the battlefield. Her Anzacs are simply following orders and not employing any great resourcefulness in doing so, perhaps because, as Light Horsemen, they were confident their skills would carry them through the war unscathed: as Louis puts it, "Ride? They could ride. They could shoot the left eye out of a fly" (71). Brazier, too, reiterates the phrase (26), but disparages that his highly skilled men have been turned into "common soldiers" (2). Ordered to dismount in Egypt and "brought to Anzac Cove without horses or leather leggings or plumes on their hats," none of their skills would "matter" at Gallipoli, which Brazier laments was "no country for a horseman" (19). In this "small war" against the Turks, officers reassured the men there was "[n]o need for the horses. Barely the need for the men. Battleships should take care of it" (71). They were also told that "[b]efore anyone hauled himself out of a trench and started running, the Turks would be smashed up by artillery from the battleships" (27). In addition, after they stumble upon a "nest of dead Turks," officers assure the Diggers that "at this rate [they] wouldn't have to lift a bayonet. The battle was going to be over by smoke-o" (28).

---

34   Blair, *Dinkum Diggers*, 4.
35   Suzanne Brugger, *Australians and Egypt, 1914–1919* (Carlton, Vic: Melbourne University Press, 1980), 43–44.

The Diggers' families on the home front were also victims of propaganda that (mis)informed them that their loved ones were safe, "protected by great English battleships" (74), that the Turks were "starving" (72) and the only ones incurring heavy losses. Although Walker's novel does not depict any Anzacs taking charge of events on the battlefield or displaying any particular resourcefulness, she indicates that the Turks certainly did: as Blair points out, "Australian troops had been inadequately prepared for the Gallipoli campaign," whereas the Turks were "better prepared for the engagements in the Dardanelles" (75). As a result, so distressed were they by the continuing waves of Anzacs they were obliged to mow down, they began to shout, "Stop" (130). Walker is thus correct to examine Bean's insistence that Australian soldiers were more resourceful or more enterprising than their enemies and allies with circumspection.

Walker's novel also downplays Bean's much-revered creed of mateship, which he insisted was unique to Australian forces and the key to their success. While Walker appears to gesture towards the notion of mateship when Tully asks Zettler to "sleep with him" for warmth on a bitterly cold evening, the men remain intimate strangers, and later in the novel, Tully informs Elizabeth that he cannot remember ever having met Zettler. While it is the case that older men attempt to shield the younger during the dawn attack (126, 131), their noble gestures are not expressions of mateship, but reflections of their selfless feelings that no adolescent should be sacrificed to the god of war. Moreover, Joe agrees to become a sniper so that he can work in solitude, and after the war, wants nothing to do with returned veterans. Walker's view of mateship, then, is closer to Dennis Altman's than Bean's: Altman writes that "what is extraordinary about mateship is its mythological stature: despite similar cultures of male bonding in other frontier masculinities, nowhere else has it been regarded as a feature of the 'national character': nowhere else has it been mythologised as a national tribute".[36] Arguably, in Walker's novel, the best depiction of "mateship" occurs in the close relationship which quickly develops between Bonnie and Elizabeth, for as Joy Damousi observes, "women spoke to each other through the fate of their men and forged a collective identity through absence".[37]

Walker's novel destabilises Bean's insistence that the principle of egalitarianism made it distinct to other nations, as instances of class distinctions and snobbery abound. On the day of the Light Horsemen's departure, Elizabeth twice snubs Joe Tully's working-class sweetheart Bonnie. But when the friendly Bonnie persists in trying to connect with Elizabeth, the latter's reply to her question, which consists of an incongruous patriotic outburst, prompts Bonnie to think that Elizabeth might be "briefly mad": "[r]ich people were allowed to be mad in ways that were not open to the poor" (6). Later, when Bonnie reflects upon the dangerous work she was

---

36   Joy Damousi, *The Labour of Loss: Mourning, Memory and Wartime Bereavement in Australia* (Cambridge: Cambridge University Press, 1999), 23.
37   Cited in Murrie, "The Australian Legend", 73.

forced to do as a child in the sawmills, she knows that "the rich [like Elizabeth] did not lose fingers in farm machinery" (11). Typically, as members of the working class, both Bonnie and Tully have carefully studied their "masters," but the favour is rarely returned. On the battlefield, for example, Zettler only dimly recognises Tully as the man who sweeps out the pub: had he seen him on the streets back home, he would simply have "flicked him a shilling" (24–25). Similarly, one "longing stare" at Zettler's expensive binoculars convinces Joe he could have never met Zettler; but even if he had, he would be "Joe," whereas Louis would be "Zettler," because only the rich refer to each other by their surnames (124). Tully has good reason to resent Zettler's wealth: when his doctor-father died and his mother then married a farmer, he lost the opportunity to attend private school, to ever become Zettler's equal. Had his father lived, Joe knows he would have talked differently, ridden his horse differently and never courted Bonnie (12). According to Walker, then, Western Australian society consists of an entrenched system of privilege and class.

But arguably, the most significant aspect of the legend Walker contests lies in Bean's declaration that returned soldiers "merged quickly and quietly into the general population".[38] Only recently have scholars taken issue with Bean's perception that the repatriation of veterans was easy and uncomplicated. Martin Crotty and Marina Larrson attest, for example, that "[f]or many, 'return' is one of the hardest parts of war. It is a process rather than an event, one that lasts for years, even decades, and which might indeed never be completed. Returning home requires courage, resilience, and flexibility of mind as well as the support of comrades, friends, family and government. For some veterans, repatriation is a relatively smooth process, but for others the challenges are more significant".[39] Blair, too, records that "soldiers' accounts, pension records and testimonies of family members reveal that ill-health, permanent incapacity, alcoholism, unemployment and severe depression – sometimes culminating in suicide – were conditions that characterised some of the lives of the returned 1st Battalion men.[40] Historian Stephen Garton echoes Blair's view, as war pensioners indicated that they suffered "higher rates of employment disruption, suicide, vagrancy, and marital instability" than ordinary Australians; the suicide rate for returned men from World War I was one-third higher than it was for the civilian population, as well.[41]

Accordingly, Walker's novel includes several descriptions of men who failed to merge quickly or quietly into civilian society: one depicts "men without legs,

---

38   Cited in Stephen Garton, *The Cost of War: Australians Return* (Oxford: Oxford University Press, 1996), 10.

39   Martin Crotty and Marina Larsson, eds. *Anzac Legacies: Australians and the Aftermath of War* (North Melbourne, Vic: Australian Scholarly Publishing, 2010), 3.

40   Blair, *Dinkum Diggers*, 194. Blair acknowledges that he examines only the 1st Australian Infantry Battalion, which fought at Gallipoli, France and Belgium. He speculates that because Bean accompanied the battalion on several journeys, he may have "fostered a closer relationship with the officers … that was tapped into during the collection of papers for the War Memorial" (Blair, *Dinkum Diggers*, 6).

41   Garton, *The Cost of War*, 28.

heaving themselves along on little wheeled trolleys at the side of the road" near the empty railway platform in Bridgetown (94); another describes "old soldiers begg[ing] for coins outside the railway station, some with an empty shirt sleeve or trouser leg, some in wicker chairs with metal wheels" (170–71). As Garton also indicates, "men were more likely to be vagrants than other members of the general population",[42] and true to form, Joe spends much time wandering in the bush, where "there were always other soldiers on the road" (135). Moreover, much of Joe's story on the home front takes place during the years 1920–21, a recessionary time frame characterised by unemployment. His inability to find full-time work prevents him being "on a level footing with [Bonnie]" (136), who has "land … a house and furniture" (136).

Walker's concern for the returned veteran obviously stems from her family background, for as she tells Victoria Laurie,

> My great uncle was a Light Horseman from NSW. My grandfather, his two brothers and his best mate Joe Young all enlisted, and only he survived …" [My] grandfather was at Gallipoli, "and then [was] sent back with enteric fever. He went on to France and was wounded at Pozieres, an appalling battle where a great many Australians lost their lives. Part of his face was shot away and [later] cobbled together.[43]

Once back in Australia, her grandfather married Young's sister and attempted, by posing "carefully," to hide his disfigured face in the wedding photo.[44] But he suffered other physical problems, as well: as Walker tells Jane Sullivan, many of his teeth were missing, his digestion was bad, he was often in pain, and his overall health was frail.[45] Walker also informs Murray Waldren that her grandfather did not live long enough to enjoy the paradise of "orchard and nut farm and beautiful house"[46] he attempted to build outside of Granton on the north coast of New South Wales where, as she tells Sibree Bron, she "grew up listening to stories about lost soldiers. Stories that made her long to write about the experiences of these men in [what she refers to as] that "colossal blunder in which so many young men lost their lives".[47] Two of those "young soldiers" were her grandfather's brothers, the youngest of whom died on the battlefield mere days before war's end. His body was never found, a fact that "haunted" her grandparents' thoughts thereafter. One day, they received an "almost incoherent letter" from a hospital in England, but her family was too poor to make the journey overseas to determine if he was, indeed, the "lost brother".[48] *The Wing of Night*, which took her six years to complete, is the novel

---

42 Garton, *The Cost of War*, 28.
43 Victoria Laurie, "Women Awaiting" *Weekend Australian,* 10–11 September 2005, R10.
44 Laurie, "Women Awaiting", R10.
45 Jane Sullivan, "War's Empty Spaces", *Age*, 27 August 2005, 2.
46 Murray Waldren, "Spoils of War for Novelist", *Australian*, 11 May 2006, 1.
47 Sibree Bron, "Casualties of Love and War", *Canberra Times*, 10 September 2005, 11.
48 Laurie, "Women Awaiting", R10.

Walker confesses she has "longed" to write ever since she knew she wanted to be a writer.[49] Writing this book, Waldren asserts, "sensitised [Walker] to the potential destruction of young men and women," especially to the experiences of the Western Australian Light Horsemen.[50] Their stories, of such "compressed tragedy," drew Walker to the "battle of The Nek as the underpinning of her novel because of 'its tremendous emotional charge'".[51] But the family's disasters did not end with World War I. At the time of Joe Young's death, Walker's grandmother was pregnant; she called the baby "Joe" after his dead older brother. That young Joe Young was "killed on the same day 20 years later, in New Guinea in World War II".[52]

Ironically, Walker also drew much of her inspiration from a happy war story. As she informs Susan Wyndham, while conducting research, she read about a sixteen-year-old who had joined the Light Horsemen in Western Australia as a bugler: just as he was about to embark, he plucked the emu feather from his hat and handed it to a pale young woman. Upon his return, that same young woman made a point of finding him and giving back his feather: the couple were married for more than seventy years.[53] But this story triggered some "what if's": "what if the boy hadn't come back, or if the girl had married someone else?". In Walker's novels, Bonnie does indeed marry someone else, and the "boy" (Joe) does indeed return traumatised, "wrecked, hallucinating, with great ragged holes in his memory".[54]

Jay Winter points out that "shell-shocked soldiers were the first carriers of post-traumatic stress disorder in the twentieth century", a condition

> in which the link between an individual's memory and his identity is severed. A set of unassimilable images and experiences, arising from war service, either in combat or near it, radically disturbs the narrative, the life story, of individuals, the stories people tell themselves and others about their lives ... Shell shock undermines that argument, that point of reference from which an individual's sense of self unfolds.[55]

Walker's Joe suffers from having been thrown out of a sniper hole by exploding shells, the kind of incident that Garton asserts resulted in "the worst cases of shell shock":[56] accordingly, as Walker writes, "He was ... shattered when he landed, but

---

49   Bron, "Casualties of Love and War", 1.
50   Waldren, "Spoils of War for Novelist", 1.
51   Bron, "Casualties of Love and War", 1.
52   Laurie, "Women Awaiting", R10. Walker's mother, Shirley Walker, has written two brilliant memoirs – *Roundabout at Bangalow: An Intimate Chronicle* (2001) and *The Ghost at the Wedding: A True Story* (2010) – which demonstrate the ruinous effects the two world wars had on her family.
53   Susan Wyndham, "Feather in the Cap for Perth Novelist", *Sydney Morning Herald*, 11 May 2006, 18.
54   Sullivan, "War's Empty Spaces", 1.
55   Jay Winter, *Remembering War: The Great War Between Memory and History in the Twentieth Century* (New Haven, CT: Yale University Press, 2006), 52.
56   Garton, *The Cost of War*, 143.

the broken parts crept towards themselves over the years, in the nights, on the roads in the day" (179). Arguably, Joe's fondness for the movies (where he may also be attracted to the cinematic technique of flashbacks), and his desire to produce a coherent film script (125), may arise out of his own desperate longing for an intelligible life narrative.

Joe's emotional problems do not fully emerge until he returns to civilian life, as Robert Jay Lifton argues is often the case[57] because, as Crotty and Larsson observe, "service personnel always bring the war back home with them", and they add that, "Faith in returning home is a crucial part of soldiers' vision. Homecoming completes a circular journey: it makes sense of departure. For it is only upon arrival back in Australia that the meanings of war experiences are revealed, both within the nation for which soldiers have fought, and within the households from which they have been separated".[58] Upon his return, then, Joe begins to suffer from the kind of symptom trauma therapist Judith Lewis Herman calls "intrusion." Traumatised people, she claims, tend to relive events as though they were continually recurring in the present. These memories are "preserved in an abnormal state, set apart from ordinary consciousness"[59] and, unlike normal memories, they "lack verbal narrative and context; rather, they are encoded in the form of vivid sensations and images".[60] In his recurring nightmare, Joe "travel[s] at great speed down a tunnel, a narrow ribbed space, and black liquid flood[s] the hole behind him. When he [wakes up], his clothing [is] dark with piss and he listen[s], sickened, to his own heartbeat which sounded like the footsteps of a fully laden soldier walking through earth wet with blood" (137). During the day, Joe is also filled with dread, "convinced there must be a reason for this dream, which shrank him to the size of a bullet moving through human flesh" (137). Interestingly, trauma therapist Roger Luckhurst comments that "trauma somehow is seared directly into the psyche, almost like a piece of shrapnel, and is not subject to the distortions of subjective memory".[61]

For some years, Joe is unable to remember the incident that has created such turmoil within him. Psychiatrist Richard McNally suggests that some returned soldiers [like Joe] suffer from "amnesia," which he defines as "an inability to remember certain facts and experiences that cannot be attributed to ordinary forgetting ... A diagnosis of amnesia requires an inability to remember". McNally adds that "amnesia is usually triggered by a precipitating event. An inability to remember facts and events that occurred before the precipitating event is called retrograde amnesia". But Joe also appears to suffer from what McNally refers to as

---

57 Cited in Richard J. McNally, *Remembering Trauma* (Cambridge, MA: The Belknap Press of Harvard University Press, 2003), 9.
58 Crotty and Larsson, *Anzac Legacies*, 4.
59 Judith Lewis Herman, *Trauma and Recovery: From Domestic Abuse to Political Terror* (New York: HarperCollins, 1992), 34.
60 Herman, *Trauma and Recovery*, 28.
61 Roger Luckhurst, *The Trauma Question* (London: Routledge, 2008), 4.

psychogenic amnesia, which is "caused by events whose psychological or emotional meaning produces memory loss without damaging the brain".[62] McNally points out that "[c]lassic psychogenic amnesia is characterised by sudden onset in response to stress, inability to remember precipitating events, loss of personal identity, and extensive retrograde amnesia".[63] True to form, Joe does not remember being asked to take care of a Turkish prisoner, nor does he remember shooting him. He also knows he must have shot someone or he would have been in trouble with his commanding officer, but he has no memory of having done so.

In attempting to expose readers to Joe's war experiences that have altered the nature of his memory, identity, and relational life, Walker has produced a fictional narrative that attempts to mimic or mirror the effects of trauma by forsaking conventional storytelling and employing artistic inventiveness such as non-linear sequencing that captures the uncertain rhythms and processes of traumatic experience, and which depict a psychological wound so intense it overwhelms the normal processes of memory and identity. Some of these disorienting techniques, such as the doubling or splitting of Joe's character, render *The Wing of Night* a paradigmatic trauma narrative that utilises a definitive rhythm of uncertainty, or what Roger Luckhurst refers to as "the disarticulation of linear narrative".[64]

Walker's novel contains two examples of a "doubled" or "split" character. The first concerns a biblical figure, St. Paul, who was, according to Elizabeth's father Ramsay, "like two different people" (106). As "Saul in Jerusalem," he tried to destroy Christians, whom he hated, but then he changed his name to Paul, "converted to Christianty" and devoted his life to living among those he had formerly "savaged" (107). Ramsay's interest in "what's left of a man after a huge change" (104) appears to run parallel to Walker's concern for what happens to a man who has been radically transformed by war. Although Walker's text does not indicate how or why the "doubled" biblical figure underwent such a transformation, it does suggest that Joe begins to develop a double, or second self, after he is released from the hospital. While fighting in Syria, he finds that he must shave "by touch" because he cannot "face himself in the glass" (132), and carefully guards his conversations so that he reveals nothing, perhaps because he has become a stranger to himself: "[h]is own name felt like someone's uniform, the knees bagging in the wrong places" (132).

Joe's inability to integrate his "double" on the home front is compromised by the lack of a support system, a problem McNally claims impedes recovery from the acute symptoms of traumatic stress.[65] Joe's parents are dead, he has no siblings, and Bonnie is no longer available. Moreover, Joe has no inclination to try to obtain medical help. While in the hospital after being blown out of the sniper hole, he is frightened by the nurses' talk of "nerve warfare" and wonders if the

---

62 McNally, *Remembering Trauma*, 186.
63 McNally, *Remembering Trauma*, 187.
64 Luckhurst, *The Trauma Question*, 91.
65 McNally, *Remembering Trauma*, 90.

doctor "practised nerve warfare or treated it" (37). He is also alarmed by the stories he hears about "the mind doctors with their baths and electric shocks. This one fixed you by making you face up to whatever it was you couldn't bear to talk about. Something to do with your mother or your sister or whatever it was you'd done up on the ridges at Gallipoli" (37). Joe's apprehensions are well grounded, for according to Garton, "the war provided the context for the continuation of a considerably longer struggle in psychological medicine between those who favoured physical explanations for mental conditions and those who believed that some of these problems, the neuroses, were psychological in origin".[66] Joe is also afraid that he may have inherited his mother's "disorder of the mind" (189), that his problems stem from the "disposition theory" so prevalent at the time, even though he has never displayed any symptoms of madness or degeneration and has never been in trouble with the law (127). Joe thus attempts to protect himself and hence determines that "being mad was only a problem if you talked" (153).

While Garton observes that returned soldiers hungered for "trench mateship" and that Anzac Day was "one means of satisfying this desire",[67] Walker's suggestion – that Joe wanted nothing to do with the RSL – is also typical: he steers clear of other veterans whose stories he does not want to hear and avoids organisations such as the Returned Soldiers League, even though they might offer him money and a job. Garton affirms that membership in the RSL declined sharply in the 1920s, and "less than two-fifths of all those who returned were affiliated with one of the major returned-services organizations".[68] Deeply disillusioned, Joe finds any form of violence abhorrent and cannot even kill a fish (124); summarising his feelings, he states, "[I] could have done without their war" (179).

Although Tully's future improves when he goes to work for Zettler's widow Elizabeth and they begin a relationship, having kept the traumatic experience to himself "prevents the integration necessary for healing".[69] According to trauma theorist Dori Laub,

> the imperative to tell the story … is inhabited by the impossibility of telling, and therefore, silence about the truth commonly prevails … None find peace in silence even if it is their choice to remain silent … The "not telling" of the story serves as a perpetuation of its tyranny. The events become more and more distorted in their silent retention and pervasively invade and contaminate the survivor's daily life. The longer the story remains untold, the more distorted it becomes in the survivor's conception of it.[70]

---

66 Garton suggests that Australian medical authorities consistently reported fewer cases of shell-shock among the Anzacs compared with British figures, but he queries whether Anzacs were "less prone to shell-shock" or "Australian doctors were less willing to diagnose the problem" (Garton, *The Cost of War*, 152).

67 Garton, *The Cost of War*, 51.

68 Garton, *The Cost of War*, 53.

69 Herman, *Trauma and Recovery*, 45.

As Laub suggests frequently occurs, after some years of remaining silent, Joe begins to hallucinate: he thinks he sees an aeroplane flying over Annie Crane's house and men "clustering about Elizabeth," but when he realises neither is accurate, concludes he has inherited his mother's madness (189).

Joe's feelings of insecurity intensify as the birth of his and Elizabeth's child draws near. Suddenly, he feels an urgent need to talk, to tell Elizabeth that there's "something wrong with [him]," that he has a "bad feeling" about what he might have done at Anzac Cove, and that he is afraid his mother's madness has been transmitted to him and that he will then pass it onto the child. But Elizabeth, somewhat distressed by Joe's unusual emotional outpouring, immediately dismisses his feelings. She insists he should not worry about being "an unworthy father" and reassures him that since his mother is dead, there can be "nothing of her left to harm this baby" (207). She thus fails to be the kind of sympathetic listener Joe badly needs. Inadvertently, perhaps in an attempt to avoid what Damousi refers to as "the moral codes that widows were expected to uphold, because ... their connection with the memory of the fallen made them targets of surveillance",[71] Elizabeth makes another serious blunder when she decides to have the baby in a town where no one knows her or Joe. The results are disastrous. After reluctantly depositing Elizabeth at the hospital in the unfamiliar town, Joe attempts to mask his pain and confusion by self-medicating with alcohol. Drunk, he falls asleep under a tree, is robbed, and then thrown into the local lock-up by a jailer who assumes he is a homeless "old soldier." Locked away in a dark cell, Joe encounters his "doppelganger," or "double self," who informs him that he knows "everything" Joe did at the Battle of the Nek (232). Joe's tragic ending – he hangs himself – reflects Lifton's theory that "extreme trauma creates a second self ... in extreme trauma, one's sense of self is radically altered".[72] He claims that after radical trauma, "a traumatized self ... is created," and recovery from post-traumatic effects, or from survivor conflicts, cannot really occur until that traumatised self is re-integrated. "It's a form of doubling in the traumatised person. And in doubling ... there have to be elements that are at odds in the two selves, including ethical contradictions."[73] But as clinical therapist Renee Fredrickson stresses, "repressed memories need to be identified, retrieved, and debriefed for healing to occur";[74] clearly, the process cannot be carried out in isolation.[75]

---

70 Dori Laub, "Truth and Testimony: The Process and the Struggle", *Trauma: Explorations in Memory*, ed. Cathy Caruth (Baltimore, MD: The Johns Hopkins University Press, 1995), 64.

71 Damousi, *The Labour of Loss*, 5.

72 Cited in Cathy Caruth, "An Interview with Robert Jay Lifton", *Trauma: Explorations in Memory*, ed. Cathy Caruth (Baltimore, MD: Johns Hopkins University Press, 1995), 137.

73 Caruth, *Trauma*, 137.

74 Cited in McNally, *Remembering Trauma*, 7.

75 In his review of the novel, Graham Clark notes that Walker conducted interviews with Vietnam War veterans who became "exiles in their own country". ("Paperbacks", *Courier Mail*, 27–28 August 2005, 6).

Tragic as the deaths of Joe and Louis and Annie Crane's husband are, Walker's text is also replete with other losses. When they were young, both Joe's and Elizabeth's mothers died – his from typhoid, hers from tuberculosis. Annie Crane's young daughter has knocked a scalding kettle over on herself and dies within seven days (103); sometime later, Annie's mother dies. Elizabeth also hears about the death of a young woman's husband who had been killed riding a motorcycle: "The tyres had gone halfway up the tree he collided with, then the machine fell back on him and he burned" (224). Zettler's parents also died tragically in a bush accident "when an axle worked free of a buggy wheel" (93). And as magistrate, Elizabeth's father Ramsay encounters numerous people who lead utterly impoverished lives; some are "ill and frightened women" who resort to desperate measures to prevent more pregnancies but are then charged with "foeticide" (84). Bonnie's story is, like Annie's, exceptionally sad: she marries a man who accidentally shot his brother when he was ten. Tormented at school, beaten by his father, he becomes a drunk and beats Bonnie for six months. Bonnie's story of life in the bush is heartbreaking: as she tells Elizabeth, her husband was torn between "hating [Bonnie] and hating himself," so he shot himself: "I was a stump in a paddock he wanted to clear and he was weighing up the dynamite" (65). Bonnie puts her husband's tragic story down to the fact that "there are too many guns in the bush. Children carry guns as big as themselves" (65).

Walker's depiction of bush life for women thus resembles Barbara Baynton's 1907 *Bush Studies* more than it does Bean's idyllic version. Both writers suggest that life in the bush is marred by intolerance – Bonnie is tormented by her classmates simply because she is raised by her grandmother – and by unfriendliness: bush women do not accept Elizabeth because she is clever and rich, and even the "Aussie battler" Annie Crane regards Elizabeth as a "poor useless thing" (162). (Crane's observation may be accurate, since Elizabeth's behaviour increasingly signals that she is too unstable to raise a child on her own.) In both texts, women who live alone are in constant fear of rapacious swagmen. Elizabeth notes that there are "plenty of crazed men travelling on the road just below her farmhouse" (169), and towards the end of the novel, when Ramsay comes to see Elizabeth after the birth of the baby, he is "suffused with fear" when he thinks about the "rape case" he had heard about the previous week: "A widow, alone in her farmhouse, had been raped by a workman she'd reprimanded. Beaten and raped" (250).

In Walker's text, then, the numbers of deaths that occur in the bush outweigh those in the war or its aftermath by about three to one. In drawing attention to those who have brought intense suffering and grief to families and loved ones even though they are not in uniform situates her thinking in accord with Stanley's, points to the fact that "12,000 people, the great majority civilians, died in the influenza epidemic that followed in that war's immediate wake". He questions whether these people were not "also victims of war" and concludes that "if we make a claim … for war's pre-eminence based on how many Australians have lost their lives fighting, perhaps we ought also to consider the argument that at least as many, or even more, have died from other causes worthy of regard".[76] Among those causes he lists infant mortality, those who die in motor vehicle accidents, or from diseases such as cancer or tuberculosis, or from drugs, or from suicide, or from natural disasters (in Australia this would include those who die in shipwrecks, heatwaves, cyclones, storms, bushfires, floods, and so on). The numbers of these dead far exceed those who died on the battlefield, but throughout the twentieth century, few "non-warlike causes have been commemorated," perhaps because they are not designated "heroic".[77] Stanley cautions that he is neither "decrying nor denigrating those who experienced war and its effects, especially on individuals and families",[78] but insists that while the lists of "everyday sufferings" are "of course part of the human condition," this does not mean they should be "less worthy of notice".[79] Walker would surely agree.

In addition, as historian Joan Beaumont argues, some war deaths are more worthy than others, as the emphasis on the Gallipoli campaign meant that those who were wounded or lost their lives in other theatres during the First World War were ignored because

> the memory of the First World War ... was one that progressively focused on Gallipoli to the exclusion of other theatres of war. This was despite the fact that at least 85 per cent of Australian deaths between 1914 and 1918 occurred on the Western front and fewer than 8,000 deaths occurred on the Gallipoli peninsula.[80]

Moreover, over the years, memories of the British, the Irish, the French, the Indians and the Gurkas were often "rendered invisible," as were the New Zealanders, who shared the acronym (Australian and New Zealand Army Corps). Beaumont concludes that "with time the contours of the Gallipoli campaign also became indistinct. In popular culture and ritual, it was the landing of 25 April (progressively accorded a capital L) that dominated the myth."[81]

In a similar vein, historian Marilyn Lake stresses that "the mythologising of Anzac as our national creation story and the popular re-writing of history that ha[s] occurred as a result ha[s] effectively marginalised other formative experiences, especially cultural, social and political achievements in the making of the nation". The kinds of stories which have been "sidelined," she writes, are of "nation-building, oriented not to military prowess, but to visions of social justice and democratic equality". Moreover, she adds that "surely Australians who had fought for sexual

---

76 Peter Stanley, "Monumental Mistake: Is War the Most Important Thing in Australian History", in *Anzacs Dirty Dozen: 12 Myths of Australian History*, (Sydney: UNSW Press, 2012), 267.

77 Stanley, "Monumental Mistake", 271.

78 Stanley, "Monumental Mistake", 263.

79 Stanley, "Monumental Mistake", 269.

80 Joan Beaumont, "Gallipoli and National Identity", *Culture, Place and Identity*, eds. Neal Garnham and Keith Jeffery (Dublin: University College Dublin Press, 2003), 142.

81 Beaumont, "Gallipoli and National Identity", 142.

and racial equality had contributed more significantly to securing our democratic freedoms?"[82] And while Stanley points out that while many politicians speak of the "Australian spirit" in the same breath as they speak of Anzac Day, he argues that there are "many contenders" for "evoking the Australian spirit". He suggests that a "cursory list would encompass qualities such as the stamina of convicts; the mateship of bushmen; the endurance of colonial pioneers; the boldness of settlers, the enterprise of gold-seekers; the initiative of migrants (of any period); the attachment to fairness by those who strove for justice; the egalitarianism of members of the labour movement; the resilience of Indigenous people; and so on".[83]

But as Lake and Henry Reynolds assert in the Preface, "for several years now Australia has seen the relentless militarisation of our history: the commemoration of war and understanding of our national history have been confused and deflated. The Anzac spirit is now said to animate all our greatest achievements, even as the Anzac landing recedes into the distant past".[84] Here again, Stanley adds that the commemorative aspect of Anzac has also been reformulated:

> The word that most often recurs on Anzac Day is not "remembrance," "sadness," or "grief," and still less any expression of regret that Australia committed itself as a nation to so many conflicts in such a short national history. Rather, it is "pride." Many Australians are "proud: of their nation's military history. They express pride in its volunteer tradition, in the way it "punched above its weight" in war, of the skill, courage, ingenuity and general martial proficiency that Australian troops are said to have exhibited.[85]

Sadly, when I wanted to teach Walker's courageous text, which challenges this interpretation of the "Anzac spirit," the novel had gone (temporarily) out of print. The lack of accessibility to such a text was unfortunate, for as Vickroy asserts, one of the principal aims of trauma narratives is to thwart societal disregard for painful, uncomfortable, often-controversial historical events".[86] Walker's novel publicly reconstructs the private, psychological experience of the traumatised soldier and further elicits a sobering, contemplative examination of the individual, psychological suffering of witnesses/victims. Her novel also invites readers to reflect upon their own collective responsibility in the continuing obsessive attention paid to Anzacs and the Anzac legend. Walker's *The Wing of Night*, with its subtle, refined and shrewd criticism of the powerful, persistent, recurring force such as the Anzac legend, is by definition what Vickroy terms a "truthful trauma narrative"[87] – one

82 Marilyn Lake and Henry Reynolds, *What's Wrong with Anzac? The Militarization of Australian History* (Sydney: UNSW Press, 2010), 10.
83 Stanley, "Monumental Mistake", 275.
84 Lake and Reynolds, *What's Wrong with Anzac?*, vii.
85 Stanley, "Monumental Mistake", 265.
86 Laurie Vickroy, *Trauma and Survival in Contemporary Fiction* (Charlottesville: University of Virginia Press, 2002), 3.

that deserves a prominent place on those shelves of bookshops that "groan under the weight" of the more than two hundred books published on Australians at war in the past two decades",[88] most of which insist that there is only one monolithic story of war – the one Bean wrote.

---

87   Vickroy, *Trauma and Survival in Contemporary Fiction*, xiii.
88   Lake and Reynolds, *What's Wrong with Anzac?*, 14.

Part 2
World War II Fictions

7

Damn(ed) Yankees

The Pacific's Not Pacific Anymore

Until recently, social historians and literary critics have paid little attention to the one million American servicemen who spent time in Australia between 1941 and 1945, a surprising oversight given that, at the time of the "friendly invasion", the population of Australia was only seven million. Although Dixon Wecter's "The Aussie and the Yank" (1946) and Henrietta Drake-Brockman's "The Americans Came" (1949) were published shortly after the war, it was several decades before John Hammond Moore's *Over-Sexed, Over-Paid, and Over Here: Americans in Australia 1941–1945* (1981); E. Daniel Potts and Annette Potts' *Yanks Down Under 1941–1945: The American Impact on Australia* (1985); Dennis Phillips' *Ambivalent Allies: Myth and Reality in the Australian-American Relationship* (1988); Rosemary Campbell's *Heroes and Lovers: A Question of National Identity* (1989); and Anthony J. Barker and Lisa Jackson's *Fleeting Attraction: A Social History of American Servicemen in Western Australia During the Second World War* (1996), appeared. These historians provide detailed accounts of the tensions over fighting prowess, money and women, which heated up shortly after the Americans arrived, but their efforts to determine the impact the Americans had on Australian culture and way of life proved remarkably elusive, leading Potts and Potts, for example, to conclude that the effect of the American presence on Australia is "much more difficult to establish than their contribution to victory in the Pacific".[1] The historians also suggest that contact with Americans served to sharpen Australians' awareness of their own identity,[2] but to what extent most are unable to say, in part because they fail to take into account the existence of the powerful "Australian male heroic tradition" that had been, according to Campbell, holding sway for decades (Introduction). She asserts that the overwhelmingly masculine monopoly of the

---

1   E. Daniel Potts and Annette Potts, *Yanks Down Under 1941–45: The American Impact on Australia* (Melbourne: Oxford University Press, 1985), 404.

2   See Henrietta Drake-Brockman, "The Americans Came", *American Quarterly* (Spring 1949), 57; John Hammond Moore, *Over-Sexed, Over-Paid, and Over Here* (St. Lucia: University of Queensland Press, 1981), 281; Potts and Potts, *Yanks Down Under*, 404.

Australian national identity was being called into question before the war, for many of the circumstances that had supported the national image were changing:

> The economy was shifting from primary to secondary industry, taking with it the very heart of the association of the national myth with rural life. The Depression had forced many men into the humiliating experience of powerlessness. An increasing number of non-British migrants were entering Australia. Above all, the overwhelming masculine monopoly of the culture was being challenged by a feminist dimension – the arrival of the "new woman", changing work patterns, falling birthrates, and the growth of suburbia with its orientation to domesticity and family life.[3]

Campbell further observes that while it seemed likely that World War II would "restore the environment which had allowed the male role of hero to flourish", she concludes that it did not, because the "presence of the Americans contributed to a questioning of sexual roles and expectations, race relations[4] and delineations of the Australian way of life that had been spelled out in various depictions of an Australian national identity".[5] According to Campbell, the war "marked a critical point in the male-female relationship in Australia and its disintegration of the hero myth".[6] I have quoted Campbell's remarks at length because I wish to demonstrate that several of the women's fictions that emerged soon after the war – Henrietta Drake-Brockman's *The Fatal Days* (1947)[7] and Florence James' and Dymphna Cusack's *Come in Spinner* (1951) – do not accord with any of these historians' analyses, including Campbell's. They do, however, conform with Michael McKernan's assessment that the Americans had little impact on Australians, who "proved remarkably resistant to change",[8] for Drake-Brockman's and Cusack/James' texts fail to discard or revise national values, particularly those pertaining to the impoverished relationships between women and men. Like their Great War predecessors,[9] these women writers re-inscribe the values of the masculine bush ethos, bolster yet again the fighting prowess of the almighty Anzac, and once more assign women a subordinate place in Australian society. Only one novel, Zora Cross' *This Hectic Age* (1944), questions national stereotypes.

Because Drake-Brockman's and Cusack/James' novels take place during different periods – *The Fatal Days* covers 20 February to 6 March, 1942; *Come*

---

3   Rosemary Campbell, *Heroes and Lovers: A Question of National Identity* (Sydney: Allen & Unwin, 1989), 2–3.
4   None of the texts I discuss here incorporate the issue of race relations to any extent.
5   Campbell, *Heroes and Lovers*, 5.
6   Campbell, *Heroes and Lovers*, 3.
7   Moore refers to Drake-Brockman's novel as *The Fateful Days*, and then indicates he has not read it by making remarks that bear no relation whatsoever to the work (Moore, *Over-Sexed, Over-Paid, and Over Here*, 273).
8   Michael McKernan, *The Australian People and the Great War* (Melbourne: Nelson, 1980), 206.
9   See Chapter 1.

in Spinner eight days in October 1944 – they offer a fascinating overview of the American presence in Australia. *The Fatal Days* opens at a time when Australians are feeling especially vulnerable: the newspapers have begun to list Australian casualties in the Mediterranean; Singapore has fallen; the Japanese have bombed Darwin, raided Port Moresby and captured Rabaul. Suddenly, the Australians comprehend that their show of British loyalty – they have shipped both their arms and their armies to the other side of the equator – has rendered them defenceless in the face of enemy attack. Realising that they can no longer count upon Britain (now fully occupied fighting for her own survival) to protect them, they are enormously relieved when the Americans agree to come to their aid.[10]

Owing to a shortage of accommodation in Melbourne, when the government asks the citizens of Ballarat to billet 5,600 GIs, they accept eagerly, their dominant emotions relief and gratitude. Avid cinema-goers, particularly of American films,[11] Australians are prepared to regard the newcomers as their celluloid saviours. Women's enthusiasm for the Yank ingress was fuelled particularly by the persistent rumour that Clark Gable would be serving in Melbourne. Although Gable never showed up, it scarcely mattered, for in *The Fatal Days*, all GIs possess star qualities. Routinely handsome and clean-shaven, the Yanks also sport superbly tailored uniforms that display to advantage their fighting-fit bodies. These American glamour boys stroll about the town with an easy confidence, their courtesy and politeness charming everyone they meet.

Compared to the local heroes, depicted uncharacteristically in this text as glum workaholics,[12] the khaki-clad soldiers are fun-loving and uninhibited in their pursuit of pleasure. The Golden City comes to life when the GIs fill the dance halls and teach enthusiastic young women how to "jitterbug". These virile young doughboys are not merely getting in one last fling before battle, however; they also prove to be sensitive and caring young men who respond sympathetically to their host family's problems.

Once Drake-Brockman secures her Yanks firmly on Australian soil, however, she uses their presence to mount a prolonged assault on the real enemies of Australia – not the marauding Japanese, but her countrymen/women who suffer from the "cultural cringe." She takes careful aim at those Australians who regard their food, alcohol, books, and art as inferior and consistently purchase imported products; and at those who are convinced their public buildings and housing

---

10 Dennis Phillips argues that the Americans came to Australia not to help fend off enemy attack, but to mount a counter-offensive into the jungles of New Guinea and ultimately the Philippines (Phillips, *Ambivalent Allies: Myth and Reality in the Australian-American Relationship*, Ringwood, Vic: Penguin, 1988, 14).

11 Potts and Potts, *Yanks Down Under 1941–45*, 26; McKernan, *The Australian People and the Great War*, 185)

12 A number of historians suggest that the Yanks found the Australians' cavalier attitude to war frustrating. Moore writes that the Australians were eager to serve, but only from Monday to Friday, and then only if they were not required to forfeit leisure time, beer or horse racing (Moore, *Over-Sexed, Over-Paid, and Over Here*, 231).

standards are inferior to the Americans'. Those whom she clearly wishes to kill off in her narrative display no interest whatsoever in the history of their own country. In this text, the real "saviours" of Australia are not the Yanks, but the home-grown nationalists.

Drake-Brockman further employs a number of strategies to convince both Australians and Americans that there is nothing inferior about life Down Under. She ensures, for example, that the Americans utter few discouraging words: a few find the lingo curious and the country parched-looking, but only one complains about his accommodation. In the main, a resounding chorus of approval fills the air. Drake-Brockman writes in a few discerning high-ranking officers whose major role is to laud the superb quality of Australian wines and sherries, praise the fine designs of the buildings and their tasteful interiors and commend the literature, particularly Henry Handel Richardson's goldfields novel, *The Fortunes of Richard Mahony*. She also takes the local denizens and the GIs on a number of walks, calling in at the zoo so that the Yanks can marvel at the uniqueness of wallabies and Tasmanian devils, strolling past the Arch of Victory and the heroic monuments to Burke and Wills and Peter Lalor, touring the gold fields and visiting Adam Lindsay's home, where the GIs learn about the English-born poet and the much-loved Australian writers Banjo Paterson and C.J. Dennis.[13] At times, however, *The Fatal Days* reads so much like a travel book that readers may be forgiven if they forget that the Americans have come to Ballarat to defend Australians in their darkest hour, not to sightsee.

At the same time as Drake-Brockman affords the Yanks opportunities to applaud all things Australian, she sees to it that one of her central characters, the elderly Mrs Vike, does not return the favour; on the contrary, she spends a great deal of time pointing out the numerous differences between Americans and Australians, but always casting the Yanks and their society in a poor light. She observes, for example, that when the Americans went in search of freedom, they found a "beautiful, friendly country" awaiting them (78), whereas when the First Fleet landed at Botany Bay, they encountered a harsh land that required "unrelenting human will" to conquer (80). She asserts that although religion may have played a large role in America (as it did not in Australia), the latter have nonetheless gone the Americans (and the British) one better by developing an extensive network of social programs and a peerless educational system. Moreover, at the same time as she praises Australians' deep reluctance to use military force against its own civilians, she criticises American employers for assaulting men who wish to form unions and describes America as a violent society (two of her Yanks hail from Chicago, home of Al Capone) where car thieving and knifing is commonplace and clear evidence of moral decay. Mrs Vike also downplays the obvious social stratifications in Ballarat in order to put forth her view that although money may be the "social yard-stick" in America and "inherited wealth"

---

13   Henrietta Drake-Brockman, *The Fatal Days*. Sydney: Angus & Robertson, 1947), 161. All
     subsequent references are to this edition and appear in parentheses in the text.

the rule in Britain, Australia is an egalitarian society "without class distinctions" (218). None of the congenial Americans takes umbrage at her insults, though; one low-ranking soldier even contributes to his countrymen's pitiable image by insisting that Hollywood creates a false impression of American life, and then confesses he was raised in poverty (123). Ultimately, Mrs Vike concedes that the Americans do possess one outstanding trait – an intense desire to learn as much as they can about Australian politics, customs and history.

Unwittingly, however, Drake-Brockman undermines her own point that the citizens of Ballarat are unenlightened about their history, for her city teems with civilians who readily deliver lengthy treatises on the Diggers' glorious victories at Sovereign Hill and Anzac Cove, the places from which the Digger spirit, so central to the formation of Australian national identity, originated. Mrs Vike herself provides a voluminous history of the Eureka Stockade, an event she stresses carries the same kind of "symbolic significance" as the Magna Carta and the Gettsyburg address (77); her granddaughter Rhea and the working-class Mrs Andrewartha further champion the event, although less formally. Rhea proves to be a veritable fountain of information, holding her American date in thrall – at midnight, no less – with another substantial lecture on the pre-eminence of the nation's prime ministers.

Overall, *The Fatal Days* reads more like a series of essays championing the events and players at the Eureka Stockade and Anzac Cove than it does a work of fiction. Most frustrating is that Drake-Brockman's female characters crow about identity-forming events that absent(ed) women, glory in a political adventure: disseminating values she did not help formulate, Drake-Brockman facilitates her own marginalisation as a woman writer. She also reinforces traditional perceptions that women's experiences are unworthy material for a national literature and hence bolsters the power of the patriarchal culture that denounces women as "Other." Drake-Brockman should have observed what happened to Great War women writers: they received no praise for backing the attack, and their books sank rapidly into oblivion. So, too, did *The Fatal Days*.

This was not the case for Cusack/James' *Come in Spinner*, which won the 1946 Sydney *Daily Telegraph*'s prize for best Australian novel; although it underwent heavy cutting before the manuscript was eventually published in 1951, it has remained in print ever since, a remarkable feat given that it had been considered politically adventurous in its representation of both class and gender. In 1989, when an unabridged edition at last appeared, the book again received rave reviews, as did the four-hour, made-for-television miniseries, first aired in 1990. *Come in Spinner* shares several similarities with *The Fatal Days*, for Sydney, too, is enlivened by the Yanks. And like Drake-Brockman, Cusack/James also take pot shots at the cultural cringers who feel Australia must continue importing Brits to "keep up the stock",[14] or who derive their cultural and artistic standards from New York or London. The writers also invite several erudite Europeans to inform Australians that they suffer needlessly from a "national inferiority complex" (405), for they consider Sydney "heaven" (400). Not all their Yanks come from auspicious backgrounds, either; one's father has been out of work for years, a circumstance exacerbated by the lack of unions and social programs in America.

It may initially appear, too, that like Drake-Brockman, these writers provide little scope for social change because they do not depict their female characters actively employed in the war effort. Only one minor character enlists in the Australian Women's Army Service (AWAS), but the writers provide no details about the nature of her work. This may seem like a curious omission, given that by 1944, according to Anne Summers, there were 49,000 women in the Services and 3,000 in the Australian Women's Land Army. The numbers of women in employment (often doing men's jobs or working in the munitions industry or other defence works) had risen by thirty-five per cent, to 840,000 in 1944.[15] Cusack/ James' central characters Claire, Deb, and Guinea are gainfully employed, but at the Marie Antoinette beauty salon in a posh Sydney hotel.[16] Their work as manicurists, hairdressers, and masseuses may seem overly traditional for a feminist reading, but by situating their women in a beauty salon, the writers appear to have been examining a significant change in women's lives that Marilyn Lake describes (in another context) as "the historically changing nature of femininity itself".[17] Lake points out that in the 1930s, "a new understanding of femininity, one that revolved around sexuality, sexual attractiveness and youthfulness" had emerged.[18] While women were being lured into the workplace by 1939, because of the "important constructors of femininity" – advertising, the cinema, the rise of consumerism – they were not necessarily gaining a new sense of financial independence, self-reliance and autonomy, but were being offered instead "the adventure of sexual romance".[19] Femininity, Lake argues, had also become "the charm of youth".[20]

But as Lake also stresses, if a woman wished to have sexual appeal, she must not only be young, but she must look young[21] – hence the new advertisements for face creams and other products that had not formerly promised to obliterate the signs of ageing.[22] The thirty-eight-year-old Claire has developed her own extensive line

---

14   Dymphna Cusack and Florence James, *Come in Spinner* ([1951], North Ryde, NSW: Angus & Robertson, 1988), 121. All subsequent references are to this edition and appear in parentheses in the text.

15   Anne Summers, *Damned Whores and God's Police: The Colonization of Women in Australia* (Ringwood, Vic: Penguin, 1975), 416.

16   Marie Antoinette was considered irresponsible and frivolous, a description that fits the clientele at the beauty salon. For more information on Marie Antoinette, see *A History of Their Own: Women in Europe From Prehistory to the Present*, eds. Bonnie S. Anderson and Judith P. Zinsser (New York: Harper, 1988): 42–43.

17   Marilyn Lake, "Female Desires: the Meaning of World War Two", *Gender and War: Australians at War in the Twentieth Century*, eds. Joy Damousi and Marilyn Lake (Melbourne: Cambridge University Press, 1995), 61.

18   Lake, "Female Desires", 18.

19   Lake, "Female Desires", 62.

20   Lake, "Female Desires", 62.

21   Lake, "Female Desires", 65.

of cosmetics bearing the Marie Antoinette symbol (20); while she knows that these products can never make her look truly young again, her clientele hope against hope that makeup, hair dye and massages can disguise wrinkles and sagging skin, cover thinning grey hair and take off pounds. Claire and the slightly younger Deb are also cognisant of their fading beauty, their "only capital" (70), and intensely aware of the male gaze, for as Lake writes, whereas women had formerly looked into mirrors to assure themselves that they looked their best, "[m]en's entry into the frame signifie[d] an important shift as femininity [was] now explicitly defined in terms of heterosexual desirability".[23] Women were incited to be "attractive, alluring, exciting – objects to men's positioning as subjects",[24] for by the 1940s, "femininity was increasingly defined in terms of (hetero)sexual attractiveness".[25] To retain their men's affections, both Claire and Deb know they must keep slim and wear eye-catching fashions, no matter how uncomfortable or costly, of the fact that no man worries what he looks like: even a middle-aged overweight man, still considered in his "prime," can attract a woman half his age (24).

Cusack/James are critical of a few other injustices that prevail in the wartime climate. They argue, for example, that it is unfair that men do not have to take the consequences for their actions, proposing that if venereal disease is an occupational hazard for men, pregnancy should be for women. They lament that an unmarried pregnant servicewoman, forced to endure shame and the threat of dishonourable discharge, dies because she cannot obtain a safe abortion, whereas the serviceman receives nary a reprimand. They further interrogate why young women presumed to be promiscuous are arrested and locked up in reformatories when licentious soldiers go unpunished, a set of circumstances that would not exist were women making the laws. The writers also contend that the Manpower Regulations, brought into effect in 1942 to conscript women into essential employment, were in part responsible for women's immorality, because those they assigned to reserve occupations in mills or factories were so poorly paid they were forced into prostitution. Others are victims of the white slave trade; coerced into brothels, argues one character, these women, often only sixteen, are "as much victims of war as if they'd been hit in an air raid" (551).

Summers also echoes the kinds of inequities in the conscription process Cusack/James identify: although the policy insisted that women who were not gainfully employed were to be conscripted into essential employment, in practice, only working-class women were, a situation borne out in *Come in Spinner*.[26] Cusack/James also underscore women's fears that they will suffer loss of income and pensions if asked to relinquish their jobs at war's end.

---

22 Lake, "Female Desires", 67.
23 Lake, "Female Desires", 65.
24 Lake, "Female Desires", 65.
25 Lake, "Female Desires", 63.
26 Summers, *Damned Whores and God's Police*, 417.

Come in Spinner also highlights the fact that by October 1944, the threat to national safety having evaporated, the Yanks, only a few of whom are still regarded as decent men, have worn out their welcome.[27] The refrain in the air is no longer the euphoric "The Yankees Are Coming", but the acrid "Yankee, Go Home,"[28] in part because Australian men feel as if they are second-class citizens in their own country, unable to get drink or taxis upon demand and forced to listen to the Yanks boast that they are mopping up the Pacific single-handedly (179). The most conflicts arise, however, when Australian men (represented primarily in the text by the Anzac Kim Scott) discover that all is fair in love and war, for local women prefer to date Yanks. Australian men should not have felt ambushed, however, for they had routinely preferred to spend their leisure time with mates, not dates, and in both *The Fatal Days* and *Come in Spinner*, they refuse to make commitments, keeping their lovers dangling for years, even decades. What enrages Australian men most, however, is that for the first time, women were challenging the double standards that had previously allowed only men the right to enjoy premarital or extramarital love affairs. Accordingly, they employ a number of strategies to maintain the sexual status quo, to force women to return to the old order, when courtship patterns were fixed, less indeterminate. Aside from blaming every problem on the Yanks, they also charge that doughboys "get away with murder" when the police haul away a fornicating Australian, but the American goes scot-free, and accuse GIs of having too much money, of "wanting only one thing" and of using liquor to get it. Rarely do they admit defeat by confessing to their shortcomings as lovers or their disrespect for women. Instead, they revert to familiar arguments, decreeing there are only two types of women – the chaste and the chased, or the decent and the decadent. Those who pursue Yanks are unpatriotic, "easy pickups," morally suspect, or harlots only after money. And in the end, Australian men emerge victorious on the home front, their efforts to preserve traditional gender codes having proved effective. Decent women say "No Thanks to the Yanks" because, by 1944, despite their romantic ways and lavish spending, their Hollywood charm has waned and they have dwindled into scoundrels who two-time women, steal their money and frequent brothels.

But what troubles me is Drake-Brockman's and Cusack/James' identification with the dominant ideology, their reaffirmation of the dual stereotypes. Drake-Brockman's Ena Andrewartha, bored with life in Ballarat, pursues Yanks shamelessly: but she is also callous, insensitive to the needs of others, and money hungry. (Ironically, a female "gold digger" receives no approbation in *The Fatal Days*.) It is inevitably the "decent" women – Shirley Hayes and Rhea Telford in

---

27 Drake-Brockman comments that her booksellers asked her to change the title of her novel, *When the Americans Came*, feeling it "would be sufficient to put the public off!" (Drake-Brockman, "Americans", 52).

28 McKernan writes that the Americans were frustrated by the presence of large numbers of Australian servicemen and began to wonder if Australians were "pulling their weight in the war effort or were leaving all the hard work to Uncle Sam" (McKernan, *The Australian People and the Great War*, 204).

The Fatal Days and Guinea Malone and Helen McFarland in *Come in Spinner* – homogeneously characterised by a love of the outdoors, a lack of concern for physical appearance or material goods, an unpretentious and down-to-earth manner and an ability to be a good "mate", always ready to lend a hand to a friend (or stranger) in need, who remain loyal to the Australian "bloke," no longer taciturn in these novels. In each text, only one woman forms a lasting relationship with a Yank. Drake-Brockman's Rhea is romantically linked with a GI, but only because he appreciates the Australian way of life; and by coincidence, his middle name is "Vike," so she consorts with a "kissing cousin," not a foreigner. Cusack/James' minor character Val is married to a sensitive, poetry-writing Yank, but we never meet him because he is "missing in action." Thus these writers ignore that statistically between 10,000 and 20,000 Australian women immigrated to the US as war brides (the figures vary widely depending upon the source), a mass departure which must surely have warned Australian men that they needed to reassess their concepts of virility and attitudes to women.

Nonetheless, neither Drake-Brockman nor Cusack/James seriously interrogates the courtship methods that uniformly privileged men. Moreover, neither of these texts features women warriors demanding an equitable place in a male-dominated society. Although one of Cusack/James' minor characters insists that "a bankbook's a woman's best friend" (41), the writers never seriously advocate financial independence as an emancipatory tool. Their one professional woman, Dr Dallas McIntyre, maintains an impressive lifestyle, but her declaration that "the only real salvation for women is work" (330) rings hollow since she herself rejects marriage and children, her show of independence merely solidifying the patriarchal assumption that any woman who desires a professional career must forfeit her right to a family. In addition, while the doctor argues that "work" can take a variety of forms, the model of domestic bliss she holds up is Deb's sister Nolly, now pregnant with her fifth child, married to Tom, a virile, fire-and-flood-fighting noble bushman husband who seems to have stepped straight out of Russel Ward's *The Australian Legend*. The resilient and resourceful Nolly and Tom are the "real pioneers" who struggle to put more into the country than they take out of it (154). Although the couple struggles to make ends meet, neither they nor their imaginative and fun-loving children appear to suffer hardships. In designating Nolly the ideal woman, the intellectual Dallas seems curiously out of touch with the times, for as Jill Matthews argues, this kind of figure – the "mother of the race" – was "fading fast".[29]

Cusack/James also cling to outdated notions by insisting that their other "decent" women – Guinea and Helen – marry not just Australian men, but bushmen, and lead thereafter, like Nolly and Tom, "fairy tale" lives (612). Helen already resides in the bush, cheerfully doing the mustering and trucking of two men

---

29   Cited in Lake, *Gender and War*, 63.

on her father's property, when she meets Alec, a repatriated soldier whose wounds prevent him from becoming a veterinarian. Because of the man shortage, Helen's father agrees to hire him, an opportunity he seizes because, like Roo and Barney in Ray Lawler's *The Summer of the Seventeenth Doll*, he scorns city life. Similarly, Guinea rejects proposals from a plethora of American admirers who promise her a comfortable life in the USA, choosing instead to marry the Anzac Kim (who, like Dennis' Ginger Mick, seems to have been reformed by war service), and spending her life on a farm.

Much of the novel focuses on Deb, whose move from bush to city when her husband Jack enlists causes her values to become corrupted, particularly by her association with the Anglophile Angus McFarland, a bigot and a "lounge lizard" (481) who gives nothing back to the bush property that supports his bountiful standard of living. Nonetheless, Deb is so blinded by Angus' wealth and privilege – he makes her feel like "Cinderella" (85, 89, 92) – that she overlooks his flaws and ignores Dallas' suggestion that her enchantment will end when the clock chimes midnight (92); when she marries him, he will expect her to become a "slave" who panders to his whims (336). Echoing Virginia Woolf, Dallas further argues that Angus will demand that Deb be "decorative and entertaining" and "expect her to be a kind of magnifying mirror, reflecting an image of [himself] so much larger than life that [he] never ha[s] to face the truth" (337). Dallas' observations are astute, for Deb already acquiesces to Angus' fancies and remains silent when he makes decisions for her, even though she complains when Jack does the same. Moreover, Deb's argument that Angus can provide opportunities for her daughter is undercut by the fact Luen, raised entirely in the bush, is a bright and sensitive child. Once Angus becomes her stepfather, she will become as despoiled as her mother, for Deb parrots Angus' conservative views, neglects her daughter, and rarely helps anyone in need unless shamed into it.

By insisting that wicked women live in the city and happy mothers in the bush, Cusack/James are harkening back to an old-fashioned city/country dichotomy produced by the dominant ideology during the Great War, reinforced by Charles Bean, and bolstered yet again by Great War women writers. The writers support the theory that a humble life in the bush is bodily and spiritually therapeutic, whereas an urban existence is morally harmful and physically stunting. To that end, women like Deb and Claire, who choose to live among glass and concrete, not blue sky and wattle, are acquisitive, overly concerned with physical appearance, uncharitable and associate with men mixed up in the seedy worlds of gambling, black-marketeering, race-fixing and prostitution. The urban environment is also inhospitable to children: neither Claire nor Thelma Molesworth, another profit-driven businesswoman, has any offspring; moreover, one young woman dies from an illegal abortion in Sydney and a young mother has her children taken from her because she is unable to care for them.

Although Cusack/James are timely in their depictions of the rise of consumerism and advertising, the cult of youth and their recognition of changing sexual mores, their nostalgic insistence that intelligent women can find fulfillment in the bush seems not only utterly insensitive to their needs, but also entirely inappropriate to a mid-1940s urban Australian culture. To suggest that women who wish to take advantage of the amenities urban life offers must be selfish and inconsiderate seems out of step with the directions Australian society had been taking for some time, for as Campbell comments, the milieu that had supported the legend was fast disappearing and the population was moving decisively away from the bush.[30] Possibly, having completed the novel in 1946, the writers were merely responding to the pressures of the time, for as Summers argues, the old ideas about what was appropriate for women were being forcefully reasserted: women were being "demobbed. Whether they wanted to or not, they were expected to return … to the pre-war division of labour and status and power".[31] Potts, too, writes that by the end of the war, the government "favoured a return to family sizes of 40 years earlier, when five or six children were the custom".[32] In another vein, James mentions in her Introduction to a later edition of the text that she and Cusack were "fired with Miles Franklin's burning conviction that 'without an indigenous literature people can remain aliens on their own soil'" (vii). But in promoting the bush as the only worthy site of indigenous literature, Cusack/James were not only disregarding that it was based upon principles women did not help formulate and that never made room for them, they were also overlooking Barbara Baynton's view that bush life offered women only inconceivable hardship.

But perhaps there is a simpler explanation: in the Introduction, James refers to the harmonious life she and Cusack led in a rented cottage in the Blue Mountains while they constructed the novel: "Dymphna's health began to improve wonderfully [and] the children loved the carefree life" (vi). James herself had spent the war years with her young children in Sydney, where "accommodation was a constant problem," and her work as a Public Appeals Officer for Royal Prince Alfred Hospital, which involved [her] in social functions and erratic hours "often made life complicated" (viii). Nonetheless, I maintain that Cusack/James were ultimately cowards in their own war effort for, like the dutiful women myrmidons in World War I who relegated their female characters to the bush, they, too, were taking their orders from the masculine bush myth-makers such as Henry Lawson, C.E.W. Bean, and C.J. Dennis.

The only writer to question, not bolster, national stereotypes is Zora Cross. In *This Hectic Age*, Cross takes her fifteen-year-old Eve Wilson from Milton Vale to Sydney (the symbolism is heavy handed), whom she describes as "a wicked wanton out for all she can get" (the prose is purple). And indeed, the urban setting subjects Eve to the kinds of experiences that once she could "have only connected with

---

30 Campbell, *Heroes and Lovers*, 12.
31 Summers, *Damned Whores and God's Police*, 419.
32 Annette Potts and Lucinda Strauss, *For the Love of a Soldier: Australian War-Brides and Their GIs* (Crows Nest: ABC, 1987), 45.

crime fiction",[33] as the following brief plot summary indicates: upon arrival, Eve rents a former friend's flat without realising that she is a "semi-prostitute", the kind of woman prevalent in Sydney during the war.[34] Her clientele, who assume that Eve is also a "loose" woman, take her to a wild, all-night party. Unaccustomed to alcohol, Eve drinks too much, is attacked by a jealous woman and then rescued by Tex, an American soldier. The next day, while innocently watching a movie, a "diabolical pair" of "notorious procurers" attempt to drug her, but Eve narrowly escapes. Hours later, she is nearly run over in traffic, and that night, a flabby, toothless woman who believes Eve has stolen her money threatens her with a knife. Within days, Eve succumbs to love at first sight, believing that the wealthy Paul "the prince of seducers" will bring her a "film-star's life" (109), but on their first date, he gets her drunk to weaken her defences; unsuccessful in his attempt to rape Eve, he is nevertheless arrested for running an illegal gambling house.

Given her thrilling and dangerous life, it is not surprising that Eve should be unimpressed by city life. She also finds the environment sordid: the stench of stale beer and cigarettes lingers in the air; the streets are full of "pick-up girls," the disorderly, and the derelict; women are hospitalised for "too much sex" (79); wives boast about their infidelities with Yanks, whereas others fear abusive husbands. An old woman informs her of the enormous decline in moral standards since the war: newspapers frankly discuss previously taboo diseases; movies are full of violence; people make love in public; nudist colonies have sprung up; and the streets are no longer safe for women (66).

Fortunately, Eve finds a protector in Andy Flackmore, a police officer from Bourke (he plans to return soon). Andy laments that so many women like Eve are leaving the "good old bush" (102) and moving to the city, where the streets are perilous and "girls grow up too fast" (111). But Eve declares that women have to "fit themselves for their times" and proposes a solution: make the streets safe for women (111). From the old woman, Eve has also learned that life in a city full of gardens, parks, beaches, shops, museums, and historical attractions, can be stimulating (65–66). It also provides the social milieu in which she can "do something" with her life. Although Eve's goals are uncertain, it is clear she will remain in Sydney, having already located a job. She agrees to date Andy, but other men, as well. Although Andy's strange outburst on the last page of the novel about Lone Pine and "mates and mateship" (128) appears to be at cross purposes with the text, it comes too late to be taken seriously, for throughout *This Hectic Age*, Cross has clearly set out to challenge outmoded notions about women's place in postwar Australia.

---

33   Zora Cross, *This Hectic Age* (Sydney: London Books, 1944), 30. All subsequent references are to this edition and appear in parentheses in the text.

34   Summers, *Damned Whores and God's Police*, 417.

8

"Where Have All the Flowers Gone?" in the Film Adaptation of *Come in Spinner*

A few semesters ago, while teaching a comparative literature course on Canadian and Australian women's war writing, my students and I became intrigued by the many references to flowers and bush imagery in Dymphna Cusack and Florence James' *Come in Spinner*, especially since flowers rarely appeared in our Canadian texts. As most literary scholars know, there is nothing unusual about the appearance of flowers in literature, for throughout history, as far back as Homer in the ninth century BC,[1] the world's finest poets, essayists, dramatists and novelists have drawn upon flower imagery to provide insight into the human condition and to express the truths of their times.[2] Although today we tend to associate flowers with conventional expressions of feelings as exemplified in Hallmark cards,[3] we need to acknowledge that during the eighteenth-century, a formal language that assigned specific meanings to flowers, plants and trees was devised in Turkey and disseminated largely by Lady Mary Wortley Montagu, then living in Constantinople. Before long, European writers, particularly those concerned with social issues, perceived that flowers could express certain aspects of human behaviour. In the Victorian era, writers used flowers to express a wide range of ideas focusing on the relationships between the sexes. There has never been an agreed-upon set of meanings, however: the language of flowers is merely a vocabulary list that matches flowers – that is, annuals, perennials, native wildflowers, bulbs, flowering shrubs and trees – with meanings, but the list depends upon tradition and contemporary associations, and thus differs from book to book, since every age and culture expresses its perspectives on life differently. The motivating factor is the human desire (Barthes claims in *Mythologies* that it is a

---

1   Marina Heilmeyer, *The Language of Flowers: Symbols and Myths* (New York: Prestel Verlag, 2001), 58.

2   Frances Kelly, *The Illustrated Language of Flowers: Magic, Meaning and Lore* (Ringwood, Vic: Penguin, 1992): 5.

3   Beverly Seaton, *The Language of Flowers: A History* (Charlottesville: University of Virginia Press, 1995): 136.

bourgeois desire) to find our cultural conventions endorsed by nature herself.[4] Thus the language of flowers might well be considered a cultural myth that uses nature to validate manners and morals.[5]

In a more recent post-colonial/literary context, the inclusion of flowers and their meaning is customary. Helen Tiffin posits that writers such as Jamaica Kincaid, Olive Senior and Lorna Goodison deploy gardens, flowers and flowering trees to demonstrate how the history of coloniser and colonised is invoked and reworked.[6] For her part, Kincaid confesses she knew nothing about Antiguan flowers and plants, considered dreary because the "conqueror" deemed them so. Similarly, V.S. Naipaul and Chinua Achebe have utilised the local seasons and climate to demonstrate the ways in which characters were either implicitly or explicitly maligned against an idea or normative imperial centre.[7] Likewise, as Libby Robbin posits, in their desire to have a distinctive culture that reflected the peculiarities of the environment that would aid in the development of a sense of pride in Australia free of the influence of Britain, "*The Bulletin* writers of the 1890s celebrated the bush" and viewed the city, not the wilderness, "as the centre of moral degeneracy."[8] Robin observes that by the time of Federation, "the 'biological cringe' that saw Australian birds, animals and plants as 'inferior' was being challenged, but the entrenched low status of Australian plants and animals and their absence from celebratory literary sources remained an obstacle to their full appreciation."[9] The mid-nineteenth century poet Adam Lindsay Gordon's view of Australia as a land of "scentless blossoms" and "songless birds"[10] prevailed until the 1920s, when C.J. Dennis began "writing poetry explicitly to undermine this view".[11] Before long, Australian women writers like Cusack/James began to use flower and bush imagery for their own unique purposes – mainly to validate bush values and bush life – but also drawing upon these images from the natural world to criticise several wartime institutions.

In so doing, Cusack/James were emulating the long history between nature and war, wherein Paul Fussell identifies in *The Great War and Modern Memory* the blood-hued poppy as an indispensable part of the symbolism of war.[12] While many assume that the flower's association with war began with the publication of perhaps

---

4   Roland Barthes, *Mythologies* (St Albans: Paladin, 1973), 140.

5   Seaton, *The Language of Flowers*, 136.

6   Helen Tiffin, "'Flowers of Evil, Flowers of Empire': Roses and Daffodils in the Work of Jamaica Kincaid, Oliver Senior and Lorna Goodison," *SPAN: Journal of the South Pacific Association for Commonwealth Literature and Language Studies*, 46 (April 1998): 58–71.

7   Tiffin, "Flowers of Evil, Flowers of Empire", 60.

8   Libby Robin, "Nationalizing Nature: Wattles Days in Australia," *Journal of Australian Studies*, 2002: 8.

9   Robin, "Nationalizing Nature", 8.

10 Adam Lindsay Gordon "A Dedication to the Author of "Holmby House", *Bush Ballads and Galloping Rhymes* (Melbourne: Clarson, Massina, and Co., General Printers, 1870).

11 Robin, "Nationalizing Nature", 8.

12 Paul Fussell, *The Great War and Modern Memory* (New York: Oxford, 1975), 243.

the best-known poem from the Great War – "In Flanders Fields" by the Canadian John McCrae – where the poppies "blow/Between the crosses row by row,"[13] the crimson flower's link with war and death dates back to Roman times, when either Sextus, the son of the King Tarquinius Superbus, or the king himself, slashed off the heads of tall poppies in a garden as a signal to commence the massacre of the population of a conquered city.[14] There was also a superstition that the poppies which grew on the battlefields of Waterloo (and later Flanders), sprang from the blood of the men who died there. Fussell adds that the poppy signalled "the blessing of sleep and oblivion – that is, of a mock-death, greatly to be desired",[15] and advances that the popularity of the "paper poppies," which disabled ex-servicemen fashioned at one time to commemorate those who died in Flanders and sold for the benefit of the British Legion on Remembrance Day, can be conceived as emblems at once of oblivion and remembrance: "a traditional happy oblivion of their agony by the dead, and at the same time an unprecedented mass remembrance of their painful loss by the living".[16] The British Legion apparently chose the poppy as its symbol of both sentiments because of McCrae's poem.[17]

Cusack/James draw upon these conventional interpretations, but challenge some of the traditional associations. Poppies appear midway through *Come in Spinner*, as the Anzac airman Kim Scott and his former lover, Guinea Malone, watch a grey-haired mourner place a wreath of crimson poppies and laurel leaves against the base of the Cenotaph at Martin Place in Sydney, but they disagree about the meaning of the gesture.[18] Guinea is certain that the mourner derives comfort from the wreath, whereas Kim protests that the "old geezer" celebrating World War I is only doing so out of "habit." Temporarily on leave from the action in Borneo, Kim has recently witnessed the killing of many of his mates and thus states with grim authority, "[t]here is no comfort for death" (382). Kim also wants to see all current memorials destroyed and replaced with the blood and guts of men who died in combat or of the women and children bombed in the London blitzes. Once confronted with these ugly realities, Kim asserts, people might "really do something to make certain that there'd never be a World War Three" (384). Kim also associates the poppy with its "biochemical realities," as poppies were said to grow at the door to the murky cave of Somnus, the Roman god of sleep, as did "other drowsy herbs" from whose juices the goddess of Night distilled slumbers that she "scattered over the darkened earth".[19] Moreover, the Spanish word for poppy, "adormidera", refers

---

13 John McCrae, "In Flanders Fields" (Sydney: Returned Sailors & Soldiers' Imperial League of Australia, Rose Bay Sub-Branch, 1922).
14 Kelly, *The Illustrated Language of Flowers*, 29.
15 Fussell, *The Great War and Modern Memory*, 244.
16 Fussell, *The Great War and Modern Memory*, 248.
17 Fussell, *The Great War and Modern Memory*, 249.
18 Dymphna Cusack and Florence James, *Come in Spinner*, ([1951], North Ryde, NSW: Angus & Robertson, 1988): 382. All subsequent references are to this edition and appear in parentheses in the text.
19 Kelly, *The Illustrated Language of Flowers*, 28–29; Edith Hamilton, *Mythology*, 111.

to the sleep-inducing properties of some species; it is akin to the word "dormitory," a place where one sleeps.[20] Kim compares the Returned Soldiers League (RSL) to dormitories; by offering ex-soldiers places to drink beer and "fight their battles all over again," he claims that the leagues lulled men into such complacency that few spoke out against war profiteers or went into politics. He speculates that even as he speaks, "some hardhead is planning how he'll fob off the boys with free beer and Friday night smokes to keep 'em from making nuisances of themselves" (384). Kim vows that when he returns from combat, he'll not be silenced, but "one hell of a nuisance" (384).[21]

Cusack/James also draw upon specific flowers to indicate how the war environment privileged only those who had decent wages. Since the price of flowers more than doubled during the war, not everyone could afford them. Because Guinea's family is on relief, her mother decorates the dining table with a vase of paper flowers (211) and brightens her hat with artificial field flowers. Guinea's younger sister Monnie notes that shop windows in the city are "full of flowers": "every girl, it seemed, wore flowers, shoulder sprays, single blossoms in elaborately piled hair, even little floral hats, enchanting as a dream, and the air was full of the heavy sweet perfume of frangipani" (80). Monnie knows she can never entertain such extravagance, but she longs to resemble the "glamorous women" who have orchids pinned to their shoulders. She can only afford a "basket of frangipani blossoms" with a little bit of maidenhair fern, which she gets cheaply because the fern is curling a little and the flowers are already bruised (137). She is reminded of the frangipani because, when she first met her former friend Shirley, she was wearing a posy of frangipani on her shoulder, but it, too, was "crushed and bruised" (79). Here, the frangipani and fern represent the young "maidens" who have been lured into prostitution; the heartbreaking stories Shirley and the other prostitutes tell describe their impoverished backgrounds and meagre pay as a result of the Manpower Regulations, which forced young and inexperienced women to carry out long hours of backbreaking and monotonous labour in factories and mills, but then refused to pay them a living wage (425–32). In order to survive, these teenage girls were forced to work in brothels and hence became wartime casualties.

Cusack/James depict numerous adolescent females wearing frangipani corsages, but the petals are inevitably damaged and discoloured. Throughout the novel, the lyrics to an original song with references to the frangipani (86, 188, 196) reinforce the vulnerability of women in wartime; to that end, several of the most poignant passages in the text recount the stories of how teenagers such as Guinea's sixteen-year-old sister Monnie who, because they are young and inexperienced, are

---

20 Bobby J. Ward, *A Contemplation Upon Flowers: Garden Plans in Myth and Literature* (Portland, OR: Timber Press, 1999), 297.

21 Ward's description of the poppy is the apt "like a yawn of fire." He also says that in Italian, the name of the poppy is "alto papavero", or literally a "tall poppy" (Ward, *A Contemplation Upon Flowers*, 297), now a common phrase in the Australian lexicon for shaming the influential.

exploited as cheap labour and prostitution becomes their only means of survival. Thus, whenever Monnie is forced against her will to "service" a serviceman, she either smells stale frangipani or the rustle of magnolia trees against the window (414). In the language of flowers, magnolias often signify dignity, the aspect of her very being that an American soldier steals from her when he gets her drunk in order to weaken her defences, and then rapes her, twice. But after being unjustly arrested, Monnie finds that it is the nearby "overpowering smell of magnolia in her nostrils" that recalls the horrific experience (434). Although neither the frangipani nor the magnolia has accumulated the same kind of traditional symbolism as the poppy, Seaton notes that "a flower's scent … has been a standard emblem of the human soul. Thus, the presence or absence of scent in a flower unusually determines whether it represents a favourable human quality: flowers of beautiful odour but insignificant appearance usually carry highly moralistic emblems".[22] The presence of a strong smell here reflects the reprehensible morals of the sailor: he has children Monnie's age (220). In referring to the sailor's brutal *de*-flowering of a naïve sixteen-year-old, Cusack/James highlight one of the recurring criticisms of the Americans in Sydney – their desire for very young women.

Cusack/James are also critical of the double standards that prevail in wartime: when the authorities raid the house of ill repute where Monnie is held captive, they arrest her on the charge of promiscuity, but allow the licentious soldier to go unpunished. Moreover, they stress that the conscription process was inequitable: although the policy insisted that women who were not gainfully employed were to be recruited into essential employment, in practice, as Anne Summers points out, "the single girls most likely to be conscripted were those poor or working-class girls who did not have fathers with the connections to get them an exemption. For the daughters of such influential men, the war years consisted of a whirl of parties with officers, then perhaps a few hours a week helping out at the Red Cross".[23] Accordingly, in the novel, the Manpower completely overlooks upper-class women's frivolity, never once admonishing them for failing to pull their weight.

The flowers such well-to-do women routinely choose to wear to fancy-dress balls are orchids, considered the most aristocratic flowers in the world. As opposed to the frangipani, which represent cheapness and exploitation, the orchid signifies status and artifice. The arrogant Mrs D'Arcy Twining, for example, lives (inexplicably, with several other wealthy people) at the upscale South Pacific Hotel, where the SP monogram is sprayed "like a monstrous orchid" on the thick maroon carpet (32), and where much of the action in the novel takes place. Lacking admirers to buy her flowers, she purchases a boxed "prize cattaleya" at an auction to wear to the ball (13), hoping it will add elegance to her "girlish" satin dress (119). None of the other urban socialites, including her equally pretentious daughter

---

22   Seaton, *The Language of Flowers*, 119.
23   Anne Summers, *Damned Whores and God's Police: The Colonization of Women in Australia* (Ringwood, Vic: Penguin, 1975), 417.

Denise, engaged to a British military officer, has any appreciation of flowers either. Denise, whose nickname DDT sounds like the noxious weed killer, thinks gold orchids might be suitable for her wedding (112), but she marks her estrangement from the natural world by admitting she doesn't know if they come in gold, or for that matter, if any flowers do. Val, one of the unpretentious hotel manicurists, urges Denise to choose dandelions for her wedding because the "pale gold colour" of the flower, also known as "pee-the-bed," is the same colour as Denise's dyed hair, and the "black centre" is the part (112). In advocating that DDT wear weeds to her wedding, Val utters an apt expression of contempt, but the dandelion also suggests coquetry and Denise is very much a coquet, for at this point, she is also engaged to an American officer.

Throughout the text, however, it is the well-paid and free-spending Yanks who purchase orchids in order to impress their dates. The gesture is wearing thin, for as I have suggested earlier, by October 1944, when the novel takes place, the threat to national safety has evaporated and they have worn out their welcome. Hence the yoking of the sexually rapacious with orchids, especially in springtime, is thus apt, for as Marilyn Lake writes, the "friendly" invasion had the effect of sexualising the local condition:

> War conditions ... undermined traditional restraints and disciplines. Faced with an uncertain future, people lived for the day, seizing pleasure when and where they found it. Thus the discursive construction of femininity as sexual, the incitement to pleasure and adventure, took place in circumstances increasingly conducive to sexual activity.[24]

While Ward refers to orchids as "the elite flowers of the world,"[25] he stresses that they are *very* sexy flowers.[26] The genus *Orchis* comes from the Greek word for testicles, or twin oval tubers. Moreover, according to some herbalists, orchids are a "testicle analogy and thus have aphrodisiac properties".[27] In Spanish, the pods and plants are called "vaina", a word derived from the Latin word "vagina", meaning sheath. As Ward observes at some length, other sexual associations – particularly concerning virility and the igniting of sexual desire, can be traced back to Greek mythology.

GIs from nearly all the forty-eight states wish to enflame sexual desire in the drop-dead gorgeous Guinea Malone, but the plethora of suitors are wasting their time (and money) buying her orchids, for Guinea, who also works in the

---

24 Marilyn Lake, "Female Desires: The Meaning of World War Two," *Gender and war: Australians at War in the Twentieth Century*, eds. Joy Damousi and Marilyn Lake (Melbourne: Oxford University Press, 1995), 67.
25 Ward, *A Contemplation Upon Flowers*, 265.
26 For another examination of the sex life of orchids, see Michael Pollan's "Love and Lies," *National Geographic Magazine*, 1 September 2009.
27 Ward, *A Contemplation Upon Flowers*, 275.

hotel's beauty salon, is too down-to-earth to be wooed by costly orchids (132). She gives several of the prized mauve and purple cattaleya to her co-workers, and somewhat carelessly discards the entire hothouse – a "riot of orchids, cream and brown and mauve and pink and purple, sprays of them, single perfect blooms, resting on a bed of roses and water-lilies, carnations and lily of the valley" (644) – an American colonel sends her. But even though Guinea's relationship with Kim has been temporarily derailed, his infidelity having propelled her into the arms of an amorous Yank, she is unable to stick to her bitter resolve to marry a wealthy American and hence avoid a life like her mother's ("seven kids and a husband on relief" [24]). But whenever she contemplates accepting any of the many proposals, including one from a handsome and gallant colonel, she is overcome by desolation, which manifests as a longing for the bush, especially the Scotts' farm. While Kim's parents are unpretentious, down-to-earth folk, Guinea is especially fond of Kim's aunt, a nurturing and caregiving woman who lives in a cosy old-fashioned brick cottage with an arch over the gate covered by a "riot" of wisteria (524), a flower suggestive of a warm welcome: significantly, it is Kim's aunt who offers shelter to Guinea's sister Monnie when she gets into trouble with the authorities. By the end of the novel, to no one's surprise, Guinea agrees to marry Kim. He has been reformed by his war experiences; he will operate a garage and he and Guinea will live happily in the bush. (Note that "the bush" refers to areas/regions close to Sydney, not the outback.) No longer the typical "taciturn" Australian bloke, Kim has become a kind of "sensitive new age guy" who helps sort out family problems. But careful readers will already have predicted that, in their reading of the flower and bush imagery, Kim and Guinea are destined to be together: they made love for the first time – in a haystack no less – at Kim's grandfather's farm. Guinea especially remembers the "crown" of green tulips Kim made her from the tulip tree after their initial encounter (38). In the language of flowers, a tulip tree in blossom is the emblem of rural happiness,[28] a joyful state of affairs the couple looks forward to at the end of the novel.

When Cusack/James argue that Guinea will find domestic bliss raising babies in the bush, they are harkening back to the old-fashioned city/country dichotomy Charles Bean reinforced throughout his writing, which held that wicked women (and men) live in the city and good women (and men) reside in the bush. All female counterparts to the noble bushmen, noble bush women, deplore the "cooped-up hothouse" atmosphere of the South Pacific Hotel, and at the first opportunity, escape to the great outdoors, where they stroll along the beach at Bondi and thrill to the raucous shrills of the galahs and currawongs as they prepare picnics for their families.

One of these noble bush women, Mary Parker, a minor character stationed in Queensland as a member of the AWAS, has a strong connection to the bush, but

---

28   Heilmeyer, *The Language of Flowers*, 82.

unfortunately has succumbed to an affair with an Australian (married) soldier and is now in Sydney (on her own, of course) to procure an abortion. An expert on bush flowers, Mary wanders through the city on the day of her appointment, stopping to admire the simple, ordinary flowers like sweet peas and crimson poppies and bush flowers such as "tall crimson waratahs" (554). She recalls her grandfather's outrage that people were selling wildflowers, fearing that the bush would soon be depleted and might never recover (554). After her abortion (which Guinea has helped find the funding for), Mary is cared for by Bessie, an older woman who works in the hotel and the only one willing to offer Mary shelter (the city-dwellers Claire and Deb shy away from taking a risk should anything go wrong). Bessie, a typical Aussie "battler" like Kim Scott's aunt, further signals her kindness and decency by decorating her small flat with surfeits of yellow Iceland poppies, delphiniums, and most significantly, "a great jar of frosted ruby gum tips" (588). Punished for her transgression and forced to leave the hotel, as luck would have it, she and her husband Blue Johnson, injured in both World War I and II, who now runs the elevators in the hotel, see their dream come true when an American hands them a winning lottery ticket that provides them with enough money to set up a pub in the country.

Like Guinea, another minor character, Helen MacFarland, is one of the "decent mates" who shows no interest in the Yank invasion. While she endures her father's criticism of her lack of interest in her appearance and a society woman's overt accusation that she lacks charm, she continues to make requisite visits to the Marie Antoinette beauty salon, knowing most consider her plain. Adept at running the bush farm on her own, she avoids society events but happily socialises at the Anzac Buffets, where she meets a repatriated wounded soldier for whom she quietly negotiates work on her father's property. (Wedding bells heard in the distance.)

Guinea is also obviously another of the "decent" women because she thinks like a noble bushman, displaying ready initiative in a hostile environment such as the Marie Antoinette. The most egalitarian of those who work in the hotel, she consistently criticises the "brass hats" for their failure to recognise the plight of the workers or the military leaders who do not recognise the suffering of the ordinary soldier. While most of her co-workers concentrate on the newspaper's society pages, Guinea draws attention to the casualty lists' reports. She is also anti-authoritarian and unpretentious, refusing to adhere to the rules that workers cannot attend fancy-dress balls or be seen walking across the hotel lobby.

While the text suggests that both Guinea and Helen will forever live happily in the bush, it also offers a glimpse into what that life might entail through Nolly, Deb's sister who inhabits the bush with Tom, a quintessential noble bushman. Like his counterparts, Tom is a resourceful, fire-fighting egalitarian, anti-authoritarian and irreverent. And like her counterparts, Nolly wears comfortable and sturdy clothes, eschews makeup, and spends most of her time outdoors. The couple carved out a life together in the bush after they observed the heavenly relationship between Nolly's sister Deb and her partner Jack. Despite their "living off the dole," they appeared to be living in a "Garden of Eden" (170), spending their days naked, soaking up the sun, and living off the food of the land. Witnessing the way Deb and Jack existed with only the barest essentials, bereft of material goods, Tom and Nolly found the courage to emulate the couple's lifestyle, marry, and move to the bush, where they quickly produced four children (with a fifth on the way). The children run naked, and like Deb and Jack, often fill up on the food such as the loquats Mother Nature has to offer. They are all resourceful, inventive children who get along well, the older often assuming responsibility for the younger. The story they love to be told and re-told – reminiscent of those by the beloved May Gibbs – is of a magic Christmas tree; voiced like a fairy tale, it is in fact a story about the happiness of their own lives in the bush (171). Tom and Nolly and their children live in harmony with others, with Nolly belonging to a co-op and Tom often seen rushing off to help fight a neighbour's bushfire. Cusack/James' large section on the lives of Nolly and Tom seems to suggest that the only things that matter are marriage to a man you love, a decent home and happy life for children (if it is in the bush) and the desire never to be dependent or beholden to anyone. In sum, by privileging rural life, Cusack/James seem to be working within an expanded view of the pastoral that, as William Empson suggests, includes any work which "opposed simple to complicated life, to the advantage of the former: the simple life may be that of the shepherd, the child, or the working man. The pastoral serves as an oblique way to criticise the values and hierarchical class structure of the society of its time."[29]

But when Jack enlists without consulting Deb, thereby forcing her to leave their daughter Luen with Nolly and move to the city, she gets a job at the Marie Antoinette. Initially she reflects on her blissful life with Jack during which she had turned a tiny cottage at a vineyard into a cosy home. Deb also recalls with fondness the time she and Jack spent on the dole, seeing "with her mind's eye the shack they had built out of stringy bark on the edge of the beach" (87) and recalling how they lived on the fresh oysters Jack caught on the beach. When the first spring came, they had together "watched the bursting buds on the long rows of vines, [when] the early blossoms came on the orange trees and their perfume lay sweet and heavy on the night air" (64). Luen was born at Christmas time, "when the grapes were swelling and the vines were full of the hum of bees" (64).

Although Deb becomes quickly estranged from bush life and can scarcely believe she once considered working at the South Pacific a hardship, her perspectives on bush versus city life continue to seesaw back and forth: each time she takes the train to visit Luen, she revels in the "red flowering gum trees," the "delicate mauve-blue jacarandas in full bloom [that] floated like misty clouds above close-clipped lawns," the "purple bougainvillea [that] spilled over fences," and "the Illawarra flame trees [that] flaunted their orange feathers in the sunshine" (144–45). In the language of flowers, all in some way signify marriage and fertility. Deb's sister

---

29 William Empson, from *Some Versions of the Pastoral*, cited in *A Glossary of Literary Terms*, eds. M.H. Abrams and Geoffrey Galt Harpman (Boston, MA: Wadsworth Cengage Learning, 2012).

Doctor Dallas (often the writers' mouthpiece) is a furtive supporter of bush life (even though she lives in the city and remains unmarried herself) and describes the wedding between Jack and Deb as a "partnership" that "sent down deep roots"; their breakup will be catastrophic, she predicts, "like gardens in an earthquake" (338). But much as Deb has loved bush life, when the wealthy pastoralist Angus McFarland falls in love with her, she quickly succumbs to the power of money and the luxuries it brings; never again will she be content to live with Jack in a shack by the sea.

When Deb receives news that Jack will soon be home on leave, she again conjures up earlier, happy scenes about the splendid beauty of the vineyards. But just when she begins to recall fondly the "large shabby bedroom opening onto the garden, the old iron bedstead with chipped paint and other rustling noises in the vines" (696), she is brought back to reality by the elegance of the hotel, where she rents a small room, replete with "air redolent of the Marie Antoinette perfumes" (696), which now compete in her mind with the scent of native plants. Yet,

> the very thought of Jack shook her, stirred old memories, woke old desires. Even now, by some trick of the brain, it was not the cloying sweetness of the Marie Antoinette air through which she moved, but the smell of wet earth, the tang of ripening grapes. And she knew with absolute certainty that once let her sit again at evening in the old-fashioned kitchen with the light shining down on Jack's head and Luen cuddled against him, solitude and love binding them inseparably within the circle of the lamp, she was lost. (697)

Life in Sydney is not without hardship, however: just as the young factory workers are overworked and underpaid, so, too, are the hairdressers and masseuses at the salon like Deb who must work for meagre wages at a frantic pace to satisfy the excessive demands of their self-indulgent clientele. Few of these hotel employees, who rarely leave the hotel, have any connection to the natural world, and as a result appear pale and washed-out; they all dye their hair, a sure sign of corruption in this novel. Claire Jeffries, another major character and astute urban businesswoman, has developed her own successful line of cosmetics, but without financial backing, is unable to put her products on the market.[30] Like Thelma, Claire is estranged from nature, indicated by her long hours at the hotel and residence in a nearby penthouse. Claire takes no interest in flowers and usually freshens up old outfits with artificial blossoms or relies on Guinea's generosity to share her orchids. Thelma Molesworth, a minor character, nonetheless resembles Claire, because both are with men who refuse to make a commitment. Unlike the Aussie battler Bessie, Thelma "lives in sin" with Sharlton, the hotel owner and, as her name suggests, also

---

30   Cusack/James may be drawing upon the life of the Polish-born Helena Rubinstein, who formed one of Australia's first cosmetic companies. See her biography *My Life for Beauty* (New York: Simon & Schuster 1966).

like a "mole", since she rarely sees the sun. She decorates her room with English blue irises and allows herself to be strung along on a decades-long relationship with Sharlton, whom readers will already have recognised as a complete rotter, allergic as he is to the much-revered wattle! As Robin suggests, "wearing wattle," which eventually became the "national floral emblem … provided scope for pride in Australia and its natural environments".[31] Like Bessie and Blue, Thelma and Sharlton long to open a country hotel, but they are self-centred cultural cringers who want to set up a California-style property for financial investment, and thus are unworthy of the bush.

By the same token, Cusack/James suggest that Deb will never be happy with Angus, a despoiler of nature who has turned the native scrub of his bush property at Palm Spring into a "terraced garden" (285). Angus will not permit Deb to wear flowers because he "dislike[s] the fashion" (84) and, like the other snobs in the novel, buys imported flowers to designate his social status. But whenever Angus sends English flowers such as lily-of-the-valley or lilacs to Deb's room, when they turn brown and wilt, she becomes sickened by the "stale, sweetish" smell that "make[s] [her] think of death" and prevents her from sleeping (237). A bush woman at heart, she prefers the scent of the wood violet bath salts (violets being traditionally symbols of modesty and humility) that Claire has given her to soak in (238).

Flowers aside, given the popularity of the prize-winning novel – even the abridged version never went out of print – it was puzzling that it had taken so long for the burgeoning silver-screen industry to adapt it for film. Ina Bertrand advances several reasons, among them that it was "primarily about the exploitation of women in the work force"[32] and contained references to contentious issues such as "abortion and prostitution".[33] But once it appeared, the television mini-series based on the novel received exceptionally fine reviews, with critics praising the period costumes, the music, and above all the cast, all of whom were superb.

Arguably, it was the outmoded inscription of bush values (characterised by the recurring images of bush/flower imagery, all missing in the series, apart from the orchid, which only Americans purchase), that filmmakers had to overcome in order to make their television series palatable to contemporary audiences, and they succeeded admirably. They seem to have been aware that the well-known poet

---

31 Robin, "Nationalizing Nature", 7. Robin notes that there are several other readings of the wattle. 1 September, declared Wattle Day throughout the country in 1992, "evoked childhood memories" for country mothers who remembered that many children died at wattle time from diphtheria, whooping cough, and other contagious illnesses (Robin, "Nationalizing Nature", 17). There is also another connection related to death: "in 1993, a significant tree was planted in Wattle Park: The Lone Pine, grown from the seed of the Gallipoli Lone Pine, in remembrance of fallen colleagues" (Robin, "Nationalizing Nature", 18). Wattle came to signify, like Flanders poppies, "Anzacs at Gallipoli and Australian blood on the battlefields of the Somme" (Robin, "Nationalizing Nature", 18).

32 Ina Bertrand, "'Come in Spinner': Two Views of the Forties", *Journal of Australian Studies* 18, no.41 (1994), 12.

33 Bertrand, "Come in Spinner", 12.

Henry Lawson had insisted during the 1890s that "the bush was no place for a woman"[34] and opted to produce a film that suggested that bush life for women was no longer tenable, which they might then have named *Where Have All the Flowers Gone?* Wisely, the script writers chose not to make a lot of changes in plot or location, as the mini-series continues to focus on the employees and guests at the South Pacific Hotel during one week in 1944, but with a whittled-down cast, about half of the minor characters either amalgamated with another or were eliminated entirely. The emphasis is now solely on Claire, Guinea, and Deb. The much sought-after Guinea remains just that, until Kim's persistence convinces her to marry him. Significantly, the story of how Guinea's sixteen-year-old sister Monnie was lured against her will into prostitution (and Kim's role in her rescue from juvenile detention), is aptly expanded, as is his mother's role as another Aussie battler. She agrees to take care of Monnie, who refuses to live with her punitive and judgemental mother ever again. (I have often remarked, and continue to do so here, that Australian novels are inexplicably filled with bad mothers, but quite frequently here, cruel fathers.)

Although I agree with Bertrand that "much of the ideological differences between the novel and the television mini-series are concerned with gender"[35] and that the novel became film-able in the 1980s because "the passing of forty years … had brought considerable mellowing of social attitudes and literary values",[36] I part company with some of her analysis. One of the main changes has to do with the "girl in the bush" figure who is largely "missing" in the mini-series. Guinea Malone is no longer heading to the bush with the mechanic Kim Scott, for there is no suggestion in the series that he wants to ply his trade in the countryside. The series is also critical of Helen McFarland as a "girl of the bush," for in their version, she has become a grasping businesswoman whose main aim is to protect her "rightful inheritance," which she believes will be threatened by her father's marriage to a woman half his age. Moreover, Nolly is no longer the ideal rural dweller, no longer a calm and relaxed mother with plenty of time to tell stories to her precious little "gumnuts" in the television series. In the television series, she looks haggard and worn out and relegates the caregiving to Deb's daughter Luen, which is not mentioned in the novel. She is also pregnant with her fifth child, so bush life will become harder, not easier. As well, Tom and Nolly's house (more like a shack) appears shabby and run-down, and Tom sounds priggish, frequently making unnecessary digs at Deb about the snobs in the city, inferring that the poor are somehow more noble than the rich.

The Claire in the novel continues to manage the salon and to cling desperately to the notion that Nigel, a married Australian officer (formerly a male model) whom she loves, intends to pay his wife to divorce him. He insists they will raise

---

34   Henry Lawson, "No Place for a Woman", *On the Track* (Sydney: Angus & Robertson, 1900), 85.
35   Bertrand, "Come in Spinner", 21.
36   Bertrand, "Come in Spinner", 12.

that money by gambling. As the pair slowly amasses the magic number, Claire struggles with whether to tell him she is pregnant, hesitating because she wants to be certain that his wife has agreed to the divorce. But she soon learns that Nigel, an addicted gambler, has lost the couple's money and never intended to leave his wife, to whom he is happily married, and he also has a son whom he has failed to mention. Devastated when she realises how she has been duped, Claire tries to entice a frequent admirer (not in the novel) to marry her, help raise the child, and in return, she, as a shrewd businesswoman, will help run his business. When he refuses, she arranges for an abortion, but tragically dies almost immediately of haemorrhage. Her death is rendered even more poignant when her admirer tries to make amends by offering to marry her, but it comes too late. The blame in part for her death falls on the shoulders of the conservative Dr Dallas McIntyre, who has refused to give Deb the name of a doctor who could help. The film version implies that Claire had no choice but to find someone "cheap" (read illegal), yet even scrounging the money from her poorly paid co-workers proves difficult.

That Deb will marry Angus McFarland and move to the city is clear in the mini-series, whereas the novel is somewhat open-ended. I agree with Bertrand that in the novel, Deb seems unusually naïve, innocently leading Angus on, whereas in the mini-series, she is clearly holding Angus at arm's length. Throughout the film, she appears to be genuinely in love with Jack and eagerly anticipating the time he can spend with his family on leave. But it is merely absence that has made her heart grow fonder, for as Bertrand points out, when we meet Jack in the mini-series, as we do not in the novel, he is "an emotional bully" who orders his wife (and daughter) to leave the city and move to the vineyard he plans to make profitable. In the mini-series, when Jack and his mates travel south together to Sydney, they pass by the vineyard, which is so run-down that even his "mates" regard the scheme as unrealistic. The filmmakers further underscore the foolhardy nature of Jack's plan when even the bush-lover Nolly raises her eyebrows as Jack sketches it on paper for Luen, the implication being that only a naïve child like Luen could embrace her father's design. Moreover, Jack also proves to be foul-mouthed and hot-headed, becoming physically violent when Deb refuses to leave her job in the hotel. In the mini-series, then, Deb marries Angus because she is fleeing a brutish husband, not because her values have become corrupted by the urban dweller McFarland (who is now less offensive as a widower). As Bertrand observes, the "social stigma that attaches to the 1990s wife-beater then provides an excuse for Deb legitimately (if not necessary wisely) to leave him".[37]

But it's also important to stress, as the mini-series does, that Deb somewhat reluctantly agrees to marry an older man because in the 1940s, marriage was a woman's only "career," and thus Deb's only ticket to a prosperous and stable life for her and Luen. The mini-series also addresses the pressures women like Deb faced in

---

37   Bertrand, "Come in Spinner", 20.

the 1940s, particularly in their traditional roles as wives and mothers. Throughout the film, Deb is often called upon to justify her association with Angus. When she tries to explain to her sister that Jack was behaving irresponsibly when he enlisted without consulting her – that he was never a "partner" in any endeavour – she bumps straight into one of Nolly's follies: she continues to believe in the archaic notion that no matter what, women marry their husbands "for better or worse," and that applies to her sister. Similarly, Dr McIntyre reinforces that it is a woman's duty to stand by her man, no matter how flawed he might be. And Helen, now Angus' daughter in the film, feels that divorcees are so beyond the pale that she will have nothing to do with Deb.

The TV drama also perpetuates women's need for help and guidance. Mary Parker does not appear in the mini-series, but Claire Jeffries now suffers a dilemma like Mary's. In her late-thirties and pregnant with a married man's child, Claire longs to raise it herself, but she is fully aware that in a 1940s climate, when single mothers were deemed unfit to parent, she cannot, either financially or morally. Before she dies, however, Claire delivers a hard-hitting speech to Deb and Guinea, insisting that they face "a cold, hard world" in which it is vital for "every woman to take what she can get," and viewers must agree. Claire is an attractive, hard-working woman who realises that without "advantages" – no formal training, no advanced education – neither she nor any of the women she works with can ever achieve fulfilling lives that allow them not only to survive (even without a man), but profit from their endeavours. On a more positive note, the mini-series also hints that women are beginning to regard themselves as allies, not enemies: Deb and Claire are no longer heard gossiping or backstabbing others but have formed a firm friendship that will aid them in the future. The few characters who have the most to gain are Deb and Luen, a point driven home in the last scene. McFarland, having finally won Deb to his side – she now views bush life as "squalid and insincere" – goes shopping for a gift for Luen. He purchases an enormous, British-designed doll's house that takes up the entire back seat of his huge car. While Luen appears to resent the gift – it bears no resemblance to the shack she lives in or any way of life she can identify with – she does not have any idea how fortunate she is. She will attend the best schools, live in the lap of luxury with servants at her beck and call and no doubt marry a wealthy man like her stepfather.

But as Bertrand observes, "the novel depicts explicitly not only the financial and moral dilemmas of working people during wartime, but also the corruption rife in Sydney at the time, pointing out how the wealthy manage to maintain their lifestyle with few sacrifices while the majority of the community carry sometimes intolerable burdens".[38] I would argue that the mini-series, with its depictions of how comfortably the rich live versus how shabbily the poor live, makes the same point, only better. As an outsider who has frequently visited Australia, I have often been

---

38 Bertrand, "Come in Spinner", 15.

puzzled by how frequently people refer to themselves and their social practices as egalitarian, even when the class structures are patently as rigidly stratified as those in England. While the television series managed to depict a praiseworthy nation worthy of the world's acknowledgement and respect, they also made audiences aware of its flaws.

9

Country Matters in the *Little (Southern Steel) Company*

In "On Appropriation: Two Novels of Dark and Eldershaw," Ian Saunders identifies a number of similarities between Eleanor Dark's *The Little Company* (1945) and M. Barnard Eldershaw's *Tomorrow and Tomorrow and Tomorrow* (1947) and makes the case that Dark borrowed much of the structure and plot of her novel from an outline Marjorie Barnard provided.[1] My aim here is neither to defend nor support Saunders's claim (although I do think he weakens his case by ignoring information included in Barbara Brooks' biography, which indicates conclusively that much of the material in *The Little Company* stems from Dark's family background), but to suggest that Dymphna Cusack, too, might have gathered some of her ideas from Dark in writing *Southern Steel* (1953). Even though Cusack claimed (as did Miles Franklin and other writers on the "Left") that she didn't "like" *The Little Company*[2] and told Bruce Molloy that "the novel 'never hit her'",[3] it certainly struck her in some ways, for the similarities between the novels seem too numerous to be coincidental. Admittedly, given the texts' shared historical time frames, some comparisons might be obvious. Dark's novel takes place between 1941 and 1942, Cusack's solely in 1942, with the bombing of Darwin figuring prominently in each. Both texts also document, to a greater or lesser extent, the "Yank invasion" of Australia and the advent of wartime measures such as blackouts, brown-outs, food shortages and rationing. The texts also depict women knitting khaki socks, serving enlisted men at canteens, and making their entry into war work – the munitions industry in *Southern Steel* and the Women's Army Auxiliary Corps (WAAC) in *The Little Company*. Characters in both texts also express surprise that Australia – especially Newcastle, with its massive steelworks on the coast producing munitions – should suddenly have become so vulnerable, so threatened by an

---

1   Ian Saunders, "On Appropriation: Two Novels of Dark and Eldershaw." *Australian Literary Studies* 20, no.4 (October 2002), 287.
2   Barbara Brooks with Judith Clark, *Eleanor Dark: A Writer's Life* (Sydney: Macmillan, 1998), 279.
3   Bruce Molloy, "Interview with Dymphna Cusack" *Imago* 1, no.2 (September 1989), 51.

enemy that had, until 1942, seemed so remote. Nevertheless, both novels attest to the kind of complacency that prevailed among Australians, including members of the military:[4] Cusack, for example, refers to navy men as "little pip-squeaks running around in white socks and short pants, worrying about their laundry and their liquor and whose turn it is to make love to who next",[5] and arguably, Dark's entire novel addresses the subject (although not in military terms). Both writers are also concerned about the lack of information given to citizens about the war. Cusack writes in her posthumously published autobiography, *A Window in the Dark* (1991), that young people were taught "nothing of the circumstances" that had led to World War I,[6] and that the nation had been committed to a war that most people, "except for a few well-informed specialists" (166), knew nothing about. Dark, too, lamented in an unpublished essay, "The Peril and the Solitude," that while "the novels and poetry between the wars were full of warnings about another war ... nobody took any notice, [sic] they listened to politicians instead. The world was in a mess because the politicians had no idea what they were doing".[7]

The central protagonists in each text, both men, have a lot in common: each was raised by a surrogate mother and single-parent father (dead mothers also abound in Australian women's fictions of the First and Second World Wars); as adults, each man is socially conservative and financially secure. Dark's middle-aged Gilbert Massey runs a religious bookstore in Sydney and writes on the side, often from his Katoomba cottage in the Blue Mountains: his seven novels have earned him a modest literary reputation. Cusack's thirty-something Bar Sweetapple is a top-notch metallurgist with Southern Steel; at the beginning of the novel, he and his wife Roz have just returned from a year-long stint in England and America, where Bar has been studying steel production with other experts in his field. Both men are married to status-conscious wives who have uneasy relationships with their sons (although the fathers do not). Both protagonists have brothers who are card-carrying members of the Communist Party. Both embark upon affairs with young, waif-like women on the night Japanese submarines invade Sydney Harbour in *The Little Company* and the Japanese shell Newcastle in *Southern Steel*.[8]

---

4   For an examination of the nonchalant approach Australians took to World War II, particularly in the Northern Territory, see historian Alan Powell's *The Shadow's Edge: Australia's Northern War* (Melbourne: Melbourne University Press, 1988) and Timothy Hall's *Darwin 1942: Australia's Darkest Hour* (Port Melbourne: Mandarin, 1989). Maria Gardner's historical novel *Blood-Stained Wattle* (Pialba, Qld, 1992) also documents how ill-prepared those in the Northern Territory were to defend Darwin from enemy attack. Most of these texts make the point that the "military brass" seemed to have forgotten the tradition of fighting prowess and ready initiative in a hostile environment that had been established by the Anzacs of their fathers' generation.

5   Cusack, Dymphna, *Southern Steel* (London: Constable, 1953), 166. All subsequent references are to this edition and appear in parentheses in the text.

6   Cusack, Dymphna, *A Window in the Dark* (Canberra: National Library of Australia, 1991), 165. All subsequent references are to this edition and appear in parentheses in the text.

7   Cited in Brooks, *Eleanor Dark*, 234.

Although both men soon discover that their lovers are shallow, insincere, lacking in compassion, and uninterested in current events, neither makes any effort to end the relationship because these women fulfil both their emotional and physical needs. Both men are eventually spurned by their lovers, however.

Both texts, which adhere loosely to the conventions of the social-realist novel, are also concerned with issues of class; each presents members of the working class as virtuous, morally upstanding, and inclined to give more to their country than they get in return, whereas the rich or upwardly mobile either lack integrity or are downright villainous. Dark's Gilbert, for example, discovers that his father, Walter Massey, has been a slum landlord when he inherits a number of run-down properties. Appalled to learn that these rents have paid for his affluent upbringing and expensive (although useless) education, Gilbert vows to renovate the hovels and lower the rents. Cusack's Bar, by comparison, remains haunted by his failure to have come to the aid of his impoverished sister and her family when they were evicted by a cruel landlord during the 1930s. Bar's refusal to take a stand has caused a permanent rift between him and his two brothers, but wartime events bring him to realise he was in the wrong. Both men suffer the loss of a family member caused in part by his neglect, but both are exonerated from guilt because their selfish, social-climbing wives are largely responsible for the tragedies that ensue. Although neither text can be considered feminist in its approach (and thus I would argue both writers were cowards in their war efforts)[9], Dark's is critical of a society that fails to educate women to participate fully in a democracy.[10] While each text offers brief glimpses into the lives of young, enlightened women who represent the next generation, both are minor characters: Dark's twenty-something Prudence remains silent about her father's extramarital affair, and both she and Cusack's youthful Annie are eager to engage in premarital sexual relationships; Annie also helps a friend obtain an abortion. Prudence, who privileges ideas over physical appearance and material possessions, runs her own bookstore, and the down-to-earth Annie becomes a card-carrying a member of the union at the munitions factory where she works (although the text suggests she is radical only "for the duration," since what she most aspires to is marriage and motherhood).

In both texts, the wartime climate brings each protagonist to recognise that he inhabits a world rife with social and economic injustice and that he has become oblivious to and hence alienated from his surroundings. Both texts emphasise the extent to which the central characters' lives are impoverished by their lack of knowledge about Australian history and literature. Accordingly, the wartime climate propels each male protagonist into a political and social education, or re-education, although each undertakes his journey towards enlightenment alone:

---

8   Cusack also wrote *Shoulder the Sky,* a drama about wartime Newcastle, which appears in *Three Australian Three-Act Plays* (Sydney: Australasian Press, 1950).
9   See Chapter 7.
10   Brooks, *Eleanor Dark,* 285.

Gilbert's wife Phyllis is intellectually deficient and, like Bar's wife Roz, reluctant to relinquish her place in society. At the end of each novel, the marriages appear to have crumbled. Ultimately, both protagonists come to the realisation that they have been burdened by what Miles Franklin had earlier referred to as "the non-existence of the Australian mind through colonial servility and lack of exercise".[11] Claiming that she was too "weary" to tackle the subject herself, Franklin urged Dark, who had already raised the issue in *The Timeless Land,* to undertake it.

Nowhere is the notion of "colonial servility" more evident than in Cusack's autobiography, which offers an account of the writer's lengthy career as a highschool teacher from the 1920s to 1944, when she was invalided out. Whether she was shaping young minds in Broken Hill or Sydney or Newcastle she was, according to Debra Adelaide's Introduction, "invariably ... disappointed ... that the schools in which she taught were oblivious to their surroundings and their history. Again and again she found the system she was part of, the curricula she was obliged to perpetuate, totally irrelevant to the lives and futures of her pupils".[12] Cusack also deemed the high school curriculum "insane" because she had no time to teach students "the proper use of their own language, the most important thing in any culture. We wasted their time on ancient languages which, in the main, had no use educationally and culturally" (91). Cusack was also frustrated because what she was being asked to teach varied little from what she had herself been taught: her own "high school courses had contained little about Australian history, and what there was, was written from the colonial point of view" (41). Furthermore, according to Cusack's husband and biographer Norman Freehill, Cusack found Sydney University a "colonial-minded place: no hint of anything Australian crossed the threshold. Most of the professors were English or, what was worse, Australians who were completely Europhile and completely bogged down in the past": "'[s]o far as our own country was concerned,' she remarked, 'we might have been living on the moon'".[13] In her autobiography, Cusack writes (somewhat awkwardly) that "[t]hough in the twenties Australia had ceased to be a colony for over a score of years, she was to remain one mentally for another fifty years in many respects: a sycophantic worship of everything English and a slavish denigration of anything home-grown" (37). Moreover, in "How I Write," Cusack observed that there were no lectures on Australian literature at any university until 1939,[14] and while at teacher's college, she could find no library that offered access to any Australian books (43).

Much of Cusack's despair at such literary and historical neglect stemmed from the recognition that her young country had good reason to be proud of its accomplishments. In spite of its "defects and deficiencies", from the 1850s onward,

---

11   Cited in Brooks, *Eleanor Dark*, 238.
12   Debra Adelaide, "Introduction", *A Window in the Dark*, 1.
13   Norman Freehill with Dymphna Cusack, *Dymphna Cusack* (Sydney: Nelson, 1975), 24.
14   Dymphna Cusack, "How I Write" *Westerly* 3 (1960), 32.

Australia had become "the most democratic country in the world". She praised the "eight-hour day" introduced in that decade, and observed that "[a]ll the liberal ideals of Europe were first to become a reality here".[15] In her autobiography, she further underscored that Australia was "one of the first to introduce universal suffrage for men and to give the vote to women as early as 1902" (41). Hence she was dismayed by the "colonial" type of education that taught students there was "nothing historically worthwhile in [their] own country," and no literature worth reading, either, (42) and angered that there was "no emotional involvement" with [the Australian past], no deep sense of "identification" with the land (56).

Cusack was not the only writer to complain of the "cultural cringe," which persisted well into the 1940s, as Deirdre Moore's 2005 article on the subject makes clear. Moore writes that, having won a lucrative scholarship in 1942, she planned to use it to write a "critique of the Australian novel" for her honours (English IV) thesis. Although she assiduously worked her way through fiction by Mrs Campbell Praed, Miss Ada Cambridge, Rolf Boldrewood, Marcus Clarke, Henry Lawson, Joseph Furphy, Miles Franklin, Henry Handel Richardson, Katherine Susannah Prichard, M. Barnard Eldershaw and Christina Stead, a respected scholar in the English Department at Sydney University informed her in no uncertain terms that not only was there was "so little" fiction available, working on such material would be "a waste of good critical ability".[16] He advised her to seek a more "acceptable thesis topic" in American literature, a bias Moore attributes primarily to the presence of the US troops who had "Americanised" Australia almost overnight.[17] The first Australian literature course was finally offered in 1955,[18] but the "cringe" did not end that year, for Elizabeth Webby, who held the first chair in Australian literature for sixteen years (until her retirement in 2007), found that as an honours student at Sydney University in the 1960s, she had no opportunity to study Australian literature, although she did "manage to get half a year of Australian history by 'hanging in' until third year".[19]

Cusack found this continued neglect of Australian literature and history deeply troubling for, as she told Bruce Molloy, "[a]ll great literature has come out of its own soil – it's breathed the air".[20] While she paid tribute to writers like Lawson,

---

15   Dymphna Cusack, "The 'Cultural Cringe' in Australian Universities' Study of Australian Literature" *Social Alternatives* 1 no.5 (1979), 80.

16   Deirdre Moore, "Cultural Cringe in Academe: Studying Literature in the 1940s" *Australian Literary Studies* 22 no.1 (May 2005), 92.

17   Moore, "Cultural Cringe in Academe", 90.

18   Cusack, "Cringe", 79.

19   Elizabeth Webby, "Australian Literature and the English Curriculum." Keynote lecture to the Australian Government Summer School for Teachers of English. Deakin University, Geelong, 8 January 2008. The "cringe" persisted much longer, though, as I found when I came to Sydney in 1990 to do graduate research on Australian women's war fictions. When I asked where I might find works by Australian women writers in a well-known local bookstore, I was directed to the cookbook section (!), and later informed by a University of Sydney librarian that if I wanted "that kind of material," I would have to look for it in the public libraries!"

Furphy, Franklin, Prichard, Esson and Palmer, who had produced a strong sense of "national feeling" by depicting life in the Australian bush, and also applauded "numerous poets who sang of Australia at the beginning of the century," she noted that their sentiments had "faded" during World War I, which "had reawakened a spiritual colonialism".[21] By the mid-twenties, however, the country had "bogged down into a morass of social and sectarian bigotry and educational conservatism" (41). At the same time as Cusack expressed her admiration for the "country type of novel" and wished to see it reinvigorated, she also felt that urban life had been unduly overlooked and declared that she wanted to write about the inhabitants of Newcastle[22] "as fully and authentically as our writers of the Nineties had described the life of our 'bush' ... and our bushmen."[23] In writing about Newcastle, Cusack was clearly writing against the grain, for according to Julian Croft, "the more common constructions are of the 'wide brown land,' pastoralism, Aboriginal Australia, and the anomie of the suburbs of the twentieth century. Industrial landscapes, and the communities that arose around those heavy industries, are not what most people think of when they imagine Australia."[24] But the citizens of Newcastle were reputedly delighted with *Southern Steel* (which was, according to Freehill, "the only Australian novel about an Australian industrial city during the Second World War")[25], for as Debra Adelaide asserts, they had "never before found such a favourable portrayal of their city in literature".[26]

Because Cusack took such a "voracious interest in the history of her surroundings"[27] and was so "profoundly engaged in the world around her",[28] she drew much of the raw material for her novel from her teaching assignment – one of her most satisfying, she claimed – in Newcastle. (Cusack joked that she had become such a troublemaker in the education system that "[w]hen news of Pearl Harbor broke, [the administrators] thought of the one place [she] was likely to be bombed and thus relieve them of the embarrassment of [her] existence, and sent [her] to Newcastle") (145). Although initially dismayed that the Broken Hill Propriety (BHP) was helping to fund Newcastle Boy's Technical High, she was soon relieved to discover that the company was not dictating the curriculum, but rather enabling the students "to find jobs rather than torture them into travesties of classical scholars".[29] Once freed from academic pressure to study irrelevant subjects,

---

20   Molloy, "Interview with Dymphna Cusack", 49.
21   Cusack, "How I Write", 32.
22   Dymphna Cusack, "A Sense of Worth: Dymphna Cusack on Her Life and Work" *Coming Out! Women's Voices, Women's Lives: A Selection from ABC Radio's Coming Out Show* (Melbourne: Nelson in association with the Australian Broadcasting Corporation, 1985), 60.
23   Cusack, "How I Write", 32.
24   Julian Croft, "A Sense of Industrial Place – the Literature of Newcastle, New South Wales, 1797–1997" *Antipodes* 13 (June 1991), 15.
25   Freehill, *Dymphna Cusack*, 73.
26   Adelaide, "Introduction", 19.
27   Adelaide, "Introduction", 18.
28   Adelaide, "Introduction", 22.

these young men could "see some immediate connection between school and work and their futures".[30]

Cusack also turned the people she met in Newcastle into characters who were "not even composites," but "taken directly from life".[31] Her landlords, a close-knit, solid working-class family, obviously became the Boultons, and a couple of local historians Cusack befriended, whose "ready-made phrases" – that "Australian lingo" she was so anxious students claim as their own – make their way into *Southern Steel*. The speakers of this (admittedly very clumsy) "lingo," Hoppy Sweetapple, Bar's one-legged sixty-five-year-old father, and Jummer, his eighty-one-year-old friend, engage in a series of conversations that express disappointment that Australians should be so ignorant of the richly varied, "tremendous" stories of the city and the country, both past and present. Jummer claims, for example, that Hoppy sees the story purely as "history – from convict to freeman; from wind-jammer to oil-burner" (22), whereas Jummer's stepson Emmett finds "poetry in machines and smokestacks" (22). To Hoppy's son Keir, by contrast, the story of Newcastle is about "steel and the power that goes with it" (22), whereas to another of Hoppy's sons, Rud, a Communist union organiser who campaigns for the nationalisation of Southern Steel, the story is an "endless process of change and the unendin' fight, for it's not only a special kind of steel they're making here in the south, but a special kind of people" (22–3). While many of these old-timers' stories focus on the history of the shipbuilding industry, Jummer also bitterly recalls that his father – clearly one of those "special kind[s] of people" – had been "[t]ransported for a crime that would have got him elected to Parliament today" (21), and Hoppy, whose tales are sprinkled with references to other identity-forming historical events such as Gallipoli and the Eureka Stockade, insists that these stories, including those of the pioneers' heroic struggles against a harsh physical environment, would be of "interest to anyone, anywhere" (21). Furthermore, he insists that there is so much history in Newcastle that "someone ought to write a book" (20) about it (and his point seems well taken, for Croft observes that Newcastle is "one of the oldest purely industrial sites in the world"[32]). Regrettably, Hoppy cannot produce the book because he lacks formal education, and Jummer, who possesses the necessary background (his house is "packed floor to ceiling with books and papers and note-books" [21] he intends to leave to the Mitchell Library in Sydney [183]), is now too old. But even if Hoppy cannot pen a book, he certainly possesses fine oratorical skills, for his accounts of his (mis)adventures on sailing ships hold both his grandson Darrell (Bar and Roz's son) and the headmaster at the private school in Sydney Darrell attends while his parents are overseas, completely spellbound. Freely admitting that he knows nothing about

---

29   Adelaide, "Introduction", 13.
30   Adelaide, "Introduction", 20.
31   Freehill, *Dymphna Cusack*, 49.
32   Croft, "A Sense of Industrial Place", 15.

Newcastle, the Headmaster deems Hoppy's account of the development of a big industrial city "fascinating" and the amateur historian himself "remarkably interesting" (13). In suggesting that the headmaster of one of Australia's most prestigious schools should be so unaware of Australia's history, Cusack appears to be harkening back to her own education at Sydney University, where only one professor offered any lectures on the settlement of Australia. According to Freehill, "[t]he result was that the graduates in Arts [even those who had travelled abroad] ... were rootless and discontented, knowing little of their country's history and nothing of its literature".[33] Freehill's remarks may also explain why the old-timer Jummer states so emphatically that if Australians are to "progress," it is vital to "know now how we came and where we're goin" (23), and why he is so angry that no one "cares for history and culture in this profit-gluttonous country" (21). Cusack infers, thus, that amateur historians like Hoppy and Jummer, who take so much pleasure and pride in the history of their country, are its real wartime "saviours."

One of the characters who cares little for either the history or culture of Newcastle is Bar's wife, Roz, a quintessential Cusack character who poses more of a threat to the country than the marauding Japanese. According to Adelaide, Cusack, who was "[d]emocratic to the marrow," detested snobs,[34] especially those who derived their cultural and artistic standards from New York or London. True to form, Roz, ironically a former schoolteacher, toadies up to the American officers stationed in Newcastle, displays a preference for American fashion and hairstyles, installs her family in a "Hollywoodish"-style bungalow, and resents that her servants are not as efficient as the "beautifully trained" coloured servants in America (142)! At the same time, she frowns upon the solidarity and commitment of the industrial personnel who struggle to obtain better working conditions. While Roz does not entirely object to Hoppy's re-telling of Australian history to her son Darrell, she does find his relationships with members of the lower classes (which include Bar's brothers, Landy, a fireman on a coastal ship, and the Communist agitator Rud), objectionable. Much of the plot turns on the schemes Roz (who rejects her birth name in favour of one she deems more sophisticated) sets in place in order to extricate her son and husband from Hoppy and his working-class mates. Roz attempts, for example, to eradicate her husband's past by insisting that he change his name from Keir to Bar and prodding him to leave Newcastle, a city she detests because it reminds her of her own humble origins. Although Bar goes along with most of Roz's proposals, he resists her attempts to force him to move to away from Newcastle, because his affection for the "untidy, smoky city" (4) is deep-rooted, as the first paragraph of the novel makes evident.

Having been absent from the city for one year, Bar feels a "quickening of his pulse" as the plane that brings him to Newcastle flies over the expansive landscape and he sees "the cobalt of the Pacific, with its cotton-white fringe of surf; the

---

33 Freehill, *Dymphna Cusack*, 28.
34 Adelaide, "Introduction", 11.

ribbons of old-ivory sand; the chain of salt-water lakes like crinkled silver-paper in a matrix of olive green – Terrigal, Tuggerah, Munmora; then the sparkling expanse of Lake Macquarie, with the Catalinas droning in declining circles to the base at Rathmines" (1). Bar also recalls his happy childhood, particularly the excursions to the "sun-drenched strip of Beach Cave," where he and his brothers searched "for the primitive chart instruments on the ancient middens where once the aboriginal tribes [sic] came to feast" (1). As Croft observes, Cusack not only wrote about the "heroic and beautiful power" of the city's industry, but she also offered a "bravura description" of its "natural beauty" (16). Although Bar's first reminder of the city's "natural beauty" and memories of his idyllic formative years help him recognise the extent to which Roz has sealed off his past, he is not able to sustain his resentment because Roz is able to seize the anxiety and turbulence of the wartime climate – Singapore falls on 15 February and the Japanese bomb Darwin 19 February – as an excuse to get Darrell away from his grandfather and his working-class mates. She sends her son (reluctantly on his part) to an exclusive private school in the Tablelands, where he will not likely learn much Australian history, culture, or literature, but he will make all the right connections. Fittingly, Roz's plan backfires, for while she is busy settling Darrell into the private school, Bar falls in love with Myee, (distressingly referred to as a "nymphomaniac"). When Myee returns to her husband who has been fighting in Malaya, Bar is distraught, but much of his distress stems from the realisation that Roz has effectively closed him off from his Australian roots and the values of his unpretentious working-class family and their friends. It seems likely he will divorce Roz and reunite with them.

Although Dark was not, like Cusack, an educator, she was concerned with the wellbeing of children in Katoomba during the war. She volunteered (part-time) to look after those whose mothers were in war industries, and her husband, Dr Eric Dark, offered the children free medical attention. Dark organised fundraising activities for the library and the local school, cared for evacuated children part-time, and used some of the royalties from her novels to help set up a free library for children. The Darks arranged for the state Minister for Education, Clive Evatt, to open the library, and agreed wholeheartedly with the politician's remarks that education during the Depression had suffered, and hence it was vital that it should now show "the way out of darkness into light, out of illiteracy into knowledge".[35] According to Brooks, especially after the Darks had moved from Sydney to Katoomba, the writer had become increasingly fascinated, not only with the landscape of Australia, but by the stories behind the landscape and the sense of identity that came out of living in the country at that time. Like Cusack, Dark railed against the "colonial attitude that regarded everything Australian as second rate",[36] and agreed with many of her contemporaries that Australia need not be a "second-rate colony of Europe," but an "egalitarian society and lively culture".[37]

---

35   Brooks, *Eleanor Dark*, 254–55.
36   Brooks, *Eleanor Dark*, 149.

(These sentiments echo, of course, those of the 1890s writers Henry Lawson and Banjo Paterson and Charles Bean.) Along with these writers, Dark believed that "[i]t was only when Australians came to grips with the country" that they could "fully live here, know themselves as part of the place and it as part of them".[38]

In *The Little Country*, Dark's Gilbert Massey shares her affection for the country, and he has been, albeit unconsciously, searching for what it means to be Australian. Dark infers that his uncertainty about his nation's history and his place in it has led him to a kind of "creative paralysis," or writer's block. Like the Darks themselves, who began to read history vociferously at the outbreak of war, Gilbert, too, endeavours to inform himself about the history of Australia, and his musings on the subject take up a significant amount of the text. Gilbert reflects, for example, in one of his many interior monologues, upon the numerous difficulties settlers faced when they first came to Australia: theirs was a history of "obstinate striving, of hardship, ugliness, loneliness, success and failure, effort and more effort".[39] Moreover, he recognises that their history was all about fighting, about staving off "the heat and the cold, the drought and the bushfires, the bad soil, the floods, the solitude" (67). But above all, Gilbert believes, they "fought the conception of themselves that had been imposed upon [them], the tradition of servitude" (67–8). As a result of their struggles, Gilbert concludes, they were not a "docile" people (66). Gilbert further notes that

> [t]his was not, thank God, a country living on its past, but still struggling away from it. It had begun badly; it grew up the hard way. Physically, mentally and spiritually handicapped, it had sweated and blundered its way out of the dark era when human flesh and blood, having suffered the deterioration of poverty, having endured nightmare voyages in the hell-ships of the day, had still by some miracle lived to tread a new earth, and kept enough vitality to reproduce itself. Human minds, warped, hardened, illiterate, and full of hatred, had still clung to the idea of survival and perpetuation. Human spirits, damned almost to impotence by the tradition of their own worthlessness, had kept alive, instinctively, a spark of faith in the possibility of regeneration. (66–7)

---

37   Brooks, *Eleanor Dark*, 420.

38   Brooks, *Eleanor Dark*, 149. Like Cusack, Dark also suggested that early settlers had made mistakes. In an essay titled "Australia and the Australians," she wrote that during the difficult period of white settlement, the people had invaded a land that was not "originally theirs" (cited in Brooks, *Eleanor Dark*, 294). In calling attention to this usurpation, Dark was echoing statements that have appeared in several of Cusack's fictions, such as *The Half-Burnt Tree* (London: Heinemann, 1967), and *Black Lighting* (London: Heinemann, 1964). Like Cusack, Dark also suggested that early settlers "used the land too recklessly, overstocking it till pastures became deserts" (cited in Brooks, *Eleanor Dark*, 293).

39   Eleanor Dark, *The Little Company* (1945. London: Virago, 1985), 67. All subsequent references are to this edition and appear in parentheses in the text.

Since the history (of white settler/invaders) in Australia had been so brief, the people were not caught up "helplessly" in

> the grip of a legend, or bemused into imagining that they could ride triumphantly into the future on the back of the past. Their ancestors were only their grandfathers, or at most their great-grandfathers, and such national memories as they had led them not very far from the life of their own knowledge and comprehension. (67)

It is inconceivable, Gilbert believes, that during World War II, they should go back on all they had struggled to attain in such a short time (68).

Because of their nation's history, Dark and some of her contemporaries had a "dream" about the kind of country Australia could be. Prior to the war, however, they had begun to feel that the people were letting them down: they had not "done enough to justify [their] occupation of [their] country," and not enough to justify "calling themselves Australians".[40] In part, Dark's text argues, Australians had become too contented, for while World War I proved to be a "nightmare" that awakened people, most then simply "roll[ed] over with a sigh of relief and [went] to sleep again" (18). Gilbert believes that

> those few who had not returned to their pillows, but had, with tiresome, persistent, and ill-mannered vociferousness, disturbed the slumbers of the majority with warnings, had been unpopular people – agitators, scare-merchants, warmongers. A few light sleepers (among whom he humbly recognised himself) had been roused by the clamour to listen, at first sluggishly, reluctantly, and then with rising anxiety, to the hullabaloo. Another bad dream called Depression had awakened a further batch with the shocking ruthlessness of a douse of cold water; but there were plenty who were still snoring – yes, even now, when the second nightmare was already twitching their limbs and distorting their mouths with grimaces of pain. And some, whose sleep had drifted into coma, would never awaken. Let them die in their sleep, [Gilbert] thought with sudden fury – so long as they die! (18)

It was crucial, Dark believed, that Australians shake off their smugness, because if they did not, they risked being colonised by either the Americans or the Japanese: "During the war, the American presence reminded Australians they were part of the Pacific rather than tied to Europe. They lived in a big country with a small population, hanging off the edge of the huge land masses of Asia. How could they defend their coastline?" Brooks further observes that the alarming situation contributed to Dark's choice of title: "it stood for those who defended the Christian West against the barbarians, also for embattled minority groups, for the people who stood up for their beliefs against the majority".[41]

---

40   Brooks, *Eleanor Dark*, 420.

Dark argues that Australians had become self-satisfied because they had been poorly educated, not taught to challenge established values or to think for themselves. Gilbert's education, for example, and that of his younger sister, the writer Marty Ransom, had consisted primarily of the rote learning of useless facts. Like Dickens's Gradgrind children in *Hard Times,* they had not been allowed to use their creative imaginations or taught to "question, to investigate, to read and think" (19). Gilbert recalls in particular one "little dried-up spinster" who had "not one single qualification except gentility" to run a school (25). She encouraged her students only to memorise facts, to recite worthless scraps of knowledge, and then struck them with rulers when they refused to obey her instructions (25). He concludes that the education system was a "misbegotten monstrosity" that turned its students "loose on the world at fourteen with no more sense of values than a bunch of chimpanzees" (207). Anticipating Cusack, Marty laments that even though she had been born at a momentous period in Australian history – 31 December 1900 – she had never been taught to believe that she was "living in history," or to comprehend the "significance of the events in which she had participated" (38). Both Marty and Gilbert come to realise that the education system has not equipped them to contest the values inculcated in them by their father, Walter Massey, a teetotalling, God-fearing, judgemental, self-righteous and bigoted Christian who refuses to countenance opinions or values not of his own making; he regards Trade Unions and Labor governments as "disastrous" for the country, and upholds everything British and imperialistic. (His wife was also a missionary).[42] Even the name Massey has bestowed upon his home – "Glenwood" – is hypocritical, for there is nothing "natural" about it. Rather, it is an "old, square stone house" on the North Shore that is as "solid as a gaol" (93), and just as confining to its inhabitants. (In her depiction of this archly conservative patriarch, Dark appears to have combined the personalities of the father of her husband Eric and her father, Dowell O'Reilly, both of whom presided over "repressive, almost fundamental Christian households"[43]). Although Modjeska refers to Walter Massey as "no more than a token" ("Introduction", xiv), given the harmful effect he has on his offspring, hers seems a misreading. After Massey's death, which occurs just before the novel opens, both Gilbert and Marty embark upon a kind of trip down memory lane, in which both recall that their childhood and adolescent years had been characterised by confusion, darkness, repression, intolerance and duplicity.

Much of the novel, then, concerns how Marty, Gilbert, their younger brother Nick, and Gilbert's wife, Phyllis (who became part of the family when her mother, also a missionary, was hired as Massey's housekeeper after his wife died), have turned out after such an oppressive upbringing. Phyllis, the only one who

---

41 Brooks, *Eleanor Dark*, 258.
42 For an examination of the sustained grip men like Walter Massey held in Australian educational institutions, see Leigh Dale's "Whose English – Who's English" *Meanjin* 51 (1992): 393–409.
43 Brooks, *Eleanor Dark*, 46.

acquiesces, develops into a prim, stiff, disapproving and narrow-minded adult. Conditioned by her surrogate father, Walter Massey, to aspire merely to domestic servitude and motherhood, Phyllis has become, according to Gilbert, the type of female who could be the subject of a thesis titled "Sex Ignorance and Female Parasitism as Factors in Maintaining the Capitalist Status Quo" (291). Denied formal education, Phyllis is unable to grasp any kind of intellectual content (she cannot understand Gilbert's novels and arranges the books in their living room by height); nor can she come to grips with what is happening to her family during the war. Frustrated by Gilbert's increasing neglect, she joins The Christian Watchers' Circle, where, presumably, her thinking is done for her.

During the war years, Gilbert realises that he has, for decades, been married to a woman he detests, although in a brief moment of insight, he comprehends that Phyllis is not to blame for her ignorance: "[i]nstead of being educated like a human being she has been domesticated like a cat" (132). Moreover, he recognises that he himself has "take[n] a hand in that training" (132), for he has, like his father, accepted as "natural that [Phyllis] should have no thoughts beyond caring for [his] physical comfort, and looking after the children" (132). Although Gilbert declares that when he succumbed to writer's block and recognised the need to re-educate himself, he tried to "drag" Phyllis along with him (132), nowhere does Dark indicate that Gilbert made any such effort: rather, both he and his sister Marty constantly hold Phyllis up to ridicule, ignore her needs, and treat her cruelly. Dark's condemnation of Phyllis is curious, for she had insisted publicly that we have "to find ways for women to participate in making decisions about the community and the nation, not just the family and the house" (233), yet she offered no policies or platforms or ideas of how to achieve this goal in her novel.[44] In addition, Dark's assertion (which echoed her father's), that "[i]f women's main duty is motherhood ... then men's first priority is fatherhood",[45] also rings hollow, for Gilbert pays attention only to Prudence, his "thinking" daughter who runs her own bookshop, and ignores the pretty, but empty-headed and far from virginal, Virginia. Gilbert suffers only a twinge of guilt when Virginia dies of an ectopic pregnancy, and within weeks of Phyllis's incarceration in a mental institution (she has so little understanding of the Australian bush [a sure sign of character weakness] that even her attempt to kill herself there after learning that Gilbert has had an affair fails), Gilbert and the other members of the family, including his son, seem to have forgotten either woman ever existed.

---

44   Cusack's novel is equally disappointing in its representation of women. Although she had complained that women had been left out of Australian history (Cusack, "A Sense of Worth", 64), she failed to give them any prominent role in her wartime novel, in spite of the fact that she had stressed the need to "give women a sense of their own worth" and to give them "courage" (Cusack, "A Sense of Worth", 69). Additionally, in writing novels that feature male protagonists, she was falling in line with women who wrote World War I fiction. See Chapters 1 and 4.

45   Brooks, *Eleanor Dark*, 232–33.

If Phyllis's lack of rebellion leads to madness, however, Dark points out that Nick's decision to become a Communist, which would have been anathema to his father, is also misguided. Although Modjeska argues that Nick is a "pivot for concepts and ideas," that his "position in the novel allows the exploration of political ideas, strategies, and positions" (xiv) and that "he is the only character with a clear position on a number of issues" (xiii), her reading is again erroneous for, convinced that his views are unassailable, Nick has, ironically, become just as dogmatic, unbending, judgemental, and resistant to change as was his father. As Marty reflects, while Nick's certainty may give him a kind of "rigid strength," it also leads to a "certain weakness," as well (49). In addition, Nick has not tested his theories against differing circumstances: the "one size fits all pattern" he clings to does not hold for all societies, wars, or circumstances. In creating a character like Nick, Dark seemed to be reflecting her own opinions of those who become members of any organisation, for while she was sympathetic to socialism, she "never joined any party or group, just as Eric had never joined the Communist Party. Institutions, she believed, destroyed the very ideas they were set up to propagate".[46] In *The Little Company*, then, only Gilbert and Marty manage successful rebellions (the words "rebel," "rebellious," and "rebellions" occur dozens of times in the opening pages), but they do so by sheer accident, and their victories are temporary.

As adolescents, they are befriended by Janet, daughter of the free-spirited bohemian poet and labour politician Scott Laughlin, a character Dark obviously modelled on her father.[47] Both the fictional Laughlin and the real-life O'Reilly encourage their daughters to read whatever books they like, and in both households, "[t]here were always arguments raging, and convention was less important than independent thought".[48] (Dark's father told her that the only thing she couldn't question was the weather!)[49] In *The Little Company*, the Laughlins inhabit an untidy, run-down home (ironically owned by Gilbert's father) that overflows with books, music, poetry, Australian art and outspoken friends who hotly debate the state of the nation, their discussions animated by the consumption of alcohol. Both Marty and Gilbert, who are warmly welcomed into the Laughlin household, are astounded that their home life should be so different from Janet's, but thrilled when Laughlin treats them like intelligent young people and volunteers to help foster their creativity by critiquing their writing. As a result of his encouragement, their word choices become less imitative of the British and more inclined to rhyme with "wattle." Laughlin's

---

46   Brooks, *Eleanor Dark*, 430.
47   The atmosphere in the Laughlin home sounds like the O'Reilly's. Although we never meet Janet in the novel, she, too, bears some resemblance to Dark. Both adolescents lived in houses full of "silences and tensions" between their parents (Brooks, *Eleanor Dark*, 64), and like Dark, Janet grows up "in the space between her mother's frustration" and her father's "wild impracticality and fertile imagination" (Brooks, *Eleanor Dark*, 64).
48   Brooks, *Eleanor Dark*, 64.
49   Brooks, *Eleanor Dark*, 181.

"roadside" classes, which he holds under a gum tree (112),[50] resemble those conducted in the Irish hedge schools. Gilbert's and Marty's educations are cut short, however, when Janet's mother Denny runs away with Gerard Avery (Brooks posits Avery was based on the writer Brian Penton[51]) and takes their friend Janet with her. (Denny, a pianist too burdened by domestic duties to practise, also seems modelled on Dark's mother.) Although both Marty and Gilbert continue to write after their contact with the "egalitarian society" and "lively culture" at the Laughlin household is severed, neither produces works that have much literary impact. Gilbert recognises that none of his novels had challenged "existing conservative values," and Marty (who, like Dark, gives wartime radio broadcasts and suffers from writer's block), often refers to the "dark side" of her education, to the "thick black curtain" (36) drawn between childhood and adulthood, and to the "black screen of ignorance" (38) that has governed her life.

Although Gilbert's and Marty's reading of history at the outbreak of war does lead them to discard convention, to re-shape their knowledge so that they readily see through measures such as the government's imposition of censorship and an imposed wartime paper shortage that facilitates the conservative government's printing of what it wishes to print and nothing else, their creativity remains immobilised, and springs to life only after each comes in contact with a woman from the past who reanimates those heady and exhilarating days of learning about Australia at Scott Laughlin's "roadside school." Marty is inspired to pick up her pen after a chance meeting with a former classmate, Sally Dodd, whom her father had disapproved of because the Dodds were poor, some of the many children suffering from starvation. Although Sally's contemporary hard-luck stories (she now has too many mouths to feed herself) fail to move Marty emotionally (it is somewhat disquieting that Marty sees Sally as merely a blinkered housewife, incapable in her "ant-like activity" of grasping the point that her "little life" was "determined by remote political forces" [252]), intellectually, they appear to, for after their brief conversation, Marty rushes to her typewriter, prepared, we assume, to retell the sad story of Sally's life, but not to help overcome her impoverished circumstances. Gilbert's muse is Elsa Kay, Janet Laughlin's daughter, with whom he has an affair. During their adulterous relationship, Gilbert realises that he wants to write about the Laughlins. He suffers a brief setback when Elsa informs him that she intends to write a novel about her family, but both Marty and Gilbert conclude that Elsa has neither the intellect and the stamina nor the inestimable social vision to carry it off, and the novel ends with Gilbert racing to get the words, which now flood his mind, onto paper.

But Cusack and Dark might well now be spinning in their graves, for although Cusack wrote that by 1979, all nineteen universities in the country had established

---

50 For a further examination of the significance of the gum tree in the creation of national identity, see Ashley Hay's *Gum* (Sydney: Duffy, 2002), and Libby Robin's *How a Continent Created a Nation* (Sydney: UNSW Press, 2007).

51 Brooks, *Eleanor Dark*, 266.

courses in Australian literature,[52] according to Rosemary Neill's 2006 newspaper articles, senior academics were declaring that "a new cultural cringe is infesting our universities and encouraging the neglect of Australian literature". In spite of the success of contemporary Australian writers – "Kate Grenville and Geraldine Brooks have won or been short-listed for the Pulitzer, Commonwealth and Booker prizes," and that the "teaching and translation of Australian literature" is popular overseas,[53] "British/European literary projects have claimed a bigger share of academic research grants than Australian projects".[54] Moreover, the country now boasts "just one permanent chair in Australian literature nationwide," and even that position was recently threatened.[55] The numbers of students interested in Australian literature, including those enrolled in the honours program at Sydney University, has plummeted (about half the numbers are studying the subject now as did in the late 1980s and early 1990s[56], even though "Sydney University remains the sole tertiary institution where undergraduates can major in Australian literature".[57] Furthermore, the paucity of students at other institutions appears to have led to fewer course offerings and restricted programs. In 2006, for example, Melbourne University offered only two Australian works of fiction in their first-year literary studies course, devoted no first-year subjects to Australian literature, and of the available thirty-one second- and third-year subjects, only "three were specifically about Australian writing". Even worse is the situation at James Cook University where, of the fifty available literature courses, only one was devoted to national literature.[58]

A number of academics attribute the lack of interest in Australian literature to the hijacking of literature departments by post-modern, post-colonial, and cultural studies' theorists, none of whose courses "accord canonical works, Australian or otherwise, a privileged place".[59] Elizabeth Webby (and others) blame the "marginalization of Australian fiction primarily on funding cuts"; Webby also points specifically to the federal government's preference for private schools over universities.[60] The problems seem to extend beyond the lecture halls, however, for presses that published series on Australian writers have shut down, and many classic Australian novels are now out of print.[61] The situation may not be as grim as Neill's articles indicate, however, for Elizabeth Webby's successor, Robert Dixon, who then held the chair in Australian literature at the University of Sydney, dismissed Neill's arguments as overly negative; he offered a number of compelling arguments which insist that "the study of Australian literature is very healthy

---

52 Cusack, "Cringe", 79.
53 Rosemary Neill, "Australia Neglecting Its Own Writers" *Australian* 2 December 2006, 1.
54 Rosemary Neill, "And Then There Was One: Lost For Words" *Australian* 2 December 2006, 1.
55 Neill, "Australia Neglecting Its Own Writers", 1.
56 Neill, "And Then There Was One", 4.
57 Neill, "And Then There Was One", 1.
58 Neill, "And Then There Was One", 2.
59 Neill, "And Then There Was One", 2.
60 Neill, "And Then There Was One", 3.
61 Neill, "And Then There Was One", 4.

indeed".[62] But that the "cultural cringe" issue is once again on the agenda seems to indicate that there is some reason to be concerned. Thus it may be time to re-read (and teach) *Southern Steel* and *The Little Company,* if only to remind ourselves that "country matters" as much now as it did in the 1940s and 1950s.

---

62   Robert Dixon, "Australian Literature-International Contexts" *Southerly* 67 no.1.2 (2007), 15.

10
Reality Bites

The Impact of World War II on the Australian Home Front in Maria Gardner's *Blood Stained Wattle* and Robin Sheiner's *Smile, the War Is Over*

According to historian Michael McKernan, "December 1941 was a black month for Australians".[1] They were stunned when the light destroyer *HMAS Sydney* was hit off the coast of Western Australia and the entire crew of 645 was lost, and alarmed when the Japanese annihilated the US forces at Pearl Harbor and conducted simultaneous raids on Malaya, Singapore, Hong Kong and the Philippines on 7 December,[2] for until that point, the war had seemed psychologically and physically remote. Prime Minister Curtin's radio broadcasts immediately after Pearl Harbor, which stated that "This is the gravest hour in [Australian] history. ... We are at war ... because our vital interests are imperilled," did little to dispel anxiety.[3] As the conflict in the Pacific continued to heat up – by early February 1942, Port Moresby had been bombed and Hong Kong, Manila, Penang, Kuala Lumpur and Rabaul were flying the flag of the rising sun – citizens in the Northern Territory and Western Australia had good reason to be frightened. Although many Darwinians were certain that a Japanese invasion was imminent because the Allied Forces used its docks for repairs and port facilities for supplies, others clung to Churchill's insistence that Singapore was an impenetrable fortress, capable of holding out for a prolonged period until the British arrived. But when Singapore fell to the Japanese on 14 February 1942 and the enemy captured 130,000 Allied Forces, over 15,000 of them Australian, and either killed or wounded 3,000 Diggers,[4] they were completely demoralised.[5] They would have been even more panic stricken, however, had they

---

1   Michael McKernan, *All In! Australia During the Second World War* (Melbourne: Thomas Nelson, 1983), 96.
2   McKernan, *All In!*, 96.
3   McKernan, *All In!*, 97.
4   According to McKernan, "the defence of Singapore was the most costly Australian campaign of the war. Almost one third of those captured died in captivity" (McKernan, *All In!*, 110).
5   Darwinians erroneously assumed that the Japanese wished to secure the airbase, but the Japanese intended to invade Timor and "anticipated that a disruptive air attack would hinder Darwin's potential as a base from which the Allies could launch a counteroffensive, and at the

been aware that the Federal War Cabinet had recently devised a classified plan, dubbed the "Brisbane Line," which would defend the vast Australian continent only south of a direct line from Brisbane to Adelaide, and effectively abandon northern and western Australia to the enemy.

Surprisingly, these threats to national safety have captured the imaginations of few novelists: Maria Gardner's *Blood Stained Wattle* (1992), and Robin Sheiner's *Smile, the War Is Over* (1983).[6] While both of these writers draw heavily upon military and political history to tell their stories, Gardner derives much of her material from a diary her father, Colin Gray Gardner, kept of his experiences during and after the bombing of Darwin, and Sheiner, who was a child living in Perth during the war, supplements her memories of the period with letters from and formal interviews with those who were alive at the time. Gardner confesses in her Author's Note that she wishes to "portray the truth" behind the "official conspiracy to suppress the facts pertaining to the bombing of Darwin [that] has persisted for fifty years" (n.p.), and her findings – that many innocent lives were lost because the government and military were "so un-prepared and ill-equipped" to "detect enemy movements that threatened Darwin"[7] – seem incredible today. Similarly, in her Historical Note, Sheiner draws attention to the Brisbane Line, a concept that now seems inconceivable.[8]

Gardner's novel opens on 19 December 1941, when the feeling that the Japanese are "hell-bent on taking the Pacific" (5) has prompted the government to order the evacuation of 2,000 women (out of a total population of 5,000) from Darwin.[9] Her central character, the twenty-five-year-old engineer John Gray, is helping his wife and infant son prepare for their departure on the *Zealandia*, the first of four troop ships to leave Darwin. The irony that men are waving goodbye to women and children leaving on troop ships is not lost on him. Shortly after his family's departure, John's concern for the safety of his sister, Grace, who has refused evacuation on the grounds that her work as a switchboard operator is essential, intensifies because he feels certain that Darwin has been abandoned, since "[o]nly two thousand defence force personnel" are stationed in its most vulnerable city

---

same time would damage morale" (National Archives of Australia, "The Bombing of Darwin", http://www. naa.gov.au/about-us/publications/fact-sheets/fs195.aspx).

6   Judy Nunn's historical romance, *Territory* (Milsons Point, NSW: Random House, 2002), devotes a few chapters to the bombing of Darwin.

7   Maria Gardner, *Blood Stained Wattle* (Pialba, Qld, 1992), 12–13. All subsequent references are to this edition and appear in parentheses in the text.

8   In "New Australian Novels," reviewer Katherine England suggests (and I agree), that Sheiner's text contains "enough characters, enough facts, for half a dozen novels, boiling and bursting from the pages of one (*Advertiser*, 8 October 1983: 29). But the novel raises issues frequently ignored in World War II literature, such as the discrimination African Americans faced in both Australia and the USA.

9   One of the few literary depictions of the evacuation of women and children from the Top End appears in Henrietta Drake-Brockman's "Smoke-Signals," in *Sydney and the Bush* (Sydney: Angus & Robertson, 1948: 251–68).

(13). John's apprehensions are well founded, for on 19 February 1942, Japanese forces mount two air raids (the first of sixty-four) that kill 243 people, wound between three and four hundred, sink eight ships in the harbour, and destroy twenty military aircraft and most civil and military facilities.[10]

Paradoxically, even though they feared an attack was looming (a Japanese reconnaissance plane had been sighted flying over the city the night before the raid [84]), both citizens and members of the military took a nonchalant approach to the war.[11] According to historian Timothy Hall, "Seldom can a town which had every reason to believe that an enemy attack was imminent have done so little to prepare itself for the onslaught".[12] Gardner notes that the service men based in Darwin continued to maintain the same kind of "relaxed lifestyle" as their civilian counterparts (61), but she is careful to point out that the inexperienced militia, who expected to be put on active duty, were not entirely to blame for their laxity because they were given little to occupy themselves; consequently, their morale plummeted, they began to drink heavily (61), and reports of servicemen wrecking buildings in the town centre, going "troppo," or inflicting wounds upon themselves in order to earn tickets south to Sydney became commonplace (63–64). But instead of giving these bored men something to do, the military allegedly dispatched a number of them to the Middle East (63). Those left behind spent their time "waiting" – the kind of inactivity traditionally associated with women in wartime – for something to happen, and when it did, they were literally caught off guard. As one Royal Australian Air Force (RAAF) officer said disgustedly when the raids were over, "A hundred Japanese armed with frying pans could have occupied Australia that day".[13]

Gardner lays the blame for much of the destruction directly on the "military brass," most of whom appeared to have forgotten the tradition of fighting prowess and ready initiative in a hostile environment that had earned such a powerful reputation for the Anzacs of their fathers' generation. Although Gardner indicates that the military had taken a few precautions against raids on Darwin, they did absolutely nothing to protect the harbour, which was "chock-a-block" (85) with "forty-five cruisers, destroyers, troop carriers, escort sloops, transport ships, a hospital ship, a munitions ship, and an oil tanker" at anchor, as well as a number of small watercraft (87–88). The military also failed to issue warnings to the seventy or so waterside labourers who were inexplicably rushing to install a lighting system for night loading; they and the hundreds of other civilians and thousands of marine personnel working in various capacities around the harbours were sitting ducks (88). Unaccountably, the military also appeared to have forgotten Curtin's bitter remark that the Japanese had struck Pearl Harbor "like assassins in the night",[14]

---

10   NAA, "The Bombing of Darwin".
11   In her 1945 novel *The Little Company* (Sydney: Virago, 1985), Eleanor Dark also comments on Australians' complacency during World War II (18).
12   Timothy Hall, *Darwin 1942: Australia's Darkest Hour* (1980. Port Melbourne: Mandarin, 1989), 13.
13   Hall, *Darwin 1942*, 7.
14   Cited in McKernan, *All In!*, 97.

and thus led citizens to believe that they would have "at least twenty-four hours warning" prior to a full-scale invasion, and "less than an hour's notice" before a bombing raid (78–79). What those warnings might have consisted of was unclear, for as Hall points out, unlike other nations involved in the war that had three distinct methods of advising of an impending attack, including radar (109), Darwin had only one pedal wireless "manned" by a priest at a Catholic Mission on Bathurst Island. Although his report of an "unusually large air formation" heading towards Darwin on the morning of 19 February followed an earlier dispatch from coast-watchers on Melville Island (86–87), RAAF Intelligence officers "chose to believe" that the planes were flown by Americans, even though many had turned back because of bad weather and others had already landed in Darwin (87). Moreover, what the military might have done to prevent the impending attack of 188 aircraft – which Commander Mitsuo Fuchida, the man who had led the attack on Pearl Harbor, was later to describe as "a sledgehammer to crack a nut" (89) – remains doubtful, for all the military had at their disposal were a few old planes (88). The rest, except for a few stationed sixty miles away, were unserviceable (12).

In addition, at the nearby Larrakeyah Barracks and at the RAAF station, pandemonium reigned, an unusual set of circumstances given that, according to David Walker, the soldiers of the First Australian Imperial Force (AIF) had "earned a powerful collective reputation for courage under fire" (144).[15] This stellar quality does not appear to have been reactivated, for as one former Anzac caustically remarked, "The old AIF ... would blush with shame and they would tum in their graves if they knew what happened at Darwin".[16] The soldiers at the barracks had no guns or ammunition with which to defend themselves, and because no one had dug trenches either, they were forced to hide in the hospital's newly built sewer system (114). But the most serious problem was that at both the barracks and the airbase, no senior officers stepped forward to issue clear orders (it was rumoured that the Commanding Officer flew away in a Wirraway shortly after the first raid [137]). And according to historian Alan Powell, while some airmen at the RAAF station thought they had been instructed to go half-a-mile down the track and then half-a-mile into the bush, others believed they were to travel three, or seven, or eleven miles away from the base. Consequently, hundreds of air force personnel simply went "bush" after the attacks. Four days later, nearly three hundred men were still unaccounted for.[17]

Both Gardner's Grace and John recount instances of citizens, soldiers, and politicians behaving reprehensibly after the attack. John observes that uniformed

---

15   In *Big-Noting: The Heroic Theme in Australian War Literature* (Melbourne: Melbourne University Press, 1987), Robin Gerster argues that "the Second A.I.F. proved that its legendary predecessor was no mere fluke of history" (172), but none of the literature he analyses mentions the attacks on the Northern Territory or Western Australia.

16   Cited in Hall, *Darwin 1942*, 98.

17   Alan Powell, *The Shadow's Edge: Australia's Northern War* (Melbourne: Melbourne University Press, 1988), 85.

soldiers took advantage of the chaos and openly and systematically set about looting the bomb-saturated town, and Grace is appalled to see men push and shove aside women, children, even the sick and injured, in order to secure themselves a place on the evacuation train (205). Further down the track at Adelaide River, John watches as the wife of a high-ranking Northern Territory administrator and her staff, friends, and political acquaintances thrust their way onto the train ahead of women and children (167). But those who escaped Darwin reserved their wrath for members of the media who made radio broadcasts that claimed the damage to the northern city had been "slight" and that there were "few" civilian casualties (158). Historian Tom Lewis notes, too, that the day after the attacks, citizens were outraged when they read newspapers that also concealed the extent of the carnage from the public: the Melbourne *Herald*'s headlines declared, for example, that there were only "15 killed, [and] 24 Hurt in Darwin".[18] Historian Daniel Connell further suggests that the prime minister was clearly lying when he told people that "the armed forces and the civilians comported themselves with the gallantry that is traditional in the people of our stock".[19]

As a result of these shocking deceptions, 19 February 1942 has become known as "a day of national shame".[20] At the same time, Gardner's novel attests that many ordinary citizens had themselves taken safety precautions and behaved admirably when disaster struck: these would be, of course, John, Grace, and her husband Josef Steinhardt (of German ancestry, he is accused of being a Nazi spy, even though he is openly a pacifist). Prior to the raids, John has had the foresight to purchase a large, recent-model car and to stash enough petrol to transport Grace and Josef to safety should the need arise; and during the first air attack, Josef leaps courageously into the shark- and crocodile-infested water at the harbour in order to help save his mates (92). After the invasion, and certain that Grace could not have survived the carnage, John and Josef prepare to flee, but stay behind to help with the burial of the dead. And in spite of having been seriously wounded during the air attack, John continues to be a Good Samaritan. He makes room in his car for a number of friends who are attempting, like 1,500 other Darwinians, to make the 76-mile trek to Adelaide River (nicknamed the "Adelaide River Stakes") by any means possible – on foot, by bicycle, car, or even sanitary cart. He also helps a Greek family keep their vehicle running, and he exhorts the military to put the safety of women and children first. Meanwhile, back in Darwin, Grace helps an injured police officer get to hospital before attempting to save herself.

A few weeks later, Sheiner's residents of Perth, aware of the rumours that the Brisbane Line will sacrifice Western Australia, are scared stiff when, on 3 March,

---

18 Tom Lewis, *A War at Home: A Comprehensive Guide to the First Japanese Attacks on Darwin* (Darwin: Tall Stories, 1999), 42.
19 Daniel Connell, *The War at Home: Australia 1939–1949* (Crows Nest, NSW: ABC Enterprises for the Australian Broadcasting Corporation, 1988), 48.
20 Hall, *Darwin 1942*, 205.

Broome suffers Australia's second-worst air raid.[21] Dozens of people are killed and twenty-four aircraft, including sixteen flying boats, are destroyed. Subsequent raids on Wyndham, Derby and Horn Island ensue shortly after.[22] Although the city council issued press statements discouraging panic, it reinforced residents' fears they would be the enemy's next target when it enforced brown-out rules, made air raid shelters mandatory for every home, and instructed school children to dig slit trenches and to carry air raid helmets and assemble ration packs (Historical Note n. p.). The citizens' spirits are buoyed, however, when they hear that the Yanks are coming to the rescue and welcome them as heroes. As the title of the novel suggests, the Americans encouraged Australians to believe that once they landed on Australian soil, the war would soon be over.

Initially, Australians viewed the Yanks favourably. Like Florence James and Dymphna Cusack's *Come in Spinner* (1951), Henrietta Drake-Brockman's *The Fatal Days* (1947)and Zora Cross's *This Hectic Age* (1944),[23] Sheiner's text also emphasises the GIs' physical appearance, their charming manners, and their generosity.[24] These "friendly invaders" resemble either tall, dark, and handsome "film stars" (42) whose jackets fit so tightly that they look as if they have been "ironed on" (29), or "golden-haired gods" (5) who shower local women with gifts of boxed orchids, chocolates and cigarettes, and orphans with books, gum and candy. But like her literary predecessors, Sheiner also highlights the kinds of problems that arose wherever the Americans were stationed in Australia. Because of the cash jingling in the pockets of these submariners and pilots (paid even better than the ordinary GIs), as well as their "smooth-talking ways," the Yanks readily monopolise taxis, booze, and women. Disgruntled Australian men retaliate by charging the Yanks five times the going rate for food, drink and taxis, and instigate brawls whenever the GIs boast they have come to "save" Australians.

But while citizens' fears for their safety quickly evaporate after the doughboys arrive (but children's do not: one continues to dream [and scream] at night of being chased by Japanese soldiers [133]) and they inject a new sense of vitality and cosmopolitan into the town, Kate Dorian-Smith argues that many Australians feared that the war was creating new social problems: "By mid-1942, federal and state politicians, the clergy, the police, and allied military authorities claimed Australian society was in the throes of war-induced moral and social breakdown".[25]

---

21   Gail Jones' *Sorry* (Milsons Point, NSW: Random House, 2007) contains a brief description of the bombing of Broome.

22   Staff Writers, "From the Archives 1942: Japan air attack on Broome, eyewitness account", *Sydney Morning Herald*, 3 March 2022.

23   For a critical analysis of these novels, see Chapter 7.

24   In "Consuming Passions: Romance and Consumerism During World War II," Lyn Finch comments that Australian men erred in assuming that Americans regarded women as "goods" to be bought, for consumerism was "central to American culture, 'integral to dating for American men,' and thus usually had no connotations of buying a woman." *Gender and War: Australians at War in the Twentieth Century*, eds. Joy Damousi and Marilyn Lake (Melbourne: Cambridge University Press, 112).

One social concern arose over the "ideological and material changes to women's economic and social status during the war", which stemmed from "the industrial conscription of women into the paid workforce" and had the effect of introducing "new forms of social behaviour".[26] But Sheiner's text indicates that the authorities had little to fear on that front; while the war did give young women opportunities to enter the work force, only those who procured jobs as taxi or bus drivers or worked for the military as drivers or radar operators were treated well and paid fairly, a set of circumstances contemporary writer Estelle Pinney documents in her Brisbane novel, *Time Out for Living* (1995). Sheiner's text demonstrates that the majority of women laboured in factories that were either freezing cold or unbearably hot, and there were no medical facilities or treatments available for injuries on the job, an unconscionable state of affairs given that much of the work was unsafe. Women also complained that they were impregnated by "a fog of cordite" (95)[27] and suffered severe headaches because of the noise of the machinery and the glare from fluorescent lights. Owing to inadequate equipment, they could take no pride in their work because the finished products were second-rate, unsafe for use in the front lines (95). Moreover, Darian-Smith argues, "the hierarchical structure of the Australian workforce remained basically unaltered. Managers and overseers continued to be predominantly male",[28] an observation both Pinney's and Sheiner's texts make. Male managers also objected to women's assuming extra jobs (several of Sheiner's female characters hold down two jobs) without taking into consideration that they were earning 50 to 54 per cent of men's wages.[29] Thus, it is not surprising that many of Sheiner's factory workers come to work "tipsy," in "no fit condition for work" (94). Darian-Smith further observes that Australians were alarmed at women's "new visibility," which produced "new forms of social behaviour"[30] such as "frequenting restaurants, cafes and hotels without a male escort".[31] In Sheiner's text, parents and friends of Carla Brown, a mother of two married to a philandering Anzac, are concerned that she often drowns her sorrows drinking alone at a local bar.

---

25   Kate Darian-Smith, "Sexualising Public Spaces: Wartime Visions of the City" *Australian Studies* 9 (November 1995), 22.

26   Darian-Smith, "Sexualising Public Spaces", 23.

27   Madeleine Byrne's short story "War Bride" also documents the negative effects of cordite. *Westerly* 46 (2001): 160–66.

28   Kate Darian-Smith, "War and Australian Society" *Australia's War, 1939–1945*, ed. Joan Beaumont (St. Leonard's, NSW: Allen & Unwin, 1996), 64.

29   Darian-Smith, "War and Australian Society", 64. Darian-Smith cautions not to overestimate the number of women who entered the workforce during the war, because workingclass women had always worked. By 1944, there was only a 5 per cent increase from 1939 in the proportion of all women working (63). The war enabled them to move "out of domestic service into better paid industrial positions" ("War and Australian Society", 63–64).

30   Darian-Smith, "Sexualising Public Spaces", 23.

31   Darian-Smith, "Sexualising Public Spaces", 22.

Another social problem Darian-Smith identifies was the over-consumption of alcohol,[32] and Sheiner's Yanks, who exhibit more larrikin-like behaviour than those in earlier texts, attribute their debauchery to the procurement and excessive consumption of alcohol. At the officers' club, the Bend of the Road (appropriately renamed "the Bend of the Elbow"), a giant urn gurgles with whatever mix of alcohol is available that day – rum, gin, whisky (some of it smuggled in underneath women's fur capes) – which is then topped up with pure alcohol in the form of "torpedo juice" (32). The imbibing of this "inflammable liquid," inexplicably christened "turkey wurkey" (33), quickly enlivens social gatherings, but contributes to decadency. More than half of Sheiner's servicemen who contract venereal disease attribute their promiscuity to the effects of alcohol. Although the military tries to prohibit the drinking of strong wines and spirits, to make supplies of "rubbers" readily available (42), to find suitable occupations for men's spare time and hence reduce their attendance at brothels (49), none of these measures appear to have had much affect, as women continue to become pregnant, have abortions, and men to contract venereal disease.

"Rampant sexuality" was another major societal concern, but in this instance, authorities were particularly anxious because, for the first time, "respectable" civilian women, not "camp followers" or prostitutes, were held responsible for the increase in sexually transmitted diseases (STDs) among the Australian and American military forces, and "because hospitalization meant the loss of 'fighting hours,' this was perceived as an urgent military problem",[33] a situation Sheiner's text reflects. Here, sixteen-year-olds to society matrons are openly licentious, but their profligacy should not be construed as a result of the oft-repeated phrase that Australia is a land where "the flowers have no fragrance, the birds no melody and the women no virtue",[34] but as a result of women's acknowledgement of their own sexual desires. According to Marilyn Lake, by the 1940s, young Australian women were not being "seduced into sexual relations," but actively initiating them.[35] Lake further argues that because of the influence of Hollywood films, women tended to encode Americans as sex objects,[36] and to objectify GIs in uniform, or "render them uniform",[37] and Sheiner's central character Michelle Brown (Carla's sister) conforms to Lake's theory when she engages in so many affairs that she can barely distinguish one lover from another. Lake further points out that "danger ... was constructed as an integral part of sexual pleasure",[38] and in Sheiner's text, nice guys finish last. Michelle

---

32 Darian-Smith, "Sexualising Public Spaces", 22.
33 Darian-Smith, "Sexualising Public Spaces", 23.
34 Cited in John Hammond Moore, *Over-Sexed, Over-Paid, and Over Here: Americans in Australia, 1941–1945* (St Lucia: University of Queensland Press, 1981), 3.
35 Marilyn Lake, "The Desire for a Yank: Sexual Relations Between Australian Women and American Servicemen During World War Two" *Studies in Gender: Essays in Honour of Norma Grieve*, eds. Patricia Grimshaw, Ruth Fincher and Marion Campbell (Parkville, Vic: Committe for Gender Studies, University of Melbourne, 1992), 118.
36 Lake, "The Desire for a Yank", 123.
37 Lake, "The Desire for a Yank", 121.

chooses to associate with an American pilot, a "flippant, unreliable" womaniser who takes unnecessary risks and spurns a polite and well-mannered GI (87).

But because the influx of Americans often resulted in a shortage of inadequate entertainment facilities and a "deficiency of private, interior spaces for socialising," the relationships between Australian women and American soldiers were often "initiated and conducted in the main commercial streets, in parks, and along beach fronts".[39] These encounters challenged "Australian definitions of manliness" because American men were often "openly affectionate" and "thought little of kissing or embracing women in public".[40] Sheiner's novel echoes these societal anxieties when four young Australian men bash in the head of a "bloody Yank" they find making love to an Australian woman on the river bank (10–11).[41] While feminist critics such as Anne Summers, Miriam Dixson and Rosemary Campbell have documented that Australian men routinely preferred booze, gambling and mates to dates,[42] and that their courtship and lovemaking methods were crude (in Sheiner's text, an American man claims that Australian men "just push women over and go at it" [112]), *Smile, the War is Over* also stresses that the Yanks' "non-stop romance and glamour" (113) proved so irresistible that many young women became disoriented and lost control over their lives. Prior to the war, for example, Michelle is content living on her family's vineyard near Perth, but once the GIs arrive, she confesses that their "glib way with words" have turned her life into a "picture theatre" where she lives out her "fantasies" as on the silver screen (35), until eventually she is unable to distinguish between what is "real" and what is "imaginary" (35). Surprised by how "thin" her "layer of respectability" is (114), she engages in a number of affairs until, she agrees (as did approximately 7,000 impressionable young women)[43] to follow a stranger to the new world. Like many other war brides, Michelle's motives are questionable: when the man she loves is reported "missing in action," she marries on the rebound.[44] Others succumb to the Americans' promise to make them Hollywood film stars (99) and most are, to use Margaret Atwood's clever term, "raw brides,"[45] unaware of how truly strange and different America would prove to be. Although these brides attend

---

38   Lake, "The Desire for a Yank", 118.
39   Darian-Smith, "Sexualising Public Spaces", 23.
40   Darian-Smith, "Sexualising Public Spaces", 23.
41   Dymphna Cusack's *Southern Steel* (London: Constable, 1953) similarly depicts how quickly the war transformed streets, parks, and beaches into sexualised spaces.
42   Geraldine Halls' *The Last Summer of the Men Shortage* (London: Constable, 1976) also makes disparaging remarks about Australian men's unsophisticated courtship methods.
43   Sheiner's estimate of the numbers of women who became war brides is conservative. Most feminist historians place the figure at somewhere between 10,000 and 20,000. Lake claims there were 12,000 war brides (Lake, "The Desire for a Yank", 119).
44   "War husbands," too, married for foolish reasons: one bride claims her husband married her so "that he could have a son in case he copped it in the war. Said he was scared to death of having his you-know-what-blown off, said it was the worse [sic] thing that could happen to any man" (147).
45   Margaret Atwood, *The Robber Bride* (Toronto: McClelland, 1993), 153. For an examination of British/Italian/German war brides who emigrated to Canada, see Donna Coates' "'Wish Me Luck As You Wave Me Goodbye': Representations of War Brides in Canadian Fiction and Drama" *Back*

information sessions organised by the American Red Cross, they fail to absorb that America is a melting pot (most assume they are marrying men of British stock), or that American cities could be dangerous and violent. Thus, one bride unwittingly marries an Aboriginal man (142), and another looks forward to life in Harlem, which she assumes will be "just like Perth" (142). Yet another remains wilfully deaf, certain that her husband is "kidding" when he warns her that he comes from the Ozarks, where the people speak so "funny" that she will not be able to understand a word they say, especially his ma, who "smokes a corncob pipe" (146). Still others are simply too young – no more than sixteen – to know what they are doing; once away from their mothers, they have no idea how to care for their babies (144). And there were lots of babies (the "Bridal Express" transporting brides to Sydney is nicknamed the "Perth Perambulator"), as many women deliberately got themselves "in trouble" in order to circumvent the lengthy bureaucratic procedure the American government required before granting couples permission to marry (60).

Like soldiers frustrated by having to wait long periods before getting "into action," war brides, too, had to tolerate lengthy voyages by train, sea, and then again by train before they could join their husbands. Those from Perth had to endure five days of not-so-sentimental journeys by train across "2694 miles of desert, mountains, and prairies" (144) before reaching Sydney: upon arrival, many looked more like "refugees" (150) than brides. That few of these women were emigrating for love alone becomes apparent before they leave Australia. Michelle has an affair during a brief stopover in Melbourne, and the numbers of drunken assignations between the crew and the brides on ships or shore ensure that some women are confined to the ship when it docks in Honolulu (153); others are offloaded for "openly soliciting" sailors' favours (153).

Only one war bride appears to have married wisely and well. Her officer-husband appears at the San Francisco wharf in a white Cadillac and whisks her away to "a white house with ocean frontage and all modern conveniences" in Santa Monica (155), but the rest, who have married in haste, repent in leisure.[46] In recounting these sad war brides' stories, Sheiner demonstrates conclusively that the aftermath of war proved as destructive to women as the war years had been to men. Her text thus reflects Margaret and Patrice L.R. Higonnet's argument that women's experiences of war require a redefinition of its temporal limits: "Women experience war over a different period from that which traditional history usually recognises, a period which precedes and long outlasts formal hostilities. Masculinist history has stressed the sharply defined event of war; women's time more closely reflects Bergson's concept of duree".[47] Correspondingly, shortly after Michelle arrives in

---

to Peace: Reconciliation and Retribution in the Postwar Period, eds. Aranzazu Usandizaga and Andrew Monnickendam (Notre Dame, IN: University of Notre Dame Press, 2007: 250–71).

46 In When the War Came to Australia: Memories of the Second World War (St. Leonards, NSW: Allen & Unwin, 1992), Joanna Penglase and David Homer suggest that 70 per cent of Australian–American marriages failed, although the Australian Consulate-General in Australia claims that 85 per cent survived (169).

America and her husband fails to meet her, she declares, "the war is just starting for me" (115). Although she manages to divorce her husband (whom she has not seen since her wedding day) and make her way back to Australia, the anguish she suffers is analogous to post-traumatic stress disorder, an affliction approximately 10 per cent of World War II soldiers experienced; the difference is that some ex-combatants received medical treatment, but war brides did not. Like many soldiers who turned to alcohol as a form of self-medication, Michelle, too, drinks to excess.

Sheiner utilises images from nature – gum trees – to underscore that Michelle's temporary move across the ocean amounts to a kind of deracination and, ultimately, a loss of identity. When she leaves for America, her sister Carla gives her a painting of a ghost gum that grows at the gate to the family's vineyard, which she carries with her as she wanders throughout America in search of a home, but then decides to leave behind because "otherwise there'll be no indication she was ever there" (199). This forsaking of the gum-tree painting signifies that she has lost her "Australianness," for according to Ashley Hay, the link between Australian national identity and the gum tree has a long history.[48] Prior to Federation, Australians felt that gum trees reflected "typical values found in the bush and in bush life", and during World War I, "a reference to gum trees was like a shorthand for patriotism, nationalism, and identifiable Australianness".[49] During World War II, Australians continued to have a "fondness for purely Australian things".[50] At the end of the novel, Sheiner suggests that Michelle can "never go home again," that she will never recover from the trauma of temporary dislocation.

But while Sheiner employs the gum tree to suggest that the war caused women like Michelle to lose their "Australianness," Gardner utilises the wattle, another tree that has traditionally stood in for the nation, to suggest that while some Australians might have provisionally lost their way after "blood has stained the wattle" (146),[51] they are nevertheless hardy people capable of triumphing over dangerous and harsh conditions. Gardner's John remembers hearing this remark for the first time from his schoolteacher, and thereafter he associates the wattle with a fighting spirit that

---

47   Margaret R. Higonnet and Patrice L.R. Higonnet, "The Double Helix" *Behind the Lines: Gender and the Two World Wars* (New Haven, CT: Yale University Press, 1987), 46.
48   Hay also notes that during the Great War, women often sent soldiers in the trenches gum leaves in their letters, or May Gibbs' "gumnut postcards" as reminders of home (Hay, *Gum*, 117).
49   Hay, *Gum*, 115.
50   Hay, *Gum*, 137.
51   Although Libby Robin does not mention the role that the wattle has played in literature, it is useful to note that this phrase first appeared in the final stanza of Henry Lawson's "Freedom on the Wallaby," that D.H. Lawrence included the remark in *Kangaroo* (Sydney: Angus & Robertson, 1923), that Leslie Haylen wrote a play titled *Blood on the Wattle: A Play of the Eureka* (Sydney: Angus & Robertson, 1948) and that Ailsa Craig produced a novel titled *If Blood Should Stain the Wattle* (Sydney: Currawong Publishing, 1947). Bruce Elder also used the phrase for *Blood on the Wattle: Massacres and Maltreatment of Aboriginal Australians Since 1788* (Sydney: New Holland, 2003) and Alex Miller's *Landscape of Farewell* (Crows Nest: Allen & Unwin, 2007), forcefully makes this link.

can readily combat hardship. At the end of the novel, after John discovers that Grace is still alive, he, Grace, and Josef sit "under the shade of [a] big wattle tree" in Alice Springs (204) discussing how the events in Darwin have "inflamed [their] moral sense of fair play" (207). When they hear an army major asking volunteers to "reconsider returning to Darwin at once" to help rebuild the town, all three agree that they must travel to the city and fight for the survival of the country, for if the people like them don't, "the whole country's done for" (210). In agreeing to help with the reconstruction of Darwin and the nation, they display the kinds of egalitarian principles that the wattle has stood for since the 1980s: "an egalitarian, classless free citizenry".[52]

Interest in the wattle waned until the Bicentenary Celebrations in 1988 when golden wattle was officially proclaimed as the national floral emblem. Due to the efforts of Maria Hitchcock, 1 September was declared National Wattle Day in 1992.[53] In 2002, when terrorist bombs in Bali killed 212 people, eighty-eight of whom were Australian, "everyone wore wattle". Although Robin writes that this was a "new" context in which "the wattle was about being threatened and being protected: it personalised a national agony. ... Nature (in its token form) was there to heal and represent resilience in adversity".[54] Today, all of Australia's "national sacrifices" are symbolised by "indigenous wattle".[55]

Addendum

I would like to include an Addendum to this chapter as an acknowledgement that, while no critic can be expected to include every observation or topic they identify, in order for this to be a comprehensive analysis of the two novels, the important issue of racism must be addressed. Canada and Australia both have violent and oppressive histories in their treatment of their Indigenous peoples, and drawing attention to examples of their oppression by colonisers in WWI Australian literary works plays a small but necessary role in drawing attention to the significant burdens faced by First Nations communities.

In her novel, Sheiner utilises the inclusion of both the gum tree and the wattle to underscore the extent to which white colonisers brought death, displacement, and severe cultural disruption to Aboriginal peoples. It accentuates their dispossession from the land by depicting them sitting, in groups or clusters, aimlessly on the hard

---

52   Libby Robin, *How a Continent Created a Nation* (Sydney: UNSW Press, 2007), 13. Hitchcock suggests that during World War I, the Red Cross and the Patriotic Fund sold sprigs of wattle on the streets of Sydney and encouraged soldiers to wear sprigs of wattle on their uniforms. Mothers enclosed sprigs of wattle in their letters to their sons abroad to remind chem of home (14). Wattle trees were also planted near the graves of Anzacs who died at Gallipoli (15).
53   Cited in Robin, *How a Continent Created a Nation*, 27.
54   Robin, *How a Continent Created a Nation*, 29.
55   Robin, *How a Continent Created a Nation*, 30.

pavement of Perth's main street, looking lost, as though they do not know why they are there. Because the street is lined with "a single file of white gums praying with outstretched branches" (35), the text seems to suggest that those white or "ghost" gums are expressing remorse for their bleak lives. Several passages also emphasise the role religion has played in their supplanting: "on a rise ... was the Anglican church which had been there since the first white settlers had come to the valley, taking up their pieces of prime land as if it were an 'inheritance'" (1).

Sheiner's text also accentuates the extent to which young girls' lives have been ruined by that same process of colonisation. The Brown family's Aboriginal servant Emma, for example, has been frequently incarcerated for misdemeanours (although the white men who forced her to "spot" for them go free). Her repeated stays in the local lock-up reflect the over-representation of Indigenous Australians in prison to this day, being incarcerated at twelve and a half times the rate of the rest of the population.[56] Eventually, the authorities take Emma from her mother (thereby making her a member of the Stolen Generation) and send her to a mission school in the valley. After a cyclone destroys the school, kills two children and injures twenty-five, the institution closes, but abandons survivors. Because Emma's family are all killed after the Japanese bombs drop on Broome (and she witnesses their burial beneath salmon gums, also known as ghost gums [19]), she no longer has any family to return to, and now lives "under the bridge which linked the valley with the small town at its edge" (7). Gardner's text offers another example of the natural world's reactions when the Japanese air-attacks turn Darwin into a slaughterhouse and the bush, with its "sparkling dew drops" clinging to leaves, seems to "weep" at the tragic loss of life (146).

Sheiner's text further exposes how commonplace prejudice against Indigenous Australians was by demonstrating that even ordinary, decent, well-meaning citizens like her Brown family hold racist views. For example, they leave Emma, their domestic servant for many years, to eat leftovers by herself in the kitchen, even on Christmas Day. Michelle's mother, a "good woman" in every other sense, declares that the "natives are hopeless": "the more you do for them the worse they are. They'll steal from you as soon as look" (76). Most notably, when Emma is found – inexplicably – dead beneath the railway bridge, none of the Browns know where the local Indigenous Australians are buried, if they have graveyards, or any religion of their own (41). At the same time, the otherwise sensible Carla declares emphatically that Aboriginal men molest women (171), when the text indicates that whites have been molesting and raping Aboriginal women for generations. Emma, for example, was born to a mother made drunk by the cheap plonk white men gave her in return for sexual favours (6). Emma herself has had two daughters by two different men, but only Pearl has survived. (Given that two Aboriginal children die in this text, Sheiner appears to be drawing attention to their low life expectancy.) The most

---

56   Australian Law Reform Commission, "Over-representation" (2018). https://bit.ly/3LEuJR3.

reprehensible white man is Vince, who has been incarcerated for "unlawful carnal knowledge": he rapes Pearl, Emma's daughter, and during the rape scene, Pearl "scream[s], torn and scratched amongst the spiky hakeas" (141). Not surprisingly, Aboriginal men despise Vince, whom they describe as "the one who bash our friend and fuck our women. His face like snake and body hair like rat" (178). After plotting their revenge beneath the ghost gums, they attack a man whom they assume is Vince (sadly, he's not). While they beat him, the Aboriginal women watch, significantly, "from the acacias glowing now like demons" (179). Later in the text, Emma's account of the burial of her granddaughter, fathered by an African American soldier, reflects the all too familiar story of the shabby, almost non-existent medical treatment of Aboriginal people. Sheiner's frequent associations of Aboriginal death/ghost gums/and "white" (or Japanese) invasions are appropriate (79), for according to Curthoys, "there have been hundreds of millions of Aborigines over tens of thousands of years who have inhabited Australia and their ghosts ... have filled the continent ... Tragically and prophetically, the Aborigines first to come into contact with the invading Europeans greeted them as returning spirits of the ancestral dead".[57]

Gardner's novel also makes the point that in times of crises, Aboriginal children like Emma (and then her offspring) have few resources to plan their futures. While her novel documents that after the attack on Darwin, children from the Northern Territory were evacuated south by train, she omits that they were not allowed to disembark in Adelaide, as were the other non-Aboriginal evacuees, but obliged to live in open horse stalls at a racecourse in Balaclava in the Adelaide Hills[58] and "kept under government control" there.[59] Moreover, although white children were routinely offered good educations, European parents prevented Aboriginal children from attending schools.[60] Although the evacuated Aboriginal children suffered "great melancholy and depression", they were not returned to the Northern Territory until March 1946. Similarly, Sheiner's novel points out that the rights and privileges of adult Indigenous Australians were few: bartenders refuse to serve them drinks and ushers ordered them to sit in the front two rows of the cinemas. Similarly, Gardner's Indigenous Australians were forced to sit behind the screens at outdoor cinemas. These longstanding types of displacement and dispossession resulted from a number of racist policies that meant that Indigenous Australians "were denied their rights of citizenship, and their lives were rigidly controlled by state and federal authorities. The introduction of government acts during the 1930s resulted in ... the 'climax of legislative control over Aborigines'".[61]

---

57   Ann Curthoys, "Mobilising Dissent: The Later Stages of Protest." *Vietnam Remembered*, ed. Gregory Pemberton (1990. Willoughby, NSW: Weldon, 2009), 49.

58   Hall, *Darwin 1942*, 11.

59   Darian-Smith, "War and Australian Society", 59.

60   Alan Powell, *The Shadow's Edge: Australia's Northern War* (Melbourne: Melbourne University Press, 1988), 263.

61   Darian-Smith, "War and Australian Society", 59.

Gardner's text also points out that those Indigenous Australians who had attempted to assimilate into a white world were disadvantaged during the war. At the Adelaide River, for example, an Aboriginal man who had gone to work for a white man is abandoned when his boss gets a ticket for the train to Adelaide. The white man tells him to "go bush and catch [his] own tucker". In these circumstances, one of the Darwin evacuees notes that Aboriginal people are worse off than anyone because they are "too shy" or "too proud" to line up at soup kitchens (172). Significantly, both Sheiner's and Gardner's reasons for including the many plights of Indigenous Australians during World War II may be partially explained by Curthoys' observation that contemporary historians (and presumably fiction writers as well) were "influenced by new left critiques of racism arising from opposition to South African apartheid, racial segregation in the USA, opposition to the Australian involvement in the war in Vietnam and from an emerging Australian civil rights movement" (33–4).[62] Although Curthoys cautions that "in their enthusiasm for uncovering and naming a brutal colonial past, these new histories sometimes risked portraying Aboriginal people as outside history, passive victims in a tragic narrative of destruction and despair," she also acknowledges that others began to "place greater emphasis on indigenous peoples' perceptions, understandings, and active responses to colonization".[63]

Gardner's text includes a modicum of praise for Indigenous Australians' ability to survive by pointing out that they are the only inhabitants of the country who know how to live in the beautiful but harsh landscape. Of the thousands of non-Aboriginal evacuees who make their way south to the Adelaide River by any means they can – on foot, by car, bike, truck – many attest they appreciate the "fierce incarnate beauty" of the landscape, especially the tall ghost gums, and as they prepare their morning billy, they smell the "fragrant wattle blossoms" and see reflected in the water the "tall eucalyptus and blossoming acacia" (144). As they near the MacDonnell Ranges, however, much as the travellers marvel at the splendid colours and lively sounds of birds within the varied terrain, they also acknowledge the perils of life in the outback: they are plagued by flies and mosquitoes that make sleeping difficult, and once aboard "Leaping Lena," the primitive train that transports them to Alice Springs, they either roast under the burning sun in the open carriages by day or freeze by night (181). Gardner's narrator expresses admiration for the Indigenous Australians' capacity to survive "in such a fierce country": when the travellers see them heading north, they observe that the happy children appear oblivious to the "harsh cruel environment" (196).

Sheiner too writes favourably about the Aboriginal presence in the outback. She notes the ways in which they blend into the landscape, and revel in the happy chatter in Mirninj and Nyangatjatjara among themselves (147). The towns they visit on the rail lines consist primarily of only a few buildings of rusted tin and

---

62 Curthoys, "Mobilising Dissent", 33–34.
63 Curthoys, "Mobilising Dissent", 34.

corrugated iron, with the "only sign of a tree the small specimen which had been planted near the siding and wrapped with cyclone wire for protection; it may have been a eucalypt but it drooped from the waist, its tips shriveled" (149). Here, Sheiner seems to be suggesting that within their bleak surroundings, not even a gum tree can survive. She also affirms that in spite of the dire circumstances, the Indigenous Australians are also seemingly inured to the guards shouting "be off youse black bastards"(149).

Sheiner's text is one of the few that acknowledges the presence of numerous other "black bastards" helping to win the war in Australia. In spite of the fact that there were, by 1942, 8,025 African Americans in Australia and New Guinea,[64] Drake-Brockman and Cusack/James made little of their presence in their novels. *Come in Spinner* reflects the derogatory attitude of both white Australians and white Americans at the time. Unlike Cusack/James or Drake-Brockman, who ignored the destructive impact of the American intrusion on Indigenous Australian lives, Sheiner acknowledges that the local Aboriginal community was affected when the US military took over Onslow, a small town in Western Australia.

While some of these events are recounted by characters whose opinions and actions readers are meant to question, in Sheiner's text, there is much to applaud the behaviour of her two African American soldiers, Jaraud and Rodney. Now working as cooks on the submarines, both have come from impoverished backgrounds in Harlem: consequently, neither learned to swim (both lied to get into the navy), but both are quick to spot advertising in local newspapers that convince them of the biases against them. While their white counterparts can freely hire taxis, the African Americans are relegated to riding about on bikes (17). They see for themselves the depth of Australian hostility towards Indigenous Australians who, when they try to take their dates to bars and movies, are often scorned. But unlike Emma and Pearl, who do not protest their prejudiced treatment, the two African American soldiers refuse to be silenced: while in prison for crimes they did not commit, they blatantly draw attention to their victimisation by referring to themselves as "strapping nigger[s]" who happily live on "ol' cotton-picking plantation[s]" (50). Once sent to an American prison for assaulting a taxi driver, Rodney recognises that the war is never over for African Americans or Indigenous Australians and vows to study the law in order to do something for not just for African Americans, but for "black guys everywhere and for that Pearl in West Aussie" (122). He demonstrates political savvy in his recognition that he will be chosen for a GI retraining program "because they need blacks to make it look good" (124). Although the novel ends before Rodney achieves his goal, Sheiner suggests that some good might have come from the relationship during the war between the Indigenous Australians and the African American soldiers, for at the end of the novel, Pearl is teaching her son (not Rodney's, though) to swim.

---

64   Hammond Moore, *Over-Sexed, Over-Paid, and Over Here*, 210.

Both Sheiner's and Gardner's texts suggest that Australians are also unwelcoming to immigrants, even though Sheiner's "Jack the Yugoslav" is a good man who teaches his employer how to run a vineyard and treats the Brown children better than their own father does (6). But because men like him fought on the side of the Germans during the Great War, no one trusts them, especially at the goldmines around Kalgoorlie and Leonora where they "dug ore for half the wages of the Australians" (81). Jack is also resented because he is a Catholic in a "community that aspired to heterogeneous Protestantism" (81). The industriousness of the Yugoslavs, who work the land from sun-up to sundown without even a breather on Saturday for the races or the footy (81), earns them no respect. Similarly, Gardner's Josef Steinhardt, born in Australia but whose parents emigrated from Germany, is frequently the victim of racist remarks and on occasion, fights. Fittingly, Sheiner's novel also takes a dig at bigoted Americans: Australian women who arrived in America as war brides found them inhospitable and rude. Conversely, on the Australian home front, the legendary fighting prowess of the Anzacs has evaporated, and the few who do appear are either "whinging" loudly about the Yanks' tight-fitting uniforms, or resenting their smooth-talking manner that attracts the most beautiful women and subsequently leads to their being served first in bars, as well as their ability to exploit the availability of taxis. The local fighting men also freely participate in violent brawls with their "home front enemies."

In spite of what they may have learned about other cultures during the war, the Australians in these texts appear to cling to tradition, to continue to utilise the natural world as a positive force that had been in place, as Libby Robin notes, since the days of nationalism, with writers of the *Bulletin* in the 1890s celebrating life in the bush; they connected the great outdoors with "great moral fibre"[65] and urban life with moral degeneracy that could only be rescued by Australian nature itself. Surprisingly, however, Robin points out that by the early 1900s, Indigenous Australians expressed concern more publicly that they were not included in the discussions about, for example, the wattle's importance to the citizenry of the nation, which white writers such as Hitchcock insisted were "symbol[s] of Australia"[66] and which future generations would invoke as "symbol[s] of independence, nationhood, patriotism, future wealth, and prosperity".[67] Nevertheless, the wattle was not designated the "national floral emblem" until 1992, at precisely the same time as Australians had become concerned about the "appropriateness of celebrating the wattle on January 26, having been recently renamed 'Invasion Day'" by those who acknowledged the displacement of Indigenous Australians during colonisation.[68] As my conclusion to the longer essay

---

65   Robin. *How a Continent Created a Nation*, 8.
66   Maria Hitchcock, *Wattle* (1991. Canberra: Australian Government Publishing Service, 1992), 3.
67   Hitchcock, *Wattle*, 3.
68   Robin. *How a Continent Created a Nation*, 17.

indicates, the wattle once again surmounted negative associations and acquired status as the symbol of "national sacrifices".[69]

Once the novel's brother and sister ascertain both have survived the bombings in Darwin, within moments of re-uniting, they are confident they can contribute to the rebuilding of Darwin and vow to return there immediately. The wattle imagery Gardner employs is fitting given that both John and Grace display the kinds of egalitarian principles that the wattle is meant to represent. John's wartime efforts have been without prejudice: he has befriended a Japanese photographer, helped out Greeks along the way to Adelaide, and overcome his prejudice against Germans when his sister Grace marries Josef. Both John and Grace are ideal citizens – friendly, hospitable, and all other "signifiers" of the wattle because they help everyone in need, regardless of age, creed, or colour. But it is important to stress that in spite of the many references to "an egalitarian, classless free citizenry",[70] Gardner's novel nonetheless does not accurately describe the dire conditions Indigenous Australians continue to occupy, even in 2023.

---

69   Robin. *How a Continent Created a Nation*, 30.
70   Robin. *How a Continent Created a Nation*, 13.

11

Loving Thine Enemies

Representations of Italian Prisoners of War in Contemporary Australian Women's World War II Fictions

According to historian Karen Agutter,

> the relatively short history of white Australian settlement is full of deliberate acts of confinement or excluding groups of people who, for one reason or another, have been either deemed unsuitable for a settler society or regarded as a menace to it. From the time of Italy's joining the First World War on the Allied side, Italians in Australia became increasingly problematic, as the Australian government struggled to maintain a volunteer army. The long history of xenophobia towards Italian immigrant in Australia (they comprised one of the largest non-British-born groups) meant that even their status as Allies did not prevent their captivity. From the end of 1917 until the Armistice, Italian-born men were rounded up and detained pending deportation to Italy. Their incarceration, motivated by racial stereotyping and exclusion, was couched within a rubric of national defence and security.[1]

In addition, historian C. Kevin points out that while racism towards Italians had been steadily increasing before World War I, the rise of fascism in the 1920s and the large influx of Italian immigrants to Australia in the early 1920s (their numbers doubled between 1920 and 1925 in part because the United States had restricted their entry and there was a surplus of jobs in Australia) caused concern to Australian governments, who in turn began to view Italian immigration in a negative light and drew upon unemployment figures to "bemoan the rising number[s]". Kevin asserts many were not surprised that when Italy declared it would enter the war on the side of Germany in 1940, Australian police and security officers encountered no barriers to arresting Italian men since the "methods of identification, arrest and internment … formulated in August 1929" gave the

---

1   Karen Agutter, "Captive Allies: Italian Immigrants in World War One Australia", *Australian Studies* 1 no. 10, (9 December 2009), 1.

federal government the power to intern any person whose loyalty was suspect: "in most areas, Italian blood was considered reason enough for arrest, regardless of one's political persuasion. Even naturalized British subjects were arrested".[2] Historian Gitano Rando adds that the entry of Italy into the war "brought considerable disruption to the over thirty-thousand strong Italian–Australian community whose presence was seen by the Australian authorities as a serious potential threat to national security. About 4700 mainly male Italian Australians [referred to hereafter as "local internees"][3] were incarcerated in internment camps while women and children were left to fend for themselves in a hostile environment.[4] But since the majority of those who had left Italy either because of grinding poverty or their opposition to fascism posed no threats to national security, numerous critics such as Robert Pascoe have concluded that "internments were, on balance, a pointless exercise, instigated by irrational fears".[5] Claudio and Caroline Alcorso concur, writing that internment was unwarranted and unnecessary: "just like Hitler and Mussolini they scorned and despised democratic beliefs; indeed they considered them dangerous and subversive. They were fascists without knowing it".[6]

Until recently, the unjust and unjustifiable treatment of Italians and Italian Australians during World War II has been largely ignored, but six contemporary Australian women novelists have endeavoured to shed light on their treatment. Both Vilma Watkins' 1999 *Pukunja*[7] and Deborah Burrows' 2012 *A Stranger in My Street* reinforce the accuracy of the historians' arguments over the plight of the local internees. Four additional novels – Goldie Goldbloom's 2009 *The Paperbark Shoe*; Susan Temby's 2002 *The Bread with Seven Crusts*; Dale Turner's 2011 *The Farmer's Wife*; and Joanne Carroll's 2005 *The Italian Romance: A Novel* – examine

---

2   Catherine Kevin, "Italian Internment in Australia during World War Two", *Teaching Heritage*, 1.

3   Historian Joan Beaumont suggests that "local internees" were "aliens whose nationality was that of a country now at war with Australia" (3). Curiously, although she provides a list of those identified as "overseas internees," she does not mention the Italians captured in Egypt and Libya in 1941 (3), many of whom are featured in the fictions I discuss here.

4   Gitano Rando, "Italo-Australians during the Second World War: Some Perceptions of Internment" *Italian Studies in South Africa* 18 no.1 (2005), 2.

5   Robert Pascoe, *Buongiorno Australia: Our Australian Heritage* (Melbourne: Greenhouse Publications and Vaccari Historical Trust, 1987), 46.

6   Claudio and Caroline Alcorso, "Italians in Australia during World War II" *Australia's Italians: Culture and Community in a Changing Society* eds. Stephen Castles, Caroline Alcorso, Gaetana Rando and Ellie Vasta (Crows Nest: Allen & Unwin, 1982), 28.

7   In her Author's Note, Watkins writes that "[t]his is a biography of an Italian woman and her husband. The names of the Australian characters have been changed, including the names of the protagonists and in some cases left out ie.[sic] departmental employees" (Vilma Watkins, *Pukunja: A Far Away Place* [Hurstville, NSW: Parker Pattison Publishing, 1999]), 5. All subsequent references are to this edition and appear in parentheses in the text). Rando calls the work "transparently autobiographical," however, because it "relates the migration of her parents from Italy to a North Queensland tobacco farm" (Rando, "Italo-Australians", 5). I am treating it here as fiction because the catalogue publication data lists it as such. As well, the book offers a thorough overview of the problems even naturalised British citizens faced during the war.

the reception of the second largest group of Italian prisoners of war, known as "overseas internees," held in captivity in Australia during World War II. According to the Alcorsos,

> Nearly 18,500 Italian prisoners of war (POWs) were confined in Australia between 1941 and 1947 … representing a (temporary) 50 per cent increase in the Italian-born population of the country. Except for those captured in territorial waters, most were brought from the Middle East and India and their importation to Australia proved to be the largest exercise in mass labour migration yet undertaken by an Australian government.
>
> The POWs were imprisoned in approximately 30 purpose-built camps across Australia … From 1943 on, POW labour was not only used on camp or government work projects but was made available for private use by Anglo-Australian farmers.[8]

The Alcorsos add that "the labour of the POWs made a significant contribution toward the Australian economy during the war years", an observation borne out in these novels. While the fictions also concur with the Alcorsos' suggestion that the prisoners of war suffered from "depression, loneliness and boredom with the dull routine of confinement," as well as "anxiety about the fate of friends and relatives in Italy",[9] they also support Rando's contention that overall, the Italians' experiences with their employers, especially those fortunate enough to work "outside the wire," were "generally cordial".[10]

Watkins' *Pukunja* begins with a few quotations from a *Sydney Morning Herald* article[11] titled "Locked Up – Just For Being Italian," which stresses that what happened to the Italians was "wrong" (7), as "[m]any of the internees [had] migrated to Australia to escape the fascist government in their homeland" (7). The opening chapter, which records the arrest of Roberto De Conti in 1940 in Queensland, shows that the onus was not on the authorities to prove that he was a fascist; rather, it was his responsibility to prove himself innocent, an impossible task. Ironically, De Conti had emigrated from Italy with his young family because he found the fascist regime, which contributed to the collapse of his business ventures, intolerable; neither he nor his wife Carolena had any intention of returning to Italy. Accordingly, as the Alcorsos note, "men like Roberto were victims of the "ironic tragedy of being treated by the authorities as an enemy, and by implication a fascist, after leaving [their] country of birth because of opposition to fascism".[12]

---

8   Alcorso and Alcorso, "Italians in Australia", 31–32.
9   Alcorso and Alcorso, "Italians in Australia", 32.
10 Rando, "Italo-Australians", 20.
11 This article also mentions that Watkins' central character Roberto De Conti was "one of over 6,000 Italian 'aliens' who were interned in Australia during the war" (7). The numbers of Italians interned varies considerably depending upon the source.

While the De Contis' main goal in migrating was financial security, they also wanted to put war behind them. Carolena was fourteen when Germany became Italy's enemy in 1916; in 1917, her well-educated, highly respectable, and professional family had to evacuate their home in Nimis, a northern Italian town,[13] and join the panic-stricken "human stream" (31) fleeing the area. She and her siblings were terrified when temporarily separated from their parents, especially since what they were witnessing – dead horses with their "bellies ripped open from shellfire" (32), soldiers' bodies "lying in grotesque poses" (32) and "rivers that ran red with blood" (32) – was so upsetting (32). The Romanian-born Roberto had, like Carolena, also become separated from his Italian parents, who were by then living in Austria. Forced to flee or be interned, they had fled, but without Roberto, who had been arrested as an Italian of military age (43). Released in 1918 at the age of twenty-two, Roberto resumed his former studies in forestry and game keeping in Italy and married Carolena, but when political unrest once again dominated their lives, the couple, who had recently produced a son, felt they had no recourse but to leave (71). On the strength of reports that Australia was "a large open land with a spare population" (72), and that the numerous forests sounded "promising," they agreed that Roberto should seek employment in Australia in 1927 and send for his family when he could support them.

Roberto eventually found a job in Queensland that made good use of his education, experience and innovative ideas and before long was able to send for his family. As many immigrants discovered, however, in order to succeed in Australia, they had to overcome an exhausting array of obstacles: the struggle to master a new language; the lack of an extended family to provide much-needed support; the tyranny of distance that prevented visits with loved ones; the hardships of the Depression, including the rise and fall of the tobacco crops Roberto carefully cultivated on his farm; the adjustment to an intensely humid and often unpredictable climate that produced dust storms, bushfires, floods, and cyclones; and the presence of daunting new enemies in the form of deadly snakes, insects and crocodiles. The De Contis were, however, grateful for the Britishers' "spirit of generosity and goodwill" (140), the friendliness of the fun-loving Australian people (105), and captivated by the strange yet exotic beauty of the Australian landscape. By 1940, after their daughter was born, the couple assumed their sacrifices had paid off, and they looked forward to peaceful and prosperous lives in Australia.

---

12   Alcorso and Alcorso, "Italians in Australia", 28.

13   In "Citizenship and Naturalisation in a Historical Context: The Story of Carmelo Belfiore," David Brown notes that "Statistically, 90 per cent of the Italian immigrants before the Second World War came from either the northern districts of Italy or the east coast of Sicily" (*Under Suspicion:Citizenship and Internment in Australia During the Second World War*, eds. Joan Beaumont, Ilma Martinuzzi O'Brien and Mathew Trinca [Canberra: National Museum of Australia Press, 2008], 36). Those from other areas "simply could not meet the costs of immigrating" (36). Accordingly, most of my texts come from northern Italy.

But as Beaumont writes, at the outbreak of war, "enemy aliens" potentially became the object of suspicion. Initially only those who posed an obvious security risk, because they were members of Nazi or fascist organisations or had been identified as potential saboteurs by military intelligence, were detained. But in the mid-1940s the fear of British collapse, lurid accounts of "fifth columnists undermining resistance in Europe and Italy's entrance into the war all led to a surge in the numbers of aliens being interned".[14] The De Contis' hopes were dashed when Roberto, who had become a naturalised British subject in 1932 (Carolena in 1934) was, like thousands of Italian descents, "snatched from [his] family and treated like a criminal" (16). Present at his arrest, Carolena insists that her husband has broken no laws, that he is a "hardworking farmer" (10), and that the authorities are making a "terrible mistake" (11), but her protestations fall on deaf ears. The police merely inform Roberto that "under Regulation 26 of the Act," the minister may "*detain*" any person he deems to be "*acting in any manner prejudicial to the public safety or the defence of the Commonwealth of Australia*" (13).[15] As Rando suggests, since Roberto had already been interned by the Austrians for the duration of World War I, his arrest must have been "a far from pleasant prospect".[16] While the military prevented "hate-filled protestors" from gaining access to the trains that carried internees, the falsely accused were nonetheless assailed by British dissenters' threats to "Kill the bastards! Kill the dagos!" (17).

Although Roberto never learns who "turned him in," the text suggests that it was one of his fellow countrymen whose "single purpose appeared to be one of self-preservation" (171). (As Temby's text also suggests, this kind of betrayal was depressingly common.[17]) Here, the traitor is a young Italian who lived up to his reputation as "a patronizing liar, a mercenary and police informant" (171) and fabricated "a malicious and incriminating story ... to convince the authorities" that Roberto was "constantly causing arguments with [Italians] about Fascist politics," that he "held the rank of sergeant in the black shirts in Italy," and that he had "spied for the Italian Government in Romania" (173).

According to Rando, Roberto, "who was able to write English, initially objected to his arrest on the grounds that he had never acted in a manner prejudicial to the safety of the Commonwealth. In December 1940 he appeared before a three-member tribunal, but despite his protestations that he was not a fascist, the minister decided he should be transferred to Loveday in late June 1941".[18] Roberto's move, from the Gaythorne Internment Camp in Queensland to the Loveday Camp

---

14 Joan Beaumont, "Introduction: Internment in Australia 1939–45" *Under Suspicion: Citizenship and Internment in Australia During the Second World War*, eds. Joan Beaumont, Ilma Martinuzzi O'Brien and Mathew Trinca (Canberra: National Museum of Australia Press, 2008), 3.

15 Italics in the text.

16 Rando, "Italo-Australians", 7.

17 Susan Temby, *The Bread with Seven Crusts* (Sydney: HarperCollins, 2002), 400. All subsequent references are to this edition and appear in parentheses in the text.

18 Rando, "Italo-Australians", 15.

in South Australia, results in what becomes a debilitating lifelong desire for revenge, even though the conditions were not all punitive: those in charge of what was referred to as a "model" camp did not force internees to work, although some did so under guard outside the wire. Many returned to their original occupations, thereby contributing to the "self-sufficient environment" (204). But the warning – that prisoners would be fired upon should they walk within six feet of the barbed-wire perimeter – precluded any thoughts of escape (204).

Roberto spends his leisure time learning to carve decorative inlaid wooden boxes and attending lectures on noteworthy topics delivered by professionals at what the inmates refer to as "*The College*" (209). He also admits in a letter to Carolena that even though the men "*roast*" inside the iron walls and are forced to occupy cramped and crowded spaces that cause tension and frustration, they are not "*ill-treated.*" Nevertheless, he regards the separation from his family as a form of "*mental torture*" (209), particularly since prisoners of war from South Australia enjoy regular visitations from their wives. Equally exasperating is the knowledge that the paper that has promised to give him and Carolena, as naturalised British subjects, "political rights, powers and privileges" (211), is worthless, since he is branded "a Fascist and an Alien" (211) and confined for an indefinite period. Although he admits there are "*some really ardent Fascist followers*" at the camp, the vast majority are, like him, politically neutral, but "*trapped like rats*" nevertheless (205). Roberto's belief, that the system of interning people with different political allegiances in the same camps is nothing but a "recipe for conflict and trouble" (210), proves both prescient and beneficial, as the murder of a non-fascist within the camp (mention of which also occurs in Temby's novel) threatens the authorities who, fearing that more assaults may ensue, release as many internees as possible, Roberto among them (239), thus allowing him to return home in 1943.

Both Watkins' and Burrows' novels explore the frequently overlooked problem of how women on the home front coped (or failed to cope) in the absence of their breadwinners. While Rando records that Military Intelligence did not consider women a security risk and therefore interned very few,[19] he nonetheless underscores that those left at home "remember the war years as times of fear and great hardship while some suffered malnutrition, sickness, and depression",[20] all of which Watkins' Carolena endures. As Rando further suggests, women were forced to "bear the brunt of hostility towards Italians".[21] Despite Carolena's status as a naturalised British subject and her daughter Wilma's as Australian-born, the local people refer to them as "Fascist dagos" (18) and school children bully her (226). Not surprisingly, Carolena concludes that "in this country, [they] will always be called foreigners" (227). She also resents that she must report to the police station each week for a "paltry Government handout" (18), particularly when the government

---

19 Rando, "Italo-Australians", 14.
20 Rando, "Italo-Australians", 14.
21 Rando, "Italo-Australians", 14.

cuts her already meagre rations in half because her adolescent son Jim has gone to work on another property to bolster the family coffers. Meanwhile, Carolena undertakes the arduous tasks of trying to look after the animals, the garden and the plants (18).

But in 1942, after the Japanese have attacked Pearl Harbor, Malaya and Singapore have fallen and Japanese forces are threatening New Guinea (many worry Australia will be next), Roberto implores the authorities to intern his family because he fears their isolation renders them unsafe. The authorities deny his request, however (215), but Carolena's apprehension at being around "the thousands of American troops whose recent entry into the war has turned the nearby town of Mareeba into a military zone" (222), is misguided, since both she and her son find them generous and friendly (a depiction not sustained in Burrows' novel). Carolena remains frightened, however, of their aeroplanes that drone in the sky day and night, particularly when they hear nearby crashes and the dropping of bombs; she is also terrified of Japanese incursion (216). Ultimately, Carolena's story reinforces that women were held as captive by fear and uncertainty as their men. Despairing that she might never see her husband again, she now considers Australia another "hostile place" (18), even though Roberto insists that he and his family are better off in Australia (277).

By this time, although the De Contis' situation has improved, with Roberto's tobacco farm once again thriving in part due to mechanisation, the couple's happiness is marred by the permanent rift between Roberto and his son Jim, who severs all contact because he claims his father had returned from incarceration a "different man" and he does not want to be a farmer like his father. Jim's application to join the Queensland Police Service, rejected because his father is an "ex-internee" (292), shows how the past continues to haunt the present. When Roberto dies a relatively young man in 1958, Carolena reflects that while "years of internment" had doubtlessly shortened his life, so, too, had the fact that he was never able to put his dark experience behind him.

Burrows' *A Stranger in My Street,* also about the plight of "local internees," is narrated by the twenty-one-year-old Meg Eaton, who works as secretary to the Crown Prosecutor in 1943 Perth. A mystery novel,[22] it opens with Meg's accidental discovery of the dead body of her neighbour Doreen Luca, a young wife and mother, which alters the course of her life. Meg's neighbours and the authorities charged with investigating the crime immediately assume that Doreen's husband Frank Luca, an Australian-born Italian serving with the Australian Navy,[23] has murdered his wife because it is common knowledge that she has been "carrying

---

22 Burrows is a prolific writer of mysteries set in wartime. See also *Taking a Chance* (Sydney: Pan Macmillan 2013) and *A Time of Secrets: For Love and Country* (Sydney: Pan Macmillan 2015). In several interviews, Burrows also reveals that the memories of her parents' postwar difficulties contributed to her decision to tell a wartime story. See Blanche Clark, "A Novel Way to Tell Parents' War Stories," *Brisbane Courier Mail*, 23 June 2012: 21–22, and Helen Crompton's "Mystery as Wartime Perth Kicks Up Heels," *West Australian*, 3 July 2012, n.p.

on" with the Yanks who have established a Catalina flying boat base in Perth. Meg insists, however, that the slim, handsome, and elegant Frank "adored" his wife, and that he is a "gentle" man, not the sort to murder anyone. When the investigation reveals that Doreen was stabbed in the heart with a knife, Frank's accusers once again claim that he is undoubtedly the murderer because Italians like to use knives, even though they are aware that Americans also carry them. Since the authorities – pathologists and detectives – remain convinced that Frank is responsible for his wife's death, they ignore evidence revealed in the autopsy and thereby place others' lives, including Meg's and Tom's (a returned veteran also present at the discovery of Doreen's body), at risk.

Outraged by the authorities' persistent avowals that all Italians are the same, Meg asserts that it is prejudicial comments such as these which have "lead to riots ... concentration camps, and wars".[24] Her sympathies stem from a childhood friendship with an Italian girl whose family was caught up in the 1934 Kalgoorlie riots (also mentioned in Temby's novel [218]) instigated by Australian miners angry that Italian men had taken their jobs.[25] In what can only be considered a cruel irony, those who rebuilt their lives after the riots then found themselves living behind barbed wire for an unknown period. As Saunders and Daniels remark (albeit in a more general context), "since they were not arrested or arraigned in a civil court, the very open-endedness and arbitrariness made the experience traumatic and bewildering",[26] an observation that also applies to Watkins' De Conti family.

By invoking details of the Kalgoorlie riots, Burrows emphasises that the rounding up of those deemed "enemy aliens" was not the product of a phenomenon that arose during the crisis of war, but was rather, as Ilma Martinuzzi O'Brien argues, "part of a much deeper racist attitude towards Italians which had increased between the wars".[27] Margaret Bevege's observation, that "[n]aturalized subjects of enemy origin were also regarded as a threat because they had built up assets and had the local knowledge that could be useful to the enemy",[28] is reflected in both Watkins' and Burrows' novels: by 1940, Roberto's tobacco farm is economically viable; Frank Luca's parents have owned a flourishing fruit shop in North Perth

---

23   By 1942, restrictions on who could serve Australia during a military crisis – a core mark of citizenship – had become more lenient.

24   Deborah Burrows, *A Stranger in My Street* (Sydney: Pan Macmillan Australia, 2012) 122. All subsequent references are to this edition and appear in parentheses in the text.

25   For more information on the Kalgoorlie riots (a similar one had occurred in 1919), see Sarah Gregson's "It All Started in the Mines? The 1934 Kalgoorlie Race Riots Revisited." *Labour History* 80 (May 2001).

26   Kay Saunders and Roger Daniels, "Introduction: Ethnicity and Citizenship" *Alien Justice: Wartime Internment in Australia and North America*, eds. Kay Saunders and Roger Daniels (St. Lucia: University of Queensland Press, 2000), xvii.

27   Ilma Martinuzzi O'Brien, "Internments in Australia During World War Two: The life Histories of Citizenship and Exclusion" *Enemy Aliens: The Internment of Italian Migrants in Australia During the Second World War* (Bacchus Marsh, Vic: Connor Court Publishing, 2005), 25.

28   Margaret Bevege, *Behind Barbed Wire: Internment in Australia During World War Two* (St. Lucia: University of Queensland Press, 1993), 154.

for many years; and Guiseppe Gangemi has spent the last twenty years building up a successful construction company in Perth. In clear violation of the principle of *habeas corpus*, the authorities, like those in Watkins' novel, offer no reasons or documentation for the Italians' arrest. Compared to the powers-that-be in other countries, those in Australia appear to have been particularly zealous in rounding up Italians. Rando, for example, observes that Great Britain interned only 2 per cent of its Italian population and the USA less than 1 per cent:[29] somewhere around 10 per cent of Italian males in Australia were confined. These figures were, as Martinuzzi O'Brien observes, a significantly "higher proportion than one would expect in a country so far from Italy and the European theatre of war".[30]

In Burrows' novel, as in Watkins', women and children, also identified as "others," encounter numerous difficulties and restrictions, including separation from their innocent loved ones and financial hardship. Mrs Gangmei, for example, does not earn enough money to support her three children, so her son, like Watkins' Jim, drops out of school at fourteen to work in a factory. Like Carolena De Conti, she worries that such employment will affect his future. Doreen Luca is another equally disadvantaged mother: with her husband in the navy, both of his parents interned and hers dead, she is obliged to take up full-time work, but then must send her daughter to be cared for in an orphanage. Doreen's work as a hospital administrator brings her into contact with American and Australian black-market operations; before she can make good on her threat to reveal what she knows, two guilty Americans kill her.

In making the Yanks responsible for her death, Burrows' novel harkens back to Cusack and James' *Come in Spinner*. In both novels, while Australians initially welcome the Yanks with open arms as their saviours, before long, the glamour of the polite, charming, fun-loving Yanks who know how to treat women soon fades, as many are revealed to be drug addicted, violent towards women, and even murderers. Meanwhile, the Italians – good-humoured, hard-working, law-abiding, and loyal in times of crises – are all exemplary citizens. As Saunders pointedly stresses, they were also innocent: "[n]one of those interned were ever convicted of espionage, sabotage or aiding and abetting the enemy".[31]

Both texts, which document biases against Italians in Australia during World War II, unmask the stories of those whose experiences have been either neglected or problematically framed in the historical record. Challenges such as these are vital because, as Saunders and Daniels remark, at the time of their publications, "no major Australian museum has tackled an extensive exhibition on internment. The Australian War Memorial, the prestigious institution in Canberra which contains

---

29 Rando, "Italo-Australians", 18. Of the 7,711 "enemy aliens" interned (including Japanese and Germans), the vast majority – 4,727 – were Italian (3).
30 Martinuzzi O'Brien, "Internments", 15.
31 Kay Saunders, "'Taken Away to Be Shot?': The Process of Incarceration in Australia in World War II", *Alien Justice*, 166.

both the national shrine to Australians fallen in battle as well as a major museum displaying Australia's involvement in war in the twentieth century, does not acknowledge the question of widespread internment in either World War I or II".[32] They add that "when the Australian government mounted an extraordinarily expensive 'Australia Remembers 1945–1995' commemoration to mark the jubilee of the end of the World War II," there were no acknowledgements or apologies "for wrongs committed in a war supposedly to preserve liberty and justice. The past was selectively recast; so that all these values of patriotic imperialism and national heroism were ironically resuscitated once again as the conservative British derived values were vaunted".[33] Moreover, as Beaumont cogently argues,

> for most internees the war experience was negative, involving loss of liberty, dignity and (often hard won) social and civic standing. Loss is, of course, an integral part of war, particularly a war on the scale of the Second World War. But personal loss can be invested with meaning if, as was the case with the men and women of the Australian Military Forces (AMF) who served and died in battle, it can be seen by them and their families as contributing to victory and making the nation more secure. The tragedy of internment is that it cannot even be said to have done that. Rather, it served to assuage the anxieties of an Australian population who were already predisposed to an exclusive understanding of citizenship and who, in the crisis of war, turned easily (if temporarily) against those whose "crime" was their ethnicity, race, or cultural difference.[34]

These issues, particularly the prejudices that the Italian POWs in Goldbloom's novel face, find echoes in Watkins' and Burrows' fictions, even though the circumstances vary considerably. As Alan Fitzgerald remarks, Australians were "suffering a severe shortage of manpower" during the war and thus needed the physical labour the "overseas internees" could provide.[35] According to the Alcorsos, the internees were treated much better than the Australians confined by the Japanese:

> Naturally all were men, and it appears that most were fit and in good health which was maintained by fair treatment through their confinement (31). These POWs

---

32   Saunders and Daniels, "Introduction", xix. This is no longer true, as in the time since significant exhibitions and release of documents now cover internment camps and civilian internees (Australian War Memorial, *Civilian internees* 2020).

33   Saunders and Daniels, "Introduction", xix. Rando comments that numerous requests for a formal apology that would confirm that what happened to Italians was "wrong" were ignored until 1991, when "both houses of federal parliament passed unanimous motions of apology" (Rando, "Italo-Australians", 20). Because recognition at state levels also did not come until the 1990s, Rando argues that it is "perhaps no accident that many accounts of internment were not published until this time" (20).

34   Beaumont, "Introduction", 8.

35   Alan Fitzgerald, *The Italian Farming Soldiers: Prisoners of War in Australia 1941–1947* (Melbourne: Melbourne University Press, 1981), 2.

also managed to thrive while in captivity: only 101 of the 18,432 POWs died in Australia, 85 from natural causes, 15 by suicide and one was shot by an Australian officer. By contrast, more than nearly one-third of the 22,516 Australian POWs held by the Japanese died of the disease, were killed or drowned at sea between 1942 and 1945. Many of those who survived the camps were maimed for life.[36]

The Alcorsos add that although "trade unions protested against this use of cheap foreign labour, and threatened industrial action in rural areas," complaints that several of these novels raise, "the minimum POW wage was sufficiently strong" to resist any political unrest. They conclude that the labour of the Italian POWs contributed significantly towards the Australian economy during the war years.[37]

Goldbloom's *The Paperbark Shoe* tells the story of Agrippa Toad, a misshapen, five-foot tall farmer unable to enlist because there are no uniforms small enough to fit him; forced to remain on the land, he requests the aid of two POWs to help plough, seed and shear on his property located near Wyalkatchem, a small town about 200 kilometres northeast of Perth. Although it is hard to believe Goldbloom's claim that her quirky characters are "real," she stresses in her dedication that she derived them from her mother's stories about "Joan and Anthony and the Italians." The opening page of the novel further affirms that "There are people alive today in Wyalkatchem who can tell you stories about when the Italians came to the wheatbelt" (9) and that "fifty-years later, they'll still be tut-tutting over the way those Toads carried on with the enemy" (9). One of those so accused is Toad's wife Gin, who suffers from a complex genetic disorder called albinism, defined as "the total absence of pigment in the skin" (20). Gin's hair is "bone" white, her eyesight typically poor, particularly in sunshine. The couple has two feral children, Alf and Mudsey, but both parents – especially Gin – continue to grieve over the death of their first-born daughter Joan, also an "albino," who died some years ago. The thirty-year-old Gin, who narrates the story from a retrospective point of view, is six months' pregnant when the two POWs – Antonio, a robust, handsome, forty-year-old shoemaker with a wife and five children in Italy who was captured in Bardia, and John, a twenty-two-year-old labourer captured in Tobruk (38) – arrive to work on the farm.

Although members of farming communities such as Wyalkatchem were aware that they needed the "overseas internees" to help run their properties, most were apprehensive about this new "enemy within." Gin, for example, is initially "afraid of those oversexed men we'd read about, rapists in tight little bodies with hot Latin eyes, men who were capable of anything" (13) and worries that the POWs will "kill [them] while [they] are sleeping" or turn out to be "baby-eaters" (14). Meanwhile, Toad, jealous of the POWs' stature and obvious machismo, deems them "fascist pigs, cowards, and … lowly slaves in the Australian hinterland" (15). The

---

36 Alcorso and Alcorso, "Italians in Australia", 31.
37 Alcorso and Alcorso, "Italians in Australia", 32.

women in the community fear that the POWS are murderers who "killed their sons over in Libya" (9); the local men regard the POWs as dim-witted; and the military police, obsessed with the POWs' sexuality, caution Gin never to be alone with these "animals" (134). Those who claim the POWs are "spies or saboteurs" make Gin laugh, for they are "a week's journey from anywhere strategic" (52); moreover, the Toads have no telephone, no electricity, and a generator-operated wireless that works only sporadically (52). Gin also realises that none of the POWs could survive if they attempted to escape, since everyone knows the thousands of miles of "uninhabited coast" are "patrolled by sharks," and that those who have "strayed" into "the appalling red desert" have "melted into the earth" (52).

Although the government mandates that the POWs wear "freakish magenta army uniforms as a sign of their inferior status," (13) Gin soon learns there is nothing inferior about Antonio or John, who are more highly skilled, talented and cultured than the locals. The POWs quickly build themselves a clean and comfortable home much better than the one Toad built for his family; they know how to fix and repair machinery; and once the olive trees they have planted mature, often whip up delicious spaghetti dinners. To Gin's immense pleasure – she is an exceptionally talented pianist whose albinism has prevented her from winning an international competition – Antonio can read music. Both he and John are gifted vocalists who know how to use their glorious tenor voices to advantage and are often heard singing, in rich harmony, selections from Verdi's *La Traviata*. Antonio, a man who loves children (as most POWs in these novels appear to), is especially kind to Gin's offspring, who have "never met people who knelt down to speak to them" (31), gave them chocolates, or made them toys. Antonio is also a superb athlete: at a town fair that farmers have brought their POWs to illegally, female spectators admire Antonio's fit body, dark skin and eyes, as well as his prowess on the football field: one even declares he could "put his shoes under her bed any day" (220).

Gin is more than willing to let Antonio "put his shoes under her bed" because he is the only person who has ever treated her with any dignity or respect. Her father, who sailed away to Gallipoli after one glimpse of his daughter, died a gruesome war-related death; her emotionally (and perhaps sexually) abusive stepfather tormented her with stories of the treatment of "albinos" in circuses, and then, after she etched the words "Don't touch" onto her breasts, signed her into Graylands, a lunatic asylum. Even though Gin finds Toad's crudity appalling, she accepts his proposal because it liberates her from the mental institution. But Toad proves to be, if possible, an even more dismal lover and husband than those who routinely appear in Australian women's fictions. He also takes Gin for granted, expecting her to do much of the backbreaking work on the property, even while pregnant. Gin has no illusions that their marriage is anything but one of convenience: she and Toad have nothing in common except "the basic need for companionship and a joint wish for protection from the eyes and comments of the people of Wyalkatchem" (23).

By contrast, Antonio pays attention to what Gin says; assists with domestic chores (which he does not define as "hers"); transcribes music into large format so she can read it easily; recklessly and relentlessly flirts with her by bringing her flowers and grappa and serenading her with Italian arias; and helps deliver Gin's baby in a manner far less perilous and crude than Toad's in the past. Antonio also insists that she move to Italy (she starts learning Italian immediately) and seduces her by using words that are surely music to her ears: she is, he claims, "like the Venus ... like the Maria in the church, smooth white marble, perfect. There is nothing more beautiful" (126). After the birth of her son (whom she names Anthony), she embarks upon a sexual relationship with Antonio, which she justifies because she has seen Toad and John making what she quaintly refers to as "lad's love" (114).

Relationships such as Gin's and Antonio's were, of course, risky. According to Alan Fitzgerald, although POW camp orders "prohibited sexual intercourse between POWs and Australian women" and the "Australian Army made every effort to prevent liaisons forming between the Italians and the wives and daughters of their employers, it could not cope with the amorous nature of some of these lonely young men nor the compliance of some Australian women".[38] For her part, Gin fails to recognise that what she and her children offer Antonio is essentially what Bob Moore and Ken Fedorowich refer to as a means of "combating the loneliness and isolation of captivity. For those who had families in Italy, these friendships provided a useful coping strategy as they were one way of trying to salvage a bit of normality".[39] Fitzgerald concludes that it is "hardly surprising that, with girlfriends and wives half a world away, some of the Italians would be susceptible to romance".[40] Gin also fails to comprehend that, as Dorcas Grimmett comments, while the prisoners enjoyed "a certain amount of freedom and were well looked after, as time passed, they became increasingly lonely and longed for their own countries".[41] Moore and Fedorowich add that prisoners tended to regard capture as "a humiliation and a slur on their masculinity"; moreover, "reports from home served to heighten ... feelings of inadequacy and impotence".[42] As well, "incarcerated in foreign lands miles from home with no immediate prospect of repatriation, they were unable to fulfill traditional patriarchal functions such as breadwinner, protector of the family or role models for children".[43]

---

38 Fitzgerald, *The Italian Farming Soldier*, 129.

39 Bob Moore, and Kent Fedorowich, *The British Empire and Its Italian Prisoners of War, 1940–1947* (London: Palgrave, 2002), 201.

40 Fitzgerald, *The Italian Farming Soldier*, 34.

41 Dorcas Grimmett, *We Remember: The Italian Prisoners of War, 1944/45* (Kingaroy Qld: Self-published, 2001), 9.

42 Moore and Fedorowich, *The British Empire*, 5–6. See also Dale Turner, *The Farmer's Wife* (Xlibris, 2011), 108; Temby, *The Bread with Seven Crusts*, 405.

43 Moore and Fedorowich, *The British Empire*, 5–6.

But according to Fitzgerald, the POWs enjoyed "a reasonably happy time" until they began to receive news that "the fighting in Italy had reached areas where their families lived".[44] Until he receives such news, Antonio has not worried about the safety of his family because, prior to leaving for war, he had joined forces with numerous other Italians who, alarmed by the fascist atrocities they witnessed in Lucca, moved their families to what they assumed would be safe refuge in the remote village of Sant'Anna. Nevertheless, Antonio receives an alarming letter from his wife that informs him that she is so frightened of being raped by either the Germans or the Americans or the owner of the place where the family stays (202) that she has taken classes in "the art of self-defence" (202) that have taught her tactics to save herself, including "the fine art of strangling a man" (202). But at this point, Antonio merely downplays his wife's assessment of danger; he also resents her bitter comments that he is well fed and clothed when she and her children are starving and wearing threadbare clothes, and continues to pursue Gin.

Although Antonio and John have often expressed their frustration with Australians' lack of geographical knowledge and nonchalant approach to war, only when they are allowed to watch a newsreel at the town fair on the battle of San Pietro that graphically depicts old people and children *actually* dying (228), does their inability to come to their families' aid and their resentment at being prisoners of war when Italy has surrendered to the Allies become all-consuming; consequently, Antonio loses all interest in Gin. Undeterred by Antonio's sudden neglect, Gin discounts the agonising grief he suffers after a telegram informs him that the Germans have killed his entire family, followed shortly after by a letter from relatives that describes the murder of his wife and children in grisly detail. Under intense pain, he lashes out verbally and blames Gin for the deaths of his family and then violently beats her with his hands and "pieces of fractured wood" (258). But nothing Antonio says or does diminishes Gin's belief that Antonio still loves her: in fact, she can "hardly keep herself from smiling" because she "wear[s] the uniform of the conqueror" (252). (Goldbloom's use of military language is superb throughout.) Once he has nothing left to live for, Antonio asks Gin for a gun and bullets and disappears into the bush. Having remained convinced that Antonio is alive and well in Italy, she carries on with her plans to travel there (secretly funding her journey by playing piano in the local hotel) and feels certain that she will stumble across Antonio on the streets of Lucca or Sant'Anna.

Elizabeth Webby's comments that "in the final chapter, with its abrupt switch from … grotesque comedy … to the historical realism of the massacre of Antonio's wife and children, we are in very different fictional terrain. Gin is forced to reassess Antonio's feelings for her, but the reader is forced to question the overall success of Goldbloom's novel", are fitting because the shift to realism, at times also resembling travel writing, is admittedly disconcerting.[45] But only Gin's eventual awareness of

---

44 Fitzgerald, *The Italian Farming Soldier*, 111.
45 Elizabeth Webby, "The Year's Work in Fiction" *Westerly* 55 no.1 (2010), 129.

the magnitude of this carnage can bring home to her how much Antonio mourned the loss of his family. Even though she has heard Antonio's version of his dreadful war experiences and knows that John's recurring nightmares indicate that he suffers from what would be today considered post-traumatic stress disorder, and she listens to Toad's tale of his cruel treatment by his father, a World War I veteran who wore his uniform every day of his life and demanded obedience from his wife and offspring, Gin has laboured under the impression that the pain of others was secondary to her own.

Shortly after arriving at the site of the 12 August 1944, massacre at the Tuscan village of Sant'Anna di Stazzema, Gin learns that during an operation against the Italian resistance movement, the Nazis murdered 560 local villagers and refugees (including 130 children and the local priest). The villagers were utterly defenceless since the Italian men – partisans – had fled because they thought the Germans were looking for them. Incredibly, after the Nazis had killed every old man and woman and child in the village and burned down every house, shop and church, they sat down to a lunch of sausage and cheese, which they ate "in the warm glow from the houses" (277). Exercising inconceivable forethought, they had brought along a musician because they thought that the "tinkling" of his hurdy gurdy would "keep it all civilized" (276), and apparently it did, as some Nazis sang, while others enjoyed drinks of brandy: only a few were "sick, quietly, in the bushes" (277).

Although Gin tries to absorb the family's torment vicariously by sleeping in the ruins of their house, she gleans most about the events of that horrendous day from a small boy who describes "everything he saw, everything that happened that summer when Italy was invaded" (270). As Susan Sontag observes, while "harrowing photographs of atrocities inevitably lose their power to shock", "narratives can make us understand".[46] Only through narrative, she argues, can we come to "an awareness," or an "enlarged sense of how much suffering caused by human wickedness [exists] in the world".[47] In his naivety, after telling Gin his gruesome story, the boy wonders if her hair "turned white from the pain of this knowledge. From *feeling*" (270), a notion that seems wide of the mark, but is not, since Gin has never comprehended how much she has suppressed her own feelings about Antonio's grief over the murder of his family:

> I had never wanted to feel anything, to lay *feeling* on my heart and let it sink its claws deeply into the bloody beating muscle at my core. Once, long ago, all this was just a story. A love story. About an Italian man and the albino woman who loved him. Now I see Antonio's wife and his children and his village and his existence. I *feel* their reality. Now the story is alive and true and terrible. (271)

---

46 Susan Sontag, *Regarding the Pain of Others* (New York: Picador/Farrar, Strauss and Giroux, 2003), 80.

47 Sontag, *Regarding the Pain of Others*, 104.

Gin also reaches two other key conclusions: that Antonio was wrong to accuse her of killing his family, and that he never loved her, a cruel fact that she learns when Antonio's lecherous brother informs her that "Gingilla" is not, as she believed, a term of endearment, but a word that connotes "plaything" or "toy" (267). Gin now sees what others have for a long time: that she has been delusional, that Italy could have never become the home she always longed for. She now knows that she must return to Australia, to "take hold of what is truly [hers]:" she must "take it up in [her] hands and do not let it go this time. Do not let it go" (279).

Joanne Carroll's *The Italian Romance: A Novel*, also about the "overseas POWs," tells a story that bears several resemblances to *The Paperbark Shoe*. Here, Lilian Malone, a young married Australian woman from an unnamed rural setting in New South Wales falls in love with Antonio Lucca, an Italian prisoner of war, who encourages her to accompany him to Italy. Carroll's Antonio, like Goldbloom's Antonio, also learns that his northern Italian family suffered at the hands of the Germans, that they transported his Jewish wife Sonia to Auschwitz and captured his adolescent son Gianni. Lilian's husband, the farmer-cum-Anzac Bernie Malone is, like Toad, devastated by his wife's determination to leave him and their daughter Francesca and pleads with her to stay. Both Bernie and Antonio had enlisted to escape unhappy marriages, but there the similarities end. Carroll's Lilian and Antonio (Nio) truly love each other and when the novel opens, have enjoyed a long and happy marriage in the richly cultured city of Rome, although guilt haunts both: Lilian for the daughter she left behind over fifty years ago, and Nio, who remains convinced that Gianni, the son he had forsaken, is alive.

Carroll's novel contains three skilfully interwoven plotlines. It begins in Rome, sometime in the 1990s, with Lilian, an internationally known writer, thrilled that her daughter Francesca suddenly attempts to contact her at a social gathering. Francesca, who stumbled across a photo of her mother on a book jacket, is conducting research for her doctoral dissertation on Australian artists (but not writers) who live in exile in Italy. Although Lilian knows virtually nothing about her daughter's life (she has never returned to Australia), she nevertheless hopes both for a peaceful reconciliation and some assurance that she will never lose her daughter again. Francesca bears too much resentment towards her mother for there to be any satisfying resolution of their relationship, however.

While the story of the fraught relationship between estranged mother and daughter occupies the largest part of the novel, the second plotline takes the form of a novel-within-a-novel that Lilian is currently writing. Titled *Romanzo*, it begins in northern Italy in 1943; loosely based on the letters of Leah, Nio's wife, which Lilian has only recently discovered, the novel may be, as Shirley Walker suggests, another attempt "to make amends for the past".[48] Narrated from the point of view of Francesco's (Nio's) fictional Jewish-Italian wife Sonia (Leah), it relays her concerns

---

48   Shirley Walker, "'Showdown in Rome.' Review of Joanne Carroll's *The Italian Romance: A Novel*", *Australian Book Review* no. 272 (June–July 2005), 46.

that her husband, who has fallen out of love with her and is now a prisoner of war in England, sends only occasional cryptic letters that do nothing to assuage her fears for the safety of her and Gianni, which have steadily increased since the Germans sent her well-connected, wealthy, Mussolini-supporter father to work in a factory and her brother and his family to a concentration camp. She is afraid because even though Mussolini has been deposed, the fascists continue to shoot people. Sonia and Gianni are relieved when Jack, an English soldier who has escaped from a camp in Germany and has fallen in love with Sonia (and she with him), offers to help them escape in the woods.

The third plotline begins in 1939, on the eve of the outbreak of war, with the local inhabitants debating Australia's role in the war. While the women express their hopes for a peaceful solution, Lilian's husband Bernie declares emphatically that "the Aussies took care of them the last time. Our boys will sort them out again, if need be".[49] Although Bernie appears eager to fight, he enlists primarily because of Lilian's refusal (or more accurately inability) to spend her time cooking and cleaning while he believes that "when a woman came into a man's life, she gave him home" (85). But the war proves to be her saviour: once Bernie signs up, Lilian fulfils a lifelong dream by landing a job on the local newspaper and training as a cadet reporter. Having found a meaningful and challenging job, Lilian is no longer listless, no longer sits around staring into space or daydreaming, but "works like a trooper" (108) devising original topics and clever angles for stories; she tells her editor that she now aspires to be a war correspondent, to be "at the coalface" (111).

Like Goldbloom's Toad and most Australian men in women's war fiction, Bernie has not a romantic bone in his body. Upon returning from combat in North Africa, he refuses to spend a night in a Sydney hotel that Lilian has arranged but insists on returning home to his mother and father. On the train to their farm, he ignores Lilian and talks only to his mates. Thus, it is no wonder that Lilian succumbs immediately to the charms of the handsome, olive-skinned Antonio, an Italian prisoner of war captured in North Africa, who utters more amorous sentiments during their brief first encounter than Bernie has throughout their entire marriage. This "Capitano da Lucca," who always speaks and writes "like a poet" (174), is a well-educated man of letters (126). In *Romanzo*, Lilian describes him as a man who comes from "noble Italian blood" (224).

Significantly, unlike Bernie, who has both a disdain for the intellect of and a firm belief that women's only function is to serve men and children, Antonio encourages Lilian to write. He offers constructive criticism of her prose but also insists that she must not stay with that "boy" Bernie because she will "never be alive. [She] will never write" (282). And in contrast to Goldbloom's false lover Antonio, Carroll's Antonio means what he says when he tells Lilian that she is "everything

---

49   Joanne Carroll, *The Italian Romance: A Novel* (St. Lucia, Queensland: University of Queensland Press, 2005), 36. All subsequent references are to this edition and appear in parentheses in the text.

[he] want[s]. Everything. Every fantasy [he's] ever had, that's [her]" (282). Antonio is everything that Lilian wants as well, but he is also everything that she needs. After the birth of Francesca, Lilian is depressed, unwilling to get out of bed, unable to care for her daughter: realising that she can only "come alive" with Antonio, she secretly makes plans to join him on the ship to Italy.

The opposition to Lilian's desire to leave her husband comes from her mother and mother-in-law, who like women in earlier World War II texts believe that women's roles were destined to be as wives and mothers. (Oddly, both Lilian's father and father-in-law are far more understanding of her desire to leave an unsatisfying marriage.) Lilian's mother tells her that her decision to leave is a "bloody thing" to do to a man who has been "off fighting" (324), and then betrays her by informing Bernie of Lilian's and Francesca's whereabouts. When Bernie finds Lilian and begs her to stay with him, she refuses; but after he breaks down and tells her about the atrocities he witnessed in New Guinea (343), how much his mates mattered to him then, as well as how much he has longed to return to his wife and daughter, she recognises his desperate need to have someone to love and care for. In an extreme act of bravery and selflessness, she leaves Francesca with her father and departs for Italy with Antonio.

Because the depiction of Italian POWs is not the focus of Carroll's novel, it provides little information about their experiences in Australia, but none of the prisoners complain about their confinement in control centres, nor offer impressions of the country, or comment on the strangeness of Australian customs. Antonio merely thanks Mussolini (whom he dislikes) for giving him a trip to "[this] beautiful country, free, gratis, and for nothing" (175). Although the authorities refer occasionally to "enemy aliens" or "dagos" or to the presence of "Fascists" (124) within the camp walls, most of their interactions with the prisoners are congenial. The commanding officer of the camp, who believes in keeping the men busy, declares that the "Eyeties" are good builders and gestures towards the mess hall as evidence (118). These POWs are, like those in the other novels, affable: several speak passable English (119); others appear keen to adopt Australian lingo. Like Goldbloom's prisoners, Carroll's are musicians whose band performances Lilian notes "ford the boundaries between the two groups" (123). Typically, the men's quarters are, like those in Goldbloom and Temby, "nice and tidy" (198).

Temby's *The Bread with Seven Crusts* offers a detailed account of "overseas internees" confinement both within the camps and on farms (as well as offering a great deal of insight in the Australian way of life). By all accounts, the conditions within the camps were as enervating as Fitzgerald noted, with one prisoner describing the camp as "an asylum of non-violent lunatics … [where] there is a continuous struggle of the nervous system against the fence".[50] Life on the farms, by comparison, subjected men to strenuous physical activity, but offered limited

---

50   Fitzgerald, *The Italian Farming Soldiers*, 126.

freedom. Fitzgerald also observes (as does Temby), that on Sundays prisoners were permitted to visit other prisoners, mainly after church, provided they wore their magenta-coloured uniforms.[51] The Alcorsos caution, however, that although "it appears that most Italian POWs enjoyed adequate work and living conditions whilst on the farms, their apparent contentment and enthusiasm for farm work needs to be understood in the context of their only other alternative: the prison camp".[52] As Temby's central character, the Italian officer Giuseppe Lazaro notes, men were homesick and longed to return home, so that "at the prison camp there was endless talk about loved homes in town, city and country" (86).

In the opening chapter, Giuseppe laments that he has spent two years wasting away at the Northam control centre in Western Australia, where he was sent after Australians captured his battalion at the Battle of Bardia on the border of Egypt and Libya in January 1941. Although the magenta prisoner's uniform makes him feel "bare, insubstantial, less than a man" (306), like Watkins' Roberto, he does not complain of mistreatment, in part because the commandant is, like his grandfather, "rotund and good-hearted" (7). Rather, he finds that most tension in the camp arises from fractious relationships between men with competing political beliefs: he himself is shunned by other officers because he has only a "lukewarm enthusiasm" (8) for Mussolini. In order to escape "the barbed wire disease" – crushing boredom, crowded conditions, political differences and animosities and disillusionment with the cause[53] – that ultimately drove his best friend and talented painter Filippo to suicide, he volunteers to work on Grey Temma Farm. The commandant warns Giuseppe that working on a farm may prove difficult because the Geneva Convention "absolves officers from work" (8), so any attempt to work with other ranks on equal terms could create problems. Giuseppe gladly takes the risk because he knows the only cure for the disease is "release into the world" (7), freedom from the feeling of being "suspended in a bell jar in space" (7). Two other volunteers sent to Grey Temma Farm are also eager to escape the confines of the prison: Enzo, a fun-loving and able-bodied young father from the Abruzzi mountains knows nothing about farming but is willing to learn; whereas Carlo, a young, angry conscript and hard-core Mussolini supporter deliberately sets out to offend all humans.

On the long dusty journey to their farms, some of the other captives fear that they will be guarded by tall Australians like the "fierce and bloodthirsty" (5) soldiers who came at them during the Battle of Bardia "in never ending waves through machine gun fire" (5). Giuseppe is not frightened of the enemy on his home turf and assures his compatriots that "Australians are Europeans like themselves and that the Aborigines are peaceful and few" (5). According to the Alcorsos,

---

51   Fitzgerald, *The Italian Farming Soldiers*, 94.
52   Alcorso and Alcorso "Italians in Australia", 32.
53   Fitzgerald, *The Italian Farming Soldiers*, 93.

Italian POWs were [also] valued by the Australian government over and above German POWs precisely because it was felt that the former made better workers. Hence in 1944 the War Cabinet dropped its earlier acceptance of German POWs and from then on accepted only Italians.[54]

The Italians' long history as loyal workers in Australia has induced the farm's owner, Max Nash, to apply for Italian rather than Japanese or German prisoners (196) because he "knew their ways," and that "they worked fast and for very little" (196).

Since he had left Italy willingly and with no intention of returning (86), Giuseppe is receptive to the notion of what it might mean to inhabit a new settler culture and curious to learn why Australians appear to have such a special relationship with their seemingly hostile land. Initially, he finds the extreme contrasts in landscape – the "lush vertical geography" (428) of Lake Como near the Swiss border where he grew up versus the "dry horizontals" (429) of Australia – disquieting. His home, "on the side of the mountain looking into the valley was the Garden of Eden, more beautiful, the most beautiful" (86). But he also recognises that "the beauty of a place isn't everything" (355): "it comes at a price" and may even be useless because "You cannot eat scenery or build houses with it" (355). Having been confined so long behind barbed wire, space and peace are vital to his survival: on his first glimpse of the farm at dawn, "he felt free for the first time since he had been drafted into the army" (21). Australia, he now comprehends, is not the "place-less" land most Europeans thought it was, if only because it lacked their geopolitical definition. But he believes that even if "there is no beauty" (86) in the flat, arid, Australian land, it "offered a better life because there were not more people depending upon it than it could sustain" (355).

Giuseppe's growing love for Australia stems in part from his miserable childhood in Italy, where his deeply devout mother had taken "her joy and her life from the spiritual world. The world of the dead" (85). Fortunately, his grandparents had taught him that the living were also worth loving. His cheerful nonna, who was "alive in this world, not waiting for the next" (85), introduced Giuseppe to the worlds of history, politics, law and music, and his nonno to fishing and sailing. Giuseppe's father also convinced his son that he had "some intellectual ability" and must therefore gain a "passport to a better life" (87) by obtaining a university education, which he does by studying structural engineering in Trieste. But here, in this prison of a "new secular world" (9), Giuseppe "hopes to find a life without need of holy vision, without relying on the help of the dead" (9). He is "delighted that in Australia, the saints are alive. They play football and tennis. God is a cricketer. A great batsman with many runs on the scoreboard. The Holy Virgin is nowhere to be found. *Joie de vivre* here is *joie d'esprit* there" (85).

But the promise in the land he discerned early on also promises to be hard earned, the people pitted in "an obstinate battle against nature" (9), with nature

---

54 Alcorso and Alcorso, "Italians in Australia", 32.

often the victor. For example, Hal Fischer, a young neighbouring farmer who intended to fund his university education by means of a bumper crop finds "that grasshoppers had devoured both his crop and his opportunities" (60). Yet as Giuseppe also observes, there were people like Max who "loved" the place even though strangers might find it inhabitable and never believed that it "was unsuitable for agriculture" (428). Although Giuseppe comes to understand that a farmer's life amounted to "a game played with the elements, a gladiator sport" (429), he nonetheless values it because "it was a land that allowed few people to exist on it but rewarded those who did with freedom of spirit" (429).

Giuseppe also becomes aware, as Libby Robin writes, that "Australia is a new nation within an old continent".[55] When he queries the absence of Aboriginal people or questions their interpretations of constellations or rock paintings, Max utters only condescending or patronising comments that indicate that he knows and cares little about their spirituality or, as Robin might suggest, he does not seem to have any "increasing reasons to respect and value the wisdom of the other Australians who have dwelt in the arid zone for 50,000 years" .[56] In another demonstration of his ignorance, as someone raised in a "new world," Max reveals that he knows nothing about the history of his own property beyond the twenty years he has lived on it (147). But when Giuseppe gets a glimpse of the Indigenous Australians who live in crude shanties on the edge of town and probes why they do not live in the town, Max explains that they receive only "keep," not wages for the work they do, so they have no choice. Suddenly, Giuseppe realises "that there is something worse than being a prisoner of war" (297).

Much as Giuseppe is intrigued by the inhospitality of the harsh land, he is equally captivated by the hospitality of Max and his mother. Temby's novel replicates historical fact here, for as Kevin comments, interviews with former POWs reveal that "friendships often developed between the employing families and the POWs. Some of the workers were included in family holidays and many shared with them their evening family dinner".[57] In another marker of the goodwill that existed until after war's end, the host families offer the prisoners parcels of clothing to take back to their families or present them with small gifts (426). The Alcorsos comment that "it seems that generally the relationships between the two groups were friendly and often warm. The Italians were typically treated in an egalitarian manner, and often almost like family members",[58] which also reflects the views expressed in Temby's novel. Mrs Nash and her son uphold the much-vaunted Australian principle of egalitarianism by allowing the prisoners to sleep in their house, a belief that further extends to relationships between landowner and prisoner: Max, for example, "smiles and speaks to the prisoners without contempt

---

55   Robin, *How a Continent Created a Nation*, 1.
56   Robin, *How a Continent Created a Nation*, 100.
57   Kevin, "Teaching Heritage", 2.
58   Alcorso and Alcorso, "Italians in Australia", 33.

and with friendliness" (15), and while Max expects everyone to work hard, he works the longest and hardest (34). Giuseppe is surprised to learn that the principle of egalitarianism extends even to equal pay, that in Australia, "it is possible to have the right to proper payment for hard work" (137).

While Max and his mother insist upon being on a first-name basis with the prisoners, the Italians are somewhat taken aback to learn that they expect the prisoners to respond to anglicised names – Enzo becomes Vince, Carlo Charlie, and Giuseppe Lazaro Joe Lazarus. But instead of being insulted or regarding the re-naming a manifestation of colonial privilege, Guiseppe believes that the Nashes are merely attempting to be inclusive and "decides that a change of name is no sacrifice if he is to be released into the world" (3). (Hereafter, for the sake of brevity, I will also refer to the prisoners as Joe and Vince.) As the only one of the POWs who speaks good English, Joe is pleased to find that Max and his mother are curious about the prisoners' backgrounds, their capture and their opinions about the war in Europe. As Fitzgerald observes, because men had the chance to work with civilians away from barbed-wire camps, they began to feel more normal than they had in years.[59] In an echo of the Alcorsos' views, Joe feels grateful for freedom and "a family of sorts," which is more than "he could have expected" (68).

Like the Italian prisoners of war in the texts already discussed who are in every way commendable, so, too, are Joe and Vince. Joe has perfected his English by studying in London and is far more cultured than his Australian counterparts. He reads the poetry of Leopardi and Gabriele d'Annunzio, plays Beethoven and Mendelssohn on the piano, as well as contemporary works by Noël Coward and Cole Porter (33). Both Vince and Joe are well-mannered, polite, good-humoured and tidy, qualities that quickly earn the respect of Max and his mother. Both undertake a variety of arduous, even "cruel" work without complaint. Although Vince works with his hands and thus contributes to the conventional view that he is a typical Italian, he has tremendous stamina and works like a "demon." Joe works equally hard, but his quick thinking and risk-taking during a bushfire saves lives and turns him into a local hero. Charlie is the only Italian of bad character to appear in any of these texts, but when he attempts to start his own "war in the wheatbelt" (62) by stealing sticks of gelignite, Max rushes him to the control centre, where he remains an unpleasant troublemaker.

While the Nashes find the Italians polite, cheerful, and having fine work ethics, the townspeople reject Joe's engineering expertise when rebuilding the town hall damaged after a severe dust storm because they believe that the Italians "could be tolerated as manual labourers ... as people with knowledge and experience they did not exist" (149). Even though Joe's advice proves invaluable, a police officer puts Vince's injury in a farming accident down to "inexperience" (251) comparable to Italians' lack of "stamina" in North Africa (251). He also insists that Australians

---

59   Fitzgerald, *The Italian Farming Soldiers*, 94.

would not be so well treated in Italian prison camps (253). Sheep shearers, unaware that the prisoners speak English, refer to Joe and Vince as "bloody dagos," "fascists" and friends of Hitler (303), and complain loudly that the prisoners are undercutting their wages and taking their jobs. Most of these skirmishes quickly blow over, though, because the Italians invariably demonstrate they are quick learners and hard workers.

But having been the brunt of so many demeaning remarks, Joe asks himself "whether the hardships of the land made the people more resentful of the newcomer or whether it was the same here as everywhere" (221). In his desire to understand and articulate the complexity of the differences between Australians and Italians (215), Joe (like many of us) struggles to come to terms with the complex and contradictory meanings of Anzac Day which, as Peter H. Hoffenberg suggests, lie "at the very centre of national identity and civic religion".[60]

Joe muses that

[i]n another country, a national day to mourn those who had died in wars would be a day of prayer and weeping. Here, it is a day of celebration. He had thought when he first came to this country that it was a place that worships life and not death. But he finds it is not so … It is the nature of this country to make bad luck and defeat into a virtue. (463)

But when he meets Max's sister Eddy, who returns from four years of nursing in the Middle East and New Guinea, Joe also sees the many differences in women's codes of conduct. Whereas Eddy freely speaks her mind, in Italy, "Women spoke out only in old age" (245). Whereas women in Italy submit to authority, Max's wife Alice refuses to be bullied by her wealthy father, who disapproves of her marriage. And while Italian women wear skirts out of "custom and femininity" (313) even if inappropriate to their work, Eddy dons men's clothes to work in the fields. But the old world's ways are, as the other novels indicate, preferable when it comes to relationships between women and men. Like Carroll's Antonio, Joe enjoys "women's talk" and finds the lack one of the most punishing aspects of internment. While Max is one of the "shy and introverted" (109) Australian blokes feminist critics like Anne Summers and Miriam Dixson identify as insensitive, even hostile, to women,[61] Max's wife Alice informs him that Joe is "the first man I've ever had a real conversation with. He didn't get up and have an important job to do if I introduced a topic that interested me" (366).

---

60 Peter H. Hoffenberg, "Landscape, Memory and the Italian Prisoners of War, 1915–1918" *Journal of Contemporary History* 36 no.1 (2001), 114.

61 Max is clearly a misogynist: he believes that women "wanted men to kill other men to save the country and starve in concentration camps and work clearing land like draught horses and down mines until they died from dust on the lungs and then talk about flower-arranging and hair-dos" (366).

But while Italian men may be happy to spend time with women, some women (like Eddy) are not so prepared to spend time with them. The relationship between Joe and Eddy gets off to a bad start when she returns from nursing in New Guinea. Like Goldbloom's Gin, Eddy regards Joe as someone who could "come in the night and chop her with the axe. Shoot her with the .22 rifle" (48). She also thinks "he might have fired a gun that caused the fatal wounds of a soldier she had tried to keep alive" (40). Moreover, believing that Max and her mother have "lost sight of who was the enemy" (45), she is furious that Max and her mother have "adopted" (48) the prisoners and barely speaks to Vince and Joe for months (181). In her mind, they are "dagos and wops" (286). But Eddy fights other battles on the home front. Like Carroll's Lilian, Eddy remains an "abiding disappointment" to her mother because she has "never developed the culinary art of the supernaturally weightless sponge cake" (255). Analogous again to Lilian, Eddy finds domestic chores repetitive and boring and suffers from combat envy, but Eddy also suffers from the cultural cringe. For her, "the war was more than a chance to leave the backwater of the world, the most forgotten and insignificant place on earth. She wanted to work beside people from other nations and see how she measured up. She wanted to measure up … She wanted them to know that there are serious people living in the antipodes, not just kangaroos" (60). Judging by her courageous actions during the war, Eddy more than measures up (283). She has become a nurse, not because she sees herself as the "ministering angel," as Joe puts it, but because nursing "was the best paid of a very narrow set of options. She had no taste for teaching and secretarial work was deadening. She was practical and efficient and it called for that" (283–84).

While Joe recognises early on that Eddy is "a challenge he felt equal to" (252), Eddy takes much longer to realise that he has many fine qualities, but her careful observations reveal that he never "pulls rank" on Vince; that he is a kind and gentle man who would never willingly hurt anyone; and that despite the common belief that all Italian men are "hot-blooded and irresistible" (261), he does not initiate their first sexual encounter, nor does he make any moves thereafter "until [Eddy] sanctioned [them]" (379). Most impressive is that like Carroll's Antonio, Joe does not "want her to conform, to do what other women did" (437) but treats her "as though she were a man, an equal" (437). Ultimately, however, it is Joe's love of the land that convinces her that he is the right man for her: "[Eddy] saw that he had become part of the space, the light, the air. Only then did she look at him with acceptance" (429). For his part, Joe knows that with Eddy, "he did not feel any pressure to be what he was not, to conform, to live up to a social formula. All he had to do was be alive, and with her he was one hundred and fifty per cent alive" (357). Eddy's gradual recognition of Joe's strengths accompanies her increasing tolerance for difference: in response to a farm woman's comment about the "dagos" being untrustworthy, Eddy reflects that "if people took the trouble to get to know others they could not feel superior" (263), a sentiment she re-phrases when Max objects to her relationship with Joe.

But as the text suggests, war's end is not the blessing many believe it will be: instead, it brings an assortment of problems that Joe wishes to discuss but Eddy dreads. Obstacles such as responsibility and guilt, which both share but in different ways, stand in the way of their futures together. Joe's concerns over family members in his "own faraway country" materialise in the form of letters from his sister that confirm that their father has been shot (362). As Joe grieves the loss of a father he has barely known, the war ends, and he is bound by the rules of the Geneva Convention to return to Italy. Aware that he is responsible for three starving women – his mother and two sisters (427) – he cannot ask Eddy to come to Italy, not only because it is "broken" (408), but because she could never learn to "live like an Italian woman. Her character was formed on the edge of an unpeopled interior. Her culture, though European, was not weighed down by the constructions of power and tradition" (428). For her part, Eddy is unable to make a commitment to Joe because of Hal. She and Hal had never been anything but friends and she regarded him as a father-figure ever since her own disappeared when she was a child. But once Hal returns from Burma having greatly suffered mentally and physically as a prisoner of war, Eddy begins to view her affair with Joe a "betrayal." Her search to find meaning in Hal's sacrifice causes a serious rift between her and Joe, in part because "she had the traditional country person's suspicion of the city person, whose work, however boring or irksome, was soft compared with that of the farmer (397–98). Her belief that those who survived the Burma Railway should be recognised as "saints" also rankles with Joe, in part because his participation in only one battle before becoming a prisoner of war has left him with a sense of "humiliation and lost self-respect and the anguish of knowing [his] family is in danger and [his] country in ruins" (405). In sum, each sees the other's loyalty – hers to a deeply damaged Burma railway prisoner and Joe's to those "who lived in his own country's ruin" (409) – as perfidious.

Their attempts to plan their futures together are also complicated by Joe's recognition that at war's end, "despite their hard work and companionship, the Italian prisoners had become a nuisance. He felt discouraged. It was all such a waste" (348). But the lovers are further torn apart by Max's discovery that his sister is having an affair with Joe, which brings Joe to realise that "the war, pervasive to the most obscure place, had become personal. Max wanted to judge how personal. A friendship between two men was acceptable to him, but an attachment between a man and a woman overstepped every boundary" (348–49). Given the respectful and collegial relationship that has existed between these two men until war's end, it seems curious that Max should now regard him as "a deceitful bastard" (323), and that he should be so opposed to Joe's becoming "one of us" that he sends him back to the camp to live behind barbed wire again.

Tim Cresswell's work on "place" helps sheds light on how expectations about behaviour in an "obscure place" may become charged with meaning. His book contains two central themes: "the first is the way in which space and place are used to structure a normative landscape – the way in which ideas about what is right, just, and appropriate are transmitted through space and place. Something may be appropriate here but not there".[62] Max's insistence – that Joe should have "kept clear" of Eddy had he any feelings for her – insinuates that his love for her is "inappropriate," out of "place." Cresswell emphasises that "the geographical setting of actions plays a central role in defining our judgement of whether actions are good or bad".[63] Hence from Max's perspective, because Joe's labour is no longer required, he has "no place" in Australia and should return to his "home" in Italy, where he belongs; the "rules" of war are on Max's side. While some Italians petitioned the government to allow them to remain in Australia, the Alcorsos observe that their attempts were futile, since "the terms of the Geneva Convention made it obligatory to repatriate all POWs even if they wanted to stay. Eventually, as ships became available in 1946 and 1947, Italian POWs were shipped back to Italy to reconstruct their disrupted lives".[64]

Cresswell's second theme is transgression. He argues that "to have transgressed … means to have been judged to have crossed some line that was not meant to be crossed";[65] hence, as Max believes, Joe has crossed a "boundary" by having an affair with his sister. Cresswell then advances that "place plays a significant role in the creation of norms of behaviour and thus in the creation of deviance" and that "the ability to define what constitutes appropriate behaviour in a particular place" constitutes a form of power. Those who wield that power may label deviants "outsiders". Cresswell defines that word "commonly used to describe people new to a place or people who do not know the ways of a place. The use of the term *outsider* indicates that a person does not properly understand the behaviour expected of people in a town, region, or nation".[66] Closely linked to the notion of transgression is resistance, which Cresswell argues "seems to imply 'intentionality' – that is purposeful action directed against some disliked entity with the intention of changing it or lessening its effect. The resistance of an action therefore appears to be in the intention of the perpetrator, in the eagerness to overcome or change some obstacle".[67] In the novel, Joe is the perpetrator, Hal Fischer the obstacle.

After Joe's mother dies and his sisters are married in Italy, he joins the large number of Italians who, with the help of sponsors (Joe's is the camp commander), make their way back to Australia. Attempts to contact Eddy by letter fail, but once he learns that Eddy has married Hal and that they have a daughter, he is distraught, but too decent to initiate action. His informer, Alice, relays the news that Eddy is deeply unhappy because Hal refuses to see a psychiatrist and treats her and her mother badly. With Alice's help, Joe and Eddy meet; when Joe sees how despondent

---

62   Tim Cresswell, *In Place/Out of Place: Geography, Ideology, and Transgression* (Minneapolis: University of Minnesota Press, 1996), 8.
63   Cresswell, *In Place/Out of Place*, 9.
64   Alcorso and Alcorso, "Italians in Australia", 33.
65   Cresswell, *In Place/Out of Place*, 23.
66   Cresswell, *In Place/Out of Place*, 25–26.
67   Cresswell, *In Place/Out of Place*, 22.

Eddy is and simultaneously realises Claudia is his daughter (his father's name was Claudio), "intentionality" takes over, with Hal the "disliked entity" whose effect on Eddy and Claudia must be eradicated by divorce. Joe has finally found a battle he desperately wants to win and does. The future looks promising: Eddy and Joe will marry and raise their daughter together; Max admits he should not have meddled in Eddy's life and ultimately comes to see Joe's true worth.

Dale Turner's *The Farmer's Wife* offers a depiction of a woman from the "big mining town Kalgoorlie" who finds that the "place" she instantly dislikes – a remote farm in Western Australia – becomes a home she never wants to leave, in large part because the home is of her making.[68] Like Temby's Eddy and Carroll's Lilian, Lil is another spirited woman who refuses to heed her husband's advice, in this case that she sit out the war with his family in Melbourne while he fights in New Guinea. From the outset, like Lilian and Eddy, she is confident that she can, with the help of neighbours, family members and women in the community, many of whom are entering or re-entering the work force, keep alive her husband Ted's dream of owning Wandoo, the mixed farm he bought near Narrobin, Western Australia, in 1939. Through hard work, common sense and boundless energy, Lil not only survives the war, but turns Wandoo into such a prosperous farm that she is able to pay off the loans on it and buy another larger, more substantial property before Ted returns. Lil has had to fight her own home-front battles, however, with bankers who do not believe women should be making financial decisions, and with hostile men whose anger at her success leads them to steal her sheep.

Among those who aid Lil, aside from her brother and sister who help out temporarily, are those from neighbouring farms: the young Aub learns so much from Lil that at the end of the war, he is applying to agricultural school, with the goal of becoming a farm adviser. Equally instrumental to Lil's financial prosperity is an Aboriginal family who, although they work initially only for their keep, are eventually rewarded by Ted and Lil, who offer them not only continuing employment, but the mud-brick home on Wandoo. Another of Lil's helpers is Nick, an Italian prisoner of war from the camp at Dwellingup (5). The farmers he works for often bring him to Lil's farm to help. They inform Lil that Nick feels "bad" about his capture and worries about his family back home (51). Lil then shows her goodness by replying that they must "treat him right … If he was one of our men, we would like to think he was treated right. This war is not his fault" (51). Lil does, of course, "treat him right" and often engages him in conversation, despite his "broken" English. He misses his family, especially since he knows they would thrive in this land of plenty. Like Carroll's prisoners, Nick tries to learn the Australian vernacular and eventually declares that he loves almost everything about life in Australia, especially people like Lil who are "good to him" (52). Typical of Italian prisoners of war, he enjoys playing with Lil's son Nev, who reminds him

---

68   Dale Turner, *The Farmer's Wife* (self pub.: Xlibris, 2011). All subsequent references are to this edition and appear in parentheses in the text.

of his one-year-old son (52). Nick's story, like Joe's, has a happy ending, since the neighbour who brought Nick to Wandoo is aware of the Australia's need to "increase its population" and offers to sponsor Nick's application to return (108). Nick, who regards Lilian as "one fine lady," senses that she will no longer be "just a housewife" (108) when her husband comes home, and she is not. But in spite of the praise Lil heaps upon Nick's strenuous work on the farm, Ted is shocked that she allowed "an enemy" on the property and inquires whether or not she worked "alone in the paddocks" with him, a comment Lil finds overwhelmingly insulting.[69] When Ted learns that Nick intends to return with his family, he retorts that "'next we'll be asking the Japs to come and live here" (134). The ever-wise Lil suggests that it will be a long time before either can comprehend what the other has been through, but one day they will (134).

That both Turner's and Temby's novels contain former POWs who wish to return to Australia after war's end indicates, as Rando suggests, that some good may have come from "both the internment of Italian Australians and the presence of Italian POWs". He argues this had "a lasting effect on relations between Italians and Australians", providing "one of the links in Australia's transition from a traditional British society towards a more broadly based multicultural society in the quarter century after the end of the war". In 1946, for example, a new mass immigration policy led to "the influx of over a million non-Anglo-Celtic people (including some 360,000 Italians) in the next 25 years". Interestingly, "about one-fifth (some 3700) of the ex POWs – in many cases sponsored by the farming families they had worked ... were to constitute part of this intake".[70] The Alcorsos are, however, less enthusiastic about the relationship between Italian immigrants and their "host society". They argue that the results were somewhat "contradictory": "On the one hand, the war created a climate in which anti-Italian racism could flourish and was indeed encouraged by the government". Many of the local Italian population underwent "considerable individual hardship and suffering". The Alcorsos further assert, though, that "the large-scale deployment of Italian POW labour had the unintended consequence of fostering attitudes of friendship and trust towards Italians among Australia's predominantly British background and ethnocentric rural population". They conclude that the "POW episode had demonstrated how useful Italian labour could be, setting the scene for large postwar intakes from Italy. The surplus peasants of postwar Italy found in Australia a more receptive destination than ever before".[71]

Watkins' novel suggests that there may be some purchase to these statements. Although it stresses the hardship and suffering that the De Contis experienced, the ending is upbeat, which comes as a surprise, reflecting both Randos' and Alcorsos'

---

69 Ted might be more shocked to learn that one of his neighbours, a married man, has sexually harassed Lil on several occasions, certain that she is so lonely she will fall into his arms.
70 Rando, "Italo-Australians", 20.
71 Alcorso and Alcorso, "Italians in Australia", 33–34.

overall responses. Although the change is slow in coming, Roberto appears to have forgotten how much he and his family battled to regain their freedom and now insists that Australia is a "great country" that offers "equality for everyone" (327). He also recognises that the country has changed: "Children of today's immigrants have endless opportunities. Good schools with high levels of education … There will be many doctors, lawyers and professional people, coming from often illiterate parents" (327). Carolena, who also wrestled to find her place in Australia, now declares that "Australia was a great country, [sic] it was still considered the land of promise" (327). After Roberto's death, Carolena is consoled by her belief that "not only had Australia given them a life but that their efforts had developed the national economy by which thousands of Australians benefited" (346). Similarly, Temby's novel takes its title from the Italian *paesani*, who come to Australia to *guadagnare il pane*, "to earn their bread," a phrase she utilises to underscore that it even though it may be "the hardest crust they will ever earn" (11), the POWs might agree that earning it was worth the effort if they could live and work in a country that finally sees their value as hard workers and welcomes them.

Taken together, these novels point out the differences between historical and political accounts of the effects of war on internees and prisoners of war but add another invaluable perspective – that World War II benefited women in many tangible ways. Several escape a patriarchal culture by marrying Italian men who value their intelligence and skills and talents or, as Temby's Eddy puts it, see them as equals to men. Moreover, by their various roles in the running of the country during the war, many find that "anything a man can do, a woman can do too, and often better."

12

Lies, Secrets and Silences

Japanese Prisoners-of-War in World War II Australian Women's Novels

In her article on the history of Australian prisoners of war, Rosalind Hearder observes that historians have only recently rendered them the focus of serious research. She asserts that this early relative absence of interest in these stories

> implies that captivity represented a situation of stasis – men [sic] were imprisoned and nothing changed except that some lived, and some died. Nothing could be further from the truth. Constant change and flux characterised the prisoner-of-war experience – from locations, supplies of food, and medications to ever-changing captors. Quality of leadership and morale depended on how long men had been in captivity and the kinds of conditions in which they were forced to live.[1]

Historian Michael McKernan further observes that Australians seem to have "forgotten or have pushed away" the terrible accounts of prisoners in the hands of the Japanese, and then queries why "the stories of the prisoners at Changi, on the Railway, and most disastrously at Sandakan [have] not become a core element of our understanding of ourselves and our past."[2] McKernan blames the occlusion of these prisoner-of-war stories on the fact that "so much of Australia's writing about war concentrates on the fighting soldier and the immediate moment of battle" (xiv). Historian Christine Twomey concurs, pointing out that Australian "war histories are, by and large, military stories" in which "civilians, especially women and children, have long struggled to find a place within them. Civilians who were themselves directly and adversely affected by war have continued to

---

1   Rosalind Hearder, "Memory, Mythology, and Myth: Some of the Challenges of Writing Australian Prisoner of War History" *Journal of the Australian War Memorial* (*JAWM*), 40 (February 2007). https://www.awm.gov.au/articles/journal/j40/hearder.
2   Michael McKernan, *The War Never Ends: The Pain of Separation and Return* (St. Lucia: University of Queensland Press, 2001), xi –xii. All subsequent references are to this edition and appear in parentheses in the text.

remain peripheral to a national vision about war which continues to concentrate on military service and its effects on individuals and their families."[3] Twomey insists that we need to listen to the voices of civilians "if only to remind ourselves that the reach of war extends far beyond the military and their families alone" (18). These historians attest that Australian prisoner-of-war stories are multifaceted, include a much broader range of experience than has been documented to date and are hence worthy of more consideration than they have received in the past.

Recently, four contemporary women novelists have also been "doing their bit" to augment the diversities of prisoner-of-war stories, including those concerning the Japanese imprisoned on the Australian home front whose experiences have been almost completely overlooked. Cory Taylor's 2013 novel *My Beautiful Enemy* establishes that after the Japanese attacked Pearl Harbor in December 1941, the Australian government rounded up all the Japanese people in Australia – including those of mixed race or who had lived in Australia their entire lives – and interned them in camps scattered across the country. Taylor's protagonist, seventeen-year-old Arthur Wheeler, works as a guard at the Tatura (Rushworth) internment camp in Victoria, where most Japanese families were held. Arthur falls in love at first sight with the handsome Stanley (Saburo) Ueno, perhaps modelled on the fifteen-year-old Japanese member of the famed Ueno acrobatic troupe captured while touring Australia and the "beautiful enemy" of the title. Arthur never openly declares his love, however, because as reviewer Glen Nicholls assumes, he is doubly ashamed of his homosexual attraction to an enemy alien.[4] Christine Piper's 2014 novel *After Darkness* centres on Tomokazu Ibaraki, a Japanese-born doctor who attempts to overcome his guilt for having participated in the germ-warfare actions begun in Japan prior to the war by taking up a medical appointment in Broome in 1938. After the attack on Pearl Harbor, he is incarcerated at Loveday camp in South Australia, which housed single men from Germany and Italy as well, although in separate compounds. Like Taylor's character Arthur, Dr Ibaraki also loses the love of two good women because of his inability to divulge the remorse he feels over the reprehensible activities he has been involved in, which would explain what they perceive of as inaccessibility or indifference.

Similarly, Anita Heiss' 2017 *Barbed Wire and Cherry Blossoms* records the stories of members of an Aboriginal community who keep silent their hiding of a young Japanese soldier in 1944 in their air raid shelter after the Cowra breakout.[5] Heiss' text discloses that the Australian government treats their Japanese "enemies" far better than its oldest inhabitants, whose freedoms and privileges are so curtailed that they are forced to eke out marginal lives in what amounts to another kind of prison.

---

3 Christine Twomey, *Australia's Forgotten Prisoners: Civilians Interned by the Japanese in World War Two* (Port Melbourne: Cambridge University Press, 2001), 14. All subsequent references are to this edition and appear in parentheses in the text.
4 Glen Nicholls, "Desire Denied," *Books & Arts*, 13 May 2014.
5 The largest prison escape of World War II, where over 1100 Japanese prisoners-of war escaped from a camp in rural New South Wales in 1944.

Saskia Beudel's 2002 *Borrowed Eyes*, a fictional account of the real-life Australian nurse Vivian Bullwinkel's capture and subsequent forty-two-month internment in Sumatra by the Japanese, differs significantly from the accounts of prisoner-of-war stories written at the time because, as McKernan asserts, one "common feature" of this literature is that "the story ends with the end of war. [Writers] may briefly tell their readers how it was that they got home; they will not say, in any detail, what it was like to come home".[6] But in her contemporary examination of Vivian Bullwinkel's experiences as a prisoner of war (here renamed Vivien Carmichael), Beudel explores the difficulties Carmichael encounters in adjusting to life on the home front, which she begins to overcome only by sharing her war experiences with another survivor. While each of these novels takes up a fascinating, though strikingly different, aspect of the prisoner-of-war story, several additional commonalities exist: Taylor's, Piper's and Beudel's each incorporate "real" characters and specific events of history; all four feature protagonists who are, to a greater or lesser extent, traumatised by their World War II experiences; and each survivor comes to understand that a combination of lies, secrets and silences has been, in several cases, forced upon them by institutions or cultural attitudes from within their countries of origin. Only when they break their silences – and not all do – can they begin the healing process necessary for themselves and their countries.

In writing their novels, both Taylor and Piper acknowledge that they have relied extensively on Yuriko Nagata's investigations into the Australian government's broad-scale internment of the Japanese during World War II. The background Nagata provides significantly enlarges any understanding of the scale of the injustices of the times, which is as follows:

> Japan's entry into the war on December 8, 1941, directly threatened Australia's security. After war was declared between the two nations, 1141 people were quickly taken into custody. They included Japanese nationals and *Nisei* (second-generation Japanese Australians) who were Australian-born, many of them of mixed heritage … Australia also received a further 3160 Japanese who were arrested and transported from neighbouring countries that were under Allied control, including New Zealand, New Caledonia, the former New Hebrides and Dutch East Indies.[7]

---

6   McKernan, *The War Never Ends*, xv–xvi. See Betty Jeffrey's *White Coolies* (Sydney: Angus & Robertson, 1954), which was made into a feature film in 1997 titled *Paradise Road* and directed by Bruce Beresford. See also Jesse Elizabeth Simons' *While History Passed* (Melbourne: Heinemann, 1954), re-published in 1985 as *In Japanese Hands*.

7   Yuriko Nagata, "Naïve Patriotism: The Internment of Moshi Inagaki in Australia during the Second World War", *Under Suspicion: Citizenship and Testament in Australia during the Second World War*, eds. Joan Beaumont, Ilma Martinuzzi O'Brien and Mathew Trinca (Canberra: National Museum of Australia Press, 2008), 113.

Nagata stresses that while "the Japanese community in Australia was more readily identifiable and much smaller than its German and Italian counterparts," the "collar the lot" internment policy was nevertheless applied only to the Japanese in Australia.[8] During the hostilities, "ninety-seven per cent of the registered aliens of Japanese descent were imprisoned, while thirty-one per cent of Italian and thirty-two percent of German descent were interned."[9] This inequity arose "because [their] membership of [sic] a particular ethnic group placed them under suspicion of being a security risk".[10] Specifically,

> [t]here was a widely held notion that Japanese were fanatical and inscrutable, and that their "Japanese-ness" must override any possible loyalty to Australia. In addition, despite the attack on Pearl Harbor, World War Two threatened Australia's security far more directly than that of the USA and Canada.[11]

Nagata further notes that the Australian government's policy was "racially based ... a reflection of the racial mores of the time with echoes of the historical reasons for the passing of the *Immigration Restriction Act* (White Australia policy) in 1901".[12] This strategy, she asserts, stated that women would only be interned when they posed threats to national security; nonetheless, "in April 1942 seventy-eight Japanese women were being held in internment, as compared to three German and four Italian women".[13]

My Beautiful Enemy is the only novel here to address the effects of incarceration on Japanese women and children. While it indicates that a few male camp personnel occasionally threaten women's mental and moral integrity, in general, the authorities are respectful when they arrest the prisoners and then tolerate the loving relationships that develop between Japanese women and Australian men employed at the camp. Japanese women attest they want to remain in Australia because they are treated better than in Japan: food and clothing are free and they are placed under a doctor's care when sick or having babies. Moreover, Nagata's observation – that children seemed to enjoy their "communal life,"[14] is reflected in Taylor's novel: they appreciate making new friends, delight in playing popular sports such as tennis and baseball, and eagerly participate in entertainment nights with their parents and other adults. Overall, despite the Australians' (unwarranted) fears of the Japanese, Nagata claims that Japanese internment in Australia was

---

8   Nagata, "Naïve Patriotism", 112.
9   Yuriko Nagata, "'Certain Types of Aliens': The Japanese in Australia, 1941–1952", *Relationships: Japan and Australia, 1870s–1950s,* eds. Paul Jones and Vera Mackie (Parkville, Vic: University of Melbourne, Department of History, 2001), 222.
10   Nagata, "'Certain Types of Aliens'", 222.
11   Nagata, "'Certain Types of Aliens'", 218.
12   Nagata, "'Certain Types of Aliens'", 217.
13   Nagata, "'Certain Types of Aliens'", 222–23.
14   Nagata, "Naïve Patriotism", 159.

considered an "uncontroversial wartime event ... handled relatively efficiently by the authorities, with internees said to have been treated humanely and with fairness".[15] Margaret Bevege verifies that internees "stressed their high regard for the men who guarded them, and their general satisfaction with their food and treatment."[16] The management of the Japanese in Australia lies, however, in sharp contrast to the unwarranted cruelty inflicted upon the more than 21,000 Australians captured by the Japanese in World War II. As Joan Beaumont points out, "more than 7,600 prisoners – or almost a third of those captured by the Japanese – died in captivity. In contrast, only 3.2 per cent of men interned by the European Axis powers died in captivity."[17]

When it came to the release of Japanese internees, Christine Piper observed that "6 per cent were released before the cessation of hostilities with Japan, compared to 74 per cent of Italians and 25 per cent of Germans."[18] As a result, because most of the Japanese interned in Australia were repatriated to Japan after the war ended, their "ability to speak out about their experience and contributing to the post-war silence" was reduced,[19] a point Masako Fukui and Mayu Kanamori reiterate in their observation that expelling almost all Japanese people as "enemy aliens" resulted in a "severing of history and Nikkei lineage."[20] Reviewer Sally Browne also suggests that the actuality of Japanese internment camps is not widely known because Australians tend (conveniently) to overlook aspects of their history which "don't fit an orthodox narrative of the nation."[21] Accordingly, Taylor confessed to Phil Brown that she was unaware of the hardships inflicted on the Japanese interned during World War II.[22]

Taylor's novel begins with Stanley Ueno's escape from the disreputable Christian Brothers' boarding school in Ballarat. Warmly welcomed back into the infirmary at Tatura by the nursing staff, he is quickly introduced to the seventeen-year-old guard Arthur being treated for "weak nerves," headaches and stomach aches. Although the first-person narrator Arthur claims that because of his immediate physical attraction to Stanley (who has learned English in Chicago), "he would never again be able to take comfort in the common wisdom that the Japs were unlovely,"[23] but retains his prejudices throughout the war. As Lisa Hill

---

15   Nagata, "Naïve Patriotism", 113.
16   Margaret Bevege, *Behind Barbed Wire: Internment in Australia During World War II* (St. Lucia: University of Queensland Press, 1997), 377.
17   Joan Beaumont, "Prisoners of War in Australian National Memory", *Prisoners of War, Prisoners of Peace: Captivity, Homecoming, and Memory in World War II*, eds. Bob Moore and Barbara Hately-Broad (Oxford & New York: Berg Publishers, 2005): 185.
18   Christine Piper, "Prejudice flares when we perceive enemies within," *Sydney Morning Herald* August 14, 2014, 3.
19   Piper, "Prejudice flares", 3.
20   Masako Fukui and Mayu Kanamori, "The Creation of Nikkei Australia: Rediscovering the Japanese Diaspora in Australia", *Journal of Australian Studies* 41 no. 3 (2017), 388.
21   Sally Browne, "Brisbane Writers the Last World in Talent," *The Courier Mail*, 1 May 2014.
22   Phil Brown, "Holding Your Enemies Close," *Courier Mail: Queensland Life*, 11 May 2014.

claims, this kind of response was not unusual in that such beliefs had become deeply ingrained, indeed "institutionalised" by the White Australia policy[24] and, as the text further indicates, reinforced by newspaper accounts that fabricated the barbarity of Japanese soldiers. Having taken for granted that the Japanese would be deprived of all rights as ordinary citizens, Arthur is dumbfounded to learn that most of the camp personnel find the Japanese "harmless" and devote themselves to promoting their "general welfare," which includes treating the Japanese "kids" as if they were "normal" (6). Thus when the thoughtful and caring school master McMaster asks him to teach Japanese students English, Arthur approaches his assignment as if fulfilling the white man's burden (23). Much as he observes that the camp, which contains about 800 Japanese, is peaceful and the internees obedient, he remains incapable of emulating the open-mindedness, benevolence, and empathy the higher-ranked camp personnel offer the internees. Unable to declare his love for Stanley, he sublimates his frustration by writing letters he promptly burns and churning out subtle love poems published in the camp's newsletter.

Although it is tempting to dismiss Arthur as weak or even cowardly, several other obstacles prevent him from pursuing a relationship with Stanley (or any other men). Uppermost is the role his archly conservative, patriarchal and homophobic father has played during his youth because, as Jacob Bucher contends, "the role that fathers and sons play in each other's understandings of masculinity is an important one." Fathers, Bucher theorises, play "an instrumental role in socializing sons in the ways of hegemonic masculinity"; they teach not only "the standard, but become the standard of masculinity – serving as a reference point or archetype, even to the point of idolization". Arthur finds nothing to venerate in his father, however; a country policeman and World War I veteran, Wheeler is a "mean drunk" with an "explosive temper" (53) who raises his only child in a "household full of secrets and silence": as a result, Arthur becomes "secretive and silent himself" (46). He also internalises his father's rejection of homosexuals, and thereafter accepts that homosexual longings (such as the ones he has felt for a school-friend Nigel, and then Bill, a young adult next-door neighbour whom he idolises), are "sick" and "perverse" (45). Much as he despises his father, Arthur tries desperately to suppress his homosexual urges and to replicate what Bucher might refer to as his father's "hegemonic heterosexuality", which means that "at a very basic level, fatherhood is directly related to masculinity – having sex with a woman and impregnating her is a clear display of virility, and virility is a construct of masculinity".[25]

Bucher's theory is borne out when Arthur meets May, a wealthy young woman from Melbourne who volunteers for the war effort on a nearby farm. Although

23   Cory Taylor, *My Beautiful Enemy* (Melbourne: Text Publishing, 2013), 5. All subsequent references are to this edition and appear in parentheses in the text.

24   Lisa Hill, "Review of *My Beautiful Enemy*, by Cory Taylor", ANZ LitLovers LitBlog, 14 June 2013. https://anzlitlovers.com/2013/06/14/my-beautiful-enemy-2013-by-cory-taylor/.

25   Jacob Bucher, "'But He Can't Be Gay': The Relationship between Masculinity and Homophobia in Father-Son Relationships", *The Journal of Men's Studies* 22 no.3 (2014), 222–24.

not physically attracted to her, under the influence of a little alcohol and May's gentle encouragement, he impregnates her during their first sexual encounter.[26] While Arthur finds the sex act with May physically unsatisfying, he is nevertheless pleased with his performance because he is now "officially a man. With May's blessing [he'd] done the thing that needed to be done to demonstrate [his] virility" (82), even though it entailed "fak[ing] something [he] didn't feel" (99). In his adolescent naivety, he informs May that he should see a doctor who might regard his (unspecified) condition as "treatable" and prescribe something he could take to remedy it (101). In her adolescent naivety, May suggests she can "help" him. But even after May produces a son, which Bucher notes warrants to most men "an even greater display of virility and masculinity",[27] Arthur pays him scant attention. (Years later, Arthur tells May that from the early days of courtship, he "didn't know if [he] was Arthur or Martha" [231].)

The advent of war and the masculine ideal so prominent in Australia also play significant roles in Arthur's conflicted desires. Shortly after he arrives in Tatura as a low-level soldier (guard), he bemoans that this is not the war experience he envisioned: "[He'd] imagined going into battle in some exotic foreign field and mowing down the evil foe before emerging bloodied but triumphant in the dawn light" (2). Arthur has no desire to be a fearless Anzac Two, however, but has signed up because "the times" are such that strangers harass civilians not in uniform (63). Subsequently, his father, who firmly believes all young men have a duty to fight, turns the plain-clothes attired Arthur away when he shows up unannounced in December 1944 (214). Discharged from the air force because he "lacks character," an all too familiar criticism, he re-enlists in the military at the beginning of 1945, but ends up at the internment camp in Victoria where the "prisoners" have no desire to escape and nowhere to go if they did. Even after the war, Arthur refrains from talking about his military past because "men were still judged by what they had done or not done in the service of their country, and one's pride rested on this judgment" (220).

But on the opening page of the text, as a first-person narrator reflecting on the past, Arthur claims that while he had earlier blamed his unhappiness either on the war or on the three wives he eventually divorced, he had also attributed it to "the times" (2), a stance Dennis Altman finds implausible, alleging there is no reason Arthur should be "frozen in the heterosexual world of the 1940s for the next twenty years."[28] Altman overlooks, however, a key factor that hinders Arthur from satisfying his homosexual desires, which is, as Frank Bongiorno observes,

---

26 Australian women's war novels are rife with instances of young women who become pregnant during their first sexual encounter. See Joan London's *Gilgamesh* (2001), Mardi McConnochie's *The Voyagers: A Love Story* (2011), and Michelle Michau-Crawford's *Leaving Elvis and Other Stories* (2016) where, in each case, the seducers either discount the possibility that women can become pregnant on their first sexual encounter or leave town without considering their actions might have consequences.

27 Bucher, "'But He Can't Be Gay'", 224.

a "social atmosphere in the armed forces" that was "outwardly heterosexual and homophobic."[29] Accordingly, at Tatura, several guards, some veterans of World War I, "exude ... a contempt for 'poofters', 'queens' and 'pansies'" (216). A few remind Arthur of his father, whom the war had turned into a "troubled, unsympathetic loner" (63). Similarly, in his wartime study of "psychotic ex-servicemen," Bongiorno finds that "quiet, introverted youths [like Arthur] ... soon became the butt ... of veiled or open accusations of homosexuality generally intended as a joke", (216) and further contends that in the 1940s, Australia was a prudish, puritan country that had little tolerance for those "othered" by their sexual preferences, a hostility that prevailed for decades. In 1958, a criminal law lecture at the University of Sydney included the information that "Whoever commits the abominable crime of buggery, or bestiality, with mankind or with any animal, shall be liable to penal servitude for fourteen years" (259). Moreover, in the early 1970s, Sydney doctors were "still performing brain operations" to help gay men make "a heterosexual adjustment" (260). Bongiorno concludes that extreme aversion to homosexuality was "firmly embedded in Australian culture" (261); as late as 1972, "some Australian men still regarded the presence of a 'poofter' in a public place as a standing provocation for a beating or worse" (261).

Not until the 1950s, a few years after Stanley and his family have undergone a harsh, forced repatriation to Japan that has driven Arthur to abandon his family and move to Brisbane, does he begin to supress his racist attitudes, now comprehending that the "real tragedy" of the internment "stemmed from the clumsy and panicky way that the Japs had been lumped together and branded as traitors" (70). But while Arthur begins to question his racial biases, he continues to renounce his sexual orientation, even though the times, at least for young people, were changing. Stuart, a sensible, good-natured teenager who seems to have always known that his father was homosexual, asks him point blank why he never tried to find Stanley, to tell him that he was "the love of his life" (226). (Stuart is unaware of the herculean efforts Arthur made earlier to block Stanley's deportation.) Acting on Stuart's advice, Arthur learns, thanks to McMaster, who has kept in touch with families from Tatura (228), that Stanley and his mother moved to Nagasaki in 1950.

Shortly after, Arthur makes his way to Nagasaki, but nothing goes the way he wants. Mrs Ueno, now more youthful in appearance than at the camp and clearly enjoying her son's financial success as a prosperous real-estate investor in bars and restaurants, shows little interest in Arthur, and neither does the ever-enigmatic Stanley, who keeps asking why he has come. During the pair's last meeting at the train station, Arthur feels embarrassed by his confession that Stanley was

---

28   Dennis Altman, "Arthur's Quest", *Australian Book Review*, no. 352 (June
      2013). https://www.australianbookreview.com.au/arts-update/102-june-2013-no-352/
      1498-arthur-s-quest. Accessed 21 April 2023.
29   Frank Bongiorno, *The Sex Lives of Australians: A History* (Collingwood, Vic: Black Inc Books,
      2012), 215. All subsequent references are to this edition and appear in parentheses in the text.

the "bravest" and "best" person he had ever known. That outburst – the closest he had ever come to declaring his love for Stanley (255) – is swiftly undercut when he realises that people are staring and casting "furtive glances" (259) at the two young men holding hands. Significantly, it is Stanley who has taken Arthur's hand and Stanley who shouts at passers-by to stop looking. That Arthur should "squirm" at such an innocuous moment underscores Stanley's cognisance – and perhaps justification for his refusal to take Arthur's overtures seriously – that Arthur's homosexual desires will remain forever closeted. But some years later, before Stanley dies, he makes a rare, kind-hearted, and compassionate gesture by instructing his American lover to bequeath his suitcase to Arthur. It contains "The Spider's Thread," a short story by the Japanese writer Akutagawa, which contains the kind of warning a man like Stanley might make because it stresses that the central character is, like him, not a "good" man, and he wants Arthur to understand that. Although Arthur continues to live a secretive, solitary life of self-discipline that he occasionally refers to as "posthumous," he is comforted by the presence of the suitcase, kept always in plain sight.

Christine Piper's *After Darkness* tells a similar story about Tomokazu Ibaraki, whose failure to overcome lies, secrets and silences also prevents him from leading a fully developed life. Like Taylor's novel, Piper's is concerned with the experiences of Japanese civilians interned in Australia during World War II, but more specifically including those of mixed race, or *haafu*.[30] In her essay titled "Unearthing the Past,"[31] which concerns "the accidental discovery of human bones that occurred while workers were digging a pit for a new National Hygiene and Disease Prevention Research Centre in Tokyo in 1989," Piper confesses that she had been drawn to stories about Japan for a long time, so that "unravelling the mystery of the bones is [her] attempt to decipher a culture that is at once both familiar and unknown" (33). Noting that she has always "remained an outsider," she confesses that "confronting the silence of Japan is a way of piecing together her cultural heritage" (33). In her struggle to "unearth" the meaning of the past, Piper creates a first-person narrator, Dr Tomokazu Ibaraki, who becomes a kind of composite of the people who inform her investigation concerning who the bones belonged to, how they ended up in Tokyo and why the silence around the bones persists to this day. Although the bones, destined after their recovery to be cremated, are now safely enshrined in a monument erected by the ministry in 2002 (twenty-five years after the discovery and seventy years after the war), those who have wanted to return them either to the families they belong to or even the regions of China they came from, have been thwarted.

---

30   According to reviewer Mark Dapin, Taylor's marriage to a Japanese man with whom she had two sons kept her "keenly aware of the nuances in relations between Australians and Asians," in "Loving the Thing You're Supposed to Hate," *Australian* 18 May 2013.
31   Christine Piper, "Unearthing the Past," *Australian Book Review*, no. 360 (April 2014). bit.ly/3PQYIaK.

Piper's novel takes place over several interwoven time frames that begin in 1934 and end in 1989, with a Tokyo newspaper account of the discovery of the bones. The novel also moves through different settings – Tokyo, Broome and the Loveday internment camp. Some reviewers have suggested that because Piper suspends the source of the traumatic events that have shaped Dr Ibaraki's memory, identity and relational life until near the end of the novel, it falls into the mystery genre. But since the plot structure is fragmented and Ibaraki suffers numerous flashbacks that derive from his scientific work in Tokyo, it may perhaps be more appropriately classified as a trauma narrative since, as Roger Luckhurst asserts, "no narrative of trauma can be told in a linear way: it has a time signature that must fracture conventional causality."[32] But as trauma theory by western critics does not take into account the specific characteristics of the complex Japanese culture, it is vital to re-assemble the events as they unfold within a linear timeline, beginning with references to some of the country's most basic tenets that firmly mould Tomokazu's behaviour. According to Yuki Tanaka, the Japanese seem "to have placed a higher value on the concepts of duty and fealty to the nation than on the concept of rights and liberties ... thus [d]uties were always to one's superior: the duty of a family to the father, of the father to the state, and of the state to the emperor. The chain of responsibility was conceived of as predominantly uni-directional, from subordinate to superior".[33] Piper's text suggests, then, that Dr Ibaraki can only become a fully functional, ethical and compassionate human being if he frees himself from these restraints, which can be attained if people inhabit, even temporarily, a country less rule-bound, less demanding of the need to adhere to rigid, unchanging principles, and more tolerant of diversity and cultural difference. Surprisingly, in this novel, that country is Australia. Although I agree with Sue Kossew's argument that the novel chronicles yet another of the "shameful" or "dark chapters" in Australia's past[34] and certainly the unjust internment of innocent Japanese people attests to that "sorry" past, it is the time Ibaraki spends in that country that marks the beginning of his long journey towards inner peace and salvation.

Within the linear structure of the novel, Piper's initial description of Tomokazu Ibaraki marks him as a man who faithfully adheres to the "chain of responsibility" by becoming head of the family at seventeen after his father, a famous Tokyo doctor, dies.[35] Destined to, but also desirous of following in his father's footsteps, Tomo excels in medical school. Shortly after graduation, he acquiesces to his mother's suggestion that he marry a woman named Kayoko, but at no point does he utter any expression of love or desire for her, his main concerns only that she be pleasant looking, and

---

32   Roger Luckhurst, *The Trauma Question* (Oxford and New York: Routledge, 2008), 9.
33   Yuki Tanaka, *Hidden Horrors: Japanese War Crimes in World War II* (Boulder, CO: Westview Press, 1996), 201.
34   Sue Kossew, "Revisiting the Haunted Past: Christine Piper's *After Darkness*", *Australian Humanities Review* 61 (May 2017), 1.
35   Christine Piper, *After Darkness* (Crows Nest: Allen & Unwin, 2014), 33. All subsequent references are to this edition and appear in parenthesis in the text.

accomplished – here as musician and trained bookkeeper. But before marrying, he realises that medicine was not the self-sacrificing profession he had visualised because the sick continued to die and he had no power to prevent their deaths. Pleased to be offered the opportunity to work at a new medical research unit within the Army Medical College, he is somewhat surprised to learn that the qualifications for the job are loyalty and discretion, not knowledge of or experience in the field of biological/medical research, but does not inquire why. By not asking questions, Dr Ibaraki tolerates what Philip A. Seaton, in his work on several "orthodox" interpretations of Japanese war memories, suggests is a "supposedly Japanese characteristic conformity" or an unwillingness to challenge authority.[36] Seaton adds that Japan is a "relatively homogenous nation in which the conformist nature of Japan's group society makes it difficult for Japanese people to hold conflicting views".[37] Fittingly, whenever Dr Ibaraki has any misgivings about his work – and they are myriad – such as why he should be "studying the effects of typhoid fever, [when] a vaccine was already available" (117), he does not seek clarification. Nor does he challenge why the next stage of his work – specimen analysis – led by the reputedly gifted microbiologist Ishii Shiro, should again require no special skills or training, but merely devotion to duty, discretion and most of all, "confidentiality." Sworn to secrecy, Dr Ibaraki has no idea that he has been recruited to work with Unit 731, headed by Ishii, which Piper describes as follows:

> [it] was the secret unit of the Army Medical College that developed biological weapons and experimented on living humans, starting in 1932 in the Japanese colony of Manchuria, and later in Guangzhou, Beijing, and Singapore … Test subjects were referred to as *maruta*, or "logs," originally as a joke because the Unit 731 compound was disguised as a lumber mill, then the term persisted … About three thousand people were directly killed in the experiments at the Unit 731 compound alone … The total death toll resulting from the spread of disease is estimated to be between 250,000 and 300,000.[38]

Because Ishii's work violated the principles of the 1925 Geneva Convention, he executed it primarily in Harbin because, as Tanaka acknowledges, it was "difficult to carry out in Japan".[39] Contemporary historians now believe that "the bodies of murdered test subjects were sent from China to the Tokyo laboratory for further analysis".[40]

---

36   Philip A. Seaton, *Japan's Contested War Memories: The 'Memory Rifts' in Historical Consciousness of World War II* (New York: Routledge, 2007): 3.

37   Seaton, *Japan's Contested War Memories*, 3.

38   Piper, "Unearthing", 33.

39   Yuriko Nagata, *Unwanted Aliens: Japanese Internment in Australia during the Second World War* (St. Lucia: University of Queensland Press, 1996), 136.

40   Piper, "Unearthing the Past", 36.

Piper's novel describes Dr Ibaraki's horrified response to the initial shipments of crates containing the gruesome bodies of murdered test subjects in large specimen jars, which he helps unload. Sickened, he rushes home where, like Lady Macbeth, he attempts to scrub his hands clean of imaginary blood and hopes that a hot bath will absolve a conscience involved in physically and morally abhorrent work. But having pledged secrecy and continuing to cling to the principles of discretion and deference to authority, he keeps his concerns to himself. Shortly after, when he learns that Ishii, whose meteoric rise through the military ranks now makes him a Lieutenant-Colonel, will discuss his work at the Army Medical College, Ibaraki is thrilled by the opportunity to meet him. After swearing his audience to secrecy, Ishii calmly and matter-of-factly describes the ghastly details of his experiments on the "maruta" and then passes around disgusting black and white photos, the last depicting a child's hands with black fingertips.

Upset by these images, Dr Ibaraki again attempts to rush home to wash them away but is intercepted by Ishii and Kimura, who have spent the afternoon drinking with a few high-ranking members of the committee bullied into accompanying them to a "geisha night" at a "tea house"[41] and insist that Dr Ibaraki join them. During the evening Ibaraki witnesses Ishii's misogyny (he intimidates and insults the mistress of the house and demands she produce his favourite fourteen-year-old geishas);[42] recalls rumours that Ishii exploits junior workers; and tolerates Ishii's condemnation of Tomo's father as an inferior doctor, content to merely heal the sick. Most shocking is Ishii's declaration that great doctors know that "sometimes a few lives have to be sacrificed to save thousands of others" (191). Throughout these venomous comments, Ibaraki remains silent. Arriving home late and again wanting only to banish the memories of the sickening photographic images from his consciousness, he learns that Kayoko is pregnant but cannot rejoice with her because when he thinks of their baby, he envisions only the image of a child's blackened fingers.

Two months later, when a second, even larger, shipment of subjects arrives and two young nurses are asked to help move the bodies, they appear reticent because, Dr Ibaraki assumes, they recognise the nature of the work. Even though he feels "stained by [his] association with the laboratory" (194), when one nurse recoils in horror,[43] he takes over, but what he sees is appalling. As he lifts a male child's light body out of a crate, he notices it is covered in blisters and he has a tag around his

---

41   Piper's essay claims that Ishii's birth in an influential family rendered him "adept at manipulating others for his own benefit" (38).

42   Tanaka declares that Ishii's unsavory treatment of women is regrettably typical: "Japanese men hold women in contempt and have no qualms about exploiting their sexuality" (Tanaka, *Hidden Horrors*, 79). He notes that when the Japanese set up a Recreation and Amusement Association (RAA) for the occupation forces in 1945, many of those forced to work in the brothels were high-school students who had been coerced to work in munitions factories towards the end of the war. One of these brothels was managed by the mistress of General Ishii Shiro (105).

43   Toyo Ishii (no relation to Shirii, a nurse at the Army Medical College), offered details of the work she was required to do (although not experiments on humans) and some information on what she

neck (195). Confronted later that evening by Kayoko's insistence that he must quit smoking, drinking and visiting brothels once the baby is born, he makes no attempt to defend himself. Hence the doctor's concern is not that Kayoko is distressed by her husband's neglect, but that she might not forgive *him*. When Kayoko suffers a miscarriage and her mother blames Ibaraki for her daughter's mistreatment, he thinks only of his own misery: "she has no idea of the things [he] had to do each day, the secrets [he] had to keep … She didn't understand the sacrifices [he] had made to serve the nation – to help ordinary people such as her" (202). As well as assuming no responsibility for Kayoko's miscarriage, he has also forgotten that Kayoko had insisted she did not believe in secrets between husbands and wives and had warned him never to underestimate her. Tellingly, he has also disregarded that during an outing to a park on *setsubun*, a day that tolerates role reversals, Kayoko had fiercely defended two young women whom authorities were treating unfairly. The text infers here that had Ibaraki informed Kayoko of his work, she would likely have insisted he resign immediately.

In spite of the horrendous revulsion he continues to feel, Ibaraki persists in believing he is contributing to a ground-breaking and vital scientific endeavour. Pleased to be asked to cut into a middle-aged man's body that has been injected with bubonic plague, he obeys, but then refuses when ordered to perform a dissection on the child he had lifted from the specimen jar, apparently only then comprehending that he is being complicit with a Japanese wartime atrocity that requires him to employ germ warfare that will kill thousands of "others" in order to save Japanese lives. That he should repudiate the command is surprisingly rare, however, since as Tanaka acknowledges, even though doctors in Unit 731 performed "unthinkable" operations, testimonials revealed that they approached their work forthrightly and could rid themselves of any guilt or pain by creating a "logic" that validated their actions and enabled them to act "dispassionately".[44]

Tanaka's conclusion – that "the willingness to dispose of certain lives … coexist[ed] with the desire to help save the lives of others", accords with what Robert Jay Lifton labels a "coexistence of conflicting desires," or "doubling",[45] which Tanaka suggests Nazi doctors adopted. Working in conjunction with Ishii, dubbed "the Joseph Mengele of Japan",[46] Japanese doctors were able to create what Lifton calls "an Auschwitz self" so they could "experiment on and eventually kill prisoners without experiencing guilt".[47] Furthermore, Unit 731 doctors became numb psychologically by not only dehumanising the prisoners, but by referring to them by numbers instead of names. This kind of "psychological distance … prevented the doctors from empathizing with their victims". Both groups also had an "external

---

saw in the morgues. Although she wanted to see a memorial built to preserve the bones, she did not "intend … to proactively testify" and died in 2012 (Piper, "Unearthing", 37).

44 Tanaka, *Hidden Horrors*, 162.
45 Cited in Tanaka, *Hidden Horrors*, 162.
46 Piper, "Unearthing the Past", 38.
47 Cited in Tanaka, *Hidden Horrors*, 162.

figure – the emperor and the fuhrer – to help them deal with whatever feelings of conflict might arise". The Japanese regarded "their work ... as an expression of their loyalty to the emperor ... a godlike figure who could solve any problems. Ultimately, any internal conflicts could be resolved by understanding that they were doing what the emperor ... would want".[48]

But after Dr Ibaraki's inability/refusal to obey instructions, he discovers that Major Kimura intends to fire him, a penalty that harms his "pride"; although Ibaraki pleads (incredibly) for another chance, Kimura merely insists that he must take the secret of what he knows to the "grave" or face the "shame" it will bring to his family if he speaks up (211). This concept of saving face: "the dichotomy at the heart of Japanese culture: the conflict between *honne* (personal feelings and desires) and *tatemae* (public façade)",[49] is crucial to understanding why Ibaraki would concede. Without Kayoko at his side (she now lives with her family) and anxious about his future, he decides to take up a position as head of a small hospital in faraway Australia that his brother-in-law has informed him about.

From the outset, Dr Ibaraki finds everything about Australia pleasing, including the strange "clash" of colours in Broome, where "rich red sand" meets an "azure" sea and "lush greenery" (46). He appreciates that the town, with its many amenities, is "civilized," and that Asiatics, Brits, Malay, Chinese, Japanese and Ceylonese appear amicable (there is a "Japtown," however). The newly arrived doctor also enjoys socialising, upon invitation, with the town's upper crust, such as the president of the Japan Association, who introduces him to his nurse, Sister Bernice, from a nearby convent. Initially impressed with her warmth and "kind-heartedness," he is thankful she possesses the bedside manner he lacks, evident when he experiences a flashback while attempting to complete a difficult operation on a young Malay man and Sister Bernice immediately takes over. But when the patient, angry that his "girl" has been dating another man, takes umbrage at the doctor's request that he be quiet, he retorts, "What do you know about love?" (82), a comment the doctor admits "cut to the deepest part" of him (82).

Unwittingly, this stranger has identified Ibaraki's estrangement, or evidence of the "empty centre" that explains, among other problems, Ibaraki's lack of humanity, which Hayao Kawai and Takeshi Ishida explain as follows:

> The empty centre ... embodies a situational logic for conflict avoidance, not necessarily conflict resolution. The end result is temporary pacification, not permanent reconciliation ... [T]his is because they are resolved [sic] of the vacuous centre which filters out moralistic sentiments. The Japanese are therefore inclined to perform situationally appropriate actions divorced from genuine feelings ...[50]

---

48 Tanaka, *Hidden Horrors*, 163–64.
49 Piper, "Unearthing the Past", 34.
50 Cited in Piper, "Unearthing the Past", 37.

Accompanied by a lack of awareness of the suffering of others, the "empty centre" obviously prevents Ibaraki from remembering both events and people from his past. None of his previous conversations with his Tokyo co-workers, for example, had ever addressed feelings, emotions, or matters of the heart, but rather focused exclusively on baseball. Moreover, he does not recall playing with Kayoko as a child; he does not recognise the happy-go-lucky Broome taxi driver Johnny Chang when they meet again at the Loveday internment camp in South Australia; he cannot identify any of his former patients, nor has he kept in in touch with his only brother after he enlists. Upon learning of his brother's death, he writes a brief letter to his mother that offers little, if any, consolation. Significantly, after Sister Bernice reveals painful details about her life, Ibaraki acknowledges only that as a child, he had been unable to make good lanterns! But once removed from the strict confines of Japanese culture, Ibaraki becomes almost sociable, able to converse easily and pleased to earn the trust of the pearl divers and other community members. While these might seem like modest accomplishments for an educated man with his skills, his sudden ease with others constitutes a big leap forward.

But these good feelings are shattered by several events, the first occurring when Sister Bernice innocently asks about the significance of a wooden tag she has found in the copy of *Robinson Crusoe* Ibaraki loaned her. Startled, Ibaraki snaps that he resents her "intrusion" into his life (159). While it is tempting to assume that Ibaraki's insubordination serves as a constant reminder of past atrocities, it is the "empty centre" that has apparently erased the incident from his mind. Although he soon realises that Sister Bernice could not possibly have understood the tag's significance (159), his callous reproach has created a permanent rift in their relationship and Bernice now becomes aloof. Even though she makes the startling confession that (like Kayoko) she might have been willing to defy authority, to give up her religion for him, he rudely dismisses her and the two never meet again (222).

The second, even more tumultuous event, occurs after the Japanese attack on Pearl Harbor, when Ibaraki is captured and eventually sent to Loveday internment camp. After the riotous colours of Broome, he finds the barren and treeless landscape disconcerting, and the barbed-wire enclosure, with its bright night lights, distressing, as are the overcrowded circumstances that result in the revolting smells emanating from the concrete latrines and ablutions blocks. At daybreak, however, he is pleased to find not only plentiful supplies of food, but relaxed, friendly and sympathetic military personnel, in particular McCubbin, who could be a clone of Taylor's Riley or McMaster. Much as the general atmosphere of the camp is casual and welcoming, the internees, like those at Tatura, are warned that the guards will shoot any escapees. But as Nagata points out, overall camps like these ran smoothly because of their formal committee system: Japanese leaders, used to exercising their authority and control over others' lives, were older, spoke good English, and were socially competent, many having worked in big NEI companies.[51]

During the early days of camp life, Dr Ibaraki is thrilled when the former executives of prosperous companies approvingly inform him that had he arrived earlier, he would have been appointed to the management committee (11). Clearly Ibaraki is regressing here, having apparently learned nothing from the past; convinced that these men can do no wrong, he clings to the familiar ideals of discretion, reverence for tradition and subservience to superiors. He ignores any suggestion that the men in charge are not good leaders, even when the nationalists engage in petty and pointless acts of sabotage, such as proposing that Ibaraki should "deliberately make patients ill," an order that makes him feel "weak" as it conjures up images of "blackened limbs and rotting flesh" (28). The nationalists also conceal information about Japanese defeats by informing the internees that Australian newspapers are full of lies. Yet in true Sisyphean style, Ibaraki continues to remain silent, to simply do his duty, apparently because he believes "[i]t is better to be discreet and present a partial truth than risk conflict" (103). Tanaka observes that while

> [d]uty was always seen in highly sentimental terms – up to and including one's duty to die for the emperor – [the] terms of such duty could be highly arbitrary. Apart from duty to one's superiors, there were no clear guidelines as to whom one owed responsibility. Nor was it clear what demands could be made on an individual – in the name of duty – by the different people in the hierarchy. Hence the notion of 'national duty and responsibility' in general led to a collapse of responsibility in particular.[52]

Such admiration for these higher-ups, however, prevents Ibaraki from questioning radical differences in the prisoners' attitudes to their homeland, and because he will do anything to "save face," he does not want to be seen as an ally of "outcasts" like Johnny Chang, even though he remembers him as outgoing and congenial (41).[53] But Ibaraki's refusal to take responsibility for Johnny's friend Stanley's injuries – he has been beaten simply for being Japanese – and then his laying the blame at Johnny's feet, has severe consequences, as Stanley is ultimately killed in large part as a result of Ibaraki's failure to treat him when he should have.

Once Ibaraki is forced to assemble evidence that his loyalties to the nationalists have been "misguided" (235), he undergoes a series of epiphanies that lead to his

---

51   Nagata, *Unwanted Aliens*, 138.
52   Tanaka, *Hidden Horrors*, 201.
53   The fictional Ibaraki, who finally recognises that Johnny is not a troublemaker, assures him that he will be welcomed back to Broome (Ngata, *Unwanted Aliens*, 242), but when the "real life" "Johnny Chi from Broome" returned in 1946, he found his house and restaurant destroyed, his taxi "commandeered" for the army (227) and he was not welcomed as a former citizen (227). He was, nevertheless, the only ex-Japanese internee who spoke publicly about his experiences. By the end of the war, the Japanese population of 300 in 1941 had dwindled to nine, with Johnny Chi one of them (227).

questioning why, "somehow, [he] always failed the people [he] cared about" (236). Suddenly he comprehends that his entire career as a doctor has been a failure, that he had been "wrong to leave the kindness of the human touch to Sister Bernice and others," and unexpectedly realises that "in keeping [his] silence, [he] hadn't exercised the very quality that makes us human: our capacity to understand each other" (150). At the memorial service for Stanley, Ibaraki makes a rare emotional speech that depicts Stanley as a young man who "had a pure heart and rarely criticised other people, despite the hardships he suffered" (252). At the same time that Ibaraki recognises his role in Stanley's demise, he also acknowledges that the interned Australians (as he now calls them) are better citizens than the cruel and sadistic committee leaders: they are fun-loving, good-humoured, not afraid to display emotion or confront injustices and are, in true Anzac fashion, egalitarians who refuse to bow down to those who claim "superior" status. The Australians are also cognisant of the pain and suffering war brings. When Ibaraki's brother is killed in the Philippines, for example, both Johnny and McCubbin offer their heart-felt sympathy, whereas the nationalists stress that Tomo should be "proud" of a brother who died "fighting for the Emperor" (135) and sacrificing himself for others. His comment, a chilling reminder of Ishii's words that some must be sacrificed [read Chinese] so that others [read Japanese] can be saved, offer Ibaraki cold comfort. When presented with the opportunity to be repatriated as part of the prisoner exchange and early release program that, according to Nagata, freed primarily prominent people,[54] Ibaraki is reluctant to move from the place he now calls "home" because that means leaving behind some genuine friends like McCubbin (273). As he boards the train at Barmera, he reflects on how much he will miss "the sunrises and sunsets – the vivid wash of light" (274) of Australia, but not the racist slurs mothers of small children hurled at him on the train on route to Loveday (3),[55] and now as he departs (275). As his ship draws near Tokyo, however, he feels optimistic; drawing upon images of Australian nature, he vows to "regrow from the embers of [his] former life, like a mallee tree destroyed by bushfire" and "never look back" (281).

While Ibaraki does inevitably "look back," he has yet to realise that self-absorption has blinded him to his mother's sorrow and he is also unprepared for his first meeting with Kayoko, which he arranges after finding work at a hospital on the outskirts of the city. Learning that she is working for the war effort and not yet ready to return to him, he is despondent but says nothing. That same year, the Americans attack Tokyo, leaving the hospital where he works "filled with burn victims and the stench of their scorched flesh" (285). Although he has resumed

---

54 Nagata, *Unwanted Aliens*, 97.

55 In "Prejudice flares when we perceive enemies within," Piper remarks how horrified she was when she heard the story of a Japanese family from Darwin about to be interned in Sydney, who were being subjected to local Australians screaming obscenities at them. Admitting that the contemporary news headlines are full of "racist taunts, bus rants and assaults," she "wonders whether we've come very far at all" (Piper, "Prejudice flares", 3).

surgical work and gradually gains confidence in his skills, he still feels helpless when he learns that there is nothing, not even anaesthetics, which might relieve sufferers from their "their terrible agony" (285). But his pain is not yet over, as these "black and blistered bodies" that merge with memories of the bodies he had dissected years earlier are now accompanied by the heartbreaking news that Kayoko has been killed during an air raid.

While the last sections of the novel initially depict Ibaraki taking stock of a contented, uneventful life with friends and family as well as purposeful work, they also reveal that he is not ready to bring into disrepute the reputation of the man renowned as "the gifted medical pioneer" Ishii Shiro, who recently died peacefully in the arms of his family (291). By contrast, a letter from Sister Bernice – written in 1942 but not delivered until 1948 – which contains Biblical quotations that express her sorrow that she had not been able to release him from his "unsaid" grief (294) and wished that he had "shared a little more of [him]self" (293), he now surprisingly commits the letter to memory. Just as Taylor's Arthur finally recognises that his "real life had somehow evaded [him], branched off at a crucial junction and carried on without [him] in a more rewarding direction" (269), Ibaraki, too, comprehends that he had "clung to the ideal of discretion, when it was courage – and forgiveness [he] had needed all along. [His] silence had been weak" (294). He also laments that both Kayoko and Bernice had brought "light" into his life and had been willing, as he had not, to challenge authority, but he had forsaken them both by clinging to obedience, duty and silence. Dr Ibaraki finally breaks with those restraints by composing a letter in 1989 to the editor of the newspaper that promises "to reveal something the Japanese people should know" (295), to finally "tell all, despite having been ordered years earlier to take any description of his duties at the ironically named "Epidemic Prevention Laboratory" with the Army Medical College in Tokyo headed by General Ishii Shiro to the grave (295). Once word spreads that Shiro was responsible for Unit 371's unspeakable work, Ibaraki knows that disgrace will doubtlessly fall to him and his mother's college-age grandchildren who will be "taunted" by their friends, but he vows to speak, to overcome his long silence and to explain his actions so that "[in] time, it will be worth the shame" (294).

Read together, Piper's essay and novel emphasise that had someone with Dr Ibaraki's knowledge come forward in 1989, the bones would have been identified, returned to their families, received proper burials, and most significantly, exposed Ishii as the thoroughly evil man behind the overwhelming tortures and deaths of so many innocent human beings. But as Piper notes, even those such as the human rights lawyer Norio Minami, who fought tirelessly for the preservation of the bones and continues to agitate for change, have been silenced. It has been more than three decades since the bones were discovered and then enshrined in a memorial, away from public access.

Heiss' *Barbed Wire and Cherry Blossoms* presents another example of how young Japanese men were forced into perilous conformity during World War II.

The inspiration for her novel began during a trip to Pearl Harbor in 2014 when, as she informed Keira Jenkins, while watching Japanese tourists wander about the exhibitions, she suddenly realised that Japanese prisoners' and Aborigine peoples' experiences during World War II were similar: both had been occupying a camp "with a mission manager and living on rations, segregated from the whites in town".[56] Heiss also observed that "sometimes the people living in Erambie (the Aboriginal mission outside of Cowra) were treated worse than the Italian and Japanese POWs".[57] As Imogen Mathew claims, that insight immediately convinced Heiss to produce a novel that teaches readers about "Aboriginal culture, history, and politics."[58]

The novel opens on 5 August 1944, with a "Prologue" narrated by Hiroshi, a twenty-five-year-old Japanese soldier captured in New Guinea and then interned in the Cowra internment camp in New South Wales. Hiroshi has found his life as a captive in the compound since 5 June 1943 to be "utopian," especially when compared to his government's having left him and his fellow soldiers bordering on starvation. Although still slight, Hiroshi has gained weight in the camp[59] and, like Piper's Ibaraki, feels relaxed around the congenial guards. The opening comments detail his reluctance to join the approximately 1,000 Japanese soldiers who plan to break out of the camp, a getaway he considers unwarranted. But like Piper's Ibaraki, he acquiesces and votes with the others who want to flee the camp because, as his father had insisted, once at war, Hiroshi should die rather than strive to return to Japan, because "it is better to die with honour than live with shame" (xix).

Hiroshi's bellicose father has spoken "passionately" about how Japan, a small country, could and should become a world leader: he has supported both Japan's invasion of China in 1937 and Prime Minister Hideki Tojo's attack on Pearl Harbor in 1941, and now expresses pride at Hiroshi's enlistment and service in New Guinea. But while Hiroshi's father supports his nation's aggression, he has never fought himself and thus has no idea of the kind of cruelty fighting men are capable of inflicting upon their enemies. Hiroshi suffers recurring nightmares as a result of the violence he has been forced to witness, but he has also observed the damage

---

56   Keira Jenkins, "A Story of Two Camps" *Koori Mail* 10 August 2016.
57   Jenkins, "A Story of Two Camps". Another instance where Australians appear to treat their enemies with more respect than they do Indigenous Australians occurs in Piper's novel. While en route to Tokyo, Ibaraki learns that the Japanese ambassador on board is transporting boxes containing the ashes of the naval officer killed in the 1942 midget-submarine attacks in Sydney so that the Australian government can return them to the families in Japan (276). Shortly after, Ibaraki reads the "shocking" news that the Australian authorities had given the Japanese officers a funeral with "full naval honours," which he "interprets as treating their enemies with more respect than their own people" (227).
58   Imogen Mathew, "Love in the Time of Racism: 'Barbed Wire and Cherry Blossoms' Explores the Politics of Romance," *Conversation*, 7 September 2016. https://theconversation.com/love-in-the-time-of-racism-barbed-wire-and-cherry-blossoms-explores-the-politics-of-romance-64126.
59   Anita Heiss, *Barbed Wire and Cherry Blossoms* (Cammeray, NSW: Simon & Schuster, 2016), xix. All subsequent references are to this edition and appear in parentheses in the text.

Japanese officers inflicted on their subordinates during training. Hiroshi's father, by contrast, knows nothing about the Japanese government's failure to send sufficient food supplies, which rendered the men too weak and depleted to fight the enemy or avoid capture.[60] Not surprisingly, Hiroshi often wishes that he had either died in New Guinea or could return to a time before war, "back to where the dread of the unknown did not destroy his sense of peace or sanity" (113), as well as back to when he could appreciate his mother's "peaceful" approach to life. Even though Hiroshi's father expresses hope that his son will never have to fight, Hiroshi knows that his wishes are futile because Japanese people (like Piper's Ibaraki) are "forced to think and act the same … [and] must not hold ideas that differ from the majority," because "[a]cting with harmony is of the utmost importance" (114).

His father's resolve that his son become a soldier does not, however, upend Hiroshi's aspiration to live, to see his family again, or to continue his longing to study English and become a poet. Accordingly, even though he realises his chances of survival from the breakout are slim – especially hampered because he knows nothing about the terrain – he must join it. Climbing over the barbed-wire fence, he runs for his life and is, miraculously, rescued by a dark-skinned man who, noticing his distress, invites him to hide out in his nearby air raid shelter. Thus begins the story of a young Japanese man who, previously unaware of the existence of Aboriginal people, lives out the war in their embrace.[61]

Heiss' decision to use her novel as a teaching tool starts with how Aboriginal people reach consensus through the democratic process, a theory that finds Banjo Williams, who has rescued Hiroshi, seeking permission from his family and other members of the close-knit community to keep the prisoner safe until war's end. While stressing similarities between the two groups, Banjo also argues that the prisoner needs their help, has never done them any harm, and wants to escape the prison *he* is in, and so does the Aboriginal community (6); perhaps even more significantly, Banjo stresses that it is not their way to turn in an innocent man. But his brother Kevin (who carries a grudge because Banjo's wife Joan had rejected him years ago), makes several mean-spirited (but often accurate) arguments against

---

60 Tanaka writes that "there is a certain amount of Japanese writing suggesting that Japanese forces committed acts of cannibalism in the Philippines and New Guinea during the Asia–Pacific War", "when their supplies had been completely cut off". Victims of cannibalism "were Japanese soldiers who had been killed in battle or who had died of various illnesses" as well as "Australian soldiers" (Tanaka, *Hidden Horrors*, 112, 114, 115). Mandy Sayer's 2011 novel *Love in the Years of Lunacy* also raises the issue of Japanese cannibalism in New Guinea.

61 Although Heiss' Japanese POW executes a safe escape and survives to war's end, according to Harry Gordon, none did. While there were "many versions" of what happened on 5 August 1944, the facts are that "[a]part from the 231 Japanese who died, four Australian soldiers were killed – stabbed or bludgeoned to death, according to the office record – 107 Japanese and four Australians were wounded, and 334 prisoners actually escaped from confinement. Within nine days of the outbreak, 25 of the escapees were dead, and the rest captured by soldiers, police and local farmers hunting either singly or in vigilante groups." See Harry Gordon, *Die Like the Carp! The Story of the Greatest Prison Escape Ever* (Stanmore, NSW: Cassell Australia, 1978), 8.

guarding the prisoner, beginning with what we now know to be a grotesque understatement – that the Japanese are mistreating Australian soldiers in captivity (4). Kevin also points out that nearly a dozen of Erambie's enlisted Wiradjuri men are currently fighting the Japanese and probably being forced to work for them[62] and raises the problematic issue of Aboriginal men who fought in World War I but were "denied the right to be Australian citizens" after the war (6). Nevertheless, Joan dismisses Kevin's final argument that his mission lacks sufficient food for its inhabitants and there is not enough left to feed a foreigner by reminding him that the Wiradjuri always "share" what they have (8). As Gaynor Macdonald might argue, Joan's readiness to divide up their minimal amount of food is characteristic of Wiradjuri people, who consistently want to "be able to respond to demands [to share]," even when their generosity "requires access to resources that others value and will demand." Macdonald notes that because of their willingness to distribute their food regardless of their circumstances, the Wiradjuri have been accused of being part of a culture that "gave everything away to kin and therefore couldn't get on in life", but she firmly asserts that their detractors simply did not "understand demand sharing".[63]

Before putting the issue to a vote, Banjo advances his strongest argument – that the POWs and Aboriginal people are fighting a common enemy – which underscores how disempowered, dishonoured and imprisoned the latter are within their own country. In sum, he declares that he wants equal pay with "white fellas doing the same job"; does not want to live "in fear" that his children will be taken away; and wants to be like "white people," who always have "enough food and … water and electricity" (7). His comments point to another characteristic of the Wiradjuri people – their longstanding desire for Aboriginal autonomy. Macdonald observes that during the nineteenth-century encroachments Wiradjuri people experienced, the expectation that "change" would be reduced to "loss of tradition" and would then lead the way to their becoming "useful poor dark-skinned members of a lower working class". But despite the immense changes the Wiradjuri have endured, they have continued to reproduce themselves as *Aboriginal persons* and Macdonald thus concludes that "personal autonomy and demand sharing as characteristics of Wiradjuri personhood … are essential for understanding how they have negotiated change of all kinds". Overall, she argues that the innovative strategies the Wiradjuri adopted to preserve their culture was the "strength of the

---

62 Elizabeth Rechniewski acknowledges that "[d]espite the obstacles that were put in the way of their enlistment, and despite the discriminatory policies to which they were subject, hundreds of Australian Aboriginal volunteers ('Black Diggers') served in the First World War and thousands in the Second." See Elizabeth Rechniewski, "Remembering the Black Diggers: from 'the Great Silence' to 'Conspicuous Commemoration'?" *War Memories: Commemoration, Recollections, and Writings on War*, eds. Stéphanie A.H. Bélanger and Renée Dickason (Montreal: McGill-Queen's University Press, 2017), 388.
63 Gaynor Macdonald, "Autonomous Selves in a Bureaucratised World: Challenges for Mardu and Wiradjuri" *Anthropological Forum* 23 no.4 (2013), 401–02.

desire for distance from the world of the white fella".[64] After Banjo's side easily wins the vote, Banjo suggests that Mary, his seventeen-year-old daughter, will take Hiroshi his nightly rations because he can no longer negotiate stairs as a result of his "gammy" ankle (read untreated) (12) and Joan is too busy as a working mother (read poorly paid) for the priest and church.

Overall, Heiss' novel carefully reveals the complex and multi-layered nature of the historically constituted social and political relationships Indigenous Australians have found themselves enmeshed in through the gradual unfolding of the loving relationship that develops between Mary and Hiroshi. But what begins as five-minute nightly exchanges of stories across cultures on subjects as diverse as rabbits (Aboriginal food and Japanese folklore), baseball, footy, music, literature, history, geography and landscape, soon leads to lengthier and weightier discussions on matters such as citizenship, equality and participation in war. During one of their encounters, Hiroshi asks Mary if Australian people are, like the Japanese, "forced to think and act the same" (114), and if young Australians' dreams are ignored, as they are in Japan. Mary responds that Indigenous Australians are "like prisoners in our own home" (118); they encounter many more difficulties than "whites" in achieving their dreams and living "full lives," largely because the government appoints mission managers who then have complete control over Aboriginal peoples' lives. Because there is no mechanism for Aboriginal people to express their identities or make decisions through governance or any kind of political structure, they have no choice but to obey their "boss[es]" (here nicknamed King Billie), who act as their agent of social control, as well as a tool of assimilation and cultural destruction. According to Mary, manager John Smith (King Billie)

> tells us what to do, where we can go. He decides whether we can leave here and who is allowed to visit, who we can marry, what time we have to be at home, if we can go to the city … So it's kind of like being in a prison … because we have rules and regulations with someone in charge to boss the "captives" around. (42–43)

Mary further discloses that Blacks cannot vote or drink alcohol legally, receive no pensions or maternity allowances, and are segregated from white people in public places such as theatres and even where they live. Missions like Erambie, situated close to Cowra, provide white people with ready access to Aboriginal labour, while ensuring that Aboriginal people continue to live outside of town or, as Anna Doukakis notes, nonetheless keeping them "out of sight."[65] In essence, Heiss' text suggests that these (inevitably white) men are paternalistic, ethnocentric and culturally insensitive; they believe that Aboriginal people are their racial and

---

64 Macdonald, "Autonomous Selves", 400–01 (italics in original).
65 Anna Doukakis, *The Aboriginal People, Parliament and "Protection" in New South Wales 1856–1916* (Sydney: The Federation Press, 2006), 13.

cultural inferiors, incapable of managing their own affairs, and thus require the protection of the government. These managers regard Indigenous Australians as primitive, child-like, inherently lazy, excessively dependent upon the state and overall, the source of their own problems. One of their stock phrases – that Aboriginal people are "no one in [their] own land" (13), resonates throughout, ironically demonstrating that Indigenous Australians definitively understand concepts of human rights and justice, as their decision to save Hiroshi displays.

Over the course of his nightly discussions with Mary, Hiroshi learns that the government's system of control keeps Aboriginal people mired in poverty and suspended in a prison-like environment like the Japanese POWs; if they want the same rights as white people, they must "assimilate, be more like them" (117). In the state of New South Wales, where Cowra and the Erambie mission are located, the government policy, or the *Aborigines Protection Act 1909*, can remove many of the restrictions on their lives, but the price is high. Even though they can apply to be "non-Aborigines" and receive an "Exemption Certificate" (118), their freedoms are thereafter curtailed: they must leave the mission, not see their families and never socialise with other Aboriginal people without certificates (118).

Another of the major lessons that Heiss' novel teaches is the extent to which mission managers regarded education for Aboriginal people as a waste of time. Mary's siblings baulk at attending the mission school because, as Joan rightly observes, the teaching is "second-rate" but presumed "good enough for the Black kids" (65). When Mary is forced to quit school and work for the Smith family in order to bolster her family's coffers, she recognises that her future opportunities are forever limited because the authorities assume that domestic work is "all … Aboriginal women are good for" (43). Mary has no means of satisfying her thirst for knowledge since Aboriginal people have no access to current newspapers; library loans are not free; and lacking electricity, few have radios. But when Hiroshi, desperate for news, innocently asks Mary to bring him newspapers, Mary concocts lies about wanting to practise her reading and convinces Mrs Smith she not only wishes to read the news, but to also become familiar with the work of Australia's best-known writers such as Banjo Paterson, Henry Lawson, Mary Gilmore and Louisa Lawson. In return, Hiroshi teaches Mary *haiku* by the famous sixteenth-century Japanese poet Bashō.

Once Mary gains access to newspapers, she finds proof that whites make no effort to keep Aboriginal people informed of activities and decisions that have a direct bearing on their lives. She has not previously known of government plans to "either rebuild or relocate Erambie Aboriginal Station" because the "camp is a disgrace" and the "homes … little better than humpies" (174), a description that infuriates Joan, who knows that women do their best to keep their homes clean and tidy, because even the "slightest speck of dirt" (dust storms are frequent) could cause them to lose their children. Moreover, they now realise that the government's justification for their dislocation – they are gradually assimilating and hence their numbers are dropping – amounts to wishful thinking that Indigenous Australians are doomed to extinction and thus will cease to be a problem (175). When Kevin learns of the government scheme, he declares that "It's all about land. They took the land that was ours. Then they moved us onto this land, and now they want to *take* this land from us too" (176). Kevin is right: in the late 1700s, non-Indigenous people began stealing their land, which the following excerpt in an article from the New South Wales Office of Environment and Heritage documents:

> the spread of settlement across New South Wales by non-indigenous people gradually pushed Aboriginal people off their land. NSW governments responded in many cases by setting aside parcels for the sole use of Aboriginal people. Across the state, Aboriginal reserves were created as a political response to the dispossession of Aboriginal people from their land.[66]

Historian Elizabeth Rechniewski summarises the effect the loss of their land had on Aboriginal people as follows:

> The federation of Australia in 1901 was intimately bound with the aim to acquire the legal means to ensure a "White Australia," a policy aimed in part against the presence of the Chinese and other foreign workers such as the Kanakas. It also entrenched the subordination of Aboriginal peoples that had allowed progressive annexation of their land from the earliest days of settlements. Upon the outbreak of WWI, Aborigines were not citizens (though a few had the vote because of particular state legislations), were often forced to live on missions, and were subject to the control of the "Protector" of Aborigines. They experienced daily discrimination, exclusion from public places and services, and occasional violence.[67]

When Hiroshi queries whether Aboriginal people fought to preserve their land, Mary informs him that they have always fought but unsuccessfully because there are more whites than Blacks, and white people have guns that will always defeat Blacks, who have only "spears or fists" (94). Furthermore, "white people have been shooting Aboriginal people since they arrived" and hence the Wiradjuri's land is "scattered with massacre sites" (93). Ultimately, when Joan hears of the plan to remove Aboriginal people from Erambie, she insists that they will leave only if physically removed, thereby attesting to their deep attachment to a place that has been their home for generations (176).

Mary's reading of the papers further apprises her of the new immigration policy the government intends to instigate postwar, again without consulting Aboriginal people: "Immigration will be a big thing after the war ... only white

---

66 "Living on Aboriginal Reserves and Stations," New South Wales Office of Environment and Heritage, https://www.environment.nsw.gov.au/chresearch/ReserveStation.htm.
67 Rechniewski, "Remembering the Black Diggers", 389.

immigrants will be invited within Australia's gates to settle and raise families of future Australians" (207). Mary, at this point deeply in love with Hiroshi, panics at the thought that he will not be able to stay and marry her, and also realises that the White Australia policy is still influential, as miners continue to protest that non-whites are taking their jobs (207). To ensure that Indigenous Australians can never become their equals, they force them to write tests in English when they apply for jobs (208). Bitterly, Banjo comprehends that nothing in their lives will change if the "prime minister say[s] that Australia will forever remain an outpost of the British race" (208).

Banjo is also disturbed at war's end when he and his family gather to hear King George VI's announcement on their neighbours' radio that the Germans have lost the war and "freedom and independence and liberty" are now restored to the Allies. The King asks listeners to remember all of those in the services "who have laid down their lives" (194). But as Mary informed Hiroshi earlier, the matter of Indigenous Australians who fought or wished to fight is also fraught because Aboriginal people are not "citizens": they cannot vote and cannot go to war overseas because "[they] have to be Australian to fight for Australia" (94). According to Mary, when Aboriginal men tried to enlist for the same reasons as their white counterparts in World War I – the desire to travel, to defend their land even though it would never be theirs (94) – they were rejected. But when the government needed more soldiers and conscription was voted down (twice), the government allowed "half-castes" (those with one white parent) to enlist (95). When Hiroshi queries why Aboriginal men would want to fight for a country that deprives them of the right to be citizens, Mary replies that they wanted to demonstrate loyalty to Australia and prove that they were courageous warriors (95). But as Rechniewski points out, even though many fought, their contribution was overlooked, in part because of influential men like C.E.W. Bean (there he is again!) who, at war's end, "exhorted his fellow countrymen and women to complete the work begun on the battlefields," to create "the greatest and best country in the world," which he described as "an Anglo-Saxon nation of free, happy brilliant people".[68] She then concludes "there is no room (and indeed no mention) in his vision of Australia for the Aborigines".[69] Or, as Kevin puts it, "Our mob [are] fighting for a White Australia, not an equal Australia" (106). Ultimately, Banjo stresses that no English monarch will be his leader: "his leaders were his ancestors – his father and Uncles and those who stayed on Wiradjuri country and fought invasion" (194).

The gross inequities between Indigenous Australians and prisoners-of-war during World War II make apparent that the war has not benefited them, as it has other "prisoners." Whereas the government considers Aboriginal people untrustworthy, it deems the Italian POWs happy, dependable men who require little supervision (79). In captivity, unlike Aboriginal people, Italians are free to

---

68   Cited in Rechniewski, "Remembering the Black Diggers", 395.
69   Rechniewski, "Remembering the Black Diggers", 389.

ride bikes, go to movies and pubs and make their own grappa (9–10). They are encouraged to present plays, operas and concerts on stage. Moreover, when the local white people choose Italians to work on their properties, they also reward them by giving them "midway meals and ... electricity and running water" (17). While the Indigenous Australians' dissatisfaction with so many inequities is understandable, tension also arises between the whitefellas and the Italian prisoners when the latter (like their depiction in Goldbloom's and Temby's novels) quickly establish themselves as proficient shoe repairers, plumbers, painters, woodworkers, carpenters, gardeners, fruit and vegetable growers and cannery workers (53). Joan begrudges that Italians are excessively praised for their talents as excellent builders when Aboriginal peoples clearly possess the same skills (108). Moreover, when women claim that Italians are irresistible, beautiful singers who are "okay on the eye" (180), their men become jealous and accuse Italians of being "philanderers," a comment not far from the mark, since at least one young Australian woman is pregnant. The local Diggers are aggrieved that they are losing their jobs to the lesser-paid Italians (105) and demand that they all be sent back to Italy (106). Hiroshi, too, is angry that Italians in captivity can send letters to their families and the Japanese cannot. But Aboriginal peoples also envy the good life offered to the Japanese: they can play sport whenever they like, suffer no food shortages and feast on rice and fish from New Zealand (56). Banjo, who has been moved to tears when he sees Japanese soldiers hanging in the trees, cannot fathom why they want to kill themselves and others, especially when the living conditions in the Japanese war camps are superior to those the Indigenous Australians in Erambie must tolerate (103). Moreover, a double standard prevails, which Kevin poses by asking Banjo to "imagine if we burnt down our huts and shot white people. What do you think might happen?" (103). The response is obvious.

Overall, Heiss' novel emphasises that the government's systems of poor education, minimal health care and chronic food shortages, deny Aboriginal peoples self-respect and human dignity. It insists that if these entrenched systems of inequality carry to this day, Aboriginal peoples can never achieve independence, prosperity or happiness, despite being assiduous, conscientious, and clever: Banjo is a skilled carpenter, and the Erambie mission has produced legendary footy players, popular "crooners," and other talented musicians like Banjo and his relatives. Consequently, Heiss' Aboriginal peoples, who have studied their "masters" assiduously, have no trouble duping the manager (an appeal to his massive ego works) into smoothing the way for Hiroshi, once discovered, to be repatriated to Japan without penalty or pain. As to the star-crossed lovers? At war's end, they remain just that.

Saskia Beudel's *Borrowed Eyes: A Novel*, continues the pattern of reliance upon the lies, secrets and silences between central characters, but the novel is unique in its challenge to what McKernan earlier considered a "common feature" of World War II prisoner-of-war literature;[70] while many thought they already knew "what it was like to come home",[71] McKernan suggests that after years of punishment and cruel treatment, simply "get[ting] on with being civilians again"[72] was nothing like they thought it would be. The brief "real-life" summary Beudel provides in her Acknowledgements indicates why homecoming may have proved so difficult:

> In February 1942 on Bangka Island just off the coast of Sumatra, twenty-two Australian Army Nurses plus one civilian woman were ordered to wade into the sea by Japanese soldiers. They were machine-gunned in the back in waist-deep water, and Vivian Bullwinkel was the sole survivor. She spent the remainder of the war interned as a prisoner of war. *Borrowed Eyes* is a fictional account of her experiences.[73]

While Beudel records here only the tragic events that occurred on Bangka Island, references to other daunting hardships abound. For example, prior to her arrival on the island, Bullwinkel (renamed Vivien Carmichael in the book) had withstood the torpedoing of the *Vyner Brooke*, the overcrowded ship purportedly taking sixty-five of the Australian nursing sisters to Australia. Twelve died, but Bullwinkel (now Carmichael) who could not swim, stayed afloat by clinging onto the side of a small boat, which eventually transported [her] safely to Bangka Island. She lived to tell the tale of her forty-two-month internment under the Japanese.

But why Beudel should have documented some of the most shattering events of Bullwinkel's life and then declare that "the depth of her existence after the war, and of how she lives with the aftermath of her survival bear no resemblance to her actual life" (298) is puzzling. Although I rarely contact writers about their work, I did email Beudel to invite her to comment on specific aspects of the novel, which she did promptly and frankly. In her depiction of Carmichael, she explains that

> she was trying to find ways to fictionalise [her] father's POW experiences, to get some distance from them, and so the Carmichael character was a way to do that in a narrative sense. And there was also, of course, the big question of how someone lives with the aftermath of such a huge trauma as hers.[74]

Although Beudel provides a list of sources she utilised in writing her novel, she makes no mention of Bullwinkel's biographer Norman G. Manners (perhaps wisely, since his account borders on hagiography) and his claim that Bullwinkel seamlessly transitioned from all the pain and anxiety she had suffered during and after the war to a completely happy and fulfilled life in Australia.[75] He adds that she continued

---

70   McKernan, *The War Never Ends*, xv.
71   McKernan, *The War Never Ends*, xvi. Here, McKernan quotes the last words in Sister Jessie Simons' memoir, *In Japanese Hands*, which are "I was home" (xvi).
72   McKernan, *The War Never Ends*, xii.
73   Saskia Beudel, *Borrowed Eyes: A Novel* (Sydney: Pan Macmillan Australia, 2002). All subsequent references are to this edition and appear in parentheses in the text.
74   Saskia Beudel, Email exchange 6 June 2020.

her distinguished nursing career, which included frequent promotions to higher-ranking capacities; maintained regular contact with many of the nurses with whom she had been interned, and received many honours and awards, as well as the prestigious Florence Nightingale medal. In a similar manner, Margaret McAllister observes that Bullwinkel paid tribute to the nurses who had not survived the war by helping to raise funds for a memorial on Bangka Island and then attended the unveiling in 1992.[76] Bullwinkel also found much joy with her late-in-life marriage to Frank Statham. In 2000, at eighty-four, Bullwinkel died of a heart attack. Nevertheless, her alleged capacity to remain unscathed stretches credulity, particularly when Robert J. Ursano and James R. Rundell document that "the severity of the conditions was greater in World War II Pacific Theatre camps than in European theatre prisons,"[77] and that "Japanese POW camp survivors have consistently been reported to have Post-Traumatic Stress Disorder (PTSD) symptoms more frequently than other POW groups and the symptoms have been more severe".[78]

Not surprisingly, Carmichael's return to the home front bears no resemblance to Bullwinkel's. Prior to the war, Vivien had been engaged to a local farmer, but recognising they have nothing in common, she gives him up and abandons hospital work, preferring to make home visits to the aged. Irritated by her patients' assumption that she is too young to have had any life experiences worth recounting, she says nothing to correct their misconceptions. In addition, her home life before World War II was lamentable: her father, a clearly traumatised World War I veteran from an unnamed country, was always "broke" and, despite having studied architecture, unable to hold down even casual jobs. Full of self-pity and anger, he remained in poor health due to chain-smoking and self-medicating with alcohol. Sometime during Vivien's childhood, her mother vanishes, leaving her daughter to cope with a withdrawn and silent father who "dedicate[d] himself to understanding the architectonics of the vegetation of his new country" (16), of which he takes photographs by the thousands (but none containing people). Although he often takes Vivien bushwalking, he rarely speaks, other than to complain that his photos are all "shit shots" (152).

The novel offers no specific reasons why Vivien's father should suffer psychological injury, but historian Jay Winter would perhaps blame it either on the "stigma then and still now attached to mental illness in general, and to mental illness among soldiers in particular"[79] or on the result of "the relatively undeveloped

---

75   Norman D. Manners, *Bullwinkel: The Story of Vivian Bullwinkel, A Young Army Nursing Sister, Who Was the Sole Survivor of a World War Two Massacre by the Japanese* (Carlyle, WA: Hesperian Press, 1999).

76   Margaret McAllister, "Vivian Bullwinkel: A Model of Resilience and a Symbol of Strength", *Collegian* 22 (2015): 135–41.

77   Robert Ursano and James Rundell, "The Prisoner of War", *War Psychiatry* (Falls Church, Virginia: Office of The Surgeon General United States of America, 1995), 433.

78   Ursano and Rundell, "The Prisoner of War", 440.

diagnostic skills doctors and administrators had available to them when confronted with a mixture of somatic and emotional disorders that many tended to treat as malingering".[80] More contemporary medical researchers such as Tara Galovski and Judith A. Lyons observe that the veteran's isolation "creates an emotional emptiness and a serious functional loss of the father and husband from everyday life"[81] or, as Vivien puts it, what her father procured for her was "a non-story, an implacable and impenetrable silence as to his experiences" (16). Galovski and Lyons further acknowledge that the wives and children of such negative uncommunicative men may become victims of "secondary traumatization":[82] accordingly, as Vivien remarks, "[her] father's life [had] imprinted on [hers] like the meticulous photographs he wished, secretly, to become renowned for" (16) and, as the novel demonstrates, contributes to her trauma.

Anxious to find a career that would enable her to flee an unhappy home life, the fictional Vivien has trained as a masseuse (now physiotherapist) and seizes the opportunity to volunteer for the military. From the moment she enlists, however, she does not resemble any of her over 400 Australian peers that historian Hank Nelson describes as "having entered nursing when duty, idealism and self-denial were an implicit part of the calling; he adds that most were "motivated by patriotism and an obligation to use their skills where they were most needed",[83] but the fictional Vivien embraces none of these sentiments. Instead, she ignores historian Catherine Kenny's proposition that the Australian sisters retained their loyalties to Australia and pride in their military units throughout their prolonged captivity,[84] and refutes Angharad Fletcher's references to the "Digger Sisters,"[85] a phrase which, although it did not make its way into the lexicon until the mid-1980s, nonetheless corresponds with the general description of World War II nurses in captivity, which Kenny describes as follows:

> [T]he bond of friendship that these women developed merits the term "mateship." This ideal, fostered by the official historian of the First World War, C.E.W. Bean, has

79   Jay Winter, "Shell Shock, Gallipoli and the Generation of Silence" *Beyond Memory: Silence and the Aesthetics of Remembrance*, eds. Alexandre Dessinque and Jay Winter (London: Routledge, 2016), 195.

80   Winter, "Shell Shock", 195.

81   Tara Galovsky and Judith A. Lyons, "Psychological Sequelae of Combat Violent: A Review of the Impact of PTSD on the Veteran's Family and Possible Interventions," *Pergamon: Aggressive and Violent Behaviour* 9 (2004): 483.

82   Galovsky and Lyons, "Psychological Sequelae", 477.

83   Hank Nelson, "An Ordinary Bunch of Women," *Prisoners of War: Australians Under Nippon* (Crows Nest, NSW: Australian Broadcasting Corporation, 1990), 70, 71.

84   Catherine Kenny, *Captives: Australian Army Nurses in Japanese Prison Camps* (St. Lucia: University of Queensland Press, 1989), 161.

85   Angharad Fletcher, "Sisters Behind the Wire: Reappraising Australian Military Nursing and Internment in the Pacific During World War II," *Medical History: An International Journal for the History of Medicine and Related Sciences* 55 no. 3 (July 2011), 420.

come to be symbolic of Australian male associations particularly during wartime, but in this instance it was also displayed by Army nurses in captivity. (160)

As well as rejecting the notion of "mateship," Carmichael also spurns the promotion of "the egalitarian spirit," both reputedly mainstays of Bean's Anzac-legend mythology.

Alongside her lack of interest in emulating Bean's ideals, Vivien is also a self-confessed "opportunist" (18) who longs for travel and adventure. While interned, she resents the resilience, the resourcefulness and the organisational abilities the Australian nurses possess: moreover, she expresses surprise that "From among our hundreds there sprang, and I was never sure how, an Executive Committee, a Committee for Correspondence, a Committee for Food Matters, Committee for Clothing, one for Daily Necessities, Maintenance, Storage, Hygiene, Labour, Recreation" (65), but refuses to be part of the committee system or to share in the spirit of co-operation. Instead, she writes in one of her three diaries (possession of which was subversive), *When I get out of here, heaven preserve me from nagging women*" (53). After her only "mate" Iole dies at Bangka Island, Vivien remains socially isolated. She does, however, befriend Martin, an intellectually gifted adolescent in the Sumatran camp whom she teaches to draw and paint, albeit without any materials available. While watching him draw, Vivien is reminded of her own troubled adolescence and thus leaps to Martin's side when he is caught spying on bathing nuns and then swiftly relegated to the men's camp, without any protest from his somewhat cruel mother. Vivien's herculean efforts to save Martin fail, and the two lose contact at war's end.

Like the World War II Anzacs who expected they would re-integrate faultlessly into civilian life (even though most did not), Vivien subsists in a kind of "self-imposed exile" until 1952, when the bulk of the novel takes place. Living alone in a rural coastal house in Victoria near where she and her father used to reside, Vivien spends her time in solitary pursuits, either searching for meaning in the copious histories of internment, or rearranging her father's slides, which she eventually realises is "purposeless." Having considerably reduced her commitment to physiotherapy, she prefers to spend time tending plants such as ferns and orchids, but also disposing of moist decay and rotting leaves from a hothouse of her own clever design. As reviewer Joan Digby comments, "The hothouse is a metaphor for the inescapability of the past. It represents a haven for Vivien, but it is also reminiscent of the Sumatran jungle, a place of pain and fear and suffering".[86] Her actions are, as trauma theorist Ron Langer might argue, symptomatic of the Avoidance/Numbing traumatic category that includes "a markedly diminished interest or participation in significant activities; a feeling of detachment or estrangement from others; ... and the 'sense of a foreshortened future' – that is, the victim does not expect to have a career, marriage, children, or a normal life

---

86   Joan Digby, "Heads Above Water," *Australian Book Review*, October 2002, 52.

span".[87] Unlike Bullwinkel and the other real-life nursing sisters who maintained their friendships after the war, the fictional Vivien has not. While she dutifully collected the names and addresses of the nurses in one of her diaries, years later she notes they were now merely "like mementos" (145).

Vivien's postwar life becomes radically altered when she receives a request from Martin to visit her. From then on, her memory becomes a "live slippery thing, furtive as a lump of wriggling mercury" (13). Images she thought were safely out of reach, especially her experiences on Bangka Island (13), keep re-surfacing. Although initially apprehensive, once Martin arrives, she realises that they "had the same vocabulary ... A mutual repertoire" (157). Pleased they had "plenty to talk about," she is also frustrated that they often spend their time reminiscing about the past by "*not* talking about it" (187). While there was something "calming, or reassuring, about that combination, [Martin's] presence was also like a trigger, or an ongoing series of triggers, to [her] memory of those times" (187). Soon she realises that Martin's life eerily resembles her father's: he, too, drinks and smokes too much; leads a peripatetic lifestyle that prohibits him from settling into any career or occupation; regularly cheats on his girlfriend, and most alarmingly, has attempted suicide (200). Vivien is quietly exasperated, in part because she "didn't know much about his life before or after the war" (187) and, like her father, Martin refuses to talk about the past, insisting instead that "talking doesn't help. It's just people being self-obsessed, creating more and more words that go nowhere, achieve nothing" (262).

But eventually, and only after they begin walking together in the natural world – (Vivien hates walls, Martin hates houses) – especially on the evening when they sleep among the dunes and bleached middens of her childhood, Martin slowly begins to answer Vivien's questions, particularly about what happened to him prior to the time he spent in the internment camp. His stories – one that finds him and his younger brother (whom he assumes responsibility for) stumbling over dead Indonesian bodies after the Japanese who caught them looting had hacked off their arms with swords and then hung them in trees as warnings to others – are grisly (235). While relaying more equally grim stories, Martin casts Vivien in the role of listener, which numerous trauma therapists such as Judith Lewis Herman insist is crucial to the healing process. She argues that trauma sufferers (like Vivien, her father, and Martin) who insist on "keeping the traumatic experiences to themselves, prevent the integration necessary for healing".[88] But when Martin refuses to listen to Vivien's stories, she postulates that he considers his trauma more significant than hers. Nevertheless, she remains determined to tell her story, as her refrain – "I tried to tell him" – indicates. Martin pays no heed, however, until he accidentally stumbles upon a copy of the testimony she gave at the Australian War Times

---

87   Ron Langer, "Combat Trauma, Memory, and the World War II Veteran," *War, Literature & the Arts: An International Journal of the Humanities*: 23, no. 1 (2011), 51.

88   Judith Lewis Herman, *Trauma and Recovery* (New York: Basic Books, 1992), 45.

Board of Inquiry that describes the horrors she sustained, about which he has known nothing. But having kept quiet for so long, "what Vivien fear[s] most all along happens [when] the knot unravels all at once. And that's too much for anyone" (257). For his part, initially offended that Vivien had never talked about her shocking experiences, Martin is now outraged by her restraint (211).

Somewhat mysteriously, Vivien confesses that she was not satisfied with the trial because she was forced to provide only the responses His Honour wanted to hear, which consisted of "empirical evidence. Names. Identificatory characteristics. Hard evidence" (269). In suggesting that Vivien was prevented from speaking forthrightly both about the nurses' unspeakable experiences on Bangka Island, and then back again on the home front, where a journalist has blatantly manipulated the facts of her internment (41), Beudel may have been more prescient than she knew. (In her email, she attests that she "did not know about either the rape of the Australian nurses or the fact that they were forbidden to mention it," and hence her "characterization of Carmichael was not affected.") But because Australians were under the impression that Bullwinkel had told "the truth" at the tribunal, they were shocked when it came to light in 2017 that the Australian government had prevented her from telling "the *whole* truth" (emphasis added). Prior to her death, Bullwinkel had confessed to a broadcaster that "most of the nurses" had been "violated" before being shot, and that abiding by the command to remain silent was "torture".[89]

Unfortunately, Bullwinkel did not live to tell that "whole truth," which came to public attention in 2017, when military historians Lynette Silver and Tess Lawrence and biographer Barbara Angell began to investigate why the government had found it necessary to muzzle Bullwinkel. Silver claims that until 1955 rape was still a "hangable offence for perpetrators in New South Wales," and "senior Australian army officers wanted to protect grieving families from the stigma of rape," which was a "fate worse than death".[90] Barbara Angell's forensic work on the nurses' uniforms (primarily the [re]placement of buttons) revealed evidence that the nurses had been violently attacked, and Silver found verification that the Australian government had committed an "act of censorship" when officials ripped a key account of what happened to the nurses out of the available evidence.[91] Yuri Tanaka, who wondered why the Japanese shot the nurses in the ocean when the soldiers they slaughtered with their bayonets were left lying on the beach, concludes

---

89 For more information on the issue, see Gary Nunn, "Bangka Island: The WWII Massacre and a 'Truth Too Awful to Speak'," *BBC News* 18 April 2019. https://www.bbc.com/news/world-australia-47796046; Tim Barlass' "Australian Nurse was Ordered to Keep War Crimes Secret," *Sydney Morning Herald* 8 April 2019. https://www.smh.com.au/national/australian-nurse-was-ordered-to-keep-war-crimes-secret-20190322-p516jg.html; Lynette Ramsay-Silver's *Angel of Mercy: Far West and Far East* (Sally Milner Press, 2019) also contains information about the events at Bangka Island.
90 Nunn, "Bangka Island".
91 Nunn, "Bangka Island".

that the commanding officer was "clearly aware that assault and murder of POWs and nurses violated the Geneva Convention and thus … took steps to destroy any evidence by disposing of the nurses' bodies in the sea". He adds that while "the contempt with which women are held in Japanese society and the exploitation of their sexuality by Japanese men" is well known in the case of the massacre, but since "traditional male ideology hold[s] that war is absolutely and exclusively a male activity", they may also have been "bewildered by the unfamiliar sight of more than twenty women in military uniform in the front line of the war". In their defence, the nurses had worn Red Cross armbands and had raised a Red Cross flag to indicate they were non-combatants, but obviously to no avail. Unfortunately, the commanding officer committed suicide before any official investigation of his role occurred.[92]

Whereas much of Vivien's trauma stems from the authorities' refusal to allow her to speak the truth, once evoking the notion that she is "sick of [her] own memories" (47), she strives to see, as the title suggests, "through someone else's eyes for a while" to "remember someone else's memories for a while, see if that were possible" (47).[93] Martin's visit has provided her with an audience (albeit a small one), to confide in and to unveil the *whole* truth to. He, on the other hand, has relied upon Vivien's having taught him to draw, and thereafter continues to utilise various types of art as coping mechanisms to deal with the emotional pain wrought both as a child and now an adult. His ability to create art rather than merely observe it serves as a means of evading frustration and unfulfilled desires. Although Vivien has taught him formal aspects of the visual arts such as shading and realism, once sent to the men's camp, he no longer relies on those specific instructions, but uses his imagination to produce, for example, a watery drawing of destroyed buildings, giant insects, guards with guns and a distraught boy like himself hiding amidst human wreckage (80). It is only through art (in varying forms such as experimental installations), that Martin produces what Vivien regards as his stubborn reticence – and that is to create, through art, a "nonverbal" means of dealing with his deeply rooted trauma, and as a method of managing it as well. The work of art Vivien describes provides evidence, or at least an interpretation, of his surroundings and experiences during his internment in the men's camp. In short, he makes evident his inner predicaments – primarily fragmented trauma memories – as he works through a variety of artistic undertakings.

In attempts to come to terms with his past, he deploys a surfeit of tactics, one of which deals with *found objects* (190) that inspire him to gather the remnants of his past and try to make sense of them. Obsessed with patterns, he seeks them in objects such as ashtrays, which offer a means of utilising various aspects of his past

---

92   Yuri Tanaka, *Hidden Horrors*, 87–88.
93   I am heavily indebted to "the eyes" of my former graduate student Hebe Tocci Marin, whose work on this novel in the English Department at the University of Calgary has provided me with a much better grasp of the significant role that art plays in this novel than my own.

such as fragmented memories of his childhood and responsibility for his brother; of abandonment by his cruel German mother and always-absent father; and his lack of a homeland after learning he is not welcome in Indonesia, but the configurations remain incommunicable or undecipherable. Some of his efforts that have led only to failed attempts subject him yet again to thoughts of failure and inadequacy.

But Martin does finally enjoy a sense of success with his camera obscura, which an adult Chinese teacher introduced him to. Understanding how it works helps Martin begin to come to terms with his past and he now teaches Vivien the same technique. His use of the camera obscura helps Vivien distance herself from the traumatic past, and then (hopefully) reach a kind of emotional steadiness. Overall, Martin teaches Vivien to recognise that vital to the healing process is an ability to view harmful, even traumatic incidents from a different angle, perhaps by utilising emotional distance to render them bearable. While this procedure is not quite Vivien's idea of employing "borrowed eyes", it is not far off, and leads to the novel's ending on a happy note, with the clever use of an artistic device that performs as a curative, or healing component for the lessening of trauma.

Accordingly, at the end of the novel, after a three-month stopover with Vivien, Martin is packing to leave for America, where he plans to study agriculture. He expresses hope that this current plan will sort everything out, and it might, since we now know that veterans returning from the Vietnam War and more contemporary conflicts find gardening therapeutic and restorative.[94] Martin has invited Vivien to join him and his girlfriend in America, and she might. At is transpires, she is also planning to leave the region without saying where she is going, but it matters not. In the past, she has been, as Martin has informed her, "too still," (219) but now that she has had the opportunity to tell her story, to break her silence, to expose historical lies, she is now in movement, in flux, open to whatever the future might hold.

Beudel's novel is important on several fronts: initially, she attempts to present a war experience that is much more complex and multifaceted than that "uniformity" handed to the Digger Sisters, given that it is folly to suggest that all nurses could possibly assume the same identity (although Beudel writes that when finally freed, the nurses were given identical haircuts and identical polka-dotted dresses). The authorities' intentions were more purposeful, however, because they wished to disguise the nurses' skeletal bodies as a result of the inadequate diets forced upon them and hence their having succumbed to deadly diseases such as beri-beri, malaria, typhus and dysentery. But most certainly, the stories of those who returned severely traumatised, the ones currently left out of history, were obviously not all the same. Beudel's novel about a fictional Bullwinkel makes a significant contribution to the prisoner-of-war literary genre since, as Yuri Tanaka emphasises,

---

94   The curative effects of gardening for war veterans appear in Helen Heritage's *Borrowed Landscape* (Createspace Independent Publishing Platform, 2010) and in Dymphna Cusack's *The Half-Burnt Tree* ([1969], Crows Nest, NSW: Allen & Unwin, 2012).

until very recently in Japan, the term 'war crimes' conjured up images of the inhumane treatment or murder of enemy soldiers, especially prisoners of war. By describing and perceiving women as civilians who held the 'home front' during the war, commentators seem to have perpetuated the belief that women were not the direct victims of war.[95]

As Beudel's novel indicates, little could be farther from the truth.

---

95   Tanaka, "War, Rape and Patriarchy", 79.

13
No Hell Like Peacetime
Going (Down) Under in the Land of the "Fair Go"

In her review of Andrew Leigh's *Battlers and Billionaires: The Story of Inequality in Australia* (2013), Gillian Terzis declares that "no Australian legend has endured the ages quite like the 'fair go' … Bigger than Bradman and Phar Lap combined, egalitarianism is as central to Australian identity as exceptionalism is to the United States".[1] In his Introduction, Leigh provides a few additional examples of the "fair go," such as that Australians don't like tipping, or that beaches have no private areas, so whoever gets there first claims the space they want. He adds that Australians sit happily in the front seat of taxis, and the word "mate" is a "universal leveller" (unless you're a woman).[2] More seriously, Leigh also points out that during World War II, there were marked differences between the ways Australians and British troops working on the Thai-Burma Railway responded to the conditions they were forced to endure. Whereas the Aussies pooled their allowances and lived "by the principle of the fit looking after the sick, the rich looking after the poor," the Brits "kept their own allowance and divided up their tents according to rank" (2). Their adherence to class structures resulted in dire consequences, as "cholera and dysentery killed all but twenty-five of the 400 British men" (2). But while Leigh asserts that "egalitarianism goes deep in the Australian character" (3), he concludes that "an egalitarian spirit is no guarantee of true equality" (4). In other words, "just because we call each other 'mate,' it doesn't mean we have an equal distribution of incomes" (4). Terzis agrees, noting that while the wealthy are highly visible, "those who are less visible – the working poor – or those in abject poverty" have found their "much less romantic" stories "eclipsed by the tale of Australia's remarkable prosperity".[3] Similarly, in an article comparing Australians' and Canadians'

---

1   Gillian Terzis, "'Shooting Through: An Ambitious Treatise on Social Stratification in Australia.' Review of Andrew Leigh's *Battlers and Billionaires: The Story of Inequality in Australia*", *Australian Book Review* no. 354 (September 2013), 14.
2   Andrew Leigh *Battlers and Billionaires: The Story of Inequality in Australia* (Collingwood, Vic: Black Inc. 2013), 3. All subsequent references are to this edition and appear in parentheses in the text.

handling of the COVID-19 pandemic, Tenille Bonoguore proposes that "a worrying number" of Australian politicians tend to apply the "fair go" to "most people," so that "anyone who doesn't fit in – any minority, really, can be viewed as a problem".[4] But as Terzis observes, it is the "truth-telling of literature" that often "undermine[s] strategic efforts to conceal and distort economic and political realities"[5] – and I agree, as there are no shortages of literature in either country that offer accounts of grave economic and political inequality. But few, if any, of these critics call attention to writing by women, particularly in Australia where, depending upon the subject – in this case, British and Japanese war brides – they either received minimal attention or were completely overlooked. Thus, this chapter strives to counteract the omission of women's voices by drawing upon two contemporary Australian novels that challenge the narrowly-defined national past by exposing the inadequacies of the core myths of Australian society (such as the "fair go") and continuing to reveal the biases and gaps in the records of those who have been systematically silenced.

Both literary works demonstrate that World Wars I and II caused huge social disruption that dislocated families and literally tore them apart. Within their ranks were numerous impressionable young women who made the courageous decision to wave goodbye to families and friends and follow a stranger into a new world, but as historian Carol Fallows points out in one of the few books on the subject,[6] information on those "brides" has been sorely neglected: estimates must suffice. Fallows proposes that approximately 15,000 war brides came to Australia after World War I from England, Belgium and France, with a few from Egypt, but that figure also includes fiancées and children. Official figures are still lacking, but during World War II, Fallows suggests that an estimate of 25,000 war brides is "reasonable".[7] She laments that even though there have been hundreds of books written about Australia's participation in twentieth-century wars and the concomitant social, political, and historical impact on the country, such books pay little or no attention to the thousands of women who married Australian servicemen during or after those years and migrated to Australia.[8] Such dismissal is surprising, given that "even a quick flick through the newspapers from the end of both world wars finds numerous stories about brides and 'stork ships' coming into Australian ports, which makes the lack of even a mention of these women in so many history books even more puzzling". Fallows speculates that their stories may have been overlooked "because the transporting of wives, fiancées and children to

---

3   Terzis, "Shooting Through", 14.
4   Tenille Bonoguore, "Canada is fighting COVID-19 with niceness – and losing", *Globe and Mail*, 20 March 2021. https://www.theglobeandmail.com/opinion/
     article-australia-fought-covid-19-with-kind-resolve-and-its-winning-canada-is/.
5   Terzis, "Shooting Through", 14.
6   Carol Fallows, *Love and War: Stories of War Brides from the Great War to Vietnam* (Milson's Point, NSW: Bantam Books, 2002). See also Robyn Arrowsmith's *All the Way to the USA: Australian Second World War Brides* (self-pub. 2013), which contains similar comments.
7   Fallows, *Love and War*, xii.
8   Fallows, *Love and War*, ix.

Australia was handled in an ad hoc fashion by the Australian government, unlike the United States where both a War Brides Act and Fiancés Act were passed at the end of the Second World War to establish the right of wives and fiancées to enter and live in the States".[9] In addition, as Ann Beveridge writes of the Japanese brides who came to Australia after World War II, they "were never part of an official immigration program" and "their contribution to Australia's multicultural diversity has been largely ignored". She adds that "rarely has Australia saluted the determined women over the past century who gave up their own homeland and family and sailed across the world – all for the love of an Australian soldier". Beveridge contends, however, that war brides' stories are far from the same in that some Japanese war brides were not seeking love but were desperate to leave their country because they had endured "extreme hardship, deprivation" and "life for them [and their families] had been a matter of survival".[10]

Moreover, even though many of these "brides" may have landed on a calm home front, more than a few quickly became embroiled in domestic skirmishes and acts of violence that required them to show a great deal of courage and make many sacrifices. That fewer than ten per cent (again, only an estimate) suffered defeat and returned to their homelands should not be regarded as proof that the rest "lived happily ever after," for governments provided only one-way tickets: poverty prevented many from returning. Many were "raw brides,"[11] but some more "raw" than others. One of these, from whom I partially glean my title here, "no hell like peacetime," would be the American critic Sandra Gilbert's former suffragist who "asked herself if any horrors could be greater than the horrors of peace – the sweating, the daily lives of women on the streets, the cry of babes born to misery as the sparks fly upward".[12]

But it is important to step back and consider who these women were. In her definition of what constitutes a war bride, Fallows suggests that the field is restricted, given that the only women to qualify have "married a member of the Australian forces as a result of war".[13] Accordingly, a mere two novels meet the requirements. They are Joan London's 2001 *Gilgamesh*, which tells the story of an English woman who marries an Australian soldier at the end of World War I, and Helen Heritage's 2010 *Borrowed Landscape*, which recounts the story of one of

---

9   Fallows, *Love and War*, x. Jessie M.G. Street, one of Australia's most notable pacifists, ensured that American servicemen provided for their Australian wives and children by enlisting the aid of Eleanor Roosevelt, who extended the same rights to women married to all American personnel in all countries. For more details, see Jessie M.G. Street's *Truth or Repose* (Sydney: Australasian Book Society, 1966): 224–38.

10   Ann Beveridge, "War's Bride and Joy," *Daily Telegraph*, 15 May 2003: 048.

11   Margaret Atwood, *The Robber Bride* (Toronto: McClelland, 1993), 153.

12   This heart-breaking comment appears in Sandra Gilbert's essay "Soldier's Heart: Literary Men, Literary Women, and the Great War," which appears in *No Man's Land: The Place of the Woman Writer in the Twentieth Century*, eds. Sandra Gilbert and Susan Gubar, (New Haven, CT: Yale University Press, 1989), vol.2, 270.

13   Fallows, *Love and War*, x.

the 650 Japanese women who married an Australian serviceman during the post-World War II occupation of Japan. Excluded, then, is the English bride Stella in Gail Jones' 2007 *Sorry*, because her husband, who served in World War I and shortly after brings his new wife to Australia, is English; also eliminated is Simone Lazaroo's 2000 *The Australian Fiancé*, which takes place at the end of World War II, because the fiancé has not fought in any war, nor does his unnamed Singaporean fiancée become his bride. (Much literary attention has been paid to both fine novels.) But there may be another reason for the paucity of war brides' stories (if I am, indeed, correct that there is one), and here I refer to historian Suzanne Davies, who makes the familiar argument that "the carefully cultivated mythology of the Anzac hero, like all militaristic mythologies, depends for its survival and strength on a selective and exclusionary construction of the past".[14] Within this enduring Anzac mythology, "it is men who are privileged as the authentic actors and knowers. Their experiences and memories of war, especially those of battle, are revered as offering "the 'truest' record of what war really is".[15] Moreover, suffering is the privilege of men: "That women should be recognised as victims or as participants in war contravenes the Anzac mythology".[16] Throughout my embarrassingly long study of Australian women's war fictions, I have learned that the Anzac legend has not been a subject women writers have wished to tackle, although this oversight is being challenged by some whose work appears in this larger study. Brenda Walker's 2005 World War I historical novel *The Wing of Night,* for example, undercuts the heroic Anzac tradition and calls attention to the much-overlooked dark sides of war, and both Mandy Sayer's 2011 *Love in the Years of Lunacy* and Sara Knox's 2007 *The Orphan Gunner* depict women stepping from the margins to the military – occasionally even into Anzacs' roles as soldiers and pilots during World War II – and proving that, as I've suggested elsewhere in this volume, anything a man can do, a woman can do better, sometimes even effortlessly so.[17]

Thus London's *Gilgamesh* reflects Terzis' comment that "inequality rose throughout the nineteenth century to the 1920s where it reached its apex"[18] by validating the extent to which the Australian government's soldier settlement scheme failed its returned veterans and their families after World War I.[19] But before examining that violation of the principle of the "fair go," a synopsis of the

---

14 Suzanne Davies, "Women, War and the Violence of History: An Australian Perspective", *Violence Against Women* 2 (1996), 360.

15 Davies, "Women, War and the Violence of History", 365.

16 Davies, "Women, War and the Violence of History", 361.

17 Although there has been considerable attention paid to the promiscuous relationships between Australian women and American servicemen in novels such as Dymphna Cusack's *Southern Steel*, Cusack's and Florence James' *Come in Spinner*, Henrietta Drake-Brockman's *The Fatal Days* and Mandy Sayer's *Love in the Years of Lunacy*, the only novel I am aware of that tells stories of the approximately 7,000 (the figures vary widely) Australian women who married Yanks and moved to the United States, is Robin Sheiner's novel 1983 *Smile, the War Is Over*, discussed in Chapter 10.

18 Terzis, "Shooting Through", 14.

story is provided. London's novel begins at a convalescent hospital south of London just a few days away from the Armistice (3). While awaiting his discharge for a leg wound, the Anzac Frank Clark meets the English Ada, who volunteers to visit recuperating soldiers in hospital. Both Frank and Ada are about to turn thirty and are hence vulnerable, at the time of life when they are thinking about falling in love, settling down, and starting a family before it is too late. After Ada tells Frank that "she had been orphaned very young [and] grew up living alone with her older brother," who had "died early in the war, at Ypres" (4), not surprisingly, when Frank asks her "what she would like to *do*" when the war is over (4), she replies that she would "like to go far away to a country where there will never be another war" (4). Frank instantly declares, "That's where I'm going" (4), and within seconds, asks Ada to "come home with him" (4) and she instantly says "yes." Although Frank's leg has healed, the text implies that his other complaints – "insomnia" and a "craving for isolation," or even war-weariness – may be symptoms of trauma. But Frank, a former schoolteacher, is certain that once he gets to Western Australia, where he is keen to "take up land", to live a life characterised by "Fresh air, honest toil, taking orders from no man" (6), his problems will be solved. (Frank appears to have imbued historian and war correspondent C.E.W. Bean's dictum that the good life was to be had only in the bush.)

Once the couple (now joined by their daughter Francis) reach Australia, Frank again acts rashly by joining the soldier settlement scheme, for as Fallows writes, although it "was organized by state and federal governments to help soldiers re-settle on their return home," and "it provided the men with land and equipment to farm it at low rates of interest, many of the more than 16,000 farms failed. Often the land was unsuitable for farming … and many [like Frank] lacked the expertise to make it work".[20] Fallows' comments – that many of those who fell for the scheme "found themselves in a landscape and way of life they could never have imagined"[21] – apply equally to Frank, for as historian Stephen Garton explains, the government land scheme "was devised to open up the wilds of southwestern Australia. Land, parcelled into blocks, was given to a group of 20 or 30 settlers who would initially work together to clear each home block and build each other a house. Every man was made a loan by the Agricultural Bank to get him started, repayable over thirty years". And as the propaganda of the times claimed, "if all went well for you, you could end up owning your own land much sooner, in a matter of five or six years. The scheme was called Group Settlement".[22] (The word "scheme" is telling.) But Frank's block of land was not what he envisioned, given that it was "the outmost,

---

19   Joan London, *Gilgamesh*, Sydney: Picador, 2001. All subsequent references are to this edition and appear in parentheses in the text.
20   Fallows, *Love and War*, 108.
21   Fallows, *Love and War*, 107.
22   Stephen Garton, "The Last Battle: Soldier Settlement in Australia 1916–1939", *Australian Historical Studies* 48, no. 3: 7.

cut off from the other farms by a belt of national forest … It was the least arable of the blocks, but the most picturesque" (7).

But if Frank's life endeavour to make a "go" of that land proved unimaginably difficult, so, too, did Ada's. She had lived with her White Russian sister-in-law Irina and nephew Leopold in a London house always full of visitors, mostly Russians, but constantly a "lively crowd" (5); moreover, Ada would have had ready access to bookstores, cafes, museums and shops, at every corner. It's doubtful she could ever have envisioned the isolation, the incredible loneliness of life in the bush. (It is important to keep in mind that her problems occurred in an era that was pre-Skype and the internet, so that ways of keeping in touch with friends and relatives other than by letters, which took weeks, if not months, to make it across the pond, simply did not exist.) That Frank and Ada's "home" was unsustainable becomes evident when their property is finally listed in 1927 on a map as Nunderup, having not appeared previously because "there was nothing there" (8). When the horses Frank was entitled to from the government (to be paid for later of course) fail to thrive, Frank decides to go into pigs, but he has no idea how to build them a shelter and is too proud to ask for advice or help from other farmers. And because he keeps running out of cash, he must often delay work on his own projects to hire himself out. Thoughtlessly, Frank fails to understand that having always been an urban dweller, Ada was also totally unprepared for the kinds of help he expected from a farmer's wife. (He complains she doesn't know how to wield an axe!)

By the time Frank and Ada come to live on their own block, they have two daughters who are nearing school age. A son was born but died soon afterwards, while they were still camping in a hut, waiting for their house to be built (7). As I have written elsewhere, houses and the concept of "home" are routinely important considerations in war brides' stories: home is a place where women do not feel like immigrants; home is a place where they can escape the helplessness and insecurity evoked by oppressive landscapes.[23] Ada has no such home: the one Frank eventually builds is only a marginal improvement on the hut. But even after the house is finished, Ada remains grief-stricken and weeps constantly. His wife's unhappiness fills Frank with "dread," as does his awareness that "She could go quite wildly out of control" (7). While his frustration with Ada increases, he has no grasp of how much she suffers. Like many husbands who have often claimed to be perplexed by what their wives do all day, he, too, asks,

> What *did* Ada do? Mooned about … Rested like a lady in the afternoons. After the boy, she seemed like half an invalid. Headaches. Woman troubles … She seemed to

---

23 For a further examination of how war brides view the concept of home, see my "Wish We Luck As You Wave Me Goodbye: Representations of War Brides in Canadian Fiction and Drama by Margaret Atwood, Mavis Gallant, Norah Harding, Margaret Hollingsworth, Joyce Marshall, Suzette Mayr, Aritha van Herk and Rachel Wyatt", *Back to Peace: Reconciliation and Retribution in the Postwar Period*, eds. Aránzazu Usandizaga and Andrew Monnickendam (Notre Dame, IN: University of Notre Dame Press, 2007): 250–271.

spend her mornings doing the washing … She was always trying to keep the girls clean. She fed the chooks, collected the eggs. Kept the stove stoked with the wood he chopped. She could never get the hang of the axe. She never left the clearing, she was afraid of the bush. She was afraid of snakes, fire, the dark, of getting lost. Afraid of bloody everything. (11)

(Frank does not place Aboriginal people on his list, but Ada is also afraid of them.)

Although the narrator mentions that the Clarks could have attended church services, gone to dances or to the pictures, it is unclear whether Frank, with his desire for isolation, ever encourages Ada to socialise. One place she does regularly visit with her daughters, however, is the nearby Sea House, a hotel built in the style of a two-storey English manor house, where she sits in the gardens, "like a governess on a nature ramble. It was the only place with any romance in this country, she said" (8). (That lack of romance in Australia quickly becomes a familiar refrain.) But eventually Ada, who *couldn't take the life*, as went the other common refrain, stops talking, Frank is again unsympathetic, resentful that she is unable to help him with even the simplest chores on the property; moreover, his daughters are still too young to work, and he is too proud to ask for help from other farmers. But while Leigh states that the poor are often distanced from politics, Frank is the exception: as the Depression worsens and more and more farmers are unable to repay their loans, he goes to meetings in the local hall and declares he and the others are nothing but "indentured slaves to the government, paying blood money to open up the country for them" (9).

But eventually Frank must admit that he has not been the only returned soldier sold what might be termed "a bill of goods," since "by 1933, more than half of the settlers had abandoned their land" (14). He also realises that his political involvement has gotten him nowhere; exhausted by the futility of his efforts, he comes close to exercising the privilege almost exclusively available to men – that is, to leave (or in the vernacular of the day – to "shoot through" or "do a runner") – but does not. The text also hints, however, that he is so intent upon changing his and his family's lives that he nearly succumbs to drowning himself, but when he watches his distraught daughters watching him "waving" from the shore (an image that conjures up Stevie Smith's famous poem, which ends with the words "not waving but drowning"),[24] he comes to his senses and realises that the "great adventure" has come to an end. He informs his daughters that their mother is homesick, that he will endeavour to take the family back to London, where Ada had lived "like a princess," and where the girls could receive a decent education. Not realising that Ada has lost her grip on reality, he intends to ask her forgiveness, but dies before he can execute his plans. Although the narrator gives no precise reason for Frank's premature demise, by 1930, he appears to comprehend that "there was hardly any

---

24   Stevie Smith, "Not Waving but Drowning," *Collected Poems of Stevie Smith*, New York: New Directions, 1972.

part of his body, ribs, legs, back, hands, that hadn't been injured by war or labour" (13). The text implies that Frank has simply given up, thereby leaving the hopelessly incompetent English war bride Ada to raise their daughters on her own, but it is the girls who must assume responsibility for their mother. (In another contravention of the "fair go," there are no references in the text to any of the reputably ever-friendly "mates": neither the farmers nor their wives ever take the slightest opportunity to extend a helping hand to any member of this miserable family.)

Shortly after Frank's death, when Leopold and his Armenian-born friend Aram come to visit (their story in part an inter-text with the ancient epic *Gilgamesh*), Leopold is surprised to discover that "there is not a trace of the Ada of his earliest memories, a presence around which his mother Irina was always happy, a presence which he remembered as light, playful, sensual" (24). Like Frank, Ada has also given up: for some years, her only lifeline had been the Christmas package and letters Irina has sent, but now, after so many years of desolation in the bush, she leaves the packages and letters unopened. Careful readers will recall the omniscient narrator's prescient comment on the first page of the novel – that "[Frank and Ada] should really never have met" (3) – which is borne out by our recognition that Ada has been clearly traumatised by the death of her child, but the manifestations of that grief are her refusal to wash, eat, work, all tropes that have been employed exhaustively in the description of mentally unsound women throughout history. Ada exhibits classic symptoms of female insanity in the form of insomnia, paranoia, muteness, depression and the failure to parent. Ultimately, she ekes out the remainder of a very despondent life, perpetually calling to the chooks, staring into space and always wearing a hat.

While London's story of Ada and her daughters continues in a tragic vein, as the daughters' futures are severely compromised by their parents' failures, this fictional story, when compared to historical fact, is sadly not unique. According to Garton, while nearly 40,000 World War I veterans obtained properties under settlement schemes, in many cases, "the land did not give adequate return". Historians have since concluded that the scheme was marred by "official incompetence, lack of planning and supervision, inadequate and barren land, drought and flood, poorly trained and inexperienced settlers, serious debt, rising costs, and falling prices for produce".[25] One declares that the settlement schemes were a "complete failure" and an "episode of which the nation was more than a little ashamed, for hardship and deprivation was not the way in which a grateful nation had intended to repay the diggers for their deeds of valour".[26] In the end, veterans were betrayed by their country that rewarded them for their service by encouraging them to apply for what sounded like a "fair go," but sadly never was.

In a similar vein, Helen Heritage's 2010 novel *Borrowed Landscape*[27] reinforces the mistaken belief that because war neuroses were deemed psychological, they

---

25   Garton, "The Last Battle", 118.
26   Garton, "The Last Battle", 119.

continued to prevail during and after World War II and hence removed many veterans' ability to take advantage of the "fair go." In the opening lines of the novel, the adolescent narrator Louise reflects upon how devastated her Melbourne family was by her father's years at war: "The Pacific War ruined my family as effectively as a dropped bomb ... My father went to war when I was a baby of nine months and he returned in 1946 when I was six years old. He returned a ruined man, ruined because of what had happened to him while fighting the Japanese in Papua New Guinea" (5). Her father's experiences remain a mystery until the end of the novel, but it is clear from the outset that he suffers, as does London's Frank, from trauma: like so many returned soldiers, he self-medicates with alcohol and cannot be left alone for long periods because he might harm himself. Although he is frequently hospitalised for lengthy stays and returns home temporarily subdued and easier to handle, family members lament that he was "only a shadow of how he should have been" (41). Shortly before her father dies – prematurely, like London's Frank – Louise learns that while fighting in New Guinea, he had become a sort of father-figure to a reckless but charming twenty-year-old named Danny. When Danny is killed and the battalion attempts to rescue his body, which they discover to their horror has been cannibalised, they come under enemy attack, but Louise's father heroically sends his men back to camp and single-handedly fends off the enemy, for which he receives a Distinguished Conduct Medal. Nevertheless, he never overcomes the feeling that he should have done more to protect Danny.

When he returns to the home front, he is no longer able to concentrate and hence cannot hold down his former job as an accountant. The family might have managed to climb out of poverty had the government given, as Louise claims, "full pensions to men who could prove that the damage occurred directly *because* of the war experience, not *before* the war – in short, that [these men] were mentally whole before active service and that it was the active service which had directly caused their mental health problems" (208). But as Louise discovers, "how to prove this was well-nigh impossible. Added to this cruel irony was the view that if one man saw the same service and coped, why should another man fall apart? Such punitive official views had no understanding that a man could be rendered mentally ill from the very act which had earned him a medal for bravery" (208). The family is also forced to conceal the real reason behind the father's illness because many people at the time agreed with the government's assessments that men who "had war neurosis were weak and cowardly" (6). Like London's novel, Heritage's underscores how little care or attention was given to those wounded in mind: for them, there was no "fair go."

Heritage's novel draws attention to another wartime inequity – the treatment of Japanese women who married Australian servicemen during the postwar Allied occupation of Japan and accompanied their husbands to Australia after World

---

27 Helen Heritage, *Borrowed Landscape* (Melbourne: Waxflower Press, 2010). All subsequent references are to this edition and appear in parentheses in the text.

War II. Keiko Tamura affirms that both Australian men and Japanese women grew up in communities where neither could have imagined the circumstances that would lead to marriage. Since the 1930s, the Japanese had been becoming more militaristic: they were in the process of expanding their interests in Asia and at the same time generating hostility towards Britain and the USA. Australians, by contrast, in the 1930s as well, were living in a remarkably homogenous country that was over 90 per cent British by birth or descent. The White Australia policy was "strictly enforced" and "fear of invasion by Asian hordes was high". Inter-marriage, considered problematic, was rare in both countries.[28]

After Japan surrendered in August 1945, Tamura writes that "the country was occupied by Allied Forces, beginning in early 1946 and until the signing of the Peace Treaty in 1951".[29] From early 1946, American forces, which consisted of 430,000 men, were scattered throughout various prefectures in order to control the Japanese population of 70 million. By February 1946, Australian soldiers began serving in Japan as members of the British Commonwealth Occupation Force (BCOF), which consisted of troops from Britain, Australia, New Zealand and India.[30] Most of the Australian contingent was situated around Kure, about forty kilometres east of Hiroshima, which had been devastated by the atomic bomb. The main duties of these 11,000 Australian servicemen were to "disarm the Japanese forces and demilitarise depots and various establishments in the occupied areas".[31] Before long, Australian servicemen were forced to revise their views, having believed that the Japanese were violent and cruel, mainly as a result of the Japanese atrocities inflicted on Australian prisoners of war and the bombing of Darwin. All of that negative perception began to change, primarily because although these troops were supposedly under a strict no-fraternisation policy with the Japanese (which the Americans apparently did not invoke), it did not prevent many hundreds of servicemen from becoming romantically involved with Japanese women,[32] most of whom they met at Kure, where as many as 20,000 had been offered jobs as waitresses, canteen workers and interpreters, at the BCOF camp. As Tamura points out, the Australian cohort were "fresh young volunteers who

---

28 Keiko Tamura, *Michi's Memories: The Story of a Japanese War Bride* (Canberra: Australian National University Press, 2011), 1.

29 Tamura, *Michi's Memories*, 2.

30 Australian War Memorial, "British Commonwealth Occupation Force 1945–52", 2 June 2021. https://www.awm.gov.au/articles/atwar/bcof.

31 Tamura, *Michi's Memories*, 2.

32 According to Suzanne Davies, "in 1993, Professor Yuki Tanaka, a political scientist working at the University of Melbourne, was denounced after he drew attention to the involvement of Australian servicemen in the rape, prostitution, and brutalization of Japanese women during the allied occupation of Japan following World War II" (Davies, "Women, War and the Violence of History", 360–61). As Davies notes, "predictably the involvement of Australian soldiers in the sexual violation and exploitation of Japanese women has been officially denied" (361). Moreover, "that women should be recognized as victims or as participants in war contravenes the Anzac mythology that positions them either as part of the property to be defended or as the steadfast but safely removed supporters of the cause" (361–62).

had not been old enough to fight during the war"; hence the opportunity for the "young and the restless" to serve in Japan suited them well because they were also seeking adventure.[33] That 650 Japanese women left their country not knowing if, or when, they would ever see their parents, siblings or friends again, required what Fallows refers to as an "extraordinary reserve of courage; it was apparent that these women believed wholeheartedly in the strength of the love and commitment they shared with their husbands and were prepared to step into the unknown in pursuit of happiness".[34] By the end of 1956, the ban on Japanese immigration was lifted when the Treaty of San Francisco came into force. At that time, Japanese women could obtain Australian citizenship, but since Japanese law did not then recognise dual citizenship, these women had to surrender their Japanese nationality to take up Australian citizenship.

But as Tamura argues, "the opposition women faced in immigrating to Australia did not solely come from the Australian government. Most experienced strong opposition from their [communities and] families when they made the decision to marry Australian servicemen",[35] a situation borne out in the story of Hanaka MacDonald in *Borrowed Landscape*. Her thoughts, italicised throughout the text, indicate that she knows that "*People in the community whisper about women like her, saying we only went with the foreigners so that we would be given food and gifts and that we were no better than prostitutes*" (95). Moreover, her aunt and two cousins, with whom she lives during the war, believe that women should not work, even though Hanaka has already sold off most of her possessions to feed them, and knowing they will surely starve if she does not find a job. Her aunt insists that marriage to an Australian will damage their reputations, that "*It will go against our name. It will lessen the chances of your cousins to marry into good families. Your father [now dead] would never have allowed it*" (55). But her views are groundless, for as Hanaka knows, there were few opportunities to marry:

> *So many men dead on foreign ground, so many boxes containing their ashes waiting for collection throughout the country. The men who did return alive were shunned even by their own families, who were shamed that the soldier had chosen to surrender rather than death – every soldier had been issued a hand grenade to ensure he would end his own life rather than be captured* (53).

Tamura points out that Japanese war brides like Hanaka arrived "in the 1950s when waves of migrants from Europe were also arriving in Australia and when the government's policy was assimilation".[36] The fourteen-year-old narrator Louise, who lives in a leafy (but working-class) Melbourne suburb, claims that Australia

---

33   Keiko Tamura, "How to Become an Ordinary Australian: Japanese War Brides' Reflections on Their Migrant Experience," *Oral History Association of Australia Journal*, vol. 24 (2002), 2.
34   Fallows, *Love and War*, 81.
35   Tamura, *Michi's Memories*, 61.
36   Tamura, *Michi's Memories*, 61.

was comprised mainly of people from Anglo-Celtic stock and that she can identify only three "Others" – one Jewish man and two Chinese men. But the times were changing, as postwar immigration was bringing large numbers of Eastern Europeans and Italians to Australia. They were not warmly received either; adolescent girls like Louise were informed that "foreign men were more hot-blooded and not as easily controlled as the native-born and were warned to think carefully before agreeing to go out with them" (14).

Somewhat surprisingly, Tamura takes the position that war brides "were generally welcomed warmly but, at the same time, expected to assimilate quickly into Australian society. It was assumed each would have the protection of her husband and his family and she would not encounter major problems adjusting to the new culture, the new language and the new way of life". Tamura adds that "the women themselves retained the traditional Japanese expectation of brides, which held that she would adapt quickly to her husband's household and to the Australian way of life".[37] But one of the problems was that, as Tamura recognises, these women had no way to comprehend what exactly that "Australian way of life" was. Notwithstanding that Hanaka had few opportunities to mix with a wide range of people, the Japanese bride's comments, which continue to appear in italics throughout the text, further indicate how truly unreceptive Australians were to foreigners: a man spits at her as she walks by, butchers and bakers stare at her in "horrible" ways (15), and she knows the Chinese greengrocer seemingly hates her because of what he deems the "'terrible actions' of the Imperial Army in China."

While Amy Bentley argues that the Australian media presents war brides as willing to assimilate and in fact already in the process of assimilation (Hanaka was certainly trying to "fit in"), they were relying on pre-existing stereotypes of Japanese women that emphasised their difference and attempting to "contain them" through several strategies such as denying them any particularity or individuality.[38] Many of the women (notably Cherry Parker, the first Japanese war bride to be admitted into Australia), took on English names or anglicised versions of their names and gave their children English names. Many of the brides like Hanaka attended a "bride school" in Kure (Christian in faith) where they were taught how to dress and what to cook in "the proper Australian way",[39] but again without any real understanding of what that is. By 1956, and because of the numbers of new applications, the Menzies government felt it necessary to hold classes for prospective wives, to provide basic information about Australia. But if *Borrowed Landscape* is anything to go by, that "basic information" was insufficient: Hanaka learns to make "shepherd's pie" (a confusing food since there are no sheep – and hence no shepherds – in Japan) and trifle. She also discovers that rice was only to

---

37 Tamura, *Michi's Memories*, 61.
38 Amy Bentley, "Japanese Women in Australia from 1890–1950s; positioning Japanese War Brides in the Australian National Imaginary" (master's thesis, University of Sydney, 2003).
39 Bentley, "Japanese Women in Australia", 103.

be used in "rice pudding." In addition, much as Louise and Hanaka faithfully pore over the *Australian Women's Weekly* in search of clues of the elusive "Australian way of life," they mainly discern that women take medicine when they are "nervy," which manifests itself in an inability to look after the house, and hence the "bride" cries often (21). Aside from being taught tasks like "home craft, social customs, geography, and English," they were frequently shown photos, such as one of Cherry Parker, which showed "her being received into a loving family of 'the right sort'". These photos also regularly depicted "brides dressed in western clothes".

As Bentley further argues, "the media emphasized assimilation," which consisted of the brides' "willingness" and more importantly their "ability" to become good wives and mothers. Correspondingly, they referred to the "brides" using "collective nouns, wives or brides" that "denied their particularity and individuality" and were often described as "girls" rather than women, which "denoted" a process of "infantilization." Moreover, the word "girls" not only hinted at the notion of "child brides," but articulated their existence only in relation to men.[40] Not surprisingly, Hanaka does not wish to confront her husband on any of these issues because, as she tells Louise, "a Japanese woman will never show her private grief" (126), and she does not.

But while Tamura proposes that many of these war brides may have been legally admitted into the country, she fails to acknowledge that many accounts indicate they were far from welcome, a situation borne out in Heritage's novel. During her relationship with the young Louise, Hanaka confesses that her Australian family does not want her as a daughter-in-law and hence they go out of their way to make her uncomfortable in hopes that she will return to Japan. Louise feels sorry for the deeply unhappy war bride Hanaka, and for good reason. Louise knows that her aunt Maggie was a "great hater" of the Japanese, calling them "harlots" and then considering the men who wanted to marry them "deviants" and "a bloody disgrace to their country" (10). Hanaka's mother-in-law, who insists that Hanaka call her "Mother MacDonald," constantly criticises her cooking while keeping up a steady stream of racist remarks, often telling her outright that "these mixed marriages rarely work" and doing her best to force theirs apart. When Hanaka reveals that she is having a baby, her mother-in-law declares that once her son Alan "realises he has a coloured baby rather than the blue-eyed blonde Carol O'Connor [the classic "girl he left behind"] could give him, I think you'll find yourself back in Japan" (140). Other family members are equally disapproving: her sister-in-law, whose husband was killed by Japanese troops in Papua New Guinea (PNG), refers to the Japanese as "sub-human savages" and "bloody murderers" (65), and refuses to have anything to do with her sister-in-law. When Louise tries to encourage Hanaka to tell her husband about the family's treatment, Hanaka informs her that Alan believes that his mother and sister-in-law will "come around," (141) that Australia is changing

---

40   Bentley, "Japanese Women in Australia", 105.

(131) and will no longer regard the Japanese as an enemy of the Australian people, and does nothing.

One of the hardest and most frustrating aspects of Hanaka's new life in Australia is that her new family is unaware of how much suffering Japanese people have endured during and after the war – and that is because they never ask. Thus, they remain unaware of the past misery of these Japanese brides and have absolutely no idea that during the war years, everyone was starving: rice was unobtainable except on the black market and it took many years before it became available and affordable to ordinary people. Despite (or perhaps because of) being told to add grasshoppers and acorns to their diets, many died slowly of starvation. Hanaka's father, a scholar who taught his daughter English, commits suicide because Japan's military expansion had so depleted the country's resources that it was impossible for his illness to be treated properly. Worst of all, however, is that when Hanaka dares to marry an Australian soldier, her aunt disowns her.

Initially, Hanaka is pleased to be befriended by a small group of neighbourly Quaker women, but she is equally distressed when they insist that she describe in detail the problems she faced in Japan during the war, or when they continue to press her on the issue of mental illness. Meanwhile, Hanaka claims she will not challenge her mother-in-law because it is her job to please her, and more seriously, she is frightened that her mother-in-law will use "mental problems" against her and have her deported because she is not yet a citizen. Hanaka's life does improve briefly when a Japanese war bride appears and the two immediately become friends, but sadly only temporarily, as her new-found friend moves to Brisbane. Once that friendship ceases to exist, Hanaka continues to slip into melancholy and eventually tries (unsuccessfully) to kill herself. This desperate act finally mobilises Alan to make a change: the couple moves to Brisbane, then to Japan for a few years, and then back to Brisbane, where Hanaka becomes a well-known artist.

For most of the war brides whose stories appear in nonfictional accounts, the postwar years appear to have been "the best of times." To be sure, there are a few brides who confess they found it difficult to adjust to the lack of culture or poverty or to rural hardship, but the historians primarily insist they are rare exceptions, and the accounts tend to be brief and sketchy, leaving readers to fill in the gaps. Tamura, for example, recounts the story of a war bride who complains that her husband would not allow the children to share family dinners with their parents, but such rather meagre information about the Japanese women's misery may also be a result of the editors' reluctance to probe too deeply. Another writer considers that war brides display a kind of stoicism in their lack of complaints about their circumstances. It may be the case that by leaving such incomplete thoughts or troubling facts dangling without apology or explanation, these writers may be reminding us of a time when people simply pulled up their bootstraps and got on with things. But even in the brief examinations of two literary war brides whose fictional lives in Australia depicted "the worst of times," there are no doubt others who believe that the truth may lie somewhere in between. One thing is certain –

neither novel suggests that returned veterans or war brides were, if ever, recipients of the "fair go."

In the subtitle to her article on the results of the "fair go" during the pandemic, Tenille Bonoguore draws attention to one of Canada's best-known national myths (Canada, she claims, "sings itself a lullaby of 'niceness'"), which she then compares to the Australian concept of the "fair go," finding both "precariously balanced" on an equally "hallowed idea".[41] But in the end, she suggests that neither "fair" nor "nice" are sufficient criteria and suggests a "third way," much harder to obtain, which stresses "kindness" yet is also "much more radical":

> It requires deep empathy and a willingness to make sacrifices. It speaks honestly about difficult things and is open to difficult things said by others. It helps people understand not just why sacrifices need to be made, but what we'll gain by making them. (7)

It is difficult to imagine a world wherein people make kindness a key concept to live their lives by, but it's perhaps worth a "go" in trying times such as a pandemic, which has stubbornly refused to go away. When we think on the lives of deeply wounded war veterans or desperately sad war brides and how they coped or failed to in earlier decades, we might also remember the words of the great writer Henry James, who famously said "Three things in life are important: the first is to be kind; the second is to be kind; and the third is to be kind." Or, as Mark Twain also insisted, "Kindness is all."

---

41   Bonoguore, "Canada is fighting COVID-19 with niceness – and losing", 6.

14

The New "Anzacs Two" Make their Debut in Contemporary Australian Women's Fictions

> Women, I suppose, have their own war stories. Stories they
> keep to themselves, stories that don't get celebrated in pubs and
> marches and boozy two-up games.[1]

In "Remembering Romance: Memory, Gender, and World War II," Kate Darian-Smith observes that "[m]uch has been written about the gender bias of Anzac mythology, with its celebration of an archetypal warrior masculinity, characterised by bravery and nobility of sacrifice, male bonding and the eroticism of the flirtation with death … Australian World War II literature was preoccupied with proving that Anzac was no pejorative 'myth' at all".[2] Darian-Smith's further suggestion – that "the authentic experience of warfare remained that of the warrior soldier"[3] throughout the twentieth century – is precise, particularly in terms of women's literature, as seemingly few novelists displayed the courage to challenge the Anzac mythology. But by the twenty-first century, a few fearless women writers such as Mardi McConnochie (*The Voyagers: A Love Story* [2011]), Mandy Sayer (*Love in the Years of Lunacy* [2011]) and Sara Knox (*The Orphan Gunner* [2008]), began to imaginatively reconstruct the events of World War II from a temporal distance and bring to light important concerns about the cultural, racist, sexist and colonial biases their predecessors' fictions had overlooked. In these women-centred narratives, writers seek to interrogate and challenge the blinkered national past and to venture beyond its boundaries, to expose the inadequacies of the core myths of Australian society and to devise an entirely new set of stories that have been omitted from "master narratives" such as the Anzac legend. Their novels indicate that daring, intrepid women were every bit as capable as men of contributing to the

---

1   Mandy Sayer, *Dreamtime Alice* (Sydney: Random House, 1998), 263.
2   Kate Darian-Smith, "Remembering Romance: Memory, Gender and World War II", *Gender and War: Australians at War in the Twentieth Century*, eds. Joy Damousi and Marilyn Lake (Cambridge: Cambridge University Press, 1995), 119–20.
3   Darian-Smith, "Remembering Romance", 120.

war effort in that each novel features women who do not shy away from danger, but in Anzac terms, exercise "ready initiative" by saving numerous lives and hence becoming "sheroes," or the new "Anzacs Two."

One fierce defender of the need to acknowledge women's contribution to the "action" in World War II is Mandy Sayer. In her memoir *Dreamtime Alice*, Sayer confesses that as an adolescent, the war stories she commended were about "an adventurous uncle who saved a battalion in Europe, or a father who wasted away in jail for refusing the draft, or a mysterious grandfather who suddenly vanished one day and was never seen again" (264). By the time she came to write her memoir, she realised that her mother's and grandmother's wartime stories were equally compelling. Months before the outbreak of war, for example, her grandfather moved to Tasmania, his departure leaving her grandmother Florence (Dolly) with four children to provide for. Dolly responded to these dire circumstances "as she had always done" (263) through dint of hard work, to which she was no stranger, having gone to work in a factory at the age of twelve. Employing military language to depict Dolly's home-front war efforts, Sayer advances that her grandmother "went into battle against hunger and poverty" by investing in detergents and brushes, arming herself with weapons such as mops and dusters, putting her youngest in a pram, and going "from door to door … asking people if she could scrub their floors" (263). She also "marshalled" her "allies" – fruit-shop owners, butchers and bakers – who ensured she always had food on the table (263).

While Sayer admits that she "laboured under [the] misconception" for some time that these "fragments of feminine history" were of little significance, she eventually comprehended that it was her dauntless and resolute mother (also forced to raise children on her own) and grandmother who "possessed the most tenacity during those long and arduous years" (265). But at the same time, she also recognised that the "ending[s]" of their stories were always tragic. Her conviction, that women must create their own happy endings, is central to her novel, as it is to McConnochie's, both set partially during World War II in Sydney. In her review of these novels, Jo Case observes that these writers exploit "the power of war to break down social barriers and give women new opportunities",[4] as it also does in Knox's *The Orphan Gunner*.

McConnochie's novel begins in 1938, Sayer's in March 1942; both feature musicians who embark upon extensive and often dangerous "voyages" during the war – McConnochie's Marina from Sydney to London, Shanghai and Singapore (including the Changi women's prisoner-of-war camp), and Sayer's Pearl from Sydney to New Guinea – to search for the American men with whom they have fallen in love. That both fictions contain the word "love" in the title is not surprising (the book covers feature kissing couples, but from opposing angles), for as Darian-Smith found in her study of eighty women from Melbourne asked to share

---

4   Jo Case, "Romance Hits a Musical Note", *Sydney Morning Herald* 21 May 2011: 1.

their memories of World War II, they did so "through a dominating narrative of heterosexual romance", which "provided a narrative structure that enabled the women to comprehend their own lives and constitute their own identities in a culturally meaningful way". Moreover, as they recounted stories of falling in love, "they were telling stories of their youth," a "transitional period of their lives". Like McConnochie's Marina and Sayer's Pearl, many confessed to "forming sexual relationships"; "their war was a time of excitement, adventure and the romance of growing up". But even though women, finally subjects of their own stories, reminisced about their friendships or jobs they held, it was men who "provided both the catalyst and the rationale for dramatic action". At the same time, "war injected the experiences of youth with a new urgency. Young men were painfully aware of their own mortality, and in the charged emotional atmosphere young women were conscious of the impermanence of their relationships with men. It was imperative in wartime to live life to its fullest and to find pleasure where one could".[5]

Much of that pleasure, as historian Marilyn Lake explains, came about as a result of the "historically changing structure of femininity itself ... one that revolved around sexuality, sexual attractiveness and youthfulness ... reinforced by women's experiences of World War II."[6] While Lake covers several areas of those experiences, such as women's entry into "men's jobs," which "generated refreshing acknowledgement of female capability," she also lists advertising, the cinema and a rise in consumerism as vital factors that convinced women that for the first time, they "could argue for their own sexual rights, for their rights to sexual pleasure,"[7] which, by the late 1930s, was "constructed as excitement, adventure, and danger": in other words, "femininity was beginning to cast off its passivity as the incitement to pleasure took its course".[8] But as Lake also points out, "the stationing of foreign troops in a country has the effect of sexualising the local female population". The objects of desire for many Australian women – those newly engaged in the pursuit of life, liberty, and happiness – were the Americans based in Australian cities during World War II, where war conditions "undermined traditional restraints and disciplines".[9] Lake insists that the arrival of American troops in 1942 led to a kind of "moral madness," with "frequent reports of adolescent girls having sex with soldiers".[10] While many authorities were anxious to condemn lower-class young women who demonstrated a desire for a sexual life, Lake insists that "many of

---

5   Darian-Smith, "Remembering Romance", 122–125.
6   Marilyn Lake, "Female Desires: The Meaning of World War Two," *Gender and War: Australians at War in the Twentieth Century*, eds. Joy Damousi and Marilyn Lake (Melbourne: Oxford University Press, 1995), 61.
7   Lake, "Female Desires", 62–63.
8   Lake, "Female Desires", 66.
9   Lake, "Female Desires", 67.
10 Marilyn Lake, "The Desire for a Yank: Sexual Relations Between Australian Women and American Servicemen During World War Two. *Journal of the History of Sexuality* 2 no. 4 (April 1992): 621–33.

them c[a]me from the best homes and ha[d] a good education";[11] moreover, "young women and girls were not always seduced into sexual relations; they also actively initiated them".[12]

McConnochie's heroine Marina, just nineteen when the novel opens in 1938, demonstrates how her life is profoundly disrupted by the wartime climate. A classically trained pianist, she has recently accepted an invitation to study at one of London's most prestigious music schools and thereafter envisions a glamorous career on the international circuit. Routinely described as a respectable, talented, innocent young woman, when invited by her best friend, the extrovert Roma, to go on a blind date with Stead, an American sailor, Marina atypically accepts the offer. Roma, admittedly surprised, rationalises that her friend has decided, in the vernacular of the day, to "let down her hair" and "have some fun".[13] The incitement to sexual pleasure plays a large role in both novels, as both Pearl and Marina fall in love – and lust – almost at first sight, with rural, poverty-stricken, uneducated Americans without families: Marina with the merchant seaman Stead, and Pearl with the talented African American saxophonist, James Washington, who has played with the likes of Artie Shaw, Count Basie, and Benny Goodman, but who also enlisted in the US army after the Japanese attack on Pearl Harbor in 1941, and is now one of the million or so Yanks either spending time in or passing through Australia during World War II. While at first glance neither suitor seems particularly suitable, it matters little, since neither female protagonist is class conscious (these writers may be drawing attention to the oft-cited Australian principle of egalitarianism). Like the subjects of Darian-Smith's and Lake's studies, McConnochie's Marina is "excitable and ready for adventure" (35), "desperate to see the world" (21), and perhaps seeking some "fascinating rhythms." During Stead's three-day shore leave, the couple makes a mandatory visit to Luna Park, the site of numerous (in literary accounts) sexual encounters, which Stead's friend declares "never disappoints." Stead and Marina's only sexual encounter occurs, however, on their third date in Stead's tramp-steamer *Fortuna* just before he sets sail with nary a backward glance.

As Lake observes, women like the fictional Marina's few moments of romantic bliss come at a cost marked for women only (75), since she discovers en route to England weeks later that she is pregnant. She is both surprised and disappointed to learn that not one woman of her own age, doctors, or even family members, expresses compassion for her plight: her roommates become "distant and polite" (62), as if fearful that her condition was infectious (62). The ship's doctor ignores the "double standard that punished women while it let men go free"[14] by blaming

---

11 Lake, "Female Desires", 67.
12 Lake, "The Desire for a Yank", 623.
13 Mardi McConnochie, *The Voyagers: A Love Story* (Camberwell, Vic: Viking, 2011), 5. All subsequent references are to this edition and appear in parentheses in the text.
14 Lake, "Female Desires", 71.

Marina for her fall from grace, callously informing her that "[she has] made [her] bed and now ... must lie in it" (47). He advises her to have her baby at Hawthornden House, a home for unwed mothers near London, give it up for adoption, and get on with her life (as if it were that simple). Her equally hard-hearted, driven Parisian artist-sister Bea, who meets Marina in London, claims she can be of no help, since she would be evicted from her Parisian flat were it discovered she had an unwed mother on the premises (127). (The text implies that Marina does not want to end up like her lonely and miserable sister who has clearly forsaken love, marriage and motherhood in her pursuit of art, and daringly strikes out on her own.)

No one Marina encounters regards her predicament as anything but scandalous, and no one mentions the possibility that she and Stead might have fallen in love: nonetheless, the much-travelled Stead has fulfilled Marina's craving for information about the wider world (21), and Marina's musical skills and the unfamiliar pieces she plays have left him mesmerised (9). Reluctant to part on their last evening together, the couple makes a rash (unfulfilled) promise to rendezvous on New Year's Eve in London. But five years lapse before Stead, who has signed on with the United States Marine Corp in 1939, makes it back to Sydney. (Marina has written Stead numerous letters but sent the only one that describes her plight; it remains unanswered.) Having finally realised that no other woman measures up to Marina, Stead pays a visit to Marina's mother while on shore leave in Sydney. The text infers that Stead assumes she has been patiently waiting for him and is now startled to learn that Marina disappeared not long after she arrived in London. He is even more stunned to hear from Roma that Marina may have disappeared because she was pregnant. Even though Stead has clearly had other "conquests," he has remained remarkably (perhaps wilfully) naïve in his assumption that women cannot become pregnant after their first sexual encounter. But upon his return to Sydney, he seems to have awakened to the fact that the war had "changed things":

> It meant there were girls ... enjoying a kind of freedom, a kind of life that would not have been possible before. War work has released them from their families, released them from the old rules, given them an independence that was unimaginable before. (139–40)

But while Stead enjoys the luxury of observing how the chaos of war has changed "things," nothing has changed for Marina. Like thousands of unwed mothers before (and after) her, she is obliged to shoulder her burden alone. On her journey to England, she briefly considers an abortion – illegal at the time – but is so frightened by the appalling primitive and filthy conditions on offer that she cannot go through with it, even though it would allow her to resume her plan to become a concert pianist. Ultimately, she recognises that there are no "good" decisions. Returning home is out of the question because she has disappointed women like her mother who had lost husbands or fiancés after the Great War and who then decided to focus their resources on their work and their children (50). Marina also realises that the mother of an unwed and pregnant daughter could never again show her face in public, and the child would face "the ignominy of life as a bastard" (53). Aware that there was no shame worse than a middle-class teenage girl's fall from social and moral grace, Marina makes her way to Hawthornden House, where doctors, nurses and parents "collude" to ensure that young, unmarried women, whom they deem unfit to parent, are not allowed to touch or see their baby, or even know what sex it is.

As Barbara Kay suggests happened to Canadian women in similar plights, Marina is ultimately coerced into handing over her "illegitimate baby at a time when abortion was illegal, birth control was difficult to access, single mothers were deemed unfit to parent," and so vulnerable they were "least able to mount a vigorous protest".[15] But although Marina falls victim to a forced adoption in England, had she become pregnant in Australia, her situation would have been no better, as the acknowledgement of the suffering unwed mothers like Marina endured has been a long time coming. In 2013, Australian Prime Minister Julia Gillard "delivered a historic national apology in parliament … to the thousands of unwed mothers who were forced by government policies to give up their babies for adoption over several decades",[16] and notably committed five million dollars "to support services for affected families and to help biological families reunite".[17]

After the stressful birth and theft of her child, Marina's sister encourages her to re-apply for the scholarship, which is granted, but with only one week to practise, she performs dismally, thereby confirming her status as a "colonial" inferior. (For his part, Stead spends the rest of the war developing a growing appreciation of music as he struggles valiantly to find Marina, a search he describes in alternating chapters.) After undergoing such a painful experience, it is not surprising that Marina should succumb to a breakdown. "Defeated, diminished," uncertain of how to resurrect her "shipwrecked" life, she attempts to re-invent herself by contacting a man named Harry West in London, whom she has been told might offer her a job in London, which he does. Attracted to her youth and beauty, Harry soon asks her to travel with him (as his lover, of course) to Shanghai, and to play popular swing tunes of the sort performed at the Sydney Trocadero while outfitted in similar "beautiful evening gowns and dresses" for the international crowd at his Golden West nightclub, most of whom are fleeing Nazi Germany. Although initially thrilled to be wearing costly robes and precious jewellery and flattered by the attention the crowd gives her, Marina quickly discerns there are many problems with Harry: while claiming to be a happily married family man who lives in London, he makes it clear to Marina that their liaison is temporary, and it will end whenever it suits him.

---

15 Barbara Kay, "Culture, Statistics Back up Churches" *National Post* 23 April 2012: A3. https://www.barbarakay.ca/Pages/article/Culture_statistics_back_up_churches.

16 Associated Press in Canberra, "Julia Gillard apologises to Australian mothers for forced adoptions", *Guardian* 21 March 2013. https://www.theguardian.com/world/2013/mar/21/julia-gillard-apologises-forced-adoptions.

17 Associated Press, "Julia Gillard apologises", n.p.

More dangerously, Harry is a ruthless, corrupt, disreputable gangster who murders (or has murdered) anyone who crosses him.

Once the wartime events threaten to curtail his privileges, Harry vanishes, but not without ensuring (somewhat implausibly) that Marina receives a first-class ticket to London and a wad of cash. At that point, Marina realises how low she has sunk: although she had slept in Harry's bed and taken his money, she had never loved him; hence she had been Harry's whore, not his mistress (169). Telling no one of her plans, Marina simply vanishes, but suddenly begins to yearn for her old life, especially for Sydney – its sunlight, its harbour, its soft damp air (173) – so with the money Harry has given her carefully sewn into her undergarments, she sets sail for home. On a brief stopover in Singapore, she catches a glimpse of Stead's *Fortuna* and becomes almost giddy at the thought of seeing him on his return within a few days, but the pandemonium that occurs during the fall of Singapore forces her to abandon her plans, obey safety rules, and board the boat to Sydney.

But before long, her ship is attacked. Noting the insufficient numbers of lifeboats, Marina courageously leaps into the water where, as a strong swimmer (of course), she takes over from a man who confesses he cannot swim and manages to drag fourteen of the drowning people, including a mother and child, out of the freezing water and onto a lifeboat. After several days at sea, she and the infant Gracie, whose mother Marina tried desperately to save, are the only survivors; rescued by the Japanese, they are transported first to a small internment camp and then shortly after to the infamous Changi prisoner-of-war camp. Somewhat implausibly, Marina and Gracie manage to survive the crowded conditions and the lack of medical supplies and food better than the others, thanks to Harry West's money. While interned in Changi, Marina witnesses the healing power of music. As she gladly plays the popular wartime favourites she had formerly dismissed as "rubbish," she now comprehends that

> [i]n the camp, where so much had been stripped away, music gave [the prisoners' lives] a richness, a vividness, a beauty and a fullness of feeling that it was all too easy to lose. Music was a window onto another world, a life beyond war; music spoke of joy and sorrow, of sex and yearning and pleasure, of comfort, of home, and it spoke in a way that went deeper than words or ideas. Music was not an idea, it was a feeling, and it moved you in the deep place, beyond thought. (239)

Having survived the camp and about to depart for Sydney with Gracie in tow, Maria experiences the sorrow of having a second child snatched from her when a young man who claims to be the child's father appears and declares his desire to take her back to his family in England.

While Marina has been spending time in Changi, Stead has been immersed in the madness of war: he has witnessed the "terrible slaughter" of the Normandy landing (179), the fall of Berlin (180) and escaped injury, as his friend Slick has not, after their ship has been hit many times (180). Stead has also heard the dreadful news about the bombing of Hiroshima and the Japanese release of the English, Dutch, French and Americans from internment camps, which he has visited in hopes of finding Marina (181). Having gleaned from a few who knew Marina that the *Princess Greta*, which had been carrying her to London, had sunk without any survivors (189–91), he gives up all hope of finding her. But all is not lost, for Marina soon discovers that Stead is on her boat and planning to live in Sydney. The story ends as romances should, with the Epilogue informing readers that love has triumphed, with the couple now married and living happily ever after in Sydney. Great swells of music.

Pearl's story is in many ways a mirror image of Marina's. When the novel opens in March 1942, Pearl, who plays tenor sax, is about to turn eighteen; like Marina, she has also studied at the Sydney Conservatorium of Music, but is now playing alto sax with an all-girl swing band at an elegant Sydney nightclub that boasts a posh clientele, where the wartime climate has allowed women to perform regularly (and for decent wages) for the first time. As Kay Dreyfus points out, after Japan's invasion of New Guinea and its attacks on Darwin, men left their civilian jobs and volunteered for the armed forces.[18] Some recruits were musicians hired to entertain the troops, so there was plenty of work for women musicians.[19] Dreyfus stresses that the girls had to be highly skilled[20] and adds that both boys and girls who excelled usually came from families who valued music and viewed it as a career possibility.[21] Both Pearl and her twin brother Martin fit that description, as both were literally born on the musical stage: her mother had gone into labour while playing percussion in the orchestra pit of the orchestra of the Tivoli Theatre in Sydney.[22] Although Pearl's working-class family provides her with a decent home, money is always in short supply. Oddly, both and she and her conservative-leaning mother frequently quarrel, but for reasons unexplained in the text, only her father supports Pearl's desire to play music.

While Marina goes from being a "good" girl to a "bad" girl, Pearl moves from being a "bad" girl to a "good" girl. A brash and adventurous eighteen-year-old, she smokes cigarettes and dope, drinks, swears and is definitely a risk taker. Both she and her twin brother play dance tunes on the saxophone at the Trocadero, but long to play jazz. Their opportunity to do so arises after the "friendly invasion," which finds them making their way to the run-down Booker T. Washington Club, the one place that permits African American soldiers to perform and dance (but only with the Aboriginal and Pacific Islander women the American Red Cross had recruited [13]). Just as African Americans are banned from the Trocadero, Pearl and Martin are not welcome at the Booker T. Washington Club and gain entry only because

---

18   Kay Dreyfus, *Sweethearts of Rhythm* (Surry Hills, NSW: Currency Press, 1999), 9.
19   Dreyfus, *Sweethearts of Rhythm*, 14.
20   Dreyfus, *Sweethearts of Rhythm*, 10.
21   Dreyfus, *Sweethearts of Rhythm*, 11.
22   Mandy Sayers, *Love in the Years of Lunacy* (Crows Nest, NSW: Allen & Unwin, 2011), 32. All subsequent references are to this edition and appear in parentheses in the text.

Martin is having an affair with Roma, an Aboriginal woman who works at the club.[23]

Upon hearing the talented African American saxophone player James Washington play jazz, Pearl immediately falls in love, and on her first date with James the next day, embarks upon a passionate wartime love affair that she initiates, an act which might seem overly bold, but Lake notes was quite common.[24] As part of her seduction, which takes place at Luna Park on the night of the Japanese submarine attack on Sydney Harbour (37), Pearl insists that James help improve her musicianship on the alto sax. While both Darian-Smith's and Lake's accounts stress the importance of women becoming sexualised as a result of the American presence, they overlook that by June 1942, "the largest contingent of black GIs [had been] sent to Australia,[25] a situation that arose when Prime Minister Curtin, who "fervently supported white supremacist policies",[26] had been forced to look to America for protection after the attack on Pearl Harbor.

Like Darian-Smith and Lake, Pearl is remarkably naive, evident in her issuing of an invitation to James to her birthday without giving any thought to how her mother Clara, not known for being open minded, will respond. (Because she feels unwelcome, Roma turns down the invitation to Pearl's birthday party.) But Clara's shock, accompanied by disapproval, is anomalous here, since although historians had earlier argued that the Australian government and its people wanted the "white Australia policy" strictly enforced, historians E. Daniel Potts and Annette Potts argue that relations between black Americans and Australians were "cordial" and that overall, as the letters they sent back home indicated, "thousands of black servicemen" received warm receptions[27] into Australian homes. Aubrey, Pearl's father, heartily welcomes James, and when the latter asks for elucidation of the White Australia policy, Aubrey treats it lightly when he denies that it was not set up to keep "coloureds out," as James presupposes, but the Chinese from the goldfields (60). Clara, by contrast, is irritated when James presents Pearl with a phonograph recording of Sonny Clay's Colored Idea band (World War II was the first conflict to take place in the age of electronically mass-distributed music); she proclaims primly that Clay and the others had been deported for "loose morals" and "lewd behaviour" (59). But Martin quickly explains that the recording also "denotes" why

---

23 While it may be coincidence that each novel contains a woman named "Roma," the name was in the news because after local white women refused to dance with African Americans stationed in the small town of Roma, several US American soldiers retaliated by stabbing Australian soldiers (Kay Saunders, "In a Cloud of Lust: Black GIs and Sex in World War II" in Damousi and Lake *Gender and War*, 185.

24 Lake, "Female Desires", n.p.

25 Kay Saunders, "Conflict between the American and Australian Governments over the Introduction of Black American Servicemen into Australia during World War Two" *Australian Journal of Politics and History* 33 no.2 (1987), 44.

26 Saunders, "In a Cloud of Lust", 180.

27 Cited in Sean Brawley and Chris Dixon, "Jim Crow Downunder? African American Encounters with White Australia, 1942–1945" *Pacific Historical Review* 71 no.4 (November 2002), 611.

Pearl is so "colour-blind": he reminds Pearl that even though she had been terrified when Aubrey had taken them to see Clay's band as small children (58), her fears evaporated when the band started to play, a comment that implies both that Pearl's love of jazz stemmed from that moment, and that the skin colour of the players – or anyone else – from that moment on never mattered.[28] A few pages later, James attempts to inform Pearl about the severity of the racial prejudice he has lived under in the United States, notably that it was the "fear of black sexuality" that led to his "granddaddy's" being hung from a tree for whistling at a white girl (69).[29] James further underscores how much skin colour matters when he recounts his experiences travelling with esteemed bands such as Benny Goodman's, which indicate there is no justice system in that country and the police are part of the problem. He also explains that mixed marriages were "illegal in thirty-three states," and that couples who attempted to marry would be immediately thrown in jail (84). Although the details of his life as a black man in America are traumatising and Pearl does recognise that she has been naive and selfish, she never "broaches the subject again" (72), making the flimsy excuse that James was a "complicated man" whose history she could never understand, and focuses instead on talking about music.

But when James learns that that there is no law in Australia preventing him from marrying Pearl, he decides maybe the country "ain't so bad" (84). Following protocol, he asks his southern US commanding officer for permission but learns he must wait two months for a reply; the CO then confines him to the base in a geographically isolated area outside of Sydney (which Saunders and Taylor suggest was common practice).[30] But the recognition that black lives did not matter only sinks in when Pearl, disturbed by James' lengthy absences, comes looking for him and is shocked to discover that while white troops live in tidy, clean huts and have the use of several recreational facilities, African American troops inhabit a "stinky shantytown" the white troops call the "zoo" (92). Until then, Pearl has been unaware that African Americans were permitted to perform only "non-combative, manual duties" that thereby "confirm[ed] their status as menials capable only of hard physical routine labour"[31] such as James' digging of "defecation pits" (93).

---

28 Several reviewers have commented on Sayer's irritating habit of introducing nearly every character by their skin colour, which I share. Equally disappointing is that while Sayer consistently poses questions about race and injustice throughout her text, it is unclear what she is attempting to convey about these complicated issues. The conclusion, which draws upon Colin Johnston's (Mudrooroo's) disapproval of cultural appropriation, is too underdeveloped to be taken seriously. For more on Johnston's story, see Anita Heiss' *Dhuuluu-Yala: To Talk Straight* (Canberra: Aboriginal Studies Press, 2003).

29 Sayer alludes here to the Emmett Till case, in which the fourteen-year-old Till, falsely accused of grabbing a white woman, whistling at her and making sexual advances, was brutally tortured and then killed. For more information on the crime, see "FBI to Revisit Emmett Till Case 63 Years After His Killing," *Globe and Mail* 13 July 2018: A6. *Till*, a 2022 movie, also tells Till's story.

30 Kay Saunders and Helen Taylor, "The Reception of Black American Servicemen in Australia during World War II: The Resilience of 'White Australia'" *Journal of Black Studies* 25 no.3 (January 1995), 335.

There was, then, as Saunders argues, a "huge discrepancy between the United States' political rhetoric about engaging in this war to preserve liberty and freedom while maintaining internal segregation within the armed services".[32]

What Saunders ignores, however, is that Americans were terrified of what Blacks might do were they issued guns which, as James puts it, was that they "might band together and turn. Run off with ol' Tojo" (244). Brawley and Dixon also observe that "the Pacific War exposed tensions *between* nation states but also revealed tensions and contradictions *within* nations. In the United States, the racially charged war against Japan and the struggle in Europe against 'race pride' brought into graphic relief the continuing subjugation of black Americans".[33] Accordingly, "when African Americans did suffer racial discrimination in Australia … it was chiefly at the hands of white Americans who sought to regulate African American access to public space with patterns of formal and informal segregation that would have been painfully familiar to most black Americans".[34]

As the relationship between Pearl and James deepens (Sayer again stretches credulity once Pearl discovers an abandoned mansion near Sydney Harbour where the lovers conveniently have their trysts), when James learns that the southern CO is transferring him to Queensland (which was, according to Saunders, the state where "racial attitudes were highly repressive" [335]), he sends a thoughtful "Dear Pearl" letter that insists she must not "throw her life away" on him. The letter devastates Pearl, especially since Martin has enlisted in an entertainment troop touring Australia, thereby leaving her with no one to talk to. Like McConnochie's Marina, alone, vulnerable and desperate (Pearl's friend Nora has married and moved to the Blue Mountains), she tries to kill herself by drinking her taxidermist father's embalming fluid. Rescued and placed under the care of psychiatrist Dr Hector Best, better known as the Master of Lunacy, Pearl struggles with his ill-chosen treatment, reminiscent of the infamous Dr Mitchell's in Charlotte Perkins Gilman's "The Yellow Wallpaper." Dr Best claims that Pearl, like many other "girls" during wartime, suffers from an "acute nervous condition," which leads to their "great fear of dying" (107). The "cure" consists of "rest, peace, and quiet," as well as copious amounts of rich food that render Pearl so listless that she can only lie in bed and gaze at "at the embossed roses woven around the borders of the pressed metal ceiling of her room" (109). Most damaging to her mental state is Dr Best's insistence (and proof that his moniker is not accurate) that Pearl quit her job at the Trocadero and give up playing the saxophone altogether. Because Pearl, like Marina, is powerless to resist, she agrees to marry the sexless and oppressive Dr Best, even though he treats her more like an adoring uncle than a suitor (146). But when she accidentally learns that both James and Martin will be serving in New

31   Saunders, "Conflict", 24.
32   Saunders, "In a Cloud of Lust", 180.
33   Brawley and Dixon, "Jim Crow Downunder?", 609.
34   Brawley and Dixon, "Jim Crow Downunder?", 611.

Guinea – Martin to entertain the troops but stepping into a soldier's role if required and James to continue in service capacities – Pearl knows she can do better than a Best. By wearing Martin's uniform, Pearl believes she can escape from a feminine identity that would threatened to "ensnare and even engulf her" (30): or, as Julie Wheelwright puts it, "Freedom was only one costume change away".[35]

Immediately prior to Martin's departure, Pearl sees her wedding dress hanging on a hook next to her brother's military uniform and suddenly realises, with stunning clarity, the gender roles the siblings are destined to perform and offers to don Martin's uniform, assume his identity, and go in search of James. Otherwise, she will be "entombed" in Hector's terrace house, "starching shirts and polishing furniture" (151). As Wheelwright suggests, like other women who choose to live out an adventure that transgresses sexual boundaries,[36] Pearl decides to "unsex" herself which, according to Matthew Teorey, not only allowed women like her to "gain ... access to male space and authority", but "confounded the contemporary conception of womanhood by cutting their hair, putting on uniforms", and "liv[ing] out an assertion of personal agency and a denouncement of contemporary assumptions about femaleness".[37] Opportunely, Pearl is no stranger to cross-dressing: she and Martin have swapped identities as school children; she has studied cross-dressers in Australian history (and most recently she attends, undetected, a contemporary Artie Shaw concert in Martin's uniform). Oddly, Pearl makes no mention of the cross-dresser she knows, the "unusually beautiful" Roma, reputedly a fabulous dancer "who used to do impersonations of Jimmy Cagney in *Yankee Doodle Dandy*" (154).

Surprisingly, when Pearl proposes that she go to war in Martin's place, he openly confesses that he is frightened of combat and "couldn't kill anyone ... not even [him]self" (135). By making Martin a man who does not want to fight, Sayer boldly challenges the monolithic nature of the Anzac legend, which held that *all* Australian men were uniformly brave and eager to get into the fray. Martin, however, immediately agrees to travel as a woman and hide out with Pearl's friends in the country for the duration. Before she departs, Martin gives Pearl a few quick lessons in how to obey orders, how to shoulder a rifle, how to salute and how to swear (161). In order to ready herself for duty, Pearl relieves herself from the bonds of womanhood by shearing off her golden tresses. Although she feels a mixture of excitement and fear, like Marina, she simply vanishes:

As she approached the sandstone walls of Victoria Barracks, she felt at once terrified and intensely alive. She was moving towards everything she now knew she

---

35 Julie Wheelwright, *Amazons and Military Maids: Women Who Dressed as Men in the Pursuit of Life, Liberty and Happiness* (London: Pandora, 1989), 51.

36 Wheelwright, *Amazons and Military Maids*, 13.

37 Teorey, Matthew. 2008. "Unmasking the Gentleman Soldier in the Memoirs of Two Cross-Dressing Female US Civil War Soldiers." *War, Literature & the Arts: An International Journal of the Humanities* 20 (1/2): 74.

couldn't live without: the adventures she longed to have, the jazz she yearned to play, the only man she'd ever love. As she passed through the gates, it was as if she'd stepped over some invisible line that divided her past from her future, separated one fate from another, and no matter what painful death or glorious reward was ahead, there was no turning back now. (57)

Pearl's feelings echo those of the fearless, often euphoric young *male* soldiers heading to battle in traditional Australian war narratives. But as Wheelwright argues, although the desires and motives of real-life cross-dressing women were as diverse as their literary counterparts, the "thread that pulls these stories together is women's desire for male privilege and a longing for escape from domestic confines and powerlessness".[38] Much as Pearl has "enlisted" to find James, she is also freeing herself from the stifling confinement of her mother and Hector Best on the Australian home front.

Initially, Pearl's invasion of the male space presents few obstacles. She spurns an advance by the gay soldier Moss, and a few days later avoids detection when, about to reveal Pearl is a "girl," Moss is killed, leaving behind his prized alto sax, which she immediately seizes. Once confronted with her first glimpse of the damage war has wreaked on Port Moresby, which was "a rubble of destroyed buildings, shopfronts pockmarked with bullet holes, [and] shattered windowpanes" (184), Pearl is upset but as yet oblivious of the massive toll it takes on human life. All of that changes during her first military event in the Owen Stanleys, where she is brought face-to-face with an audience that consists of bruised and broken men with bandaged heads, missing limbs and others, aided by makeshift slings and crutches, moving along slowly to their seats. Her sudden recognition of the transcendental power of music and its restorative powers resembles Marina's:

> As she stared at these men, her own problems receded, became remote and insignificant. She had her health: all her limbs were intact; she'd never had to face, repeatedly, the threat of her imminent death. It occurred to her that these men needed music as much as they needed morphine or antibiotics, and, as she began to play, as she followed the circumlocutions of each chart, as she saw the glowing faces of the wounded men, a kind of urgency welled up through her until nothing else mattered but trying to ease their pain. (192)

As reviewer Rowe notes, the veracity of Marina's and Pearl's encounters in McConnochie's and Sayer's novels results in "the slow reconstruction of a stronger and more complex self"; both heroines "do not pick up the trails of their lovers until they have undergone this lone process of self-discovery" (1), which arguably comes through the stark recognition of the pain of others.

---

38   Wheelwright, *Amazons and Military Maids*, 2.

But Pearl's acknowledgement of the devastation war brings seems short-lived, as the last section of the novel becomes increasingly unconvincing, particularly when the problematising of gender boundaries becomes more complicated. After a brief stay in Port Moresby (which includes a bombing attack on the warehouse where the American comedian Bob Hope and the Australian soprano Gladys Moncrieff perform briefly with the Australians), the troops fly to the Huon peninsula, an area framed by the Solomon Sea where, after Pearl overcomes the smell of the corpses (too many to be buried), she enjoys a reprieve from war by swimming, fishing with Charlie and his gay friend Blue, or arranging experimental musical variations.[39] Aside from feeling she is on an "endless holiday," she relishes in the fact that there was no Clara or Hector to "tell her what to do" (201). But eventually finding herself not quite on a "battlefield," Pearl proves her worth as a soldier on more than one occasion: the first occurs when she shoots in the leg a Japanese enemy dressed in an American army uniform who has been stealing food and medicine from the camp supplies but has eluded capture.

In late January 1944, just as Pearl is congratulating herself on how well she has negotiated military life – she plays music she loves on an instrument she loves and no one asks questions about her identity – her unit is ordered to make their way by barge from Finschhafen to Lae, a severely damaged town the Allies have taken, but with an awareness of Japanese presence. Orders are to split into two: one unit to stay in Lae to help the Allies repair the damage to the town, and the other to travel into the "remote areas" to entertain the troops who lived near combat zones, lacked sufficient supplies, and had nothing to entertain them: "It would be tough, exhausting and extremely dangerous" (202), with only five chosen to regale soldiers who long for "lots of song-and-dance routines, comedy, magic acts" (208). Pearl nonetheless volunteers to audition, her desire fuelled more by the rumour that she might encounter American camps on the way to Nadzab where Americans (including James) might be found than any aspiration to amuse the troops, which she knows will be difficult: if she impersonates a woman, she will be "far too convincing" (206), unable "to sound like a man trying to sound like a girl, which wasn't the same as a girl trying to sound like a man" (226). Drawing inspiration from her father's rendition of some vaudeville songs (213) that she belts out while disguised in "tarty" female attire, Pearl satisfies the recruiters and is ordered with the others to make their way to Nadzab.

Much as Pearl faces numerous horrendous conditions as her war experiences seemingly never end, she manages to survive in part because, as Wheelwright points out, there is plenty of evidence in previous centuries to indicate that "women could withstand the hardships of the ship or army camp",[40] and Pearl proves no exception: she is forced to wade through flooded rivers full of mud and snakes

---

39   Curiously, Sayer depicts her "queers" enduring only harmless teasing or silly jokes, when in reality they were tormented.

40   Wheelwright, *Amazons and Military Maids*, 14.

and swamps infested with leeches and swarms of buzzing mosquitoes; put up with the stench of enemy and allied corpses too numerous to bury; watch out for the pygmies who steal supplies, as well as cannibals rumoured to be in the area; and bear up under extreme hunger and exhaustion. While some of the men in her unit suffer PTSD, others dysentery or malaria or shots under enemy fire, thanks to Dr Best's insistence that she down frequent doses of quinine, Pearl remains able-bodied and does a better job of soldiering than Martin ever could have. In her second act of military prowess, she once again becomes the brave and resourceful Anzac her twin could never have been: exercising "ready initiative," Pearl manages to save the lives of a small Australian troop led, of course, by James Washington, who has defected from the American army because he wants to fight and is good at it. (As he eventually tells Pearl, the Australians "didn't care if [James] was black, blue, pink, or purple, as long as [he could] hit a target" [247]). While glancing through her binoculars, Pearl becomes aware of an impending Japanese attack on the Australians, but lacking any obvious means of warning them, she blows on her saxophone and thus alerts them of the danger. (Apparently there is some truth to this story, but the sax player was male.) Her quick thinking thwarts the Japanese attack. Markedly, by the end of the numerous battles she has fought, her troubadour/combat unit consists only of her and the black tracker Wanipe (who has always known Pearl is female), hired to carry the entertainers' equipment.

Pearl's efforts to find James soon materialise, but the two enjoy only a brief sexual reunion before he is shot and killed by his CO who may (or may not have) believed he was an enemy, but since this is his second attempt, probably the latter. Both incidents go unreported because everyone knew no one would believe the words of a black man against a white officer (274). But after returning to Sydney, Pearl discovers she is pregnant, a circumstance which returns to the frame narrative, with the "Coda" revealing that Jimmy, "Australia's First Indigenous Crime Writer" (318), is Pearl's son, not nephew. She has communicated her life story via recently discovered cassette tapes, which end with the "order" that her son "Pretty up" his mother's story and "Make it sing" (7), but the tale Jimmy produces does neither: instead, it hits numerous sour notes, particularly in how the cross-dressing narrative ends. Heilmann observes that cross-dressers like Pearl who have focused on "the attainment of individual fulfilment" often find upon their return to female occupations that they face "fatal consequences" for their professional lives (86), but these unfortunate outcomes do not apply to Pearl, who has not only continued to play jazz but created a legacy of her own: a "new American style of bebop – the style she had been taught to play by James – to Australian musicians" (2). One of Jimmy's friends, a jazz historian, emphasises the magnitude of her contribution when he reveals that he is writing a book on Australian jazz which, based on Pearl's recordings and papers housed in the National Archives in Canberra (2), will contain an entire chapter devoted to Pearl's work.

But nevertheless, there are reasons Pearl's supporters feel let-down, believing she has become a "coward" in her own war effort. Instead of using her "male identity" for specifically political purposes by trying to effect larger structural changes in society, as Heilmann suggests, Pearl deems it "unthinkable" for a returned soldier to raise a "bastard black child" (319). Instead of "soldiering on" in protest of the social mores of her times, the once "feisty" Pearl succumbs to her mother's plan that she give birth in secret in a country home (319) and then relinquish the care of Jimmy to her mother and father, who volunteer to raise the boy under the guise that Martin is the father and his Aboriginal girlfriend Roma the mother, who has recently given birth to a blue-eyed boy and then conveniently died.[41] But more wrong notes render the ending implausible, since neither Martin nor his family appear to have had any connections with Roma's Aboriginal family or any other Indigenous group, and Pearl's mother, earlier described as "conscious of the family's reputation in the local community" (53–54), would likely not be keen to raise a mixed-race child. The myriad improbabilities of the ending do not warrant further effort, particularly once they wander away from the cross-dressing narrative.

Knox's *The Orphan Gunner*, another romance but this time between two women, nevertheless has a lot in common with *Love in the Years of Lunacy*. It, too, relies upon a frame narrative that begins in the present, when Olive Jamieson, an Australian WAAF during World War II, returns with her irritable husband Norm to Lincolnshire, where they both served; structured largely around Olive's memory of "her" war, it concludes with an epilogue set in 1958 in New Zealand that finds Olive visiting Lofty, a kiwi gunner who, like Pearl's friend Charlie, has helped her and her cross-dressing friend/lover negotiate the war from a man's point of view. Both novels introduce powerful heroines like Pearl and Evelyn who acquire access to another world where, for the first time, they enjoy the social power and privileges of men by stepping into the clothing and identities of their faint-hearted, fearful of combat, volunteer brothers. Both novels suggest that had the war not offered their characters a "shot" at emancipation and release from the bonds of womanhood and domestic confinement, their futures would have been bleak. But as cross-dressers, they experience war in ways they could never have done as women; as a result of their exemplary performances as warriors in the jungles of New Guinea or in the air as pilots and gunners, they become the new Anzacs Two who prove conclusively that anything a brother can do, a sister can do better. But unlike their brothers, whose battlefront performances as Anzacs were rarely placed under scrutiny, Wheelwright points out that women warriors carried an extra burden, as any women who cross-dressed had to endure "endless self-imposed tests of their masculinity, proving over and over again that they measured up"; accordingly, while their brothers have the chance to avoid the battlefield, their sisters, now women Anzacs, earn the respect, trust, and admiration of their fellow (male) soldiers. Wheelwright observes that "male approval among

---

41 Apparently Jimmy's son (whom we never meet) inherits his grandmother's musical talents as a prize-winning choreographer with the Bangarra Dance Company (154).

her comrades became the ultimate sign of the cross-dressed woman's rejection of her femininity and security of her acquired privileged position".[42]

The plot turns on the story of Olive, a young Australian woman sent to England shortly before the outbreak of World War II by the wealthy land-owning parents of her best friend, Evelyn McIntyre, to bring their daughter back to a life of gendered conformity. On her journey overseas, Olive recalls that a few years earlier, Evelyn's mother had caught her daughter cross-dressing as a cricketer and immediately forbade her to leave the house for weeks. By the time Olive saw her again, "she'd changed. She'd been reined in: ... Evelyn ha[d] assumed a proper style, but a perpetual air of dissatisfaction was its price".[43] When Olive arrives in England, she learns that Evelyn takes a particular pride in the fact that the renowned (and fascinating real-life) female pilot Amy Johnson had asked her to join the Air Transport Auxiliary (ATA), and then "ratified her as an aviatrix" (80). As a result, Evelyn has become an exceptionally skilled pilot and flight instructor who loves flying, is good at it and wants to "keep doing it" (55). Although Evelyn is, like Pearl, motivated to "escape the boredom of domestic life," unlike Pearl, she is equally anxious to do something "useful" such as "getting a country ready to deal with the war that's coming" (57). In this regard, she joins the ranks of the other trouser-clad women in history who, according to Wheelwright, were also "compelled" by a similar sense of "urgency" to do their bit for the war effort. Wheelwright further adds, however, that most cross-dressers (like the fictitious Pearl) throughout history have not set out to overcome women's oppression, since "one rebellion against the constraints of [their] gender does not translate into a broader social analysis of oppression".[44]

While Wheelwright's observations clearly apply to Pearl's desire to masquerade as a man, Wheelwright would, I believe, view Pearl's actions as constituting merely "a process of imitation rather than a self-conscious claiming of the social privileges given exclusively to men for all women".[45] Wheelwright adds that "to expect [cross-dressers] to challenge an institution [like the military] in which they held such a precarious position is unrealistic",[46] but Evelyn nevertheless proves to be a harbinger of the women's movement in the mid-twentieth century, as she continues to rail against the powers that relegate women's roles in war to the support of and control by men. She encourages a young servant to "throw off the burdens of [her] sex" and sign up because, she insists, with all of the men in the services or reserved employment, "they'll eventually need more people for non-operational flying and will have nowhere to get them" (96). Evelyn's optimism and common sense prove premature, however, for once war "breaks out," she is denied the opportunity to be

---

42 Wheelwright, *Amazons and Military Maids*, 51.
43 Sara Knox, *The Orphan Gunner* (Artarmon, NSW: Giramondo, 2007), 42–43. All subsequent references are to this edition and appear in parentheses in the text.
44 Wheelwright, *Amazons and Military Maids*, 11.
45 Wheelwright, *Amazons and Military Maids*, 11.
46 Wheelwright, *Amazons and Military Maids*, 10.

a fighter pilot or to serve in any aircrew capacity, and even her work ferrying planes is jeopardised. As she remarks disparagingly, "It's just so bloody unfair given the hours I've put in. Along comes this fellow from the Civil Aviation Authority and that's the end of inessential flying and inessential flyers. Just like that. Of course, inessential flyer means any woman who happens to be doing it" (80). What Evelyn seeks most in the wartime climate is change, a new challenge: she tries "talking to pilots of the Atlantic Ferrying service – those men who flew Liberators on the long haul from the Coast of Canada to England," but is told that "no women flew that route" (220).[47] Dismayed by the lack of opportunities for highly skilled women, she tells a male friend, "I'm fighting the same war as you, but with the blood squeezed out of it" (221).

Like Pearl, Evelyn eventually gains access to the masculine world of privilege by stepping into her brother Duncan's trousers. The process takes much longer because, unlike Martin, who avoids fighting at all costs, Duncan is threatened by his sister's success and abandons veterinary studies in Australia to become a pilot like his sister. But he "washes out" of the elementary pilot school because he is terrified and sick on every flight. Still desperate to be part of the action, he volunteers to become a high-in-demand gunner, but not only does his airsickness continue, he is also devastated by the suicide of the wire operator and ravaged by the (falsely) reported death of his lover, an American pilot. As Evelyn observes Duncan's increasing exhaustion, his serious weight loss, and hears him weeping in the shower, she comprehends that "if he refused to fly he'd only spend the remainder of his war sweeping out hangars or sluicing down ablutions blocks" (243). Thus in order to save him from being labelled LMF (lacking moral fibre), or from the more serious charge of "malingering," since the general consensus is that being a gunner is "not that hard" (261), Evelyn concocts a plan to save Duncan from future harm and humiliation: she will "unsex herself," learn what a gunner's job consists of, and assume Duncan's role at the rear of the plane. Meanwhile, Duncan will sail back to Australia under Evelyn's gender-neutral name. When Olive protests that the plan is "absurd," that Evelyn will have to live as a man in a crew hut, the latter quips, "'If I can bomb Dresden and Leipzig, shaving shouldn't be a challenge" (288). But when Olive then accuses her of tackling a job she is not trained to do, Evelyn replies confidently, "'I'm not afraid of this. I can do what my brother can't. The war provides no other options, nor any other means – *honourable* means, that is," (262) and even Duncan confesses that "she'll probably do a better job at being me than I ever could" (270). And she does. Like her real-life counterpart Amy Johnson, Evelyn has an all-consuming determination to prove that women can be

---

47   While Canadian women pilots were certainly not readily welcomed into the military, 166 managed, under the auspices of the ATA, to fly brand-new single and twin-engine aircraft to operational squadrons all over Britain and Europe. See Amanda Huddleston, "Canadian Women in WWII," Greenwood Military Aviation Museum. www.bit.ly/3rpcckA. Accessed 25 April 2023.

as competent as men in a hitherto male-dominated field, "even if [in her case] she[] show[s] it only to two people" (318).

While Pearl swelters in the heavy humid air of PNG, Evelyn flies in the dark cold of winter, as Bomber Harris (also known as Butcher Harris) commands that the Allies would have to "knock out" Berlin during night raids in January and February (298), but the Irvin Jacket and trousers, as well as the May West flying suit, prove little better than the skirts she has been required to wear while flying as a woman. The men's flying suits expose parts of her body to the freezing conditions so that she "quickly los[es] all sensation" (298); moreover, her brother Duncan has also insisted she must learn to "do without goggles" whenever the plane is most vulnerable, which means there is nothing to keep the cold out of her eyes "the whole time the aircraft was over Europe," and "blinking" proved "agonizingly painful" (280). Of course the pilots tried to avoid "flak" while trying to get to targets "no one could see" (280), but Evelyn, like her cross-dressing counterpart Pearl, remains cool and "unrattled." What she finds most difficult, though, is not being in charge: "it's as though I'm being dragged along in the darkness outside," she laments (280). She also fears, too, that if she must bail out over Germany and is caught, "she would almost certainly be shot as a spy. Not for her the prison camp, and the duty of escape" (302). But while Duncan's health and body deteriorate under stress of flying, Evelyn looks more youthful than ever, thriving as she does on the new challenge, and proves to be so good at her job that her squadron leader notes she could be "put up for a commission," which she has refused because an interview is part of the promotion (317).

This fascination with cross-dressers like Pearl and Evelyn over the centuries has prevailed into World War II, as Wheelwright might argue, "partly because they live out an adventure that transgresses sexual boundaries".[48] The emancipation of the cross-dressing woman has traditionally defied the constraints of the Victorian separate spheres ideology and provided provocative material for writers. Accordingly, cross-dressers began to appear more frequently in the fictions about the "new woman" because, as Ann Heilmann remarks, the subject of cross-dressing "enabled writers to challenge patriarchal essentialism by exploding the category of gender. If women could exchange female and male costumes at will and 'perform' masculinity without being detected, then both masculinity and femininity were socially constructed roles, not inherently biological facts".[49] In other words, biology was NOT destiny. Wheelwright further notes that those who cross dressed "were unconventional women who spent their lives rebelling against their assigned role before they pursued a male career. Most could only conceive of themselves as active and powerful in male disguise".[50] In the late nineteenth and early twentieth century, young women who chose to cross dress (the "best-documented" cases are those

---

48   Wheelwright, *Amazons and Military Maids*, 13.
49   Heilmann, Ann. "(Un)masking Desire: Cross-Dressing and the Crisis of Gender in New Woman Fiction" *Journal of Victorian Culture* 5 no.1 (Spring 2000), 106.

of soldiers and sailors)[51] did so because, as Marjorie Garber posits, "Whatever the specific semiotic relationship between military uniforms and erotic fantasies of sartorial gender, the history of cross-dressing within the arms forces" remains a complex form of gendered social resistance.[52] Hence the military, partly enabled by the regularity created by the wearing of uniforms, is one of the spheres particularly conducive to female cross-dressing. Wheelwright also observes that women's ability to "deceive officers and recruiters in gaining admission into the ranks" rests upon a number of assumptions about "constructions of sexual difference": that is, "the women who so easily disguise themselves make transparent those fixed and immutable barriers between the sexes. They blur distinctions and raise questions about how they are maintained".[53] As Garber further posits, the military uniform is the extreme of sexual inversion, as few would deny the soldier (or airman) is held up as the epitome of masculine identity within traditional western society. The cross-dressing woman desires something she cannot have as a woman in a society that would exclude her from war and the work of war memorial – men's work.

But Evelyn's good luck comes to an end. One night, the squadron leader orders the crew to fly low over Berlin during a full moon "so bright it was like daylight" (336), and the outcome is, predictably, disastrous. The plane is hit by flak while attempting to return to base, and those not seriously wounded plan to parachute out, but Evelyn asks for permission to try for an emergency landing because, as she has told Duncan earlier, "[t]he[se] planes are worth their weight in gold, and so are the people who fly them" (96). On that fateful night, Evelyn's concern for the survival of "the expensive bit of machinery" is uppermost. She "demonstrate[s] a superb bit of flying" and executes a "perfect three-point landing," thereby prompting the flight engineer to comment on "how well the RAF trained its gunners to fly a Lancaster, and land it, when push comes to shove" (348). One of the gunners watching from the ground declares, "I don't know how 'e did it, but when they patch 'im up I'll be first in line for lessons" (349). Upon landing, the plane bursts into flames, and Evelyn survives only briefly. The nurses in the burn unit at the hospital discover her gender when they attempt to remove her uniform, parts of which have fused with her skin (350). The attending physician cannot resist making an ugly accusation by claiming that she may have "lacked heart" at the end because "She was just a girl" (350).

---

50 Wheelwright, *Amazons and Military Maids*, 19. Liz Bissell notes that "it is only when Evelyn assumes Duncan's identity that Olive's sexual ambiguity resolves itself; the eroticism of Evelyn's flirtation with death intensifies their relationship, and her assumption of male identity allows the women to conduct a visible and socially 'acceptable' relationship" (Liz Bissell, "'Private Desires'. Review of Sara Knox's *The Orphan Gunner*", *Australian Women's Book Review* 19 no. 2 [2007], 13). Until this point, Olive had engaged in several serious flirtations, but the cross-dressing Evelyn remains the love of her life.

51 Wheelwright, *Amazons and Military Maids*, 8.

52 Marjorie Garber, *Vested Interests: Cross-Dressing and Cultural Anxiety* (New York: Routledge, 1992), 55.

53 Wheelwright, *Amazons and Military Maids*, 28.

Shortly after, Olive, who works as an operator with the WAAF and is thus responsible for "letting a crew go up with someone who'd never been trained as a gunner, and who wasn't in the RAF" (354), is immediately informed by the wing commander and the most senior WAAF officer on the Station that the rumours about the "bogus gunner" being involved in an on-Station romance (with Olive, he now realises), amount to "a poor show under the best of circumstances," but "we're not writers for the gutter press, so that part of it is your business. The rest of it, alas, is not" (355). Had Evelyn survived, he would have told her she had done a "marvellous piece of flying to get that Lancaster down," and then called the police, but "Now no one beyond the four people in this room will ever hear that commendation. And neither should they. Imagine what Lord Haw-Haw would make of the information that we had a woman in our bomber crews. Not to mention the questions in the House. Unconscionable. Furore at Australia House is quite enough for me to be going on with" (355–56). He emphasises that "even if your friend acted heroically at the end, the fact she was in a position to do so stinks to high heaven ... she was no ... hero" (356).

Wheelwright's observation – that "happy endings are all too rare in these stories"[54] – is borne out in these texts. Within days of Evelyn's death, Olive learns that Duncan has died on the ship sunk on the crossing to Australia, hence the attempt to save his reputation has been futile and now there is nothing, not even plaques engraved with their names to commemorate the siblings' commitment to the war effort. By contrast, Sayer's Pearl's attempt to become a soldier ends better, even though she is discovered bathing in the river by her commanding officer. Outraged that he now realises he has had a "woman under his command" for eleven months, he declares he will report it immediately. But when he tells Pearl that both she and her brother will be court martialled, she advises him to remain silent: "How's the brass going to react when you tell them I've been posing as my brother ... when they find out you can't tell a boy from a girl?" (293–94). Pearl then informs him she is going to Hazden (where James Washington is) and that "no one's going to stop her" (294), and no one does, but the officers' anger in both novels indicates how vigorously the military rejected the notion that women could step so easily into men's jobs.

Wheelwright observes that during World War I, debates raged on both sides of the Atlantic about whether women were fit to become combatants because "photos and reports of women fighting as soldiers, disguised as men or serving in an all-female battalion in Russia began to filter back to Britain and North America" (9). Some felt that the relationships between the sexes would be harmed; more doggedly, a Harvard professor declared that "the average, normal woman ... is biologically more of a barbarian."

---

54 Wheelwright, *Amazons and Military Maids*, 19.

Unleashed, it was feared, a monstrous regiment of women might dominate the earth. But as women were increasingly catapulted into traditionally male spheres of work during the war, the female soldier came to symbolise the ultimate liberation. It was falsely assumed that entry into the military, the most masculine of occupations, would herald a new dawn of equality. If women could now defend their country, went a popular argument, they must be guaranteed political power.[55]

Nevertheless, as Wheelwright acknowledges, although the nature of warfare, military organisation and its relations to general society have undergone significant changes in recent history, the fundamental beliefs – that "war allows men to assume their role as patriarchs; to become the defenders of the nation, the protectors of 'their' metaphorical and actual women and children. It confers a homogeneity upon their aims, pursuits, identities and rewards them with a short-lived glory" persist. Arguably, even today, with Canadian, Australian and American women no longer excluded from participation as combatants, they are still considered "deviants" trying to enter an arena where "fighting remains the test of masculinity, a chance for men to assert their control, their capacity for domination, conquest and even immortality".[56] Women's presence, then, threatens to compromise the essential character and integrity of such a masculine endeavour. The reception of these last two novels bears out this stance: reviews by both women and men of Sayer's novel have focused on jazz and race relations and entirely ignored Pearl's success as a cross-dressing soldier. Similarly, Knox's superbly researched and well-written novel has been almost entirely ignored: I am aware of only a few reviews, none of which address Knox's challenge to the Anzac legend. Even though Wheelwright observes that stories like these of gender inequality illustrate that "with courage and imagination, women have always found ways of overcoming the most seemingly impossible restrictions",[57] these novels have clearly not had much impact in Australia.

---

55   Wheelwright, *Amazons and Military Maids*, 9. The quoted professor was Dr Dudley A. Sargent.
56   Wheelwright, *Amazons and Military Maids*, 17.
57   Wheelwright, *Amazons and Military Maids*, 20.

Part 3
The Vietnam War

15
Coming Home
The Return of the (Australian Vietnam War) Soldier

According to Stuart Rintoul, "almost fifty thousand Australians went to the Vietnam War between 1962 and 1972. Five hundred and one died there, two thousand four hundred were wounded physically. Most of them were scarred. Few who went to Vietnam came away uninjured."[1] In spite of this large number of damaged men, Peter Pierce claims they have been ignored, for "in Australia, there is no extensive literature portraying returned servicemen from Vietnam as outlaw victims".[2] The Australian veteran has had a "slighter literary role" than in the USA, Pierce contends, and "usually figures as psychopathically harmed" in a handful of works the critic considers to be "exceptions": David Williamson's play *Jugglers Three*, (revised and re-published as *Third World Blues)*, C.J. Cairncross's novel *The Unforgiven*, and Gabrielle Lord's thriller *The Sharp End*. Pierce also acknowledges that Georgia Savage's *Ceremony at Long Nho* [sic] includes many "deep ambivalences about Australians at war",[3] but he does not mention her concern over the plight of the wounded veteran. Nor does Pierce seem aware that it is primarily women writers who have cared about how soldiers were treated once they were "back in the world," for he ignores entirely that Dymphna Cusack's *The Half-Burnt Tree,* Marian Eldridge's *Springfield* and Finola Moorhead's *Still Murder* all address, to a greater or lesser extent, the reactions of Australian soldiers to their Vietnam War experiences.[4] (These texts do not accord ideologically, however. Cusack, Moorhead and Lord promote the view that Australian soldiers were duped

---

1   Stuart Rintoul, "Preface," *Ashes of Vietnam: Australian Voices* (Richmond: Heinemann, 1987), ix.
2   Peter Pierce, "Australian and American Literature of the Vietnam War" *Australia's Vietnam War,* eds. Jeff Doyle, Jeffrey Grey and Peter Pierce (College Station: Texas A&M University Press, c2002), 134.
3   Pierce, "Australian and American Literature of the Vietnam War", 134.
4   Dymphna Cusack, *The Half-Burnt Tree* (London: Heinemann, 1969); Marian Eldridge, *Springfield* (St. Lucia: University of Queensland Press, 1992); Gabrielle Lord, *The Sharp End* (Rydalmere: Sceptre, 1998); Finola Moorhead, *Still Murder* (Ringwood, Vic: Penguin, 1991); Georgia Savage, *Ceremony at Lang Nho* (Ringwood, Vic: Penguin, 1994). All subsequent references are to these editions and appear in parentheses in the text. Georgia Savage's *Slate &*

into fighting a pointless war and hence their texts are critical of American imperialism, male violence and religious hypocrisy. Eldridge and Savage avoid overt commentary on the war itself, although they do honour the Australian soldiers' participation in combat.) Drawing upon the works of a number of trauma theorists, I will demonstrate that these novelists display a thorough understanding of the various types of traumas returned soldiers suffered: the trauma of war itself; the trauma of an unwelcoming homecoming; and the trauma of post-traumatic stress disorder (PTSD).

According to Paul Fussell, "every war is ironic because every war is worse than expected".[5] When these Australian men enlisted, either as conscripts or volunteers, they believed they would be fighting in a conventional war, or "a proper war like my Dad fought in," as Moorhead's Peter Larsen puts it. In the kind of conflict he refers to, the Allies, situated behind clearly defined front lines, relentlessly advanced against readily identifiable enemy forces. Lord's Harry Doyle soon discovers that in Vietnam he was fighting in a guerrilla war "without fronts or flanks," where "the war surround[ed] [soldiers] like the jungle surround[ed] [them]" (159). Although Aphrodite Matsakis remarks that this was not the first guerrilla war fought in the twentieth century, it was the first "in which guerrilla warfare predominated," and the tactics made it "particularly savage": soldiers were constantly exposed to "specialized, well-hidden booby traps, often aimed directly at castration or dismemberment". Permanently crippling or disabling wounds such as castration and amputation were sustained at a far greater rate in Vietnam than in previous wars – "300 per cent higher than in WWII and 70 per cent higher than in Korea".[6] Moorhead and Savage introduce veterans in wheelchairs, although not as central characters. Eldridge and Cusack recognise that the size of the "tall, big-boned Aussie," which had rendered him a formidable foe in previous wars, was now a liability: only the slender and nimble Vietnamese could negotiate the marshes and swamps, so that even the jungle became an enemy.

Another difficulty soldiers faced was the lack of clear boundaries "to demarcate friends and foe".[7] In both Eldridge's and Savage's texts, Australian soldiers are killed because they do not suspect that the children running towards them with outstretched hands presumably offering gifts or the slow-moving old men on crutches clutching coke cans are carrying explosives, even though as Jonathan Shay writes, "[e]very familiar item of the physical world could be made to be or to conceal an explosive by the Vietnamese".[8] The absence of an easily discernible

---

Me and Blanche McBride (Ringwood, Vic: Penguin, 1983) features a Vietnam veteran, but because he exhibits few symptoms of trauma, I am omitting the text from my study.

5   Paul Fussell, *The Great War and Modern Memory* (New York: Oxford University Press, 1975), 7.

6   Aphrodite Matsakis, *Vietnam Wives: Facing the Challenges of Life with Veterans Suffering Post-Traumatic Stress* (Baltimore, MD: Sidran Press, 1996), 40.

7   Robert S. Laufer, "War Trauma and Human Development: The Viet Nam Experience", *The Trauma of War: Stress and Recovery in Viet Nam Veterans*, eds. Stephen M. Sonnenberg, Arthur S. Blank and John A. Talbott (Washington DC: American Psychiatric Press, c1985), 39.

enemy fuelled the paranoia that became characteristic of the Vietnam War: as Lord's Harry says, "Some men became walking time bombs" (162). Thus Cusack's Paul Murray, unable to identify whether the peasant men, women and children wearing black trousers, floppy tunics and conical hats are Vietcong or Allies, fires at them all, because "It's them or us" has been drilled into him (87–89). Similarly, Eldridge's Angus Springfield quickly discovers that "If you didn't blow the bastard's brains out in a frenzy of rage or grief within the first few minutes he was safe" and could later kill (70, 286). In order to justify the killings, the authorities dehumanise the enemy. Cusack's Paul is informed that he must exterminate the Vietcong because they are like "fleas and lice that carry plague and typhus" and are the destroyers of civilisation and Christianity (83). (Paul is cast into confusion when a Vietnamese family whose village he has torched saves his life [82].)

Because of the fear and anxiety they experience in combat, soldiers may intentionally wound or kill non-combatants. As Laufer points out, the Vietnam War "created a milieu which encouraged the military and the individual soldier to justify a personal broadening of the 'rules of war'" so that soldiers might succumb to an "abusive use of violence," raping women, mistreating or killing civilians and unarmed combatants such as prisoners of war, destroying entire villages, even mutilating the dead.[9] Thus Moorhead's Peter Larsen, a "basically decent sort of bloke," commits a truly vile act: he rapes a ten-year-old Vietnamese girl "because he was visiting his own pain and terror on a small helpless human being who had no redress, because he embraced the values of the racist warmongers responsible for his own terrifying situation".[10] And although Cusack's Paul Murray performs at least one good deed – he ensures that a child who has had her legs blown off obtains medical treatment (115) – he nevertheless participates in the destruction of a village containing innocent women, children and old men, pours chemicals on the earth that cause defoliation and drops napalm as a form of retaliation against the Vietcong's booby traps and elephant pits. Paul also remains silent when his fellow soldiers use water torture on women and apply electrodes to an adolescent's testicles because they believe he has killed one of their mates. Even though these procedures sicken him, he does not protest. These kinds of "meaningless acts of malicious destruction," observes Judith Lewis Herman, render soldiers most vulnerable to lasting psychological damage.[11] So Larsen is never able to forget raping a child: he spends the rest of his life atoning, becomes sexually impotent and is generally unfit for human society.[12] Those who witnessed horrific acts also suffer guilt: Lord's

---

8   Jonathan Shay, *Achilles in Vietnam: Combat Trauma and the Undoing of Character* (Toronto: Maxwell Macmillan, 1994), 34.

9   Laufer, "War Trauma and Human Development", 39–42. See also Shay's chapter on the "berserk state," in Sonnenberg, Blank and Talbott *Trauma of War*, 77–99.

10   Denise Thompson, "Finola's Dilemma, or; If Literature and Politics Don't Mix. What Am I Doing Here?" *Southerly* 55 no.2 (1995), 120.

11   Judith Lewis Herman, *Trauma and Recovery* (New York: Basic, 1992), 54.

12   Thompson, "Finola's Dilemma", 120.

Harry Doyle remains forever haunted by the sight of his mate raping a dying woman. Moreover, according to Patrick J. Bracken, veterans experienced difficulty "processing" these horrifying events because they conflicted with their deepest assumptions about the world and their place in it.[13] Many of the soldiers do not realise the extent to which their own standards of humanity have been overthrown until they return to the home front.

Back in Australia, Paul attempts to comprehend why he followed bloodthirsty soldiers blind to all but violence and destruction. He realises that he had gone along with barbaric acts because he believed, as did they, that they should be fighting in Vietnam. As well, because these men had prolonged combat experience, he was thrilled to learn from them how to defeat the enemy. And as Herman notes, when men are in danger, they become emotionally dependent upon their leaders.[14] For Paul, when it was too dangerous to hesitate and question the morality of their actions, these men's sense of invulnerability, their indifference towards the enemy, made him feel safe. As Paul continues to reflect upon his combat experience, he begins to understand why he could not absorb the information Johnny the Nasho (clearly Cusack's mouthpiece) gave him about his country's commitment to the war. Paul recalls that, like all volunteers, he hated conscripts for several reasons: they were badly trained, they squawked about the lottery that sent them there, they counted the days until they could go home, and they were generally regarded as subversive and seditious. But unlike most volunteers who could not have located Vietnam on a map, Johnny has studied the culture and the history of Vietnam. He insists that the Americans' ignorance of and disrespect for the Vietnamese warrior culture has led them to underestimate the Vietcong, who are not "dim-witted," but are cunning warriors who have successfully fought off numerous invaders for centuries. Johnny also accuses Australians of being invaders who have no right to be on Vietnamese soil; he then compares them to the Australian settlers who tracked down and shot Indigenous Australians and the New Zealanders who did the same to the Māori people, and asks how Australians would respond were the situation reversed. Johnny also points to the kinds of abstract, noun-heavy rhetoric war makers employ. He argues that words such as "liberation" and "civilization" have lost their meaning because "civilized" people do not kill innocent women and children, destroy age-old cities and pagodas or defoliate the land. He insists that phrases like "Pacification Programmes" are euphemisms for search-and-destroy missions, and that the healthy-sounding "New-Life Hamlets" are in reality filthy concrete spaces full of malnourished, idle Vietnamese people. According to Johnny, "when [the Australians] have finished bringing Civilization and Liberation to Vietnam there'll be nothing left but scorched earth and no

---

13   Patrick J. Bracken, "Hidden Agendas: Deconstructing Post Traumatic Stress Disorder",
     Rethinking the Trauma of War, eds. Patrick J. Bracken and Celia Petty (New York: Free
     Association Books, 1998), 46.
14   Herman, *Trauma and Recovery*, 25.

one left to liberate" (85). Back on the home front, Paul sees that Johnny was right: Australians were not in Vietnam for the good of the people, for the South Vietnamese did not wish to be "saved" from communism, nor did they want to fight. He moreover wonders if Australians go into war "light-heartedly" because they have "never known the horrors of war on their own soil" (94). Ultimately, Paul recognises that he was wrong to scorn the conscripts and to despise the anti-war protesters and the conscientious objectors, because they possessed the kinds of "guts" he lacked (95). Paul's realisation, that he should have resisted his father's patriotic (and hypocritical) talk of freedom and democracy and his emphasis on "war as a fulfilment of the male role" (79) thus anticipates the frequent confessions by the American combatant writer Tim O'Brien, who claimed that he enlisted because he did not have the courage to stay home.[15]

It was not only the unique military and political features of the Vietnam War that contributed to the survivors' trauma, however; the disappointing homecoming also played a role. According to Herman, while "returning soldiers look for tangible evidence of public recognition",[16] these Vietnam vets were greeted either with apathy, derision or outright hostility.[17] Savage's photojournalist, Fiona Sinclair, argues that this antagonistic reception was unfair, because in previous wars, men also saw and participated in atrocities, but they came home "and spoke only of the glory of battle and that sort of crap. This lot had no choice: everyone knew what happened in Vietnam and they knew because of the clever little camera" (113). Vietnam veterans were, then, the only ones labelled drug-abusing baby killers, the only ones not offered societal forgiveness, the only ones left to carry the burden of national shame. Although Moorhead's Peter Larsen stresses that he and his mates believe it was patently unfair to blame soldiers obliged to follow orders because of "the stupidity of Canberra and Washington" (14), he also admits that the veterans were completely undone by the contempt shown them when they arrived in Sydney, and were further outraged by the government's insistence that veterans be "shuffled back from Vietnam in the middle of the night, debriefed in secret, and asked to keep their war experiences to themselves" (135). Cusack's Paul also discovers just how unpopular the war was when, after being horribly burned and disfigured in a napalm attack, he is forced to endure excruciating pain for nine days before he gets to an Australian hospital because, as he bitterly remarks, "no one at home thought that their wounded were worth enough to bring them back in a fast plane" (80). The walking wounded fared little better: Eldridge's Angus Springfield receives no sympathy for his permanently damaged knee, loss of hearing and "fucked-up" head,

---

15   Tim O'Brien, "The Vietnam in Me" *New York Times Magazine*, 2 October 1994, 52.

16   Herman, *Trauma and Recovery*, 70.

17   Most are unaware, however, of the extent to which their wives and lovers have also been caught in the crossfire. In Lord's *The Sharp End*, a soldier's wife is harassed so frequently by anti-war protesters that she stops admitting that her husband is in Vietnam and in Moorhead's *Still Murder*, Peter Larsen's sweetheart is so besieged by angry protest mobs that she aborts his child and, within weeks, marries a peace campaigner (162).

and is told repeatedly that he "only got what was coming to him" (72). As both Savage and Moorhead point out, Australian veterans had to wait a long time – until the Welcome Home Parade in Sydney on 3 October 1987 – before the public finally offered them honour and respect.

Perhaps the most emotionally incapacitating trauma veterans suffered from though, consists of invisible wounds now commonly identified as PTSD. R.J. Spiller defines PTSD as a behavioural disorder that sets in after "a person has experienced an event that is outside the range of usual human experience and that would be markedly distressing to almost anyone," events such as natural disasters, catastrophic accidents, victimisation by criminal or state action, the death of a loved one and of course combat.[18] Matsakis observes that PTSD is "more prevalent, more long-term, and more intense among victims of man-made disasters" than those of natural catastrophes.[19] Although some psychologists propose that the symptoms of PTSD appeared on the battlefield, most, like Ghislaine Boulanger, suggest that they did not surface until the veteran had been home for more than a year, and that once the symptoms were established, they could last indefinitely.[20] Hence Eldridge's Angus and Lord's Harry find that although they may have left the war decades earlier, it has not left them, but continues to rage on in their hearts and minds long after they return home; these veterans, now in their forties, continue to suffer from a combination of intrusive memories, dreams and nightmares and flashbacks.

Recurring dreams and nightmares about Vietnam may replay real war events or probable or feared war events, but all create anxiety for the veteran forced to relive these traumatic experiences.[21] Eldridge's Angus endures gruesome nightmares depicting putrefied corpses that twitch as though they are still alive (167) and Cusack's Paul suffers from a number of what he terms "living nightmares." One brings back the "intolerable agony" (30) he experienced when his body was scorched by napalm. Just before he awakens, he sees the "three contorted black heaps like twisted scrap steel that had been his mates" (30). In another recurring dream, he sets fire to a village full of innocent women and children; he awakens just at the moment that he visualises a mutilated woman's body (she has no face) with a tiny baby (it has no body) clinging to her breast. Paul also relives in his dreams the weeks he spent with the Vietnamese family who rescued him, as well as the agonising flight back to Australia. But the dreams he dreads most depict his wife Marilyn as more enticing and passionate than ever before, when in reality, she has taken one look at his disfigured body and headed straight to a divorce lawyer. When

---

18   R.J. Spiller, "Shell Shock," *American Heritage* 41 no.4 (May/June 1990), 77. For more detailed definitions of PTSD, see Shay, *Achilles in Vietnam*, 165–67; Ruth Leys, *Trauma: A Genealogy* (Chicago: University of Chicago Press, 2000), 2.

19   Matsakis, *Vietnam Wives*, 23.

20   Ghislaine Boulanger, "Post-Traumatic Stress Disorder: An Old Problem With a New Name", in Sonnenberg, Blank and Talbott *Trauma of War*, 25, 19.

21   Matsakis, *Vietnam Wives*, 26.

Paul awakens from his jungle-dreams, he can at least console himself that the war is over, but knowing that his marital relations have also ended offers cold comfort.

According to Matsakis, flashbacks, which are sudden, vivid recollections of the traumatic event, are also common. The veteran, who suddenly finds himself back in combat, "may see the scenes of Vietnam, smell the smells, and hear the sounds".[22] Eldridge's Angus has been troubled for more than twenty years by recurring flashbacks reminding him of his failure to warn his mate Metcalf of impending disaster. Angus also suffers because men who fight beside each other in combat develop a tender, caring relationship.[23] Moreover, they tend to blame themselves for their mate's death even if they were not responsible.[24] Angus has no reason to blame himself because he was caught in a catch-22; in order to prevent his mate's death, he would have had to kill the child who carried the booby trap and at the same time violated the mates' pact never to harm a Vietnamese child. But as Stephen Sonnenberg notes, since veterans spend so much time reexperiencing traumatic events, they may unconsciously strive to master their traumas by making them come out better.[25] But this attempt to defeat a trauma can also prove destructive because veterans may easily confuse their wives and children for the enemy.[26] Accordingly, Angus mistakes an innocent child – the son of his lover – for the child who killed his mate, and almost "wastes" the boy (305).

Because these intrusive memories, nightmares, and flashbacks are so psychologically painful and physically exhausting, many veterans use drugs or alcohol to control anxiety or insomnia,[27] but the use of narcotics tends to make their problems worse by alienating them from others.[28] True to form, several of these veterans, Cusack's Paul and Eldridge's Angus, drink to excess, Savage's David becomes a heroin addict, and Moorhead's Peter grows marijuana that he sells to Vietnam War veterans because he believes he is helping them overcome the pain no one cares about. None of these veterans is offered psychological counselling. Doctors advise Cusack's Paul to undergo more skin grafts when what he needs most is help facing the future as a mutilated man, and doctors readily hand Eldridge's Angus prescriptions for pills (presumably tranquilisers) but take no interest in his psychological condition.

Perhaps because it was published in 1998, Lord's *The Sharp End* is the only text that suggests that societal institutions have become more sympathetic to victims of PTSD. When Sydney detective Harry Doyle accidentally kills an innocent man while on duty, the police force exonerates him because he has served in Vietnam.

---

22 Matsakis, *Vietnam Wives*, 28.
23 Shay, *Achilles in Vietnam*, 39.
24 Shay, *Achilles in Vietnam*, 73.
25 Stephen M. Sonnenberg, "Introduction: The Trauma of War", in Sonnenberg, Blank and Talbott *Trauma of War*, 5.
26 Matsakis, *Vietnam Wives*, 28.
27 Sonnenberg, "Introduction", 5.
28 Herman, *Trauma and Recovery*, 44.

In turn, Harry advises Angus Wetherill, a deranged veteran who has raped and murdered several women, to ask the authorities to let him serve time in a hospital, not a jail, because he, too, suffers from PTSD. (Moreover, Angus' alcoholic father, who has beaten his son as a child, is also a descendant of the brutal white colonisers who massacred nearly all of Harry's Aboriginal ancestors.) Significantly, Harry Doyle has also been traumatised when young. He was abducted from his Koori family's home in New South Wales and sent to a "terrible" institution in Adelaide where he was forced into silence. Although Harry makes a partial recovery after his mother rescues him, he nevertheless forsakes his proud Aboriginal heritage when he learns in school that blacks are "primitive" and "treacherous" (298). He cuts his ties with his mother and closes his emotions down. Angus Wetherill, by contrast, never overcomes his childhood abuse because neither of his parents shows him any love. In referring to childhood traumas, Lord's text may appear to be supporting the American Psychological Association's pre-disposition theory that, until 1980, held that PTSD sufferers had personalities that made them especially susceptible to PTSD, and that well-adjusted people would not succumb to the disorder. It seems more likely that Lord is arguing that these men's psychological, medical, social and genetic histories may govern how they react to traumatic events. The returned servicemen in these texts are in dire need of counselling, for many find it difficult, if not impossible, to return to their prewar occupations. Savage's handsome David Sinclair loses a frontal lobe (and hence his looks) in an explosion at Dalat; thereafter, he suffers permanent memory loss and never regains his skills as a photographer or finds a job that makes use of any of his talents. Similarly, Cusack's Paul's freakish appearance prevents him from resuming work in real estate, and in a less extreme case, Lord's policeman Harry Doyle realises that he has seen too much of the pain and anguish people cause one another and asks to be transferred to the Dog Squad.

Veterans like Harry and Angus also display a number of symptoms associated with PTSD, such as "hyperalertness".[29] The scent of eucalyptus conjures up to Harry the tropical rainforest at Núi Đất, and a swarm of blowflies recalls the hot, stinking days he spent in the jungle. For Angus, the sight or smell of smoke or the sound of a flaring candle brings back the memory of Metcalf's death in a bomb explosion and the "screeching" of pine trees across his roof reminds him of the screaming women who were being burned in their villages. As well, both Angus and Harry are "always on guard and overreact" to "a combat-related stimulus", such as the sound of an automobile (or tractor, in Angus' case) backfiring. Returned soldiers also tend to shun activities that remind them of their combat experience. Angus avoids bush walks because the terrain reminds him of Vietnam and he often carries a loaded weapon with him, another symptom of PTSD.[30] Moreover, some veterans

---

29 Boulanger, "Post-Traumatic Stress Disorder", 23.
30 Arthur L. Arnold, "Diagnosis of Post-Traumatic Stress Disorder in Viet Nam Veterans", in Sonnenberg, Blank and Talbott *Trauma of War*, 104–105.

who are unable to adapt to the rhythms of civilian life may "embark upon travel which is not planned and goal-directed".[31] Moorhead's Peter never settles down in one place. After Cusack's Angus returns from Vietnam for the second time, he wanders aimlessly around the outback and the Top End for several years, picking up odd jobs and engaging in a series of half-hearted affairs. Once he returns home, he confines himself to his own personal redoubt – one room in his large house – and, like many veterans, when forced into the company of other people, he tends to face outward from a corner or a wall.[32] These fictional soldiers also suffer from "avoidance phenomena," which means that they may appear "preoccupied, bored, or disinclined to action with others".[33] Typically, Angus does not join in conversations with his friends and family because he finds the topics utterly banal. After only three weeks on the home front, Angus signs on for a second tour of duty in order to be with his mates.

The majority of these veterans are also unable to feel or express emotion, especially with those closest to them. As a result, their wives and other family members "often feel rebuffed".[34] Eldridge's Belle complains that Angus is "using" her in bed (146), whereas Savage's Fiona laments that "normal marital relations" with her husband David do not resume until he has been back from Vietnam for fifteen months (263–64). Given their emotional remoteness, it is not surprising that many of these vets face marital strife upon their return from combat. Eldridge's Angus, Cusack's Paul, Moorhead's Peter and Lord's Harry are divorced; Harry is in a second marriage that is also floundering. Veterans who have supportive wives most often undergo successful rehabilitations,[35] but this is rare. When Moorhead's Paul Murphy, a veteran confined to a wheelchair, is publicly repudiated by the woman he loves, he turns into a "mean kind of guy, irreparably buggered" (15). Rejected by his wife, Cusack's Paul resolves to kill himself. Savage's text proves the exception: although Fiona is a compassionate wife, when David realises that he is a burden to her, he overdoses on heroin.

Several of the other veterans are ultimately saved by the love of good women whom they eventually come to trust. Learning to trust another person is crucial to recovery but, as Sarah Haley points out, when victims are traumatised by other human beings, not natural disasters, their trust in others may be "severely shaken or shattered entirely".[36] According to Shay, veterans will place their trust in others only after testing them frequently. Shay places a great deal of faith in the way "narrative" enables survivors to "rebuild" their character. But he cautions that narrative can "heal" only if the survivor encounters listeners who are not shocked by what they

---

31 Arnold, "Diagnosis", 115.
32 Arnold, "Diagnosis", 105.
33 Arnold, "Diagnosis", 104.
34 Arnold, "Diagnosis", 104.
35 Charles Kadushin, "Social Networks, Helping Networks, and Viet Nam Veterans", in Sonnenberg, Blank and Talbott *Trauma of War*, 67.
36 Cited in Matsakis, *Vietnam Wives*, 23.

hear. To build trust, these listeners must also refrain from judgement and neither refute the story nor blame the victim.[37] Two of the women in these texts fail to be empathetic. Angus Springfield's former wife Belle, concerned about the changes in his personality, begs Angus to tell her what happened to him in Vietnam, but when he does, she becomes frightened and cannot cope (146), so their relationship crumbles. Lord's Meg Doyle encourages Harry to talk to her, but then she "fights against what he says" (246); like Angus, he retreats into silence. But several other women exhibit compassion because they have developed sympathetic ears owing to their own experiences with trauma. Cusack's Brenda has married a good-looking pilot, only to learn after she becomes pregnant that he is a bigamist. She obtains an abortion but becomes a bitter recluse thereafter. Her only source of comfort is her garden. When it is destroyed in a bushfire, she hires Paul to restore it to native plants. Having been "burned" once by an attractive man, she is now prepared to disregard a "half-burnt" man's appearance. And since Paul has contributed to the defoliation of Vietnam, it seems fitting that he should wish to restore the garden to its natural state. Paul's life thus comes full circle: prior to the war, he had wanted to be a farmer, but his father bullied him into living off the land instead of on it. By the end of the novel, Paul appears to have established authority over his memory,[38] as his nightmares have disappeared; he now dreams only of "victory" over the garden. Similarly, Eldridge's Gita is hooked on both sex and drugs but, fortunately for Angus, she is only trying to kick the heroin habit. Angus hires Gita, who has developed a "green thumb" at a rehabilitation centre up north, to help him grow seedlings that will restore the under-storey on a Victorian property destroyed by overgrazing. After establishing trust, he tells her the story of Metcalf's death, and she helps him understand that he was not at fault. Lord's novel also concludes with a happy resolution for Meg, after being involved in a dodgy affair with the crazed veteran Angus Wetherill (which nearly destroyed her family), learns to listen without judgement.

Interestingly, although none of the (mostly American) trauma therapists I have quoted in this paper have stated that life in the Australian bush contributes to the healing of these wounded veterans, this seems to be the conclusion Cusack, Eldridge and Lord have reached, for their happiest characters either live in the bush or retreat to it as often as possible. In this sense, these texts seem decidedly old fashioned, hearkening back as they do to a city/country dichotomy that asserts that a humble life in the bush is bodily and spiritually therapeutic, while an urban existence is morally and physically degenerating. At the same time, these writers also re-inscribe the values of the masculine bush ethos. But there is one significant difference: the inhabitants of the bush are racist and inhospitable to "Others" such as immigrants, hippies or Aboriginal people. Some rural inhabitants sound as if they are card-carrying members of Pauline Hanson's One Nation Party. And as I've

---

37   Shay, *Achilles in Vietnam*, 185–89.
38   Shay, *Achilles in Vietnam*, 192.

already pointed out, the bush itself, like the veterans who seek refuge there, is also in need of rehabilitation.[39]

---

39 I delivered a shorter version of this paper at "The Vietnam War, Thirty Years on: Memories, Legacies, and Echoes" conference at the University of Newcastle (April 2005). Several Australian veterans (not all combatants) challenged a few points raised in my paper. They argued that Australians never dropped napalm; that most veterans were given Welcome Home parades; that they had never heard of veterans being returned at night to avoid hostility; and that many veterans adjusted well to civilian life. For similar arguments, see also Jane Ross' "Australia's Legacy: The Vietnam Viets," in *Vietnam Remembered*, ed. Gregory Pemberton (Sydney: New Holland Press 2002): 186–213.

16

"All We Are Saying is Give Peace a Chance"

The Vietnam War Protest Movement in Australian Women's Fictions by Janine Burke, Patricia Cornelius, Nuri Mass and Wendy Scarfe

Nearly fifty years ago, the Australian government sent thirty military advisers to South Vietnam, thereby initiating a commitment to a war – Australia's longest – which was to last for over a decade. Although Greg Langley observes that Australia's contingents were small compared to those from Thailand, South Korea and the USA, altogether nearly 47,000 Australians, including 17,500 national servicemen, served in Vietnam and the "toll of 496 dead and at least 2500 wounded or otherwise scarred was tragic". Almost as disturbing as the results of the battlefield were the shockwaves that reverberated throughout Australian society, for the war years turned out to be one of "the most turbulent periods in the nation's history". While Langley acknowledges that changes in Australian society were occurring prior to the war – "labor and immigration patterns, science, the media, international travel and education, were all being transformed, and a growing affluence and consumerism posed a challenge to old ways" – at the same time, he stresses that Australia was "a conservative, inward-looking country whose attitudes had been shaped by years of depression, conflict, and the Cold War, and characterised by a rabid anti-communism and an almost pathological fear of Asia".[1] Ann-Mari Jordens further asserts that Australians had grown accustomed to placing their confidence in the authority of the federal government, so when Prime Minister Menzies announced in November 1964, without any debate, that he was requiring conscripts to serve overseas (the first troops left for Vietnam in 1965), he had the support of the majority of the population.[2] Eventually, however, the Vietnam War became the major catalyst for a re-thinking of the whole of Australian culture and society, as the Tet Offensive, the Mỹ Lai massacre, the Kent State shooting and the increasing numbers of deaths and casualties convinced many Australians they were

---

1   Greg Langley, *A Decade of Dissent: Vietnam and the Conflict on the Australian Homefront* (Sydney: Allen & Unwin, 1992), x.
2   Ann-Mari Jordens, "Conscription and Dissent: The Genesis of Anti-War Protest", *Vietnam Remembered*, ed. Gregory Pemberton (1990. Willoughby, NSW: Weldon, 2009), 64.

engaged in a dishonourable and unwinnable war. This combination of factors –
which also included many Australians' discomfort with what they perceived as an
increasing subservience to the USA[3] – led many to feel their country was in the
wrong and hence "the 1960s and early 1970s became an era of demonstrations,
strikes, and confrontations," as public support for the war began rapidly to erode
and the "Australian way of life" challenged as "never before".[4]

The events of these tumultuous years are examined in five little-known
Australian women's fictions: Nuri Mass' 1971 *As Much Right to Live*, Janine Burke's
1984 *Speaking*, Wendy Scarfe's 1984 *Neither Here Nor There* and her 1988 *Laura, My
Alter Ego: A Novel of Love, Loyalty and Conscience*, and Patricia Cornelius' 2002 *My
Sister Jill*. To my knowledge, these are the only women's fictions to offer sustained
examinations of the Vietnam War protest movement in Australia,[5] to demonstrate
the ways in which the family unit became a home-front war zone where the war
against the war played out through verbal, emotional, and physical violence and
thus to narrate the kinds of stories that rarely appear in history books. Together
these texts chronicle what Ann Curthoys has referred to as "the politicization,
even radicalization of Australian youth";[6] recount the kinds of overt challenges to
the traditional standards of masculinity that had prevailed in Australian society
since its inception; and document the emergence of the second-wave feminist
movement.

Although Peter Cochrane argues that the "dissent and protest of the sixties was
not simply a youth rebellion, as is often suggested",[7] in these novels, it is primarily
the "Vietnam generation" – those who grew up during 1965–71, when conscription
for Vietnam was in full force – who express the most bitter resentment towards the
government and who most strenuously agitate for social change. These "post-war
baby boomers," Cochrane asserts, were an "unusually large cohort" who, as a result
of the rapid growth of the university system, were staying in school longer and
"studying new subjects such as sociology" or discovering "new challenges in old

---

3   Ann Curthoys, "Mobilising Dissent: The Later Stages of Protest", *Vietnam Remembered*, ed.
       Gregory Pemberton (1990. Willoughby, NSW: Weldon, 2009), 144.
4   Langley, *A Decade of Dissent*, x.
5   In Helen Hodgman's *Jack and Jill* (Ringwood, Vic: Penguin, 1981), the central character, Jill,
       takes up a petition to help stop the war, and then suffers a head wound from a police attack
       during a Vietnam War protest in Sydney, but the episodes are brief. The opening scene of
       Adrienne Sallay's *Loaded Hearts* takes place during the 8 May 1970 moratorium march in
       Sydney, but the instances of police brutality seem out of place because, by all accounts, the
       march was entirely peaceful. Sallay's novel focuses more on the plight of the returned soldier
       who has fought with the Americans than the protest movement. For more analysis of the
       difficulties returned soldiers faced, see Chapter 15. See also Evie Wyld's *After the Fire, A Still
       Small Voice*, which offers a sympathetic view of both Korean and Vietnam War veterans, and
       Neilma Sidney's *The Return*, which features an American soldier who deserts the army during
       his rest and recreation (R & R) leave in Sydney and then seeks refuge in the Australian bush.
6   Curthoys, "Mobilising Dissent", 138.
7   Peter Cochrane, "At War at Home: Australian Attitudes During the Vietnam War Years",
       Vietnam Remembered, ed. Gregory Pemberton (1990. Willoughby, NSW: Weldon, 2009), 168.

subjects such as the rise of left-wing Keynesianism in economics". Because this "period of extended adolescence and education … provide[d] the space for questions for identity and meaning to arise," these students were "possibly the most energetic, idealistic and visible political force of the era".[8] Hence the government's prosecution of the war "seemed alien" to the "romanticism and idealism" of youth culture.[9]

Cochrane's description of these young rebels fits Mass' Glen Rimshaw in *As Much Right to Live* perfectly. Born in 1950, Glen is a product of a new system of secondary education designed to raise standards, which requires him to spend an extra year in his Sydney high school. Mass' narrator asserts that the extended stay resulted in the crop of university entrants (of which Glen is one) being "much quieter," "more serious minded," more "mature" than their predecessors,[10] and his mother Elaine suggests Glen is a "determined and individual thinker" (207). Glen is also idealistic: his father Clyde claims Glen wants "to build a utopian world" (275). And quixotic; a "die-hard, traditional romantic" (312), says his father, and a lookalike of the romantic poet Shelley, says his mother (314). But Glen is also liberal-minded and responsive to others' troubles; during high school, he rescues Larnie, the orphaned daughter of a Jewish poet whose parents died in a rail disaster, from a cruel aunt by bringing her home and then marrying her while both are at university. Glen comes of age when Prime Minister Menzies (who first took office in 1949) commits the first troops to Vietnam, and is a rebellious arts-law student at the University of Sydney when required to register for National Service. He does so, but reluctantly, because he believes, as do the other well-read and politically astute young radicals in these texts, that his country is in the wrong. Like Glen, Cornelius' University of Melbourne students blame the nation's problems on a prime minister who has not only stayed in office too long, but is also a "war-mongering bastard," and the "worst Prime Minister the country has ever had".[11]

Conscription is the central issue that serves to politicise these members of the fictional "Vietnam generation." One is Scarfe's Jonathon Bourke, a brilliant chemistry and physics student at the University of Melbourne who, distracted by studying for exams, registers, without thinking, for National Service. But after reading the history of Vietnam and its political situation – and in spite of the fact that his eyesight is so poor he would never be conscripted – he applies for exemption because he concludes "there is no evidence that Australia as a nation is threatened by the Vietnam conflict and therefore no reason to conscript young men to fight there".[12] He insists the government has no right to abrogate his right to moral choice, particularly since the system is so "irrational" (64). The method

---

8   Cochrane, "At War at Home", 169.
9   Cochrane, "At War at Home", 174.
10   Nuri Mass, *As Much Right to Live* (Sydney: Alpha Books, 1971), 318. All subsequent references are to this edition and appear in parentheses in the text.
11   Patricia Cornelius, *My Sister Jill* (Sydney: Random House, 2002), 143. All subsequent references are to this edition and appear in parentheses in the text.

of selection, which he appropriately calls "killing by lottery," forces young men to kill "upon a pure chance happening of marbles being picked out of a barrel" (64). Furthermore, as he points out, if he kills under civil law, he will be sentenced to life in prison, but if he kills in wartime, he does so with impunity. Ultimately, although he is not a pacifist, Jonathon decides that he has a moral obligation to resist fighting and killing in Vietnam and to resist those who would force him to do so (75).[13]

Young men like Jonathon who refused to comply with the *National Service Act* were considered either liars or cowards and hence routinely subjected to a series of protracted court cases and fines. Jonathon makes three court appearances, all of which he loses because he is bamboozled by magistrates whose cunning questions prevent him from explaining himself thoroughly. Scarfe's central character Richard McGill, a family friend present at these court appearances, is shocked by the gross unfairness of the proceedings, which treat resisters worse than any criminal, for they are privy to "no jury, no defence, just gaol" (127). After losing his first court case, Jonathon forsakes his studies and becomes an "artful dodger," reduced to playing a game of cat and mouse with the authorities who conduct early morning raids at universities and houses or private homes suspected of sheltering conscientious objectors and draft dodgers, and then arrest them. Richard observes that by taking a stand on the right to freedom of opinion, Jonathon has ironically deprived himself of any free will at all. Totally dependent upon others, he is no longer able to sustain his "pride and courage," which eventually turn into "self-doubt and a remorseless disintegration of belief in the morality of his own actions, in the worth of such morality and indeed in any morality at all" (127). At the end of the novel, and despite his fear of being incarcerated, Jonathon has been caught, arrested, and sentenced to two years in prison for non-compliance.[14]

Similarly, Mass' Glen and his friend Mike refuse to play a part in any organisation whose purpose is killing. Mike, a medical student who respects the sanctity of human life, registers for National Service, but purposefully includes with the papers a "hostile" letter that asserts that a democratic government should not force him or anyone else to "go against his will or conscience" to fight in a war which is not only "immoral, but obsolete and a form of lunacy" (348–49) and then challenges the government to conscript him. In reply, the government informs him that if he refuses to be called up after graduating from medical school, he will go to prison for two years. While Mike labels the government's actions "fascist,"

---

12   Wendy Scarfe, *Laura, My Alter Ego: A Novel of Love, Loyalty and Conscience* (Ringwood, Vic: Spectrum, 1988), 70. All subsequent references are to this edition and appear in parentheses in the text.

13   Although Mass' novel concentrates on the moratorium marches, it also mentions schoolteacher William White's arrest, imprisonment and suspension from his job (276) and the "terrible persecution of Simon Townsend and others like him" (418).

14   In Gayla Reid's "Sister Doyle's Men," a short story in *To Be There With You: Stories of Longing and Desire* (Crows Nest: Allen & Unwin, 1996), a young man who is conscripted in New South Wales "disappears" into Western Australia. "Contemptuous" and "hostile" plainclothes and military police hound his sister about his whereabouts.

Glen argues that any system of government that does not allow for "freedom of opinion and of conscience" is not a democracy, but a "totalitarian" regime that "brainwash[es] a fair proportion of its youth into believing that they're doing a noble service by giving their lives to defend it" (401).

Like other members of the "Vietnam generation," Glen is opposed to conscription because he is convinced the Australian government is merely toadying up to the USA. He accuses Prime Minister Harold Holt of trebling the commitment of fighting forces to Vietnam in order to "win the heart of the President from Texas" (315), refers to the Australian government as "corrupt, war-addicted ... American boot-lick[ers]" (411), and refutes as folly the domino theory his father upholds as a reason to remain an American ally. Cornelius' Jill Wheatley in *My Sister Jill* has similar objections: she regards the presence of Australian and American troops in Vietnam as "unlawful" and enthusiastically swells the ranks of those who protest against the visit of President Lyndon B. Johnson in 1966, whom Holt invited to tour the eastern states. When her twin brothers are conscripted, she tells them they should refuse to fight because they will be nothing but "cannon fodder" for the Americans. Johnson has not come Down Under, she asserts, to "enjoy our beaches or our windswept plains," but because he needs Australia to send young men to fight in Vietnam, and "Nobody else is stupid enough to help him. Nobody else wants to join forces with a country that has started an illegal war" (149).

These young resisters are also cynical about the Americans' claim that they are "freedom-fighters" bringing democracy to the world. Scarfe's Jonathon argues that the Vietnamese want to run their country themselves, much as Australians want to run theirs, "without being pawns in the colonial strategy of the French or the defence strategy of the Americas" (65), and Cornelius' Jill claims that if the Vietnamese want to live under communism (which they did not), they should have the right to do so. She also claims the Americans have no intention of helping the Vietnamese: "they're there because communism scares the shit out of them" and "because communism is about equality and capitalism is about how the rich have it all and everyone else is shit" (170). Mass' narrator also argues that although the Vietnamese themselves never enter into the discussion, she believes they simply want to form "one country" (445) and argues that the Americans operate under a hidden agenda: they want to ensure that the "tungsten-rich lands of Vietnam [will] be governed in a manner favourable to their interests there" (345). Mass' Glen argues too, that Australians should abide by the wishes of the Vietnamese, who do not want Americans in their country because they have merely set up a "puppet government" to satisfy their own "corrupt ends," and have left in their wake nothing but devastation: "burnt villages and massacres and defoliation and napalm" (416). Glen is outraged that Americans have yet again employed deadly force against innocent people; he points out that "the destruction of Hiroshima was less than a two-hundredth part of what's already happened in Vietnam" (350), and he is revolted by Americans' hypocrisy: at the same time as they are withdrawing ground troops from Vietnam, they are "stepping up aerial bombardments" (432) on Laos and Cambodia. Furthermore, Glen asserts that the twenty to thirty billion dollars the US spends on genocide should go towards building schools, hospitals and nurseries in America and towards solving their own racial, economic and social problems (416). He also protests that democratic ideals are being undermined in Australia because the young do not have the right to reject acts that are cruel, immoral and "downright un-Christian" (313), such as attacking a developing nation full of poor people.

The youthful protesters in these fictions find themselves not only railing against the dictates and actions of corrupt political governments and institutions, but also fighting hostile home-front enemies – their fathers – whose values they do not share. During the Vietnam War, Cochrane remarks, the generation gap became "unusually wide"[15] and in these fictions many young people find their fathers have turned their kitchens and lounge rooms into battlefields. Cornelius' Christine claims she and her five siblings are only free to laugh, tell jokes and talk when their father is "missing"; but when Jack, a mean drunk, returns from the pub (and it is always from the pub), the house becomes a war zone where fighting, yelling, ugly outbursts and threats of attack prevail. Jack's daughters refer to him as "a ticking time-bomb" (83) and a "savage pit-bull" (22) and regard him as such a destructive force in their lives that they occasionally play a macabre game where they devise ways to kill him.[16]

Conscription once again proves divisive because fathers support the policy; they are, as Scarfe's mother/wife Laura says disdainfully, "middle-aged or old m[e]n quite safe in [their] armchairs by the fire at night and quite ready to send the young to fight and die" (90). Cornelius' Jack Wheatley, the only one of these fathers to have served in World War II,[17] is in fact eager to send the young to fight and die; he claims that conscription "is the best thing that's happened to the country for years" and declares that "young men today … need direction, training … If you're called up, you're called up. There's nothing more to say about it" (133). But Jack has plenty more to say about it: "Conscientious objectors! Cowards, Communists, should be shot" (134). He is therefore delighted when his twins, Michael and Matthew, are conscripted, even though they are physically slight and temperamentally unsuited for combat, and revels in the congratulations (and beer) his RSL mates – who were, as Jordens asserts, strong advocates of conscription[18] – bestow upon him. Heartlessly, Jack shuns Matthew when he fails the medical. Similarly, Mass' Clyde Rimshaw lacks any understanding of his son's gentle nature: he encourages Glen to register for National Service because "a couple of years of hard physical training" are "exactly what he needs" (172). Scarfe's Kelvin Bourke declares that those who

---

15   Cochrane, "At War at Home", 169.
16   In Cornelius' unpublished play "Jack's Daughters" (1989), loosely based on the same subject, one of the daughters succeeds in killing Jack.
17   In Hodgman's *Jack and Jill*, Jack, another World War II veteran, also takes a dim view of resisters, whom he calls "limp-wristed conchie[s]" (45).
18   Jordens, "Conscription and Dissent", 64.

do not want to fight are either "cowards" (90) or "stupid young fools" who will "not stop the war" (89) and because "father knows best" is the rule in his household, Jonathon is forced to leave home.

Other skirmishes arise because the young want to change the world, whereas the old merely wish to safeguard it. Glen argues that young people do not want to accept "things as they are," but to "to make the world a better place for everyone"; yet whenever they identify societal ills, their fathers tell them to stop "disturbing people" who simply "want to go on sleeping" (205), a recurring comment in several of these texts. According to Cochrane, many of these white-collar, middle-class, and affluent fathers (like Clyde and Kelvin) were content with their lives and hence "fearful of protest and change";[19] many others (like Jack) were befuddled and irritated by a shifting world they did not understand. In the postwar era, Cochrane proposes, some men found "the answer to self-fulfilment in terms of lifestyles conducted around consumer goods" but they also ran the risk of becoming "shallow" and "one-dimensional".[20] Scarfe's Kelvin is just that man: an ambitious, consumer-driven high-school principal who raises his offspring in the kind of suburban wasteland George Johnston so thoroughly denigrated in *My Brother Jack*; Kelvin also suffers from what Richard (echoing D.H. Lawrence) describes as the "contagion of emotional repression so typically Australian" (17).

Although Jack is far from repressed (he boasts constantly about how tough he had to be to survive three years as a prisoner of war in Changi) and his economic status differs from the others (his family lives in poverty because he is unable to hold down a job),[21] he, too, finds the world changing so quickly that his daughter Christine observes he is "about to crack [because] there is no keeping the world and its irritations out" (84). For example, when he discovers that George Johnston's *My Brother Jack*, which fails to laud the military mastery of World War II veterans, is on the list of books set for English, he is so outraged that he hurls the novel onto the street. Jack is also stunned when he sees a young man on television burning a registration card and another setting fire to an Australian flag; he claims these anti-war protesters "don't belong to the real world," which he predicts will soon be taken over by "little yellow bastards" (134–35) if they do not stop. Jack holds rigidly conservative and racist views: he supports capital punishment but not unions, resents that the "'whingeing Poms' and the 'Bloody abos'" think they own the place" (133), and complains that women who dress in saris should "fucking well fit in" (84) if they want to live in Australia.

---

19 Cochrane, "At War at Home", 168.
20 Cochrane, "At War at Home", 169.
21 Stephen Garton argues that men like Jack found war "an exaggeration of manliness" and hence assimilating to the "more domestic and sedentary life of the modern breadwinner" proved difficult ("War and Masculinity in Twentieth Century Australia," *Journal of Australian Studies* 56 [1988], 93). His recurring nightmares and alcoholism suggest he may be suffering from PTSD. Indicative of the times, he is offered no counselling or medical treatment; doctors tell his wife Martha not to let him talk about his feelings, the kind of response we now know was misguided.

On the surface, the comfortably well-off Clyde Rimshaw seems a cut above Jack Wheatley, but Clyde, too, is an unthinking patriot, a firm upholder of law and order, and hence guilty of outmoded thinking. Having earned a law degree while working with the Sydney police force, Clyde sides with his government's commitment to war (and everything else) and adheres strictly to the accepted wisdom of the times which, as Cochrane stresses, entails "a willingness to settle for the way things are".[22] During heated debates with Glen, Clyde reiterates that it is every citizen's duty – including his son's – to obey his elected officials and the laws they have carefully constructed over time, even if they are bad laws, and moreover, that anyone who wishes to criticise or change the law must do so within its existing framework. But Glen, who grows increasingly exasperated with the repetitive nature of his father's arguments, eventually accuses his father of behaving like Adolf Eichmann, who justified his crimes by declaring that he was only acting on orders from his leader.[23] During these numerous and prolonged debates with his son, however, Clyde wonders only once if his years of service in the police force have caused his thinking to "calcify" (173).

These middle-aged fathers are also, to a greater or lesser extent, tyrants and bullies. Clyde believes that violence is occasionally justified and spanks Glen even as an infant. As Glen matures, Clyde practices what might today be termed "tough love." When Glen fails to do well in school, Clyde puts him through such a rigorous program of study that his mother-in-law calls him a "bully and a tyrant [who runs] his home like a police state" (124) and his wife Elaine claims (prophetically) that "even killing [his] own son doesn't matter" (128). Scarfe's Richard observes that his father Kelvin maintains a "constant bullying attitude to his family" (51); and both Kelvin and Ben, the husbands in *Neither Here Nor There*, display violent tempers and strike their wives and children (not always their own) for what they construe as disobedience or insubordination. Jack Wheatley is the most abusive husband and father, however; although he believes hitting a woman is "cowardly," he shouts that his wife Martha is "stupid" so often that Christine claims "it's like the boards of the house have responded to the years of his bellowing with their cracked and peeling curls of paint" (199). As well, Jack plays roughly with his offspring and watches for signs of vulnerability in order to give his perpetual insults more sting. Because Jack always needs money (he smokes and drinks even when the family has no food), he forces the frail fourteen-year-old Johnnie to take on a physically demanding job that nearly kills him, and because he has a disdain for the intellect, he makes Jill quit high school, even though she is an excellent student with a bright

---

22   Cochrane, "At War at Home", 170.

23   Langley writes that protestors defended their positions "on principles of individual conscience which harked back to the Nuremberg judgments of World War Two ... One of the central principles of Nuremberg was that obeying orders is not a defence. This implies that a moral imperative is placed on individuals to find out the consequences of government policies and their role within them" (Langley, *A Decade of Dissent*, xi–xii).

future in the sciences. Lonely and frustrated by her lack of knowledge and work at low-level positions, Jill attempts to educate herself by reading student newspapers and hanging around lecture halls at the University of Melbourne.

By contrast, the sons of these insensitive and mean fathers are motivated by an intense humanity; they detest violence, vengeance or coercion of any kind and want to make the world a kinder, gentler place. Thus they repudiate fighting, do not condone "legitimized murder," refuse to be intimidated by a national mythology that places the Digger at its centre, and reject their fathers' preoccupation with the Anzac legend, which Stephen Garton claims is "saturated in manhood".[24] As Cochrane observes, for members of the youth culture, "going away to fight" was no longer the "apotheosis of citizenship and manhood"; instead, young men began to

> challenge the integrity of the soldier, to question the established connection between citizenship and military activity in Vietnam, to break up the strict standards of masculine conformity which had prevailed, it seemed for eons. For many observers (and some soldiers), the Vietnam War would seriously discredit the style of aggressive masculinity that had been kept alive (and culturally dominant) by a succession of "just wars" and the Cold War, for decades.[25]

Mass undermines this established masculinist/military ethos by creating Glen as a pacifist almost from infancy. Small for his age, he evades sports entirely and declines, even when bullied, to fight or defend himself except by the unusual strategy of talking excessively. During high school, he is quiet and studious, writes poetry and has only one "mate," the equally bookish and scholarly Mike, with whom he spends time reading. As adolescents, the not-so-dynamic duo become moderately famous for their social-action songs that take aim at subjects such as parliamentary servants and their perks, acid rain and the assassination of JFK. Glen, who composes the lyrics, also writes the occasional love song, a sure indicator that he is not a typical Australian bloke. While Mass' Clyde wishes his son would defend himself on the playground, Scarfe's "aggressively masculine" Kelvin has explicit ideas about what constitutes the character of "real boys": they must love "dirt," "football," and "camping" (31), and want to study "proper" subjects such as physics, chemistry and maths (48). Kelvin dismisses his younger son Michael's passion for painting as "recreational fribble" and the literature and history Jonathan loves reading as mere "scribbling" (42). Laura believes that she cannot "save her sons" from this "tribal society" that removes children from their mother's influence and places them under a "totalitarian world of male values," and acquiesces (31).

Although it seems risible today, another of the ways in which the rift between the generations played out was through hairstyles which, during the Vietnam War,

---

24   Garton, "War and Masculinity", 86.
25   Cochrane, "At War at Home", 176.

took on a kind of symbolic importance. According to Donald Horne, "for three generations, short hair had been a symbol of manliness, virility and national virtue in a country where long hair symbolised the evils of an impractical but arrogant intellectuality, or of a boozy and morally lax bohemian artiness, or a plain cissiness and poofterism".[26] Cochrane remarks, too, that the authorities associated "long and ungroomed hair with uncleanliness, rampant sexuality and traitorous values. On young males it was understood in gender terms as a lack of manliness".[27] Moreover, "fashions suggested a rejection of the culturally dominant ideals of masculinity"; thus the "coloured shirts" and "flared trousers" worn by the young also challenged "traditional standards of masculinity"[28] and "had a lot of older people worried".[29] Among the worried is Clyde Rimshaw, who considers his son's lengthy tresses and green velvet jacket with billowing sleeves unmanly. In his defence, Glen argues that young people should not be "ostracized" or "persecuted" as criminals because they simply want to try "something new" and insists they have the right to dress as they please (298). Another of the anxious fathers is Jack Wheatley; like Clyde, he associates long hair with the feminine: when he spots a young man with hair on his collar, he "yells bullishly … 'Get a haircut, you poofta'" (84). Jack also finds his son Johnnie's "pretty" appearance – particularly his long curly locks – an "immense flaw, something close to an abomination" (20).

Another contentious issue that divided the generations was the right to protest. Jack Wheatley finds the idea so upsetting that when he catches Jill walking home with a resister after a demonstration, he throws her out of the house, permanently. Clyde Rimshaw's reaction is less extreme, but he holds fast to the view that neither Glen nor Larnie should participate in moratorium marches. Although Glen acknowledges that these forms of public protest are technically illegal, he contends that democracies have only ever been won by people breaking the law, and demonstrating in the streets is a well-tested tactic. When Clyde argues that the streets are to be used by *all* people, not just those who will disrupt ordinary life for one day, Glen retorts that no one gets upset when "royal visits, and returning soldiers, and Anzac Day parades often do this" (411). But when Glen insists that the protesters have agreed that they will be peaceful, that there will be no ugliness or violence on their part, Clyde answers that Glen cannot make such a "positive statement on behalf of the goodness of thousands of people" (409).

Although Clyde, now Metropolitan Superintendent of the police force, is unreservedly against the right to protest, Malcolm Saunders points out that because opinion polls continued to suggest that the majority of the population supported the government's decision to send troops to Vietnam and to conscript its young men, the federal government was not overly concerned about anti-war

---

26   Cited in Cochrane, "At War at Home", 172.
27   Cochrane, "At War at Home", 172.
28   Cochrane, "At War at Home", 179.
29   Cochrane, "At War at Home", 172.

demonstrations until the late 1960s.[30] Thus it regarded protests such as those against Johnson's visit to Australia as "minor irritants" which represented only a "small minority of the community at large". When the government "bother[ed] to attack the peace movement, it fell back on the familiar strategy of denouncing it as Communist-inspired and Communist-controlled".[31] But the federal government nevertheless paid close attention to the "law and order" issue Richard Nixon developed to help him win the 1968 election. In his platform, he declared that the USA had become "the most lawless and violent in the history of free peoples" and promised that, if elected, he would not only bring an end to the war, but would "adopt a program of general domestic repression".[32] Inspired by Nixon's success at the polls, the Australian federal government began to devise their own "law and order" tactics and encouraged the states to follow suit. Both levels of government continued to claim that communists were controlling social protest, but then, adopting Nixon's strategy, they attempted to frighten people, including draft dodgers, by enforcing the *National Service Act*, which they had been reluctant to do until that point. Various levels of government further predicted that the peace marches would turn violent and result in clashes between anti-war demonstrators and police or pro-war demonstrators. But as Mass' narrator notes, some of these pronouncements were intentionally confrontational: on the eve of Anzac Day, for example, the NSW government publicly referred to those who wanted peace as "a fifth column more monstrous than anything Hitler could ever have devised" (407). The inciting rhetoric heated up even further when the minister for labor and national service referred to the moratorium organisers as "political bikies pack raping democracy," a comment Mass includes in her text and which her narrator declares has been "universally censured for its hysteria and bad taste" (407).

These incendiary tactics proved ineffectual, however, for as Mass' novel underscores, the first of the moratorium marches, held around the country on 8 May 1970, was wholly peaceful. According to Curthoys, herself a protester, the march was "successful beyond the wildest dreams of its organizers",[33] and Saunders, too, writes that the 8 May march turned out to be the "peak of the anti-war movement's activities"; it mobilised huge numbers of people (25,000 turned out in Sydney) and demonstrated that "street marches supported by tens of thousands of people held in an atmosphere of controversy and tension could still be peaceful",[34] a set of circumstances Mass' novel also documents. The success of that first march clearly threatened conservative politicians, for they immediately began to condemn the upcoming 18 September march as "lawless" and their strict "law and order"

---

30 Malcolm Saunders, "'Law and Order' and the Anti-Vietnam War Movement: 1965–72", *Australian Journal of Politics & History* 28 no.3 (1982), 367.
31 Saunders, "'Law and Order'", 368.
32 Saunders, "'Law and Order'", 369.
33 Curthoys, "Mobilising Dissent", 157.
34 Saunders, "'Law and Order'", 372.

campaign became the "principal stick" with which to "beat the peace movement".[35] Initially, as Mass' narrator observes, politicians sought to discredit the marchers by labelling them riffraff, communists, traitors and violent extremists; their slurs were further shored up by the RSL, who declared the protesters were "either abysmally ignorant or … purposefully working for totalitarian victory" (407). The most inflammatory rhetoric came from NSW Premier Robert Askin, who called protesters "just a heap of garbage," a vitriolic phrase Mass includes in her novel (410).

These protestations appear to have had the desired effect, since many civic, police and state authorities instigated repressive measures. As Mass' novel indicates, University of Sydney administrators, who had not stood in the way of the first march, became obstructionist during the second and prohibited students from gathering on the Commons. Civic authorities prevented marchers from gathering at Sydney's Town Hall, the Domain, or Hyde Park, and required them to request a permit to walk on the streets, although none had been asked for this on the 8 May march. Glen notes that this demand was simply a ruse, because when moratorium marchers complied with the rules and requested a permit weeks in advance of the second march, they received no reply. Saunders writes that many citizens believed their government was being "deliberately provocative" in hopes of increasing the likelihood of violence at demonstrations,[36] a conviction Mass clearly shares, for in her novel, the police – under the authority of Clyde Rimshaw – actively seek confrontation with the demonstrators, the authorities' senseless acts of brutality against peaceful demonstrators thus turning the march into a scene of chaos and disorder.

Mass appears to have modelled Rimshaw on the real-life Norman Allan for, according to Saunders, as police commissioner at the time, Allan "mobilized the largest force of police ever assembled for an anti-war demonstration anywhere in Australia".[37] Mass' narrator refers to Rimshaw as the "architect of brutality and shame" (480) because he appears to have been swayed by the thinking of conservative politicians who convinced him that instead of using the police force to protect citizens, he should deploy it for political purposes. Clyde's orders also lead to the somewhat melodramatic death of his son Glen who, ever since he was a child, has expressed sympathy for the underdog and the needy. Accordingly, in the midst of the confusion, Glen tries to help an elderly man who is being jostled by the crowd, but the police beat Glen and fling him onto the road, where he is then run over by a car. (Here, Mass may have intended readers to recall NSW Premier Askin's instructions to "run over the bastards"[38] who were protesting

---

35 Saunders, "'Law and Order'", 377.
36 Saunders, "'Law and Order'", 371.
37 Saunders, "'Law and Order'", 373.
38 Ian Hancock, "Robin (later Sir Robert) William Askin", *The Premiers of New South Wales 1856–2005*, eds. David Clune and Ken Turner (Annandale, NSW: Federation Press, 2006), 355.

Johnson's visit to Sydney.) Clearly, Mass constructs Glen's death as a cautionary note to the government, for in her "Dedication" to the novel, she declares that it is "responsible for building a society in which the culminating event of this story could well be not only possible, but inevitable" (n.p.). She then pleads with these "guardians of democracy [to] reorient their thinking so as to recognize that a democratic government dignifies its people rather than degrading and suppressing them" (n.p.). The "culminating event" – Glen's death – thus stresses that courageous young men had "as much a right to live" as anyone else, but they were betrayed by their nation's participation in an unnecessary and immoral war.

But as Cornelius' novel points out, those who expressed loyalty to the government also paid a high price. Michael returns from his tour of duty wounded in mind, unable to speak about his experiences or adapt to daily life: "it's like he died," observes his sister Christine (203–04). His homecoming also proves traumatic because, as Cochrane observes, returned soldiers were no longer feted as they had been in previous wars; "many saw [this war] as immoral and its perpetrators as bullies and butchers".[39] Jack Wheatley is thus infuriated when he learns that Michael has been told to make his "own way" home because the military wants "to avoid trouble with the demonstrators," and irate that he was advised not to wear his uniform home because "a lot of people don't feel very friendly towards it" (202–03). Jack simply cannot understand that in some circles, the returned soldier had now become the enemy, or that many believed that it required more courage to be a conscientious objector than it did to go to war.

In the end, the battles these patriarchs wage against their offspring result in numerous home-front losses: Clyde's "get tough" approach contributes to his wayward daughter's suicide and Kelvin's homophobia causes his youngest son Michael to take his own life. Similarly, Jack's homophobia drives his son Johnnie as far away from home as possible. Cornelius' Christine is the only one of these young radicals whose future appears promising: at the end of the novel, she has left home and is studying at the University of Melbourne. By contrast, her sister Jill, who desperately wanted an education, has becomes pregnant, married young, and at the end of the novel, is unhappily expecting another child. Wives and mothers are also losers in these combative homes. Cornelius' Martha spends her days watching television alone, having never developed relationships with friends or family because her husband Jack, a typical abuser, would never allow visitors into *his* house. Only in Scarfe's novels do women move from positions of weakness to strength, but their journeys to self-actualisation are fraught because, as Pemberton observes, the "participation of women in Australian political life was rare throughout the sixties".[40] Curthoys, too, acknowledges that it took courage to be

---

39 Cochrane, "At War at Home", 204.
40 Gregory Pemberton, "Conclusion", *Vietnam Remembered*, ed. Gregory Pemberton (1990. Willoughby, NSW: Weldon, 2009), 76.

supportive of women's issues; even during the Vietnam War, their position within the protest movement was marginal:

> We didn't even have the language to discuss it then, and words like sexism and male chauvinism did not emerge until around 1970. Women were in a very second-class position, there was no doubt about it. The spokespeople were always men, and they were very sexist men.[41]

Both of Scarfe's novels depict sexist men who dictate the way their households and families are run. In *Neither Here Nor There*, the childless primary school teacher Elizabeth Kingswell's desire to offer refuge to one of her students after his sole caregiver dies causes a permanent rift in her marriage because her husband Ben (who wants no children) refuses.

Although Elizabeth had arguably married Ben because she had admired his kindness and liberal thinking, she suddenly realises she has been in error when she attends a "radical cell" meeting and discovers her husband is "conditioned by a set of political theories" which he applies to "all actions and all events," even though they may be inappropriate to the social context, such as the Vietnam War, and may even occasionally include the condoning of violence. When she vocalises her objections and Ben belittles her remarks, she becomes increasingly disturbed, for she had not until that moment realised that she was married to a man who "fundamentally distrusts emotion … denigrates it [and who] never recognize[s] that some truths [are] derived from emotional awareness".[42]

In drawing attention to the distinctions between men's rational and women's emotional approaches to complex moral situations, Scarfe reflects psychologist Carol Gilligan's challenge to male theorists' privileging of men's reliance upon abstract concepts such as justice, right and duty, and the concomitant conclusion that women's moral reasoning tends to be primitive because it is more intuitive and concerned less with principle.[43] According to Seyla Benhabib, Gilligan argues that "women's moral judgment is more contextual, more immersed in the details of relationships and narratives. It shows a greater propensity to take the standpoint of the 'particular other', and women appear more adept at revealing feelings of empathy and sympathy required by this". In Gilligan's view, "the respect for each other's needs and the mutuality of effort to satisfy them sustain moral growth and development".[44] Both of Scarfe's novels demonstrate that Laura's and Elizabeth's compassion for others allows them to "sustain moral growth and development,"

---

41 Cited in Langley, *A Decade of Dissent*, 96.
42 Wendy Scarfe, *Neither Here Nor There* (Warrnambool: Kepler, 1984), 25. All subsequent references are to this edition and appear in parentheses in the text.
43 Cited in Seyla Benhabib, "The Generalized and the Concrete Other", *Ethics: A Feminist Reader*, eds. Elizabeth Frazer, Jennifer Hornsby and Sabina Lovibond (Oxford: Blackwell, 1992), 267.
44 Cited in Benhabib, "The Generalized and the Concrete Other", 270.

whereas their husbands Kelvin and Ben have, like Clyde Rimshaw, allowed their thinking to "calcify," and thus remain static and fail to develop with the times.

The testing ground for Scarfe's theories is the Vietnam War. Although there are exceptions, in *Neither Here Nor There* she develops a series of binary oppositions that situate male politicians, educators, ministers, social workers, political organisers and heads of families in the "abstract concept" camp. Much disagreement exists between these groups over how to conduct protests, because each faction claims to know how the community will react. Since none of their political stances is impartial, those with most institutional power become the most influential. The novel underscores how little concern these institutional representatives exhibit over the real suffering the war brings. Although these important men have both the resources and the power to aid innocent victims, particularly Vietnamese children damaged by napalm or bomb attacks, none sees that as an important role (104). As one woman's advocate for children puts it, they are simply "big men having a look at war and pushing people around. But they never have a close look at the slaughter. They can't even look at one child" (104). For the most part, these prominent men are waging a paper war, one in which they themselves are never in danger.

Both an Anglican minister, with whom Elizabeth has an affair, and her husband Ben, reveal they are willing to sacrifice the wellbeing of underprivileged Australian and Vietnamese children (both in general and individual terms) in order to satisfy their own selfish (read sexual) needs. Whenever Elizabeth mentions attempting to save wounded children, Ben insists that she is wasting her time trying to save a few children when there are thousands in need, a response that renders her insecure about her feelings and opinions. Only through engagement with other women does Elizabeth learn to find strength in her convictions. By chance, she meets a woman who has served as a war correspondent in Vietnam and has adopted a young Vietnamese girl. The woman introduces Elizabeth to others who, like her, concentrate on saving a few individual children, even though thousands are in need. They believe that "anyone who has no sympathy for an injured child hasn't got any respect for broader social issues" (104). Elizabeth is also introduced to the Religious Society of Friends, a group of Quakers who endeavour to fund medical treatment for injured Vietnamese children. The two groups disagree about the direction these children's futures should take: the Quakers wish to use the children's plights to raise governmental awareness of the problems, but they draw the line at adoption. Significantly, these women work out their disagreements through negotiation and compromise, not aggressive power struggles; their discussions always have at heart the welfare of children. (Elizabeth has earlier encountered similar feelings of good will among the nuns at the orphanage where her troubled student is placed, as well as among the female police officers in charge of disadvantaged children.)

Although Elizabeth is not certain "whether the conflict ... over Australia's participation in the Vietnam War had made her super sensitive to the attitudes of others or whether it had simply stimulated her intelligence and activated long sleeping values" (102), it is clear that she will no longer tolerate her husband's denunciation of her feelings or his violent outbursts. Although she is panicky and apprehensive about her future, she vows never again to be dependent upon others. In the final pages, she is standing on the steps of the Melbourne General Post Office handing out pamphlets designed to raise the moratorium marchers' awareness of the victimisation of Vietnamese children; her actions, she knows, could lead to her arrest, but she bravely defies the law. Scarfe's ending in *Laura* is similar: as Laura's concern for her son Jonathon's wellbeing increases, she no longer dedicates herself solely to pleasing her husband and children, but begins reading about the Vietnam War, joins the Save Our Sons (SOS) movement and, determined to defeat the Liberals (Whitlam has become her "hero"), becomes a member of the Labor Party. Arrested and jailed briefly for hitting a police officer outside the American Embassy, she remains undaunted, and continues to protest the war by standing outside Parliament House every Friday night wearing a black armband and carrying a placard.

Janine Burke's *Speaking*, the most structurally experimental of these novels, further stresses the importance of women's joining forces to combat the conservative and masculinist culture they inhabit, but with one important difference: her protagonist, Lily Wolfe, dismisses the feminist movement as irrelevant, in part because she has been raised by her father, an important member of the Communist Party, who introduces her to the male structure of politics, which she thereafter embraces. Her father's training enables her to become a prominent member of the protest movement, but even when she becomes aware that she operates within a male-dominated, sexist milieu where men either treat women as if they were invisible or steal their ideas, she ignores their blatant sexism because she earns recognition from both men and women through her genius for organising and her ability to "speak," or more often, to yell. (In her review of the novel, Sarah Dowse refers to Lily as "a sort of Weatherman of the antipodes"[45] and one of Lily's friends refers to her as the "Angela Davis of student politics"[46]). At the 8 May moratorium – which she later refers to as "the best day of her life" (65) – she incites thousands of marchers to believe that they can bring an end to the war if only they will commit themselves to doing so. Her oratorical skills seem to bode well because, as Margaret Henderson points out, "[w]omen's speaking out about their experiences and oppression has been fundamental to the modern women's movement, being used as a political tactic to confront and challenge",[47] as Cora Kaplan puts it, "the patriarchal convention that enjoined women to deferential

---

45   Sarah Dowse, "Political Novels", *Island Magazine* Winter 1985, 59.
46   Janine Burke, *Speaking* (Richmond, Vic: Greenhouse Press, 1980), 32. All subsequent references are to this edition and appear in parentheses in the text.

silence" and the "related suppression of women's speech, writing, and sexuality".[48] But Lily is neither speaking against female oppression nor for peace – the word she uses most often is "fight" – but advocating "revolution" that will change the world by bringing an end to capitalism. It takes her nearly a decade, though (the novel is set in 1980), to recognise that she has been badly served by staying "loyal to the political paradigm that oppresses her" and by "screwing" nearly every man in the anti-war movement, because "the cavalcade of cocks" (37) fails to support her when she is thrown out of the University of Melbourne for her radical politics and abandons her when she becomes pregnant.

Accordingly, when the revolution fizzles and her disillusionment with party politics reaches its peak, she has nothing to fall back on, for she has declared war on her friends (a poet, a painter, a lesbian arts administrator and a research assistant to a conservative politician) who try to support her. Throughout the novel, Burke employs military language to indicate the kind of relationship Lily has with her friends, who characterise their gatherings as "combative offensives" (63) where Lily "controls the manoeuvres and triumphs because she is a superb markswoman" (70). Lily aims most of her barbs at the women's movement, especially consciousness-raising groups, which she views as banal outpourings of emotion and gushy sentiments about love, which she calls a "minor ailment" (75). But after many failed starts at jobs in Melbourne and London, she remains so haunted by her failed past, so "mad with memories" (15), that she determines to write a history of the anti-war movement. Lily's conception of her history, however, is rambling and confused, because as Henderson points out, she lacks the "insights and experiences provided by the women's movement"[49] that would have encouraged her not to obliterate her own subjectivity. The narrative thus follows Lily's struggles with feminism and her "gradual realization of the inadequacy of her particular form of leftist politics" (135).

Before Lily reaches rock-bottom, she is saved by Raider, an Aboriginal man who is politically involved with the Aboriginal land rights movement, and who supports her efforts to write. (He is one of the few good men in these texts – Scarfe's Richard is another.) In an interview with Jim Davidson, Burke suggests that Raider is the only one "who really perceives what is happening to Lily and the way that she can get out of it".[50] Unlike Lily, he does not challenge the world to a fight, but attempts to "guard … what was his and seek … what had been stolen" and in the process, struggles to show the "white country" how "blind" they have been

---

47   Margaret Henderson, "New Angels for Storms of Progress? Two Historical Novels of Australian Feminism", *Hecate* 25 no.1 (1999), 133.
48   Cited in Henderson, "New Angels for Storms of Progress?", 133.
49   Henderson, "New Angels for Storms of Progress?", 135.
50   Jim Davidson, "No Silence Anymore: An Interview with Janine Burke", *Footprint New Writers No.1: Janine Burke*, ed. Jim Davidson (Footscray, Vic: Footscray Foundation of Australian Studies, Footscray Institute of Technology, 1987), 44.

to the effects of colonisation and how "blind" they are now to the harmful effects of uranium mining in the Northern Territory (294). When Lily expresses interest in becoming involved, he tells her it's not her "party," that "she's not running the show," and that she will have to learn to do politics differently, which she does (296). When Raider is arrested and put in prison, Lily is spurred on to actually do something. She declares a kind of truce with her friends, takes steps to help further their careers, perhaps even saves a marriage, and begins to recognise the value of the feminist movement. However, Burke seems to suggest here that the feminist movement may have had its limitations, because arguably, without the aid of the skills Lily garnered while working within male political structures, several of her friends' lives and careers might have floundered.

Lily also channels her considerable energies into Indigenous issues, a move that seems appropriate because, as Pemberton points out, Aboriginal people (like Raider) were "becoming increasingly politicized". The young radicals in both Mass and Cornelius' novels were also identifying a range of societal ills – Indigenous issues, environmental concerns such as mining in the Blue Mountains and the White Australia policy – which they intend to tackle. Although it is difficult to state whether any of their struggles (fictional or otherwise) to make Australia a better place had much impact or any sustaining power, Pemberton suggests it would be "very wrong to deny the enormous impact that the Vietnam conflict, both home and abroad, had on Australian society". He asserts "there was a growing mood of discontent with our subordination to British and American influence" and that the country eventually had to accept "that its main effective relations were with Asian nations". He also claims that the women's movement was revitalised through its experience in the anti-war movement, not just through criticism of the traditional patriarchal structures that had produced Vietnam, but also through criticism of the male domination of the anti-war movement itself. For many women, the war was the first time they were involved in political activity, certainly in a public way, often defying not only convention but also their peers, husbands and perhaps even their sons.[51]

Pemberton's observations reflect the changing gender structures that Scarfe and Burke identified in their novels, and which may indeed be one of the legacies of the Vietnam War. When I wrote this essay, the prime minister, the governor-general, and premiers in New South Wales, Tasmania and Queensland were all women who represent a political power structure that would have been inconceivable in the period covered by these novels.

But both Pemberton and Langley have also argued that changes in attitude to the military ethos may have been one of the positive lasting legacies of the anti-Vietnam movement,[52] although their comments have proven premature; as

---

51   Pemberton, "Conclusion", 233–234.
52   Pemberton, "Conclusion", 233; Langley, *A Decade of Dissent*, xii.

Marilyn Lake and Henry Reynolds claim, "for several years now Australia has seen the relentless militarization of our history ... The Anzac spirit is now said to animate all our greatest achievements, even as the Anzac landing recedes into the distant past".[53] Furthermore, in their chapter on the Vietnam War, Carina Donaldson and Lake note that the protest movement, which "celebrated a progressive, urban, culturally innovative nation committed to the goals of sexual and racial equality, an Australia that was forward looking and multicultural, rather than locked into the British tradition of its past",[54] appears to have lost the home-front battle. In her Introduction Lake argues that the time has come (again) to "proclaim ourselves a free and independent republic, enshrining not militarist values, but the civil and political values of equality and justice, which in an earlier era had been thought to define a distinctive 'Australian ethos'".[55] It would be fitting and proper were the nation's women leaders working to achieve that goal – their gender having been, after all, left out of the "getting of nationhood" at Anzac Cove.[56]

But I'm not counting on it.

---

53 Marilyn Lake and Henry Reynolds, "Preface", *What's Wrong with Anzac? The Militarisation of Australian History*, eds. Marilyn Lake and Henry Reynolds (Sydney: UNSW Press, 2010), vii.
54 Carina Donaldson and Marilyn Lake, "Whatever Happened to the Anti-War Movement?", in Lake and Reynolds *What's Wrong with Anzac?*, 89.
55 Marilyn Lake, "Introduction: What Have You Done For Your Country?" in Lake and Reynolds *What's Wrong with Anzac?*, 2.
56 War correspondent C.E.W. Bean's famous proclamation, that "in those days [the First World War] Australia became fully conscious of itself as a nation" (*The Official History: The Story of Anzac From the Outbreak of War to the End of the First Phase of the Gallipoli Campaign, May 14, 1915* [Sydney: Angus and Robertson, 1934], xlvii), celebrated an event that absented women.

17

O What a Lovely War

No More Shooting Blanks in Helen Nolan's *Between the Battles: A Novel*

It seems appropriate to conclude this lengthy examination of Australian women's World War I, World War II and Vietnam War fiction by including the only Australian woman (to my knowledge) to provide a literary account of her observance of and participation in the Vietnam War. In *Between the Battles: A Novel*, oddly not published until 2005, Helen Nolan claims that she wanted to "record a non-combatant's account of the [Vietnam] War," and adds that "while many of the events depicted in the book happened – although not always to me – the story itself is fictional".[1] Nolan's novel tells the story of a brave young Australian woman who made the decision to "serve" in the Vietnam War, even though she knew nothing about the conflict (it is unlikely that she would have heard of "the yellow peril" or "the Domino theory" and would have had difficulty locating Vietnam on a map). But it is important to point out at the outset that what Nolan has written will not suit everyone's taste, given that, as reviewer Tony Smith points out, for some, "war is such a serious business that it seems irresponsible to approach it with anything but reluctance or to regard it as anything but tragic".[2] By contrast, Nolan's protagonist, Holly Gow, views the war primarily as an opportunity for high adventure, preferably with a lot of American military officers, and easily gets her way.

In order to shed light on why there should have been such a dearth of women who may have wished to share their war stories, I turned to the American poet and autobiographer W.D. Ehrhart, whose argument about why women have traditionally shied away from discussing their time in Vietnam appears in his Foreword to *Visions of War, Dreams of Peace*, an anthology of writing by American women who served in the Vietnam War.[3] Ehrhart thanks women veterans for their

---

1   Helen Nolan, *Between the Battles: A Novel* (Canberra: Pandanus Books, 2005), Author's note. All subsequent references are to this edition and appear in parentheses in the text.
2   Tony Smith, "Review, Helen Nolan's *Between the Battles: A Novel*", *Journal of Australian Studies Review of Books*, 28 June 2005, https://bit.ly/3qwOoua.
3   W.D. Ehrhart, "Foreword," *Visions of War, Dreams of Peace: Writings of Women in the Vietnam War*, eds. Lynda Van Devanter and Joan A. Furey (New York: Warner Books, 1991): xvii–xx.

courage in contributing to the volume because, as he boldly asserts, most people assume when people think of war, they regard it as "the domain of men" and believe that "Women have no place in war". He adds that "one measure of the depth of those perceptions – misconceptions really – is that the U.S. government cannot even state with accuracy how many women served in Vietnam. That the government can be so ignorant is a source of shame and embarrassment".[4] Ehrhart insists, however, that thousands of American women (the current estimation is about 19,000) did serve in a variety of jobs such as "military nurses ... Red Cross volunteers, and workers for a variety of private organizations, just as women have served in every U.S. war". Nonetheless, "their sacrifices and suffering have been ignored and they have been forced to bear a burden of silence even male veterans of Vietnam have not known".[5] But as Ehrhart points out,

> if male Vietnam veterans were met with indifferent silence when we came home, we began to struggle against that silence almost immediately. And if what has been written by many men about Vietnam departs from that long tradition, be it a refusal to "romanticize or glorify" war, an enormous and still growing body of literature has come out of the Vietnam War, but if the amount of writing is astounding, the fact of it is not. Men wage war; men write about war.[6]

In addition, Ehrhart underscores that while men have published hundreds of books about the Vietnam War, only a small number of books by women have appeared, but "almost none has been treated seriously by the popular, literary, scholarly, or historical communities".[7] In their Preface to that anthology, editors Van Devanter and Furey echo Ehrhart's words about the dearth of women's writing, but they also draw attention to the fact that unlike men, women have come home from war and "kept quite silent. They have gone back to their 'duties', left the writing to the men".[8] Moreover, even if they wished to document what "their" war was like, they would have undoubtedly faced obstacles such as the "words of a New York publishing house editor who asked in 1979, 'What could a woman possibly have to say, especially about war, especially the Vietnam War?'"[9] Plenty, if Nolan's book is any example.

---

4   Ehrhart, "Foreword", xvii.
5   Ehrhart, "Foreword", xviii.
6   Ehrhart, "Foreword", xviii.
7   Ehrhart, "Foreword", xviii.
8   Lynda Van Devanter and Joan A. Furey, "Preface", in Van Devanter and Furey *Visions of War*, xxii.
9   Van Devanter and Furey, "Preface", xxi. Upon arrival in Saigon, Holly hears from the pilot that the "disembarking passenger" should be ready to get off, but as she prepares to do so, others on the flight – including the pilot – urge her to sit down because they "couldn't quite believe that this six-stone-four (forty kilos) female was getting off the plane to go to war" (cited in Siobhan McHugh, *Minefields and Miniskirts: Australian Women and the Vietnam War* [Sydney: Doubleday, 1993], 3).

Current estimates of Australian women's commitment to the war effort indicate that about one thousand of those women who refused to be left behind didn't "count" in their country either, nor did they talk publicly about their work for some years, and then only after being invited to do so by the Irish-born Siobhan McHugh, whose *Minefields and Miniskirts; Australian Women and the Vietnam War* appeared in 1993. In her Preface, McHugh outlines briefly how her book came about. Asked to "explore the possibility of one on Australian nurses," and immediately after speaking to only two, she "knew that here was a whole missing perspective," and she was right: her extensive research unearthed "nearly two hundred Australian women who had been involved in Vietnam". Like their American counterparts, they had lived and worked in Vietnam "as entertainers, secretaries, journalists, consular staff and volunteers, as well as army and civilian medicos – many spending far longer than the twelve-month tour of duty of most male 'veterans'". McHugh's book offered about fifty of these women – routinely referred to in Vietnam as "round-eyed" – the unique opportunity to "reclaim their place in Australia's longest war".[10]

As someone who tries to visit Australia frequently, I recognise that the words of the New York editor remain accurate, even today. Bookshelves at the Australian War Memorial in Canberra continue to groan under their weight and numbers of books by and about men at war and their wartime commitments, whereas women's writing is sparse. Moreover, novels I have identified throughout this study were scarcely, if ever, reviewed, or if reviewed, rarely favourably. In large part, I would argue, Australian women have been defeated once again by the intense adulation of the Anzacs, routinely the heroes of both world wars (and eventually the Vietnam War)[11] who have become larger-than-life legends. They have accordingly played a role in the obliteration of women's voices, which occurred both during and after the Vietnam War in a familiar pattern identified by historians Marilyn Lake and Henry Reynolds (with Mark McKenna and Joy Damousi) as "the relentless militarization of our history".[12] They emphasise that "The Anzac spirit is now said to animate all our greatest achievements, even as the Anzac landing recedes into distant past".[13]

Those "greatest achievements" have failed to include those of Australian women who worked in Vietnam during the war, however. McHugh reveals that when Australian women attempted to march with the male veterans on Anzac Day or join the Returned Services League, they were repeatedly informed they could not claim veteran status because "there were no [Australian] women in Vietnam".[14] When the women continued to march, people shouted "husband or brother?," once again confirming their belief that no women served in the Vietnam War.

---

10   McHugh, *Minefields and Miniskirts*, ix–x.
11   Australian Vietnam veterans were finally honoured at a "Welcome Home" parade in Sydney on 3 October 1987.
12   Marilyn Lake and Henry Reynolds with Mark McKenna and Joy Damousi, eds. *What's Wrong With Anzac?: The Militarisation of Australian History* (Sydney: UNSW Press, 2010), vii.
13   Lake et al., *What's Wrong With Anzac?*, vii.
14   McHugh, *Minefields and Miniskirts*, 104.

According to McHugh, after Nolan returned to Australia and volunteered to offer the country's military historian Dr Peter Edwards details depicting her two-year stint in Vietnam, he brushed her off, stating that he was writing the "*official* version of the war," thereby, claims Nolan, *consciously* excluding women's presence.[15] The chapter closes with Nolan's recognition that because she is a woman, she has been "denigrated," told her opinion is "worthless".[16] McHugh's book takes a large step towards "shatter[ing] one element of the myth" that women neither go to war nor write about it.[17]

Nolan's novel begins with a series of events that indicate that the American government was cavalier when choosing their future employees, as her protagonist Holly Gow learns when she responds to an "innocuous advertisement" in the *Sydney Morning Herald* (3) crafted to identify women who wanted to work in Vietnam. After several hours of drinking in a hotel with a "handsome" recruiter from the US post exchange (PX), Holly is finally asked what kind of work she could do and replies that she could be a "typist or anything like that" (4). Hearing nothing from the interviewer for three months, Holly is nonetheless delighted when she receives a cable URGENTLY requiring her services. Excited by "the prospect of adventure on high pay," Holly arrives with her one-way ticket to Saigon and a twenty-dollar bill in her pocket, but she is apprehensive when she finds herself at the hot and crowded airport on New Year's Eve, 1967. As the only woman in the airport, she fears that the "wall-to-wall" men are looking *at* her, but none looking *for* her. Her distress is short-lived when a group of American soldiers help transport her to the address of her new home, where she is immediately embraced by three women (one Australian) who have been waiting for her to arrive so that they could embark on their journey to a New Year's Eve party outside of Saigon, and the fun begins.

Holly's new friends inform her at the outset that she must wear her most attractive party clothes – long dresses preferred – and try "really hard to look beautiful" (11), because they will be the only women there and approximately one hundred soldiers will "treat them like royalty" (11) or what the men classify as "Precious Cargo." But the trip to their destination, which involves a bus being loaded onto a chopper, proves harrowing because as soon as it takes off, shots start coming from the ground below. While those familiar with the attacks cling to the sides of the chopper, Holly makes herself vulnerable by falling to the floor, where she instantly recognises that if she is going to survive in Vietnam for twelve months, she must "listen hard and learn fast" (9). And that she does.

Shortly after her arrival, however, Holly is confronted with a perplexing string of commonly used phrases such as "red dogs," "black cats" and "white mice," but here with special meanings. Her co-workers inform her that the dogs and cats

---

15 McHugh, *Minefields and Miniskirts*, 105.
16 McHugh, *Minefields and Miniskirts*, 106.
17 McHugh, *Minefields and Miniskirts*, xxii.

refer to specific Combat Aviation Divisions, the white mice to the uniforms the Vietnamese police wear. But her new friends also insist that Holly needs to follow the rules (apparently agreed upon by both soldiers and women), so that before she "sleeps" with any American soldier, he must inform her as to whether he is "long or short" (17). Asking joyfully whether the choice is *that* good (17), Holly learns that the words apply to the amount of time the American soldier has left on his tour. Accordingly, her co-workers caution her to avoid someone who will be in-country for a long time because he may become possessive, or someone in-country for a short time because she may fall in love with him, and he may be leaving soon. They suggest that a man with "three to four months" is ideal (17). Overall, Holly's first New Year's Eve party – one of dozens of similar gatherings to follow – exceeds her wildest dreams; but much as she has her "pick of men," she also finds that choosing one is not as easy as it sounds because, she claims, they are *all* "good-looking, tanned, virile, muscular, tall, gorgeous, and horny" (55–56). Her co-workers also encourage her to "sleep" with officers because they can requisition better goods and host better parties than the ordinary soldier, advice she follows. For their part, the party-going officers are equally delighted to meet a new "round-eyed" white woman because, as McHugh notes, they were so rare: "women stationed in Vietnam at the height of the conflict were outnumbered thousands to one by Western males".[18] Holly immediately loves these parties and underscores her pleasure by stating that "It was absolutely wonderful being able to say, like the queer at the church when given the choice of hymns, I'll have him and him and him" (55).

The talk about sex scenes that permeate the novel continue in part because, as Smith suggests, Holly is a "gung-ho nymphomaniac".[19] In the late 1800s nymphomania was broadly defined as either those women whose sexual desire was considered a disease stemming from a lack of morals and willpower, or those with the causes, which appear in most descriptions such as eating rich food, consuming too much chocolate or bourbon, dwelling in impure thoughts, masturbating, or reading novels![20] More recently, the definition has been updated and now describes a female who has an abnormally excessive desire for sexual activity, especially with different partners. That would be Nolan's Holly, who is dazzled, on the night of her first party in Vietnam, by the suggestion of what being at war will mean for her: as she watches the other women don their bikinis and "dive into the Olympic-sized blue pool surrounded by palm trees and deck chairs … interspersed through the trees," selected her sexual partner for the evening, she utters only a few sober words: "Wow! This is war" (10). Thereafter, the perpetual partying, the freedom to engage in as many sexual encounters as she wishes, the opportunity to have at her beck and call those whom she labels "sex-starved, slathering men" (15) offer "her first

---

18   McHugh, *Minefields and Miniskirts*, 50.
19   Smith, "Review".
20   Jane Ussher, "What makes a woman a nymphomaniac?" *The Conversation*, December 25, 2013. https://theconversation.com/what-makes-a-woman-a-nymphomaniac-20306.

taste of the power of a female" (15), a proclamation I will return to, but for now, Holly's declaration leads Smith to suggest that "literary bean counters might be fascinated to tally the number of servicemen Holly beds in her fifteen months or so in Vietnam but suffice to say that an alternative title for the novel might be *Between the Sheets*".[21]

Nolan's protagonist also appears to be modelled on Holly Golightly, Audrey Hepburn's character in Truman Capote's popular film *Breakfast at Tiffany's* (1961), whose name is synonymous with sex and sophistication. Reviewer Rebecca Renner suggests it also addressed the transition from the fifties to the sixties, when sexual mores strayed from the rigid monogamy of the past into the culture that produced key parties, beatniks, and the Free Love movement.[22] It was also an era when "the pill" had become readily available and simultaneously appears – at least in Vietnam – to render redundant boxes of prophylactics, which the American soldiers laughed at and deliberately left unopened. This moment in history was also significantly pre-AIDS, but venereal disease, McHugh indicates, was "rampant, as the men sought sexual release while disdaining to protect either themselves or the thousands of bar girls who serviced them".[23] (There are no references to venereal disease in Nolan's novel, perhaps because officers were not required to declare whether they had it.) As McHugh indicates, Nolan was "already hitched" to the hedonism of the age, keen to "sample whatever thrills life outside her boring Sydney suburb could offer".[24] Unlike many women who signed up for humanitarian reasons, or patriotism, or as nurses volunteering to "help the casualties of war" (3), both Nolan and her narrator Holly were, at least initially, simply "seeking adventure" (3), and there was no shortage.

Shortly after she arrives, however, Holly becomes fed up with her job as a typist, which requires a commitment of sixty-six hours per week! And a requirement to type the same letter, sometimes fifteen times, to get it right! Anxious to find something more challenging, she scours the documents that contain the list of available jobs and before long she has obtained a job working for the Public Information office, which produced two newspapers weekly and bi-weekly about Vietnam, by claiming (falsely) to have worked as a journalist for the *Australian Women's Weekly* in Sydney (27). (The novel might also be titled *Between the Lies*.) Within days, she confesses that even though she "couldn't write ... [she] couldn't be happier" (51). As someone always ready to improve situations (both for herself and others), within minutes of taking up her newspaper job, Holly orders local builders to "make a darkroom, a photo lab, editors office, main office" and "joy of all joys, their very own toilet" (53). She also devises a clever "perk" that allows her to hijack US army flights all over the country, which she does by inventing a

---

21 Smith, "Review", 1.
22 Rebecca Renner, "Was Holly Golightly Bisexual?", *Paris Review* 21 December 2018.
23 McHugh, *Minefields and Miniskirts*, 52.
24 McHugh, *Minefields and Miniskirts*, 2.

new (male) name and typing her own travel orders. While putting her travel plans together, Holly also invokes her "perk" to supply her friends with tickets so that they can continue to fly to parties. In another example of her creativity to enhance working conditions, Holly also crafts another fake name that enables her to utilise the American postal system and helps reduce visits to her designated postal service (both ineffective and dangerous), as the area is frequently bombed. Later in the novel, Holly shares her idea with the Filipino community, thereby also saving them trips to unsafe areas and saving money as well (151).

It could be argued that Holly loves her new job because she is a thrill-seeker. Norbury and Hsuain suggest that the brains in high-sensation seekers release more dopamine and less norepinephrine than low-sensation seekers.[25] As a result, the adrenaline-addicted repeatedly seek out new, exciting experiences. They also tend to be creative thinkers who like to make up their own minds, just as Holly's fascination with hazardous games and other perilous situations frequently governs her actions. Such daredevil behaviour does not always guarantee a positive outcome, as Holly finds when she receives an order to visit "the boys" on Nui Ba Den, Black Virgin mountain. Aware, as her superiors were obviously not, that the young man she is sent to work with is an opium addict, Holly is convinced to experiment with a mixture of the drug (which she claims has no effect on her) and bourbon. This combination nevertheless moves her to wave a brand-new wristwatch from the PX on her arm at the top of a crater while enemy bullets whistle by and she is captured doing so on camera (79). Not surprisingly, once her employers see the photos, they inform her that they can no longer hire someone who clearly "courts death," and her days as a newspaper reporter are over. Being fired is lamentable, however, because the topics she explored included spending time in the jungle, where she thoughtfully described a "profusion of wild life," with "tigers and elephants roam[ing] freely" and "a great variety of monkeys liv[ing] in the highlands" (74).[26] Her research also led her to learn about the creativity of the Montagnard people (who inhabit the mountainous border area between Vietnam, Laos and north-eastern Cambodia) and who produced wood and ivory carvings as well as some weaving (73), which tourists happily purchased. But not all assignments had been so stimulating: one village in the Central Highlands "had the smell of death" after Korean soldiers had beheaded a tiger, as well as four Vietnamese, and then left them in full sight (75). Much as Holly has no intention of writing about what she has witnessed, she does acknowledge that this is the first time she has begun to recognise "what the war was all about. During her stay in Vietnam, [she] had hardly seen any real action" (107), and none of it was "like it was portrayed in the movies – all guns and fighting and tough-talking men" (107–08).

25   Agnes Norbury and Masud Husain, Sensation-seeking: Dopaminergic modulation and risk for psychopathology, *Behavioural Brain Research*, 288, (15 July 2015): 79–93.
26   Nolan accuses the Americans of practically "wiping out the panda and tiger population" (cited in McHugh, *Minefields and Miniskirts*, 40).

Admitting she had not "really seen an enemy face," she had, however, "seen *evidence* of enemy activity, but never the actual enemy" (108). Based on the information provided by an American doctor, Holly estimates that 80 per cent of the soldiers sent to Vietnam never saw "any action" either and that two-thirds of the injuries were self-inflicted by accidents in bars, drunken driving, and other causes that had nothing to do with the war. She concludes that many of the men who made it home never told the truth about their war (108).[27]

Although losing her job is a serious blow, Holly finds that she loves her new work at Cam Ranh Bay as a personnel officer at the PX store, situated north of Saigon. She does not miss the city, but she misses her friends, none of whom appear to be thrill-seekers like her. One Saturday evening, for example, when they are visiting, she introduces them to a game that they wisely reject as too risky, but Holly freely exposes herself to peril and plays the game. Not long after it has begun, however, three "fellows" have broken ribs, Holly has a cut on her eye, and several other "girls" claim to be injured, so Holly accompanies them to the hospital to get "stitched up," but then admits she is too drunk to feel any pain and continues to "dance the night away" (141). Another even more serious game involves the damage done when a commander, aware of Holly's wish for a vehicle to get her around the island, shows up at a late-night gathering and offers her a very clumsy vehicle called "an armored personal carrier" that can be "all hers," but warns that it won't be much of a "joy ride" if she is sober enough to drive it. Before long, while driving drunk in the dark, Holly propels the vehicle over some important telecommunication wires that are hot lines to the local general and to another in the US, but neither she nor the other partygoers seem concerned that they could be court-martialled for their ruinous behaviour, nor do they worry that the communication wires are vital to any kinds of trouble that could erupt and would require reporting on immediately (156).

But while many of these reckless games inevitably end with gradations of disaster, Holly's desire for spine-tingling experiences ramps up considerably when she meets Garry, a "dashing Phantom pilot" (144) who proves to be as foolhardy as she is. During the day, Garry locates maps that help them "pick their way carefully through a field of landmines in search of a spot on the beach where they can swim in the nude" (144) and then make love at night after hazardous climbs to a dark water tower. Those undertakings are, however, nothing compared to their irresponsible conduct while in the air: on their first ride together in a small spotter plane that Garry has "borrowed," he renders Holly "the only female to have joined the Mile High Club in the Vietnam War" (148). But immediately after, Garry

---

27   McHugh writes that Helen's work took her all over Vietnam, and she came to see that the Vietnamese wanted to have Ho Chi Minh in charge – but they were not particularly sympathetic to the idea that the north would take over. According to McHugh, Helen believed that the Vietnamese were right – that the Americans were "mainly after Vietnam's rich oil rights" (McHugh, *Minefields and Miniskirts*, 83), and she begins to display a "gut sympathy" for the Vietcong. None of these feelings occur in the novel, however.

suddenly identifies several problems with the plane and informs Holly that they will need a miracle to land safely, which they can only do if they execute one of two choices. Garry gives Holly the chance to choose, she does, and the plane lands safely. Unruffled by that brush with death, Holly "nearly faints with excitement" at Garry's next proposal that she ride in a Phantom jet with him; warned at length of the numerous risks they would be facing before they take off, Holly typically responds with "fear and terrible excitement" (158), especially when she learns that the plane will be carrying five tons of bombs that Garry will drop on Hanoi.[28] Prior to the bombing, however, Garry enhances her joy by "flipping the plane over" so she can see Cam Ranh Bay, a sight that transported her to "[a] great feeling of complete joy [that] welled up inside [her]" (160). At that moment, "[she] wanted to sing. This was simply beautiful. Flying had never been like this before. [She] didn't want to come down again. [She] was in heaven" (160). While still in the air and still in a "high state of joy," Holly claims that "if she got her hands on Garry, [they] would have joined the Mile High Club again" (160).

But there is more to Holly than a relentless desire for a good time, for as Smith points out, "she has a deep-rooted hatred of discrimination, especially racism".[29] Not long after she arrives, she becomes aware of a "pecking order" that governs the US Department of Defense's Direct Hire program that purportedly includes her. But in the ranking of the countries meant to be working together, Holly notes that the Vietnamese were designated number one, because, after all, it was *their* country. Ranked number two was any US citizen. number three, or third country nationals (TCNs), were Filipinos, Thais, Koreans and Chinese nationals hired in-country to assist in the operation of the vast PX conglomerate. But the TCNs (which included Australians) suffer racial discrimination in their salaries and PX privileges and are prohibited from patronising restaurants unless with an American. Even more hurtful is the restriction that they are not allowed to use the commissary to purchase edible and decent food. The imposition of these rules drives Holly to view the Americans as "heartless and cruel" (25), given that the Australians' choices were so extremely limited: they could purchase basics such as snacks and canned goods or "dried fish [and] weevil-riddled rice by the sack" to accompany the expensive meats they could buy and slaughter themselves (25). Even more crippling yet is the confirmation that the Americans, doing the same work as the TCNs, are paid two-thirds more, so they could readily afford to shop at a huge supermarket and purchase anything they liked – or even a Cadillac! Once again, Holly takes matters into her own hands by informing an American officer about her drastic weight loss: in response – or perhaps in the kind of sexual trade-off Smith hints at – the officer purchases equipment for her and her housemates to cook and eat outdoors.

---

28 McHugh indicates that Holly was aware that the Americans were not telling the truth when they informed their citizens that they had "ceased bombing Hanoi" several weeks earlier because she had been on a later "bombing run" (McHugh, *Minefields and Miniskirts*, 84).

29 Smith, "Review", 2.

Later in the novel, after the death of Eisenhower, Holly hears that an American senator has arrived to see what might be done about the army base, which was full of "racial discontent between the white and black enlisted men" (134) that led to grisly results: "two white airmen had been beheaded, their bodies left in the streets" (136). One night another poor fellow "lived to tell that he had been chopped at by axe-wielding black men" (136). But much as she recognises there were increasingly serious racial problems erupting between the enlisted men, Holly reiterates her position that someone needs to "speak" for the Aussies, and that, of course, would be Holly.[30] The senator is impressed with Holly's presentation in part because she does not "speak" her complaints but has put them into a folder containing well-researched arguments and thoughtful analyses of the situation. Her work pays off, but not entirely: almost immediately, the senator raises the TCNs' pay by an astonishing increase of 60 per cent, but as Holly bitterly remarks, even with those figures, the Aussies remain the lowest paid in the country. As a result, and making no apologies, Holly begins to contribute in a "small way" to the black market, swapping Coca-Cola for Aussie beer, which the Americans really like and are prepared to pay "exorbitant price[s]" for (91). She also dupes the Americans by selling them two-dollar "slouch hats" for two hundred dollars, and then rationalises that her use of the black market is merely a means of paying the rent (91).

Essentially, much of what the novel "teaches" appears to be an extensive indictment of Americans in Vietnam, which Holly begins to learn about during the Tet Offensive in January–February 1968, when she and her co-workers are rescued by an American couple concerned that the women might be endangered in their home – and they were, but for a different reason: unaware of the significance of the Tet four-day holiday, the women had made no plans. Having little food, they spend the first few days getting drunk. Over the course of their stay with the Americans, an engineer attempts to inform them of the Americans' rationale for being in Vietnam. Their plan, he claims, is to weaken the Vietnamese dedication to communism and thus give the Americans the opportunity to "maintain a stable government, increase prosperity and provide a reasonable standard of living for all nationals" (45); if so, "the people who assisted the NVA and VC would gradually come to realise that life was OK and there would be no need for them to try to alter it" (45). Despite having been in-country for a short period, Holly comprehends that

---

30   In his review of McHugh's *Minefields and Miniskirts*, Donald A. Ritchie notes that Helen Keayes (apparently the name Nolan was using at the time) identified a "peculiar system of discrimination by which Australian women earned a third less than American women doing comparable work but more than Asian women. Despite the army's professed endorsement of equal employment rights, Keayes also found that she lacked equal commissary, PX, and postal rights" (Donald A. Ritchie "Book Reviews: *Minefields and Miniskirts: Australian Women and the Vietnam War*", *Oral History Review* 26 no.2 [1999], 171). He does not, however, suggest that she consistently and overtly challenges many of the inequities and frequently receives positive results, which then appear in Nolan's novel.

the theory, in practice, was good, but the Americans did not follow through. They did not treat the Vietnamese as equals, they stole from their own government (the military and the PX stores), they perpetuated the black market, they abused Vietnamese women and generally behaved like conquering heroes. (45–46)

Holly concludes nonetheless that "it was not the Vietnamese who needed education to bring about a higher standard of living; it was the Americans who needed to be taught the truth of equality!" (45–46).

Holly is also eager to explore another kind of shabby conduct she has heard the locals are subject to and wants to see for herself how the Americans (and no doubt Australians) respond to the "bar girls," or "B-girls, as they were called" (123). Initially offended by the sight of the GIs having "little Viet girls" perched on their knees and appalled that the men "all looked drunk and dirty and unkempt," not at all "like the men they were used to being seen with" (122), she wonders momentarily how she would cope if her country "was ever occupied by a foreign army" (123), particularly since she has heard they were "usually refugee country girls with no way of earning enough money to feed themselves in the big city other than by perching on a bar stool next to a GI and letting him buy her drinks" (123). While there is little good to say about the way these men deal with the bar girls who, according to McHugh, were indeed "treated as prostitutes," Holly is comforted by the information that they know how to protect themselves (53), and that the "exploitation wasn't entirely one way. Many became adept at conning the men, making small fortunes out of watered-down liquor and dud champagne" (53). On the spot, Holly composes a song about how a "bar girl" might describe her life, how she might stand up to a man who did not treat her well. The song, Nolan claims, eventually became well known across the country in various forms (124).

But as her time in Vietnam lengthens, Holly acknowledges her increasing admiration for the Vietnamese people, but laments they were essentially regarded as servants. As a result, she starts doing her own cleaning and hopes to learn from her *Mamasan* how she regards the politics of her country. Because Holly's new job has required her to work directly with Vietnamese people, she soon develops "respect and affection for Vietnam and its people"[31] and particularly for the women who have undertaken the work men would have done in "normal circumstances" (132). In a moving passage, Nolan writes that

the Vietnamese women carried the country on their backs during the war. They kept their families together, fed and clothed them while their menfolk were in the armed forces, and they moved the country ahead by sheer physical hard work. The women of Vietnam were truly the backbone of the country. (132)

---

31   Smith, "Review", 2.

McHugh adds that it is important to recognise that when Ho Chi Minh took over the leadership of Vietnam in 1930, he insisted that because "the oppression of Vietnamese women had dominated the country since the tenth century AD, one of his stated objectives was the achievement of equity between the sexes". In 1943, when Minh declared Vietnam a "Democratic Republic," 90 per cent of women were illiterate, still imprisoned in a dismal round of virtual slave labour".[32] But aware of his country's history, which "had once been a matriarchal society where women were honoured in language and literature," ... "it was hardly surprising then that Ho Chi Minh saw women as essential to his cause".[33] He claimed that "without women's participation, the victory cannot succeed,"[34] and he was right. In 1965, "women were exhorted to take over production and family affairs, freeing more men for the front. The response was overwhelming. All over Vietnam, millions of women learnt to handle ploughs, raise dykes, harrow the land and harvest its produce, working with rifles at the ready and firing off anti-aircraft guns whenever they came under attack". McHugh adds that "North Vietnamese women were active in civil defence, the transport of wounded and the capture of downed enemy pilots ... Women comprised about 41% of the North Vietnam forces, where intelligence gathering was as important as armed aggression, an estimated 70 per cent of NLF guerrillas were female".[35]

Arguably, Nolan's Holly is also a woman warrior who, when tested, readily proves her mettle by fending off the enemy in Ban Me Thuot, a village near the Cambodian border, where she has been sent "to check out the civilian staff there to see if all was well" (183). Having heard that there have been some "CV offenses," her boss asks Rudy, a Filipino man, to accompany her, but presciently hands Holly a Magnum pistol and offers instruction on how to use it (184). There had indeed been CV offences, which Holly and Rudy discover when one hurls a grenade into the hotel lobby where they spent the night. Almost immediately, Rudy "burst into tears" then "blubbered and cried and ran around in circles" (185) but Holly, quickly realising she will have to save him as well as herself, springs into action and places a mattress over their heads, a feat that *Mamasan* had taught her to do in order to afford the best protection when danger strikes. Holly then begins carefully negotiating the crumbling stairs, half of which are already gone. On the landing, which they must jump from, she spots a Huey chopper at the end of the street getting ready to take off and yells at Rudy to run to it. He is unaware, however, that a Vietcong is aiming to shoot and kill him, but before he realises what is happening, Holly shoots the man in "the black satin pants" in the back at close range. Thanks to Holly's quick thinking, they both make it to the chopper, but with Holly insisting

---

32 McHugh, *Minefields and Miniskirts*, 268.
33 McHugh, *Minefields and Miniskirts*, 269.
34 McHugh, *Minefields and Miniskirts*, 299.
35 McHugh, *Minefields and Miniskirts*, 270.

that the "bawling, shivering young Rudy" can never tell anyone what happened (188), even though Holly Gow is not someone who "shoots blanks."

Towards the end of the novel, Holly is devastated to learn that most of her friends are planning to leave, regardless of the likelihood that none would be issued an entry visa again. She plans to stay put, but the dangers are increasing in part due to an influx of African American soldiers who do not want to be in Vietnam: according to McHugh, "they felt they were doing the white man's work against fellow coloured people, and being killed and injured in disproportionate numbers in the process". In addition, "in 1965, Martin Luther King had declared it was wrong for Afro-Americans to take up arms against another people of colour when the country they served would not accord blacks full citizenship rights".[36] Consequently, no women in Cam Ranh Bay felt safe in this new environment, particularly given that some African Americans were taking out much of their anger on women, two of whom (one pregnant) they had shot. But learning that one of her co-workers has been repeatedly raped by the "white mice" who wrongly insist she is Vietnamese, this low point brings Holly to rethink her life in Vietnam, and before long she is homesick, having not seen her parents for nearly four years. She arranges travel to Sydney with an Australian friend, but after a few days with her parents and former friends, Holly is ready to return to Vietnam: she has no patience with a nation full of people who do not seem to understand that the Vietnamese simply wanted their help to prevent a foreign power from taking over their country. She longs to tell her Sydney friends and relatives about her Vietnamese friends, their dreams, aspirations and hopes, but knows they won't listen for long. Not surprisingly, Holly confesses that what she misses most are men in uniform. Viewing Australian men as "insipid and pallid," she claims there was something

> [i]ndefinable about men at war that was exciting. A sort of *secretive* power, as though soldiers knew more about the core of existence than an ordinary businessman. These civilians didn't laugh so hard or play so hard or work so hard as the military men. They seemed sluggish compared with their counterparts in Vietnam. (202)

In sum, Holly regards the men who attempt to flirt as "insipid and hopeless. [She] longed for [her] suntanned, tall, virile Yankees back there in the war" (203) and returns to Vietnam.

Unsure of how to avoid the officials at the airport who would immediately send her packing, she asks a friend to meet her there. He makes the simple suggestion that she "give up her luggage" and it works: the two walk straight out of the airport, and before we know it, she is (somehow unexplained) back in Cam Ranh Bay, but not for long. In perhaps her finest moment, Holly claims to be "sick to death"

---

36   McHugh, *Minefields and Miniskirts*, 59.

of American prejudice and bigotry; her anger intensifies as she tries to defend a woman who risks danger every time she comes to work because, even though she is entitled, indeed "authorized" to the same privileges as Holly, she is Vietnamese and therefore "not the type of woman [those in charge] would like to live in such nice quarters" (218). In protest, Holly does not go lightly: she refuses to attend work and moves out of her accommodation just before being fired. She also rejects a friend's offer to find her a job on the grounds that her girlfriends had all left, and "the soldiers had lost their keenness, their sense of fun, their urgency" (221). Claiming that she will "never set foot on the army base again" (220), she delivers a "parting shot" to the Americans, which goes as follows:

> These are the people who preach freedom, democracy not racial prejudice (but only against blacks) – but the dreadful catch is – PREJUDICE AGAINST AMERICANS IS PREJUDICE. PREJUDICE BY AMERICANS IS NON-EXISTENT. And they really believe this. No wonder they're losing the bloody war. (219)

Although it is perhaps not fitting to continually equate Holly with her creator, Helen Nolan, it is perhaps appropriate to conclude the story, as McHugh does, with some sense of what effect their service in Vietnam contributed to their lives thereafter. On her first night in Vietnam, Holly watches as her co-worker Penny tells the one hundred or so men to listen to her and obey her orders. "In awe" of Penny's actions and the way men complied, Holly vows to "remember how to do that" (16).While readers cannot be certain – or even guess at – what kind of work Holly might take up again in Australia, we can see that she has been developing into a much stronger, more forceful woman determined to do as much as she can to improve the lives of those around her, especially underestimated Vietnamese women. Although Holly arrives in Vietnam with professional secretarial skills, it becomes apparent that only months later she has much more to offer than being an excellent typist. McHugh observes that "those who worked and lived in Vietnam acquired a new assertiveness"[37] and suggests that "Helen Keayes, for instance, traces virtually all her subsequent success in life back to her experiences in Vietnam."[38] Nolan, "now a corporate lawyer and single mother by choice," declares that she learned while in Vietnam that she was "worth something, that [she] didn't have to put up with crap from anybody, that [she] had [her] own method of creating [her] own power base – even though [she is] a female". In part, it is also possible to consider Keayes' novel as a "writing back" to a father who did not want his clever

---

37 McHugh, *Minefields and Miniskirts*, 275.
38 Throughout her text, McHugh refers to Helen's last name as Keayes (McHugh, *Minefields and Miniskirts*, 2), which may either be her birth name or the name of the man she divorced before going to Vietnam. Oddly, although McHugh relies a great deal on Keayes' experiences, Nolan makes no mention of her in the list of people she wishes to acknowledge in *Between the Battles: A Novel*, either.

daughter to go to university because, he told her, she would just "get married and some other man would get the benefit of *his* money". He sent her off to learn how to type, and by the age of fifteen she was doing full-time work but not with any sense of pleasure. But sadly, she remarks that she knew she was being "mistreated because [she] was female," and also because "women didn't get a fair go – misogyny was rife in those days".[39] Finally, in expressing her gratitude for the fifty or so women who went to Vietnam and then shared their stories, McHugh reinforces that "for too long, we have had only a male-oriented view of what happened in Vietnam. By placing their stories on record through this book, woman have at last begun to reclaim their place in Australia's longest war".[40]

---

39   McHugh, *Minefields and Miniskirts*, 276.
40   McHugh, *Minefields and Miniskirts*, ix–x.

Conclusion – Boomerangs do come back

> We need to know the writing of the past, and to know it differently than we have ever known it; not to pass on a tradition but to break its hold over us.[1]

Before I began my research into Australian and Canadian women's writing about the Great War, I speculated about what I would find. I supposed that, given their lack of presence in the wartime canon in either country, I would not unearth many women's wartime novels. I expected the novels I did find to function as social documents, and predicted similarities between Australians and Canadians in terms of content. I presumed that the novels would be set on the home front, and that fictional women would complain about rationing and food shortages. I supposed that some women would take up jobs in munitions factories, exult in receiving pay cheques and grumble mildly when forced to return to their private homes at war's end. Moments of enlistment would be crucial, I thought, as would home-comings. I anticipated that the novels would be filled with sadness, with mothers weeping at having to relinquish their sons to battle, and with sweethearts and wives grieving over the death or dismemberment of their loved ones. I reasoned that women writers would be advocating peace, that their characters would mark the futility of combat, and all would call for an end to war.

I found almost none of the above in Australian novels. With the exception of Lesbia Harford's text, which details women's daily lives on the home front, the novels do not operate as social documents. They cannot, because much of the time, women are "missing." While I expected that men, overseas fighting the enemy, would be absent from the discourse, I did not imagine that women would be gone. Nor did I foresee finding so many Australian novels on this subject, or imagine that the books would be so similar. After reading only a few, I began to wonder who

---

1   Adrienne Rich, *On Lies, Secrets, and Silence: Selected Prose 1966–1978* (New York: Norton, 1979), 35.

this grey-eyed, square-jawed, hatchet-faced, hulking great Anzac was, and why he, and his principles of mateship and egalitarianism, kept getting in the way of the female story. I wanted to read about what women thought, felt and experienced on the home front, not about the fighting prowess of the Anzac. I was dismayed because he was so often the hero, a figure so overpowering that in some instances, he "killed" the women's narrative altogether. I cringed at women's depictions of his participation in war. I was uncomfortable at the bellicose tone of the novels, unnerved by women writers' lack of concern or compassion for the enemy, and unsettled by their praise of men who liked to fight. I was astonished that there were no Australian women writing pacifist novels, none making pleas for peace. I was also dispirited by writers' frequent reiterations that women were too emotionally and mentally inferior to be men's equals and angered by their acquiescence to confinement. I found the lack of female camaraderie disheartening, especially the insistence that women should police other women into dutiful submission to male authority. I was vexed by women writers' promulgation of Australian society as utopian, astonished that they should be so resistant to change, so certain that a return to prewar existence was possible. Overall, reading these novels was a depressing experience. I was thrilled when Lesbia Harford's *The Invaluable Mystery* made its long overdue appearance.

My frustration with these novels was exacerbated because I was reading Canadian wartime writers at same time, and was pleasantly surprised by the overtly feminist stance they take, which I had not contemplated. I was exhilarated by the vital and energetic female characters they created, and delighted at their confidence in women's ability to make social change. I was pleased that the novels function as social document, for I learned, in fiction, how Canadian women spent the war years. I knew what they read, thought and felt about their place in society as women and as writers. (I was wrong again about rations and food shortages, though.) It was an eye-opener to find women already in the labour force as librarians, journalists, teachers, and farmers, and who perceived themselves as men's equals. One emotional response I should have envisioned but didn't. This being Canada, I should have predicted that guilt would be prevalent. Fictional women feel contrite when they momentarily forget about the war and enjoy themselves; they feel chastened when they are warm and safe on the home front when their loved ones are freezing in the trenches; adolescent heroines feel repentant when they cannot honestly return a soldier's declaration of love; wives and mothers feel remorse when they recall having been insensitive to their son's or husband's needs. I did not find any expressions of guilt in Australian novels, however.

Canadian novels are more than social documents, however; they are, in subtle ways, pleas for peace, instructions on how to avoid war. Although women writers cannot fight wars themselves, they can expose war mentality: they point to the dangers of propaganda and make their characters cognisant of the hype generated by war. They admonish them to be wary of slogans that "get" men to enlist, and encourage them to see through patriotic fervour, to recognise that soldiers will find neither glory nor glamour in the trenches. One of the strengths of these novels lies in writers' promotion of non-violent ways of solving problems. While only Francis Marion Beynon draws upon overtly pacifist theories, other writers encourage their characters to solve disagreements by exploring differences of opinion through mediation. L.M. Montgomery depicts her characters making compromises, occasionally swallowing slices of humble pie, but always more anxious to foster a harmonious environment than to enact small victories or take revenge over minor matters. Throughout her novel, Nellie McClung encourages team play, arguing that much can be accomplished through collective action, and stressing that people share a deep desire for cohesion and spiritual bonding. Canadian writers promote a system of values that finds its power, not through the binary opposition of domination–subordination, but in co-operative and peaceful negotiation. In their texts, women writers reflect the national identity and shore up the qualities Canadians are best known for: peace-keeping and compromise.[2]

Canadian women writers could be termed war profiteers or opportunists because they utilise the chaos occasioned by war to improve women's status, and to make Canada a better place for all. While men are overseas destroying the world, women on the home front are devising ways to build it up. Writers are conscious of women's marginalisation in politics and recognise that women can no longer afford to be onlookers in a man's world. They insist upon bringing an end to the image of women as caregivers and nurturers, and forcefully reiterate that women deserve a place in society among men, but not as their subalterns. Canadian women writers emphasise that women are intelligent beings who have not been "allowed" to develop their talents and mental faculties to the full, and stress that it is a foolish society that denies women's unique ways of knowing. Writers express their anger that women have been denied access to public and political realms and beseech their characters to make their presence felt during the war. Each of the texts features opinionated, forthright women who function as excellent role models. McKowan's heroine takes up a non-traditional career and prospers. The novel can almost be read as a "how-to-be-a-successful-woman-farmer" manual, with a clear message to the reader: Janet can survive – and thrive – so can you. McClung's narrator is a woman who speaks with ease in public; she, like Beynon's Aleta, stimulates women to find their voices, and to "come out strong." Canadians write women's recent victories into their texts, thereby instilling confidence in others that they can be winners at social change, but they also recognise the danger of complacency. Writing in 1917, one year after prairie women received the vote, McClung recognised that women's "worst troubles" were not over, for a "second Hindenburg line" had been set up to prevent them from entering the field of politics

---

2　See Francis Marion Beynon, *Aleta Dey* ([1919]. London, Virago, 1988); L.M. Montgomery, *Rilla of Ingleside* ([1920] Toronto, Seal. 1982); Nellie McClung, *In Times Like These* ([1915] Toronto: University of Toronto Press, 1982); and Evah McKowan, *Janet of Kootenay: Life, Love and Laughter in an Arcady of the West* (Toronto: McClelland and Stewart, 1919).

and seemed harder to "pierce" than the first. But the narrator seems undaunted, almost eager to take up the challenge.

Canadian women writers were aware they were waging a war against male domination on the home front. In order to sharpen their defences, writers exhort women to develop their intellectual might. One of the oft-repeated words in these texts is "think." The novels entreat women to eschew simplistic thinking, to recognise that most issues are complex, and to reject the notion that only men can lay claim to authority. When McClung refers to the war as a "great teacher," she means in part that, without so many men around telling women what to think, they can learn to reason for themselves. Several novels deconstruct the notion of authority by refusing to tell readers what conclusions to draw. Montgomery explores problems from a variety of points of view but leaves readers free to find their own answer. Beynon, too, refuses to orchestrate her readers' opinions, but counsels them to ensure that they are in possession of all the facts, for only then can they make the best decisions. While she encourages her characters to read, she also urges them to trust their basic instincts, for personal experience is also a worthy basis from which to govern one's behaviour.

One of the most effective strategies Canadian women employ is humour, pervasive in novels by McClung, Montgomery and McKowan. Montgomery's description of a decidedly unromantic war wedding, which features a flat-faced and commonplace bride and a groom who sobs uncontrollably throughout the ceremony is a howler, as are McClung's not-so-subtle digs at men who postulate that only they are capable of running the world. By utilising wit, Canadian writers dispel the myth that women have no sense of humour. Further, their use of comedy makes the subject of war accessible, and thus an appropriate vehicle for social reform. I agree with Carolyn Heilbrun, who writes that "women laugh together only in freedom, in the recognition of independence and female bonding".[3] To writers from Down Under, there is nothing risible about war; it is a serious, weighty subject to be encroached upon hesitantly, timidly. Correspondingly, their novels are mostly lacklustre and sombre, with only a few mildly amusing moments in Stirling's *Soldiers Two*; by contrast, Mollie Skinner's *Tucker Sees India* is rollicking good fun from the start. But no Australian novels depict women laughing together in freedom. Women writers, enclosed within a stifling and repressive environment that rendered them defenceless and powerless, obviously found little funny about the war.

It is this precisely restraining environment, which I would argue, demands literary investigation. For the past several decades, women already mentioned in previous chapters (Schaffer, Dixson, Jones, Sheridan, Summers and Langer), have documented women's exclusion from the national myth-making 1890s, when writers Paterson, Lawson and Furphy were setting down what they perceived to

---

3   Carolyn G. Heilbrun, *Writing a Woman's Life* (New York: Ballantine, 1988), 129.

be the positive characteristics of the Australian male. While I do not wish to detract from these feminist critics' fine analyses, I would assert that the force of the Anzac legend has been even more debilitating to women and women writers than the bush mythology. While Miles Franklin, Barbara Baynton and Katharine Susannah Prichard wrote out of the bush milieu, their books were published, read, reviewed, occasionally even praised, but the war proved a more difficult discourse for women to write themselves into, in part because, added to the Diggers' already sterling traits, were the laudable qualities of courage, valour, duty and self-sacrifice. Moreover, the Anzac handed Australians (men) nationhood, not just a unique personality. But unlike the bush myth, which inevitably began to wane with increasing urbanisation, the Anzac legend, like a boomerang, keeps coming back, reinforcing itself every 25 April.

A number of Australian activists – Rosemary Pringle, Deborah Tyler and Adrian Howe – have argued that the national holiday does not merely mourn those who died, but annually valourises war as a heroic male endeavour, and re-celebrates the gallantry of Australian troops.[4] It is a massive commemoration of masculinity. Howe asserts that, because Anzac Day reinforces the identity of men as nation builders, in the process, it has become a vehicle for perpetuating the subordination of women in Australian culture.[5] Anzac Day festivities perpetuate the national tradition of valour and heroism, as sons replace fathers, grandsons replace grandfathers, but no daughters or granddaughters march for mothers and grandmothers killed in war. Anyone who witnesses the Anzac day celebration, as I have done, is struck by its womanlessness. National identity, as then, continues to sustain itself on a principle that regards women as superfluous, non-essential. (Helen Nolan would certainly agree.)[6] Central to the existing power structure is that women remain silent about their effacement, as the women who have tried to organise protest rallies on Anzac Day have discovered. In the past decades, women's groups that have endeavoured to share the event by honouring women raped in war or, more radically, have been confronted with anger, insult, arrest and even police brutality.[7] By demanding to be present at Anzac Day celebrations, either as protesters or participants, but not in their customary role as approving spectators, women pose a threat to sacred male rituals.

I mention the writing of social activists to point out that the Anzac legend is still extremely potent in Australian society. Anyone who goes against the myth runs the risk of appearing callously indifferent to the suffering and sacrifice of the Anzac troops at Gallipoli, a risk which may, or may not, account for why literary

---

4   See Rosemary Pringle, "Rape: The Other Side of Anzac Day" *Refractory Girl: A Women's Studies Journal* 26 (June 1983): 31–35; Mary Marlowe, *The Women Who Wait* (London: Simpken, 1918); and Ray Philips, *The White Feather* (Melbourne: Melville and Mullen, 1917).

5   Adrian Howe, "Anzac Mythology and the Feminist Challenge", *Melbourne Journal of Politics* 15 (1983–84), 21.

6   See Chapter 17.

7   Pringle, "Rape", 31.

critics have avoided examining women's Great War writing. But an exploration of this literature is crucial to an understanding of women's literary tradition in Australia, for it demonstrates, as no other writing in their tradition does, the extent to which women's voices can be decimated by a forceful dominant ideology. When critics address the question of women's relative absence or presence in Australia and Canada, they need to investigate women's wartime writing, to determine how that eradication of women's voices affected future writers.

Having been informed by the literary significance of the Anzac myth and its renunciation of women, I would advance that literary critics need to re-evaluate their tradition in light of that legend. If, as Rich suggests, we want to break the hold over the past, we need to know the writing of the past. A number of contemporary women writers are writing back to the Great War, perhaps out of the desire to furnish missing links with the past. The stories they tell are very different to those already written during the actual historical period, but we need both: we must fill in the gaps of women's experiences during the Great War with the novels written by Brookes, Marlowe and Phillips; only they can enrich our understanding of the present stories and at the same time contribute our knowledge of how a potent myth can silence a woman writer, estrange her from her own story. Boomerangs, powerful myths, do come back; in order to deflect them, we need to know where they come from, and how to gauge the force of their power.

In Canada, our understanding of the writing of the past will facilitate the passing on of a vigorous and healthy tradition. Critics have done the heritage a disservice by ignoring writers like McClung, Montgomery and Beynon, whose contributions to a vital cultural legacy have not been marked. As Woolf writes, "we think back through our mothers if we are women". [8] In assessing why Canadian women have such a strong place in our literary tradition, critics have thought back, but they have looked (until recently)[9] to our grandmothers, or great-grandmothers Catharine Parr Traill, Susanna Moodie and Sara Jeannette Duncan, not the women writers who, in this century and the last, were showing women how to write themselves into an intensely male-dominated discourse, and at the same time, teaching women how to secure powerful positions in their society. In the recent agenda to expand or dissolve the boundaries that exclude women writers, critics have argued for the admittance of marginalised women's genres like memoirs, diaries and autobiographies. Not only does such a re-reading have implications for how we read the fiction that women produced in subsequent wars, it will inform us how Canadian women writers managed to gain small victories during a turbulent historical period. Conversely, an analysis of Australian women's wartime writing will provide clues as to how women lost the literary war between women and men.

---

8   Virginia Woolf, *A Room of One's Own* (1929. New York: Harcourt, 1957), 79.
9   Modestly, I would suggest that interest in these writers has blossomed once I drew attention to the merits of their writing. Montgomery in particular has been "discovered" by numerous scholars.

Works cited

Adam-Smith, Patsy. "The White Feather." In *Australian Women at War*, 73–83. Ringwood, Vic: Penguin, 1996.

———. *Australian Women at War*. Melbourne: Nelson, 1984.

Adelaide, Debra. "Introduction." In *A Window in the Dark*, edited by Debra Adelaide, James D. McGrath and National Library of Australia, 1–22. Canberra: National Library of Australia, 1991.

Agutter, Karen. "Captive Allies: Italian Immigrants in World War One Australia." *Australian Studies* 1, no. 10 (9 December 2009): 5–6.

Alcorso, Claudio, and Caroline Alcorso. "Italians in Australia during World War II." In *Australia's Italians: Culture and Community in a Changing Society*, edited by Caroline Alcorso, Stephen Castles, Gaetano Rando and Ellie Vasta, 18–34. Sydney: Allen & Unwin, 1992.

Altman, Dennis. "The Myth of Mateship." *Meanjin* 46, no. 2 (1987): 163–72.

Arnold, Arthur L. "Diagnosis of Post-Traumatic Stress Disorder in Vietnam Veterans." In *The Trauma of Stress: Stress and Recovery in Vietnam Veterans*, edited by Stephen M. Sonnenberg, Arthur S. Blank, and John A. Talbott, 99–124. Washington: American Psychiatric Press, 1985.

As, Berit. "A Materialistic View of Men's and Women's Attitudes Towards War." *Women's Studies International Forum* 5, no. 3–4 (1982): 355–64.

Ashcroft, Bill, Gareth Griffiths, and Helen. Tiffin. *The Empire Writes Back: Theory and Practice in Post-Colonial Literatures*. 2nd edition. London: Routledge, 2002. https://doi.org/10.4324/9780203426081.

Auerbach, Nina. *Communities of Women: An Idea in Fiction*. Cambridge: Harvard University Press, 1978.

Australian Law Reform Commission. "Over-representation" (2018). https://bit.ly/3LEuJR3.

Ball, Martin. "Review of *Dinkum Diggers: An Australian Battalion at War* and John McQuilton's *Rural Australian Battalion at War*." *Australian Book Review*, no. 232 (July 2001): 36–7.

Barker, Anthony J., and Lisa Jackson. *Fleeting Attraction: A Social History of American Servicemen in Western Australia During the Second World War*. Nedlands: University of Western Australia Press, 1996.

Barlass, Tim. "Australian Nurse was Ordered to Keep War Crimes Secret." *Sydney Morning Herald*, 8 April 2019.

Bassett, Jan. "'Preserving the White Race:' Some Australian Women's Literary Responses to the Great War." *Australian Literary Studies* 12, no. 2 (1985): 223–33.

Bean, Charles Edward W. *The Anzac Book: Written and Illustrated in Gallipoli by the Men of Anzac*. Melbourne: Cassell & Co, 1916.

———. *The Official History of Australia in the War of 1914–1918*. Sydney: Angus & Robertson, 1934.

Beaumont, Joan. "Gallipoli and National Identity." In *Culture, Place and Identity*, edited by Neil Garnam and Keith Jeffery, 138–51. Dublin: University College Dublin Press, 2003.

———. "Introduction: Internment in Australia 1939–45." In *Under Suspicion: Citizenship and Internment in Australia During the Second World War*, edited by Joan Beaumont, Ilma Martinuzzi O'Brien and Mathew Trinca, 1–8. Canberra: National Museum of Australia Press, 2008.

———. "Prisoners of War in Australian National Memory." In *Prisoners of War, Prisoners of Peace: Captivity, Homecoming, and Memory in World War II*, edited by Bob Moore and Barbara Hately-Broad, 185–94. New York: Berg Publishers, 2005.

Benhabib, Seyla. "The Generalized and the Concrete Other." In *Ethics: A Feminist Reader*, edited by Elizabeth Frazer, Jennifer Hornsby and Sabina Lovibond, 267– 300. Oxford: Blackwell, 1992.

Bentley, Amy. "Japanese Women in Australia from 1890s–1950s: Positioning Japanese War Brides in the Australian National Imaginary." Thesis, Master of Philosophy History, University of Sydney, August 2003.

Beynon, Francis Marion. *Aleta Dey*. London: Virago, 1988.

Bertrand, Ina. "'Come in Spinner': Two views of the forties." *Journal of Australian Studies* 18, no. 41 (1994): 12.

Bevege, Margaret. *Behind Barbed Wire: Internment in Australia During World War Two*. St. Lucia: University of Queensland Press, 1993.

Beudel, Saskia. *Borrowed Eyes: A Novel*. Sydney: Pan Macmillan, 2002.

Beveridge, Ann. "War's Bride and Joy." *Daily Telegraph*, 15 May 2003, 48.

Birns, Nicholas. "All you have to do is look." *Antipodes* 34, no. 2 (December 2020): 222–32.

Bissell, Liz. "Private Desires." Rev. of *The Orphan Gunner*, by Sara Knox. *Australian Women's Book Review* 19, no. 2 (2007).

Blair, Dale James. *Dinkum Diggers: An Australian Battalion at War*. Carlton, Vic: Melbourne University Press, 2001.

Bonoguore, Tenille. "Canada is fighting COVID-19 with niceness – and losing." *Globe and Mail*, 20 March 2021.

Boulanger, Ghislaine. "Post-Traumatic Stress Disorder: An Old Problem with a New Name." In *The Trauma of Stress: Stress and Recovery in Vietnam Veterans*, edited by Stephen M. Sonnenberg, Arthur S. Blank, and John A. Talbott, 19–25. Washington: American Psychiatric Press, 1985.

Bracken, Patrick J. "Hidden Agendas: Deconstructing Post Traumatic Stress Disorder." In *Rethinking the Trauma of War*, edited by Patrick J. Bracken and Celia Petty, 46. New York: Free Association Books, 1998.

Brawley, Sean, and Chris Dixon. "Jim Crow Downunder? African American Encounters with White Australia, 1942–1945." *Pacific Historical Review* 71, no. 4 (Nov. 2002): 607–32.

Brooks, Barbara with Judith Clark. *Eleanor Dark: A Writer's Life*. Sydney: Pan Macmillan, 1998.

Brookes, Mabel. *Broken Idols*. Melbourne: Melville & Mullen, 1917.

———. *Memoirs*. Melbourne: Macmillan, 1974.

———. *Old Desires*. Melbourne: Australasian Authors' Agency, 1922.

———. *On the Knees of the Gods*. Melbourne: Melville & Mullen, 1918.

Brown, Phil. "Holding Your Enemies Close." *Courier Mail*, 11 May 2014.

Browne, Sally. "Brisbane Writers the Last Word in Talent." *Courier Mail*, 1 May 2014.

Bruce, Mary Grant. *Captain Jim*. Melbourne: Ward, 1919.

———. *From Billabong to London*. Melbourne: Ward, 1915.

———. *Jim and Wally*. Melbourne: Ward, 1916.

Brugger, Suzanne. *Australians and Egypt, 1914–1919*. Carlton, Vic: Melbourne University Press, 1980.

Burge, Linda Webb. *Wings Above the Storm*. Melbourne: National Press, 1944.

Burke, Janine. *Speaking*. Richmond, Vic: Greenhouse Press, 1980.

Burrows, Deborah. *A Stranger in My Street*. Sydney: Pan Macmillan, 2012.

Campbell, Rosemary. *Heroes and Lovers: A Question of National Identity*. Sydney: Allen & Unwin, 1989.

Cardinal, Agnes, Dorothy Goldman, and Judith Hattaway. *Women's Writing on the First World War*. Oxford: Oxford University Press, 1999.

Carroll, Joanne. *The Italian Romance: A Novel*. St. Lucia: University of Queensland Press, 2005.

Caruth, Cathy. "An Interview with Robert Jay Lifton." In *Trauma: Explorations in Memory*, 128–50. Baltimore, MD: Johns Hopkins University Press, 1995.

Case, Jo. "Romance Hits a Musical Note." *Sydney Morning Herald*, 21 May 2011.

Chopin, Kate. *The Awakening*. New York: Herbert S. Stone & Company, 1899.

Clark, Anna. "The Place of Anzac in Australian Historical Consciousness", *Australian Historical Studies* 48, no. 1 (2017): 19–34.

Coates, Donna. "The Best Soldiers of All: Unsung Heroines in Canadian Women's Great War Fictions." *Canadian Literature* 151, (Winter 1996): 66–99.

---. "Catch 22." In *Women and War: History of Feminism*, edited by Jaclyn Carter and Timothy Duffy, xi–xxvii. New York: Routledge, 2008.

---. "Coming Home: The Return of the (Australian Vietnam War) Soldier." *Southerly* 65, no. 2 (2005): 105–19.

---. "Country Matters in *The Little Southern Steel Company*." *Literature in Northern Queensland* 35, (December 2008): 79–84.

---. "'Damned Yankees:' The Pacific's Not Pacific Anymore." *Antipodes* 15, no. 2 (December 2001): 123–9.

---. "'The Digger on the Lofty Pedestal': Australian Women's Fictions of the Great War." *Australian and New Zealand Studies in Canada* 10, (December 1993): 1–22.

---. "Myrmidons to Insubordinates: Australian, New Zealand and Canadian Women's Fictional Responses to the Great War." In *The Literature of the Great War Reconsidered: Beyond Modern Memory*, edited by Patrick J. Quinn and Steven Trout, 113–94. New York: Palgrave, 2001.

---. "Happy Is the Land That Needs No Heroes." *ANGLICA: An International Journal of English Studies* 27, no. 3 (September 2018): 111–42.

Cochrane, Peter. "At War at Home: Australian Attitudes During the Vietnam War Years." In *Vietnam Remembered*, edited by Gregory Pemberton, 164–85. Willoughby, NSW: Weldon, 2009.

Cornelius, Patricia. "Jack's Daughters." Unpublished play. 1989.

---. *My Sister Jill*. Milsons Point, NSW: Vintage, 2002.

Cook, Tim. *The Fight for History: 75 Years of Forgetting, Remembering and Remaking Canada's Second World War*. Toronto: Penguin, 2020.

Connell, Daniel. *The War at Home: Australia 1939-1949*. Crows Nest, NSW: ABC Enterprises for the Australian Broadcasting Corporation, 1988.

Cresswell, Tim. *In Place/Out of Place: Geography, Ideology, and Transgression*. Minneapolis: University of Minnesota Press, 1996.

Croft, Julian. "A Sense of Industrial Place – the Literature of Newcastle, New South Wales, 1797–1997." *Antipodes* 13, no. 1 (June 1991): 15–21.

Cross, Zora. *This Hectic Age*. Sydney: London Books, 1944.

Crotty, Martin and Marina Larsson. *Anzac Legacies: Australians and the Aftermath of War*. Melbourne: Australian Scholarly Publishing, 2010.

Cusack, Dymphna. "The 'Cultural Cringe' in Australian Universities' Study of Australian Literature." *Social Alternatives* l, no. 5 (1979): 79–83.

---. *The Half-Burnt Tree*. London: Heinemann, 1969.

---. "How I Write." *Westerly* 5, no. 3 (1960): 32–5.

---. "A Sense of Worth: Dymphna Cusack on Her Life and Work." In *Coming Out! Women's Voices, Women's Lives: A Selection from ABC Radio's Coming Out Show*, 58–69. Melbourne: Nelson in association with the Australian Broadcasting Corporation, 1985.

---. *Southern Steel*. London: Constable, 1953.

---. *A Window in the Dark*, edited by Debra Adelaide. Canberra: National Library of Australia, 1991.

Cusack, Dymphna and Florence James. *Come In Spinner*. North Ryde, NSW: Angus & Robertson, 1988.

Curthoys, Ann. "Mobilising Dissent: The Later Stages of Protest." In *Vietnam Remembered*, edited by Gregory Pemberton. Willoughby, NSW: Weldon, 2009.

Dale, Leigh. "Whose English – Who's English." *Meanjin* 51, (1992): 393–409.

Damousi, Joy. *The Labour of Loss: Mourning, Memory and Wartime Bereavement in Australia*. Melbourne: Cambridge University Press, 1999.

Darien-Smith, Kate. "Remembering Romance: Memory, Gender and World War II." In *Gender and War: Australians at War in the Twentieth Century*, edited by Joy Damousi and Marilyn Lake, 117–29. Melbourne: Cambridge University Press, 1995.

---. "Sexualising Public Spaces: Wartime Visions of the City." *Australian Studies* 9, no. 1 (November 1995): 19–34.

---. "War and Australian Society." In *Australia's War, 1939–1945*, edited by Joan Beaumont, 54–81. St. Leonard's, NSW: Allen & Unwin, 1996.

Dark, Eleanor. *The Little Company*. London: Virago, 1985. First published Sydney: Collins, 1945.

Date, Margo. "Locked UP – Just for Being Italian." *Sydney Morning Herald*, 7 Jun 1991, 1–2.

Davidson, Jim. "No Silence Anymore: An Interview with Janine Burke." In *Footprint New Writers No.1: Janine Burke*, edited by Jim Davidson, 43–7. Footscray, Vic: Footscray Foundation of Australian Studies, Footscray Institute of Technology, 1987.

Davies, Suzanne. "Women, War and the Violence of History: An Australian Perspective." *Violence Against Women* 2, no. 4 (1996): 359–77.

Dennis, C. J. *The Moods of Ginger Mick*. Sydney: Angus & Robertson, 1916.

Digby, Joan. "Heads Above Water." *Australian Book Review,* no. 245 (October 2002): 52.

Dixon, Robert. "Australian Literature-International Contexts." *Southerly* 67, no. 1/2 (2007): 15–27.

Dixson, Miriam. *The Real Matilda*. Ringwood, Vic: Penguin, 1976.

Donaldson, Carina and Marilyn Lake. "Whatever Happened to the Anti-War Movement?" In *What's Wrong With Anzac? The Militarisation of Australian History*, edited by Marilyn Lake and Henry Reynolds, 71–93. Sydney: UNSW Press, 2010.

Dooley, Gillian. "Review for Writers' Radio." *Radio Adelaide*, 15 October 2005.

Doukakis, Anna. *The Aboriginal People, Parliament and "Protection" in New South Wales 1856–1916*. Sydney: The Federation Press, 2006.

Dowse, Sarah. "Political Novels." *Island Magazine*, Winter 1985, 59.

Drake-Brockman, Henrietta. "The Americans Came." *American Quarterly*, Spring 1949, 44–57.

---. *The Fatal Days*. Sydney: Angus & Robertson, 1947.

---. "Smoke-Signals." In *Sydney and the Bush*, 251–68. Sydney: Angus & Robertson, 1948.

Dreyfus, Kay. *Sweethearts of Rhythm*. Surry Hills, NSW: Currency Press, 1999.

Dugdale, Joan. *Struggle of Memory*. St. Lucia: University of Queensland Press, 1991.

Dunlevy, Maurice. "A Lawrencean Coupling That Set a Puzzle." *Canberra Times*, 6 January 1973, 8.

Ehrhart, W.D. "Foreword." In *Visions of War, Dreams of Peace: Writings of Women in the Vietnam War*, edited by Lynda Van Devanter and Joan A. Furey, xvii–xx. New York: Warner Books, 1991.

Eldridge, Marian. *Springfield*. St. Lucia: University of Queensland Press, 1992.

Empson, William. "Some Versions of the Pastoral." Cited in *A Glossary of Literary Terms*, edited by M. H. Abrams and Geoffrey Galt Harpman. Boston, MA: Cengage Learning, 2012.

England, Katherine. "New Australian Novels." *Advertiser*, 8 October 1983, 29.

Fallows, Carol. *Love and War: Stories of War Brides from the Great War to Vietnam*. Milsons Point, NSW: Bantam Books, 2002.

Felski, Rita. *Beyond Feminist Aesthetics: Feminist Literature and Social Change*. Cambridge, MA: Harvard University Press, 1989.

Finch, Lyn. "Consuming Passions: Romance and Consumerism During World War II." In *Gender and War: Australians at War in the Twentieth Century*, edited by Joy Damousi and Marilyn Lake. Melbourne: Cambridge University Press.

Fischer, Gerhard. "Beethoven's Fifth in Trial Bay: Culture and Everyday Life in an Australian Internment Camp during World War I." *Journal of the Royal Australian Historical Society* 69, no. 1 (1983): 48–62.

---. *Enemy Aliens: Internment and the Homefront Experience in Australia 1914–1920*. St. Lucia: University of Queensland Press, 1989.

---. "Integration, 'Negative Integration,' Disintegration: The Destruction of the German-Australian Community during the First World War." In *Alien Justice: Wartime Internment in Australia and North America*, edited by Kay Saunders and Roger Daniels, 6–7. St. Lucia: University of Queensland Press, 2000.

Fitzgerald, Alan. *The Italian Farming Soldiers: Prisoners of War in Australia 1941–1947*. Carlton, Vic: Melbourne University Press, 1981.

Fletcher, Angharad. "Sisters Behind the Wire: Reappraising Australian Military Nursing and Internment in the Pacific During World War II." *Medical History: An International Journal for the History of Medicine and Related Sciences* 55, no. 3 (July 2011): 420.

Freehill, Norman with Dymphna Cusack. *Dymphna Cusack*. Melbourne: Thomas Nelson, 1975.

Fussell, Paul. *The Great War and Modern Memory*. New York: Oxford University Press, 1975.

Fukui, Masako and Mayu Kanamori. "The Creation of Nikkei Australia: Rediscovering the Japanese Diaspora in Australia." *Journal of Australian Studies* 41, no. 3 (2017): 388.

Galovski, Tara and Judith A. Lyons. "Psychological Sequelae of Combat Violence: A Review of the Impact of PTSD on the Veteran's Family and Possible Interventions." *Aggressive and Violent Behaviour* 9, no. 5 (2004): 477–501.

Garber, Marjorie. *Vested Interests: Cross-Dressing and Cultural Anxiety*. New York: Routledge, 1992.

Gardner, Maria. *Blood Stained Wattle*. Pialba, Qld: Self-published, 1992.

Garner, Helen. "Foreword." In *The Invaluable Mystery*, by Lesbia Harford, 1–3. Ringwood, Vic: Penguin, 1987.

Garton, Stephen. *The Cost of War: Australians Return*. Melbourne: Oxford University Press, 1996.

---. "The Last Battle: Soldier Settlement in Australia 1916–1939." *Australian Historical Studies* 48, no. 3 (2017): 456–7.

---. "War and Masculinity in Twentieth Century Australia." *Journal of Australian Studies* 22, no. 56 (1988): 86–95.

Gerster, Robin. *Big-Noting: The Heroic Theme in Australian War Writing*. Carlton, Vic: Melbourne University Press, 1987.

Gilbert, Sandra M. "Soldier's Heart: Literary Men, Literary Women and the Great War." In *Behind the Lines: Gender and the Two World Wars*, edited by Margaret Higonnet, Jane Jenson, Sonya Michel and Margaret Collins Weitz, 197–226. New Haven, CT: Yale University Press, 1987.

Gilbert, Sandra M. and Susan Gubar. *No Man's Land: The Place of the Woman Writer in the Twentieth Century, Volume 2, Sexchanges*. New Haven, CT: Yale University Press, 1989.

Gilman, Charlotte Perkins and Elaine Hedges. *The Yellow Wallpaper*. New York: Feminist Press, 1996.

Gollan, Myfanwy. "A Radical of the '20s Has Her Day At Last." *Sydney Morning Herald*, 19 September 1987, 47.

---. "Review of The Invaluable Mystery." In *The Good Reading Guide*, edited by Helen Daniel, 104. Melbourne: McPhee Gribble, 1989.

Goldboom, Goldie. *The Paperbark Shoe*. Fremantle, WA: Fremantle Press, 2009.

Gordon, Adam Lindsay. "A Dedication to the Author of 'Holmby House.'" In *Bush Ballads and Galloping Rhymes*. Melbourne: Clarson, Massina, 1876.

Gordon, Harry. *Die Like the Carp! The Story of the Greatest Prison Escape Ever*. Stanmore, NSW: Cassell Australia, 1978.

Gostand, Reba. "Penguins New and Revisited" *Social Alternatives* 7, no. 2 (1988): 57–58.

Gowland, Pat. "The Women's Peace Army." In *Women, Class and History: Feminist Perspectives on Australia 1788–1978*, edited by Elizabeth Windschuttle, 216–33. Melbourne: Fontana, 1980.

Grimmett, Dorcas. *We Remember: The Italian Prisoners of War 1944/45*. Kingaroy, Qld: Self-published, 2001.

Grimshaw, Patricia, Ruth Fincher, and Marian Campbell. Essay. *Studies in Gender: Essays in Honour of Norma Grieve*, 117–29. Parkville, Vic: Equal Opportunity Unit, University of Melbourne, 1992.

Guardian. "Julia Gillard Apologises to Australian Mothers for Forced Adoptions." Associated Press in Canberra, 21 March 2013.

Gurr, Andrew. Untitled Review. *Australian Studies* (UK) 4, (1990): 127–29.

Hain, Gladys. *The Coo-ee Contingent*. Melbourne: Cassell, 1917.

Hall, Timothy. *Darwin 1942: Australia's Darkest Hour*. Melbourne: Mandarin, 1989.

Hamilton, Edith. *Mythology*. New York: Warner Books, 1942.

Hancock, Ian. "Robin (later Sir Robert) William Askin." In *The Premiers of New South Wales 1856–2005*, edited by David Clune and Ken Turner, 347–73. Annandale, NSW: Federation Press, 2006.

Harford, Lesbia. *The Invaluable Mystery*. Ringwood, Vic: Penguin, 1987.

Harmstorf, Ian, and Michael Ciglar. *The Germans in Australia*. Melbourne: AE Press, 1985.

Hay, Ashley. *Gum*. Potts Point, NSW: Duffy & Snellgrove, 2002.

Hearder, Rosalind. "Memory, Mythology, and Myth: Some of the Challenges of Writing Australian Prisoner of War History." *Journal of the Australian War Memorial* 40, (February 2007).

Heilbrun, Carolyn. *Writing a Woman's Life*. New York: Ballantine, 1988.

Heilmann, Ann. "(Un)masking Desire: Cross-Dressing and the Crisis of Gender in New Woman Fiction." *Journal of Victorian Culture* 5, no. 1 (Spring 2000): 93–111.

Heilmeyer, Marina. *The Language of Flowers: Symbols and Myths*. New York: Prestel Verlag, 2001.

Heiss, Anita. *Barbed Wire and Cherry Blossoms*. Cammeray, NSW: Simon & Schuster, 2016.

Henderson, Margaret. "New Angels for Storms of Progress? Two Historical Novels of Australian Feminism." *Hecate* 25, no. 1 (1999): 130–44.

Heritage, Helen. *Borrowed Landscape*. Melbourne: Waxflower Press, 2010.

Herman, Judith Lewis. *Trauma and Recovery: From Domestic Abuse to Political Terror*. New York: HarperCollins, 1992.

Higonnet, Margaret R. and Patrice L. R. Higonnet. "The Double Helix." In *Behind the Lines: Gender and the Two World Wars*, 31–47. New Haven, CT: Yale University Press, 1987.

Hitchcock, Maria. *Wattle*. Canberra: Australian Government Publishing Service, 1991.

Howe, Adrian. "Anzac Mythology and the Feminist Challenge." *Melbourne Journal of Politics* 15, (1983–84): 16–23.

Hodgman, Helen. *Jack and Jill*. Ringwood, Vic: Penguin, 1980.

Hoffenberg, Peter H. "Landscape, Memory and the Australian War Experience, 1915–1918." *Journal of Contemporary History* 36, no. 1 (2001): 111–31.

Howson, I. M. *Love's Sacrifice (Founded on Facts): A Book from the Trenches Depicting Undying Love*. Melbourne: Imperial, 1917.

Inglis, K. S. "An Anzac Tradition." *Meanjin Quarterly* 24, no. 1 (1965): 25–44.

Jenkins, Keira. "A Story of Two Camps." *Koori Mail*, 10 August 2016.

Johnston, George. *My Brother Jack*. London: Collins, 1964.

Jordens, Ann-Mari. "Conscription and Dissent: The Genesis of Anti-War Protest." In *Vietnam Remembered*, edited by Gregory Pemberton, 60–81. Willoughby, NSW: Weldon, 2009.

Jones, Dorothy. "Canon to the Right of Us, Canon to the Left of Us." *New Literature Review* 17, (1989): 69–79.

———. "Mapping and Mythmaking: Women Writers and the Australian Legend." *Ariel* 17, no. 4 (1986): 63–86.

Kadushin, Charles. "Social Networks, Helping Networks, and Vietnam Veterans." In *The Trauma of Stress: Stress and Recovery in Vietnam Veterans*, edited by Stephen M. Sonnenberg, Arthur S. Blank, and John A. Talbott, 67. Washington, DC: American Psychiatric Press, 1985.

Kay, Barbara. "Culture, Statistics Back up Churches." *National Post*, 23 April 2012.

Kaufman, Linda S. *Discourses of Design: Gender, Genre, and Epistolary Fictions*. Ithaca, NY: Cornell University Press, 1986.

Kelly, Frances. *The Illustrated Language of Flowers: Magic, Meaning and Lore*. Ringwood, Vic: Penguin, 1992.

Kelly, Gwen. *Always Afternoon*. Sydney: Fontana Collins, 1981.

---. "The Monument at Trial Bay." *The Newcastle Herald*, 18 March 1983.

Kenny, Catherine. *Captives: Australian Army Nurses in Japanese Prison Camps*. St. Lucia: University of Queensland Press, 1989.

Kent, David. "The Anzac Book and the Anzac Legend: C.E.W. Bean as Editor and Image-Maker." *Historical Studies* 21, no. 84 (1985): 376–90.

Khan, Nosheen. *Women's Poetry of the First World War*. Lexington: University of Kentucky, 1988.

Knox, Sara. *The Orphan Gunner*. Artarmon, NSW: Giramondo, 2007.

Kruse, Darryn and Charles Sowerwine. "Feminism and Pacifism: 'Women's Sphere' in Peace and War." In *Australian Women: New Feminist Perspectives*, edited by Norma Grieve and Ailsa Burns, 42–58. Melbourne: Oxford University Press, 1986.

Lake, Marilyn. "The Desire for a Yank: Sexual Relations Between Australian Women and American Servicemen During World War Two." *Journal of the History of Sexuality* 2, no. 4 (April 1992): 621–33.

---. "Female Desires: The Meaning of World War II." In *Gender and War: Australians at War in the Twentieth Century*, edited by Joy Damousi and Marilyn Lake, 60–80. Melbourne: Cambridge University Press, 1995.

---. "The Politics of Respectability: Identifying the Masculine Context." *Historical Studies* 22, (1986): 116–31.

Lake, Marilyn and Henry Reynolds. *What's Wrong with Anzac? The Militarization of Australian History*. Sydney: UNSW Press, 2010.

Langer, Beryl Donaldson. "Women and Literary Production: Canada and Australia." *Australian-Canadian Studies: An Interdisciplinary Social Science Review* 2, (1984): 70–83.

Langer, Ron. "Combat Trauma, Memory, and the World War II Veteran." *War, Literature & the Arts: An International Journal of the Humanities* 23, no. 1 (2011):50–58.

Langley, Greg. *A Decade of Dissent: Vietnam and the Conflict on the Australian Homefront*. Sydney: Allen & Unwin, 1992.

Latta, David. "Out of the Box." *The Book Magazine* 1, no. 2 (August–September 1987): 39–40.

Lawson, Henry. "No Place for a Woman." In *On the Track*, 85. Sydney: Angus & Robertson, 1900.

Laub, Dori. "Truth and Testimony: The Process and the Struggle." In *Trauma: Explorations in Memory*, edited by Cathy Caruth, 61–75. Baltimore, MD: Johns Hopkins University Press, 1995.

Laufer, Robert S. "War Trauma and Human Development: The Vietnam Experience." In *The Trauma of Stress: Stress and Recovery in Vietnam Veterans*, edited by Stephen M. Sonnenberg, Arthur S. Blank and John A. Talbott, 39. Washington, DC: American Psychiatric Press, 1985.

Laurence, J. H. "He Seared My Spirit." *West Australian*, 2 December 1972, 27.

Laurie, Victoria. "Women Awaiting." *Weekend Australian*, September 2005, 10–11.

Lawler, Ray. *Summer of the Seventeenth Doll*. Sydney: Currency Press, 1978.

Lawrence, D.H., and M.L. Skinner, [1924] *The Boy in the Bush*. Cambridge: Cambridge University Press, 1990.

Leigh, Andrew. *Battler and Billionaires: The Story of Inequality in Australia*. Collingwood, VIC: Redback, 2013.

Lewis, Tom. *A War at Home: A Comprehensive Guide to the First Japanese Attacks on Darwin*. Darwin: Tall Stories, 1999.

Lord, Gabrielle. *The Sharp End*. Rydalmere, NSW: Sceptre, 1998.

London, Joan. *Gilgamesh*. Sydney: Picador, 2001.

Luckhurst, Roger. *The Trauma Question*. London: Routledge, 2008.

Macintyre, Stuart. "1901–1942: The Succeeding Age." In *The Oxford History of Australia*, vol. 4, 156. Melbourne: Oxford University Press, 1986.

Macdonald, Gaynor. "Autonomous Selves in a Bureaucratised World: Challenges for Mardu and Wiradjuri." *Anthrolopological Forum* 23, no. 4 (2013): 401.

Manners, Norman D. *Bullwinkel: The True Story of Vivian Bullwinkel, A Young Army Nursing Sister, Who Was the Sole Survivor of a World War Two Massacre by the Japanese*. Carlyle, WA: Hesperian Press, 1999.

Manners-Sutton, Doris. *A Marked Soul*. Melbourne: McCubbin, 1923.

Marcus, Jane. "The Asylum of Antaeus: Women, War and Madness: Is There a Feminist Fetishism?" In *The Difference Within: Feminism and Critical Theory*, edited by Elizabeth Meese and Alice Parker, 49–83. Amsterdam: John Benjamins, 1989.

–––. "Corpus/Corps/Corpse: Writing the Body in/at War." In *Arms and the Woman: War, Gender, and Literary Representation*, edited by Helen M. Cooper, Adrienne Auslander Munich and Susan Merrill Squier. Chapel Hill: University of North Carolina Press, 1989.

Marlowe, Mary. *That Fragile Hour: An Autobiography*. North Ryde, NSW: Angus & Robertson, 1990.

–––. *The Women Who Wait*. London: Simpkin, 1918.

Mass, Nuri. *As Much a Right to Live*. Sydney: Alpha, 1971.

Matsakis, Aphrodite. *Vietnam Wives: Facing the Challenges of Life with Veterans Suffering Post-Traumatic Stress*. Baltimore, MD: Sidran Press, 1996.

Mathew, Imogen. "Love in the Time of Racism: 'Barbed Wire and Cherry Blossoms' Explores the Politics of Romance." *The Conversation*, 7 September 2016.

McAllister, Margaret. "Vivian Bullwinkel: A Model of Resilience and a Symbol of Strength." *Collegian* 22, no. 1 (2015): 135–41.

McClung, Nellie. *In Times Like These*. Toronto: University of Toronto Press, 1982.

McConnochie, Mardi and Helen Taylor. "The Reception of Black American Servicemen in Australia during World War II: The Resilience of 'White Australia." *Journal of Black Studies* 25, no. 3 (January 1995): 331–48.

McConnochie, Mardi. *The Voyagers: A Love Story*. Camberwell, Vic: Viking, 2011.

McCrae, John. "In Flanders Fields." In *In Flanders fields, and other poems*. London: Hodder and Stoughton, 1923.

McGirr, Michael. "In Short Fiction." *Sydney Morning Herald*, 19 March 2005, 12.

McHugh, Siobhan. *Minefields and Miniskirts: Australian Women and the Vietnam War*. Sydney: Doubleday, 1993.

McKernan, Michael. *The Australian People and the Great War*. Carlton, Vic: Melbourne University Press, 1980.

–––. *All In! Australia During the Second World War*. Melbourne: Thomas Nelson, 1983.

–––. "Preface." In *Big-Noting: The Heroic Theme in Australian War Writing*, by Robin Gerster, ix. Carlton, Vic: Melbourne University Press, 1988.

–––. *The War Never Ends: The Pain of Separation and Return*. St. Lucia: University of Queensland Press, 2001.

McKowan, Evah May. *Janet of Kootenay: Life, Love and Laughter in an Arcady of the West*. Toronto: McClelland & Stewart, 1919.

McNally, Richard J. *Remembering Trauma*. Cambridge, MA: Belknap Press of Harvard University Press, 2003.

Molloy, Bruce. "Interview with Dymphna Cusack." *Imago* 1, no. 2 (September 1989): 51.

Montgomery, L.M. *Rilla of Ingleside*. Toronto: Seal, 1982.

Moore, Bob, and Kent Fedorowich. *The British Empire and Its Italian Prisoners of War, 1940–1947*. London: Palgrave, 2002.

Moore, Deirdre. "Cultural Cringe in Academe: Studying Literature in the 1940s." *Australian Literary Studies* 22, no. 1 (May 2005): 90–3.

Moore, John Hammond. *Over-Sexed, Over-Paid, and Over Here*. St. Lucia: University of Queensland Press, 1981.

Moorhead, Finola. *Still Murder*. Ringwood, Vic: Penguin, 1991.

Morgan, Sally. *My Place*. London: Fremantle Press, 1988.

Murrie, Linzi. "The Australian Legend: Writing Australian Masculinity/Writing 'Australian' Masculine." *Journal of Australian Studies* 22, no. 56 (1998): 68–77.

Nagata, Yuriko. *Unwanted Aliens: Japanese Internment in Australia during the Second World War*. St. Lucia: University of Queensland Press, 1996.

———. "Naïve Patriotism: The Internment of Moshi Inagaki in Australia during the Second World War." In *Under Suspicion: Citizenship and Internment in Australia during the Second World War*, edited by Joan Beaumont, Ilma Martinuzzi O'Brien and Mathew Trinca, 112–124. Canberra: National Museum of Australia Press, 2008.

National Archives of Australia. "The Bombing of Darwin." http://www. naa.gov.au/about-us/publications/fact-sheets/fs195.aspx

Neill, Rosemary. "Australia Neglecting Its Own Writers." *The Australian*. 2 December 2006, 1.

———. "And Then There Was One: Lost for Words." *The Australian*. 2 December 2006, 1–6.

Nemeth, Tunde. "Taboo, Silence and Voice in Women's Writing: Intertidal Life as Case in Point." *Canadian Research Institute for the Advancement of Women (Ottawa)*, no. 23 (1989): 3–10.

Nelson, Hank. "An Ordinary Bunch of Women." In *Prisoners of War: Australians Under Nippon*. Crows Nest, NSW: Australian Broadcasting Corporation, 1990.

Nicholls, Glen. "Desire Denied" *Books & Arts*, 13 May 2014.

Nile, Richard, and Robert Darby. "Introduction." In *The Invaluable Mystery*, by Lesbia Harford, 5–17. Ringwood, Vic: Penguin, 1987.

Norbar. "Novelist and Nurse: Work of Miss M. Skinner." *West Australian*, 23 July 1938, 6.

Nolan, Helen. *Between the Battles: A Novel*. Canberra: Pandanus Books, 2005.

Nunn, Gary. "Bangka Island: The WWII Massacre and a 'Truth Too Awful to Speak.'" *BBC News*, 18 April 2019.

O'Brien, Ilma Martinuzzi. "Internments in Australia During World War Two: The Life Histories of Citizenship and Exclusion." In *Enemy Aliens: The Internment of Italian Migrants in Australia During the Second World War*. Bacchus Marsh, Vic: Connor Court Publishing, 2005.

O'Brien, Sharon. "Combat Envy and Survival Guilt: Willa Cather's Manly Battle Yarn." In *Arms and the Women: War, Gender and Literary Representation*, edited by Helen M. Cooper, Adrienne Auslander Munich and Susan Merrill Squier, 184–204. Chapel Hill: University of North Carolina Press, 1989.

O'Brien, Tim. "The Vietnam in Me." *The New York Times Magazine*, 2 October 1994, 52.

Pascoe, Robert. *Buongiorno Australia: Our Australian Heritage*. Melbourne: Greenhouse Publications and Vaccari Historical Trust, 1987.

Pearson, Kathleen. *Hugh Royston*. Sydney: Cornstalk, 1924.

Pemberton, Gregory. *Vietnam Remembered*. Willoughby, NSW: Weldon, 2009.

Penglase, Joanna and David Homer. *When the War Came to Australia: Memories of the Second World War*. St. Leonards, NSW: Allen & Unwin, 1992.

Perry, A. R. "The Landing: By a Man of the Tenth." In *The Anzac Book: Written and Illustrated in Gallipoli by the Men of Anzac*. Melbourne: Cassell & Co, 1916.

Philips, A. A. "Followers of the Inner Light." *Nation Review*, December 1972, 16–22.

Phillips, Dennis. *Ambivalent Allies: Myth and Reality in the Australian-American Relationship*. Ringwood, Vic: Penguin, 1988.

Phillips, Ray. *The White Feather*. Melbourne: Melville and Mullen, 1917.

Pierce, Peter. "Australian and American Literature of the Vietnam War." In *Australia's Vietnam War*, edited by Jeff Doyle, Jeffrey Grey, and Peter Pierce. College Station: Texas A&M University Press, 2002.

Piper, Christine. *After Darkness*. Crows Nest: Allen & Unwin, 2014.

Piper, Christine. "Prejudice Flares When We Perceive Enemies Within." *Sydney Morning Herald*, August 14, 2014, 3. Also published as "Japanese internment a dark chapter of Australian history".

Christine Piper, "Unearthing the Past," *Australian Book Review*, no. 360 (April 2014). bit.ly/3PQYIaK.

Pinney, Estelle. *Time Out for Living*. Chippendale, NSW: Pan Macmillan, 1995.

Pollan, Michael. "Love and Lies." *National Geographic Magazine*, 1 September 2009.

Potts, Annette and Lucinda Strauss. *For the Love of a Soldier: Australian War-Brides and Their GIs*. Crows Nest, NSW: ABC Enterprises for Australian Broadcasting Corporation, 1987.

Potts, E. Daniel and Annette Potts. *Yanks Down Under 1941–45: The American Impact on Australia*. Melbourne: Oxford University Press, 1985.

Powell, Alan. *The Shadow's Edge: Australia's Northern War*. Carlton, Vic: Melbourne University Press, 1988.

Prentice Alison, et al. *Canadian Women: A History*. Toronto: Harcourt Brace Jovanovich, 1988.

Pringle, Rosemary. "Rape: The Other Side of Anzac Day." *Refractory Girl: A Women's Studies Journal* 26, (June 1983): 31–35.

Prichard, Katharine S. "M.L. Skinner: The West Australian Writer Who Collaborated with D.H. Lawrence in His Latest Book 'The Boy in the Bush.'" *Women's World*, 1 December 1924, 18–41.

Rando, Gitano. "Italo-Australians during the Second World War: Some Perceptions of Internment." *Italian Studies in South Africa* 18, no. 1 (2005): 1–23.

Reid, Gayla. "Sister Doyle's Men." In *To Be There With You: Stories of Longing and Desire*, 13–28. St. Leonards, NSW: Allen & Unwin, 1994.

Rechniewski, Elizabeth. "Remembering the Black Diggers: from the 'Great Silence' to 'Conspicuous Commemoration'?" In *War Memories: Commemoration, Recollections, and Writings on War*, edited by Stéphanie A.H. Bélanger and Renée Dickason. Montreal: McGill-Queen's University Press, 2017.

Renner, Rebecca. "Was Holly Golightly Bisexual?" *Paris Review* 21 (December 2018).

Rhodan, Clare. "Innovation Meets Tradition in Brenda Walker's *The Wing of Night*" *Westerly* 56, no. 1 (2011): 118–32.

Rhys, Jean. *Wide Sargasso Sea*. London: Deutsch, 1966.

Ritchie, Donald A. Untitled review of *Minefields and Miniskirts: Australian Women and the Vietnam War*, by Siobhan McHugh. *The Oral History Review* 26, no. 2 (1999): 171–3.

Rich, Adrienne. *On Lies, Secrets, and Silence: Selected Prose 1966–1978*. New York: Norton, 1979.

Rintoul, Stuart. *Ashes of Vietnam: Australian Voices*. Richmond, Vic: William Heinemann, 1987.

Rixon, Annie. *The Scarlet Cape*. Sydney: Criterion, 1939.

———. *Yesterday and Today*. Sydney: Criterion, 1940.

Robin, Libby. "Nationalizing Nature: Wattles Days in Australia." *Journal of Australian Studies* 26, no. 73 (2002): 13–26.

———. *How a Continent Created a Nation*. Sydney: UNSW Press, 2007.

Rubinstein, Helena. *My Life for Beauty*. New York: Simon & Schuster, 1966.

Ruben, Olaf. "Memoirs of a Humble Sparrow." *The Australian*, 9 December 1972, 22.

Ruddick, Sara. "Preservative Love and Military Destruction: Some Reflections on Mothering and Peace." In *Mothering: Essays in Feminist Theory*, edited by Joyce Trebilcot, 231–62. Totowa, NJ: Rowman & Allanheld, 1984.

Sallay, Adrienne. *Loaded Hearts*. Sydney: Ace Press, 2010.

Saunders, Ian. "On Appropriation: Two Novels of Dark and Eldershaw." *Australian Literary Studies* 20, no. 4 (October 2002): 287–300.

Saunders, Kay and Roger Daniels, *Alien Justice: Wartime Interment in Australia and North America*. St. Lucia: University of Queensland Press, 2000.

Saunders, Kay. "Conflict between the America and Australian Governments over the Introduction of Black American Servicemen into Australia during World War Two." *Australian Journal of Politics and History* 33, no. 2 (1987).

---. "In a Cloud of Lust: Black GIs and Sex in World War Two." In *Gender and War: Australians at War in the Twentieth Century*, edited by Joy Damousi and Marilyn Lake, 178–90. Melbourne: Cambridge University Press, 1995.

---. "Taken Away to Be Shot? The Process of Incarceration in Australia in World War II." In *Alien Justice: Wartime Internment in Australia and North America*, edited by Kay Saunders and Roger Daniels, 152–67. St. Lucia: University of Queensland Press, 2000.

Saunders, Malcolm. "'Law and Order' and the Anti-Vietnam War Movement: 1965–72." *Australian Journal of Politics & History* 28, no. 3 (1982): 367–79.

Savage, Georgia. *Ceremony at Lang Nho*. Ringwood, Vic: McPhee Gribble, 1994.

Sayer, Mandy. *Dreamtime Alice*. Sydney: Random House, 1998.

---. *Love in the Years of Lunacy*. Sydney: Allen & Unwin, 2011.

Scarfe, Wendy. *Neither Here nor There*. Warrnambool: Kepler, 1984.

---. *Laura, My Alter Ego: A Novel of Love, Loyalty and Conscience*. Ringwood, Vic: Spectrum, 1988.

Scarry, Elaine. *The Body in Pain: The Making and Unmaking of the World*. New York: Oxford University Press, 1985.

Schaffer, Kay. *Women and the Bush: Forces of Desire in the Australian Cultural Tradition*. Sydney: Cambridge University Press, 1988.

Schweickart, Patrocinio. "Reading Ourselves: Toward a Feminist Theory of Reading." In *Speaking of Gender*, edited by Elaine Showalter, 17–44. New York: Routledge, 1989.

Searle, Geoffrey. "The Digger Tradition and Australian Nationalism." *Meanjin Quarterly* 24, no. 2 (1965): 149–58.

Seaton, Beverly. *The Language of Flowers: A History*. Charlottesville: University of Virginia Press, 1995.

Seymour, Alan. *The One Day of the Year*. Sydney: Angus & Robertson, 1976.

Shay, Jonathan. *Achilles in Vietnam: Combat Trauma and the Undoing of Character*. Toronto: Maxwell Macmillan, 1994.

Sheiner, Robin. *Smile, the War Is Over*. Melbourne: Macmillan, 1983.

Sheridan, Susan. "Temper Romantic: Bias Offensively Feminist: Australian Women Writers and Literary Nationalism." In *A Double Colonization: Colonial and Post-Colonial Women's Writing*, edited by Kirsten Holst Petersen and Anna Rutherford, 49–58. Aarhus: Dangaroo Press, 1986.

Showalter, Elaine. *Speaking of Gender*. New York: Routledge, 1989.

---. "Tradition and the Female Talent: The Awakening as a Solitary Book." In *The Awakening: Case Studies in Contemporary Criticism*, edited by Nancy A. Walker, 169–70. Boston: Bedford, 1993.

Shute, Carmel. "Heroines and Heroes: Sexual Mythologies in Australia 1914 –1918." *Hecate* 1, no. 1 (1975): 7–22.

---. "'Blood Votes' and the 'Bestial Boche:' A Case Study in Propaganda." *Hecate* 1, no. 2 (1975): 7–23.

Sibree, Bron. "Casualties of Love and War." *Canberra Times*, 10 September 2005, 11.

Sidney, Neilma. *The Return*. Sydney: Nelson, 1976.

Skinner, Mollie L. *The Fifth Sparrow*. Sydney: Sydney University Press, 1972.

---. *Letters of a V.A.D.* London: Melrose, 1918. First published under the name R. E. Leake.

---. *Tucker Sees India*. London: Martin, 1937.

Smith, Tony. "Review, Helen Nolan's Between the Battles: A Novel." *Journal of Australian Studies Review of Books* 29, no. 85 (2005): 141–90.

Spiller, R. J. "Shell Shock." *American Heritage* 41, no. 4 (May/June 1990): 77.

Sonnenberg, Stephen M. "Introduction: The Trauma of War." In *The Trauma of Stress: Stress and Recovery in Vietnam Veterans*, edited by Stephen M. Sonnenberg, Arthur S. Blank, and John A. Talbott, 5. Washington, DC: American Psychiatric Press, 1985.

Sontag, Susan. *Regarding the Pain of Others*. New York: Farrar, Strauss and Giroux, 2003.

Stasko, Nicolette. "Notes on Fiction." *The Phoenix Review* 2, (1987–88): 57–8.

Stanley, Peter. *Bad Characters: Sex, Crime, Mutiny, Murder and the Australian Imperial Force*. Miller's Point, NSW: Murdoch, 2010.

---. "Monumental Mistake: Is War the Most Important Thing in Australian History?" In *Anzacs' Dirty Dozen: 12 Myths of Australian Military History*, edited by Craig Stockings, 260–86. Sydney: UNSW Press, 2012.

Stirling, Chrystal. *Soldiers Two*. Sydney: NSW Bookstall Co., 1918.

Stockings, Craig. *Zombie Myths of Australian Military History*. Sydney: UNSW Press, 2010.

Sullivan, Jane. "War's Empty Spaces." *The Age*, 27 August 2005, 1–4.

Summers, Anne. *Damned Whores and God's Police: The Colonization of Women in Australia*. Ringwood, Vic: Penguin, 1975.

Tamura, Keiko. "How to Become an Ordinary Australian: Japanese War Brides' Reflections." *Australian Book Review*, no. 354 (September 2013).

---. *Michi's Memories: The Story of a Japanese War Bride*. Research School of Pacific and Asian Studies, Australian National University, 2011.

Tanaka, Yuki. *Hidden Horrors: Japanese War Crimes in World War II*. Boulder, CO: Westview Press, 1996.

---. "War, Rape and Patriarchy: The Japanese Experience." *The Asia-Pacific Journal* 18, no. 1 (31 December 2019): 96.

Temby, Susan. *The Bread with Seven Crusts*. Sydney: HarperCollins, 2002.

Teorey, Matthew. 2008. "Unmasking the Gentleman Soldier in the Memoirs of Two Cross-Dressing Female US Civil War Soldiers." *War, Literature & the Arts: An International Journal of the Humanities* 20 (1/2): 74–93.

Terzis, Gillian, "Shooting Through: An Ambitious Treatise on Social Stratification in Australia." Rev. of *Battlers and Billionaires: The Story of Inequality in Australia*, by Andrew Leigh. *Australian Book Review*, no. 354 (September 2013): 14.

Thirkell, Angela. *Trooper to the Southern Cross*. London: Virago, 1985. First published London: Faber & Faber, 1934, under the name Leslie Parker.

Thomson, Alistair. "Passing Shots at the Anzac Legend." In *A Most Valuable Acquisition: A People's History of Australia Since 1788*, edited by Verity Burgmann and Jenny Lee, 190–204. Ringwood, Vic: Penguin, 1988.

---. *Anzac Memories: Living with the Legend*. Melbourne: Oxford University Press, 1994.

Thomson, Helen. "Of Charm and Politics: Two Novels Reclaimed" *Australian Book Review*, no. 94 (1987): 15–16.

Thompson, Denise. "Finola's Dilemma, or: If Literature and Politics Don't Mix, What Am I Doing Here?" *Southerly* 55, no. 2 (1995): 120.

Tiffin, Helen, "Flowers of Evil, Flowers of Empire: Roses and Daffodils in the Work of Jamaica Kincaid, Oliver Senior and Lorna Goodison," *Journal of the South Pacific Association for Commonwealth Literature and Language Studies* 46, (April 1998): 58–71.

Tuffield, Aviva. "The Reverse of the Picture." Rev. of *The Wing of Night*, by Brenda Walker. *Australian Book Review*, no. 277 (December 2005–January 2006): 32.

Turner, Dale. *The Farmer's Wife*. XLibris, 2011.

Turner, Ethel. *The Cub*. London: Ward, 1915.

---. *Captain Cub*. London: Ward, 1917.

---. *Brigid and the Cub*. London: Ward, 1919.

Twomey, Christine. *Australia's Forgotten Prisoners: Civilians Interned by the Japanese in World War Two*. Melbourne: Cambridge University Press, 2001.

Tylee, Claire M. "Maleness Run Riot: The Great War and Women's Resistance to Militarism." *Women's Studies International Forum* 11, no. 3 (1988): 199–210.

Ursano, Robert and James Rundell. "The Prisoner of War." In *War Psychiatry*, 431. Falls Church, VA: Office of The Surgeon General, 1995.

Van Devanter, Lynda and Joan A. Furey. "Foreword." In *Visions of War, Dreams of Peace: Writings of Women in the Vietnam War*, edited by Lynda Van Devanter and Joan A. Furey, xxii. New York: Warner Books, 1991.

Vickroy, Laurie. *Trauma and Survival in Contemporary Fiction*. Charlottesville: University of Virginia Press, 2002.

Vondra, Josef. *German Speaking Settlers in Australia*. Melbourne: Cavalier Press, 1981.

Waldren, Murray. "Spoils of War for Novelist." *The Australian,* 11 May 2006.

Walker, Brenda. *The Wing of Night*. Camberwell, Vic: Viking, 2005.

Walker, David. "The Writers' War." In *Australia's War, 1939–45*, edited by by Joan Beaumont, 136–61. Sydney: Allen & Unwin, 1996.

Walker, Shirley. "The Boer War: Paterson, Abbott, Brennan, Miles Franklin and Morant." *Australian Literary Studies* 12 (1985): 207–22.

———. "Showdown in Rome." Rev. of *The Italian Romance: A Novel*, by Joanne Carroll. *Australian Book Review*, no. 272 (June–July 2005): 46.

Ward, Bobby J. *A Contemplation Upon Flowers: Garden Plants in Myth and Literature*. Portland: Timber Press, 1999.

Ward, Russel. *The Australian Legend*. Melbourne: Oxford University Press, 1958.

Waten, Judah. "The Writer and the Nurse." *Age*, 20 January 1973, 19.

Watkins, Vilma. *Pukunja: A Far Away Place*. Hurstville, NSW: Parker Pattison Publishing, 1999.

Watson, Kathleen. *Henriette Says!*. Melbourne: Alexander McCubbin, 1921.

Webb Burge, Linda. *Wings Above the Storm*. Melbourne: National Press, 1944.

Webby, Elizabeth. "Australian Literature and the English Curriculum." Keynote lecture to the Australian Government Summer School for Teachers of English. Geelong: Deakin University. 8 January 2008.

———. "The Year's Work in Fiction." *Westerly* 55, no. 1 (2010): 119–39.

Wecter, Dixon. "The Aussie and the Yank." *The Atlantic*, May 1946.

West Australian. Review. "Letters of a V.A.D." 18 April 1919, 6.

West Australian. Review. "Three New Novels." 18 September 1937, 4.

Wheelwright, Julie. *Amazons and Military Maids: Women Who Dressed as Men in the Pursuit of Life, Liberty and Happiness*. London: Pandora, 1989.

White, Richard. *Inventing Australia: Images and Identity 1788–1980*. Sydney: Allen & Unwin, 1981.

———. "The Soldier as Tourist: The Australian Experience of the Great War," *Kunapipi* 18, no. 2–3 (1996): 117–29.

Williams, Maslyn. "The Quaker Spinster's Story." *Sydney Morning Herald*, 3 March 1973, 25.

Winter, Jay. *Remembering War: The Great War Between Memory and History in the Twentieth Century*. New Haven, CT: Yale University Press, 2006.

———. "Shell Shock, Gallipoli and the Generation of Silence." In *Beyond Memory: Silence and the Aesthetics of Remembrance*, edited by Alexandre Dessinque and Jay Winter, 195–208. London: Routledge, 2016.

Woolf, Virginia. *A Room of One's Own*. New York: Harcourt Brace Jovanovich, 1957.

———. *Three Guineas*. New York: Harcourt Brace Jovanovich, 1966.

———. *The Letters of Virginia Woolf*, edited by Nigel Nicolson and Joanne Trautmann. New York: Harcourt Brace Jovanovich, 1975–80.

Wyld, Evie. *After the Fire, a Still Small Voice*. Sydney: Random House, 2009.

Wyndham, Susan. "Feather in the Cap for Perth Novelist." *Sydney Morning Herald*. 11 May 2006, 18.

Index

www.ingramcontent.com/pod-product-compliance
Lightning Source LLC
Chambersburg PA
CBHW081132020726
47504CB00010B/2050